Islam

in Modern History

Islam in Modern History

BY

WILFRED CANTWELL SMITH

PRINCETON UNIVERSITY PRESS
PRINCETON, NEW JERSEY

Copyright © 1957 by Wilfred Cantwell Smith
Published by Princeton University Press, Princeton, New Jersey
In the United Kingdom: Princeton University Press, Guildford, Surrey
ALL RIGHTS RESERVED

LCC 57-5458
ISBN 0-691-01991-6 (paperback edn.)
ISBN 0-691-03030-8 (hardcover edn.)

Printed in the United States of America
First PRINCETON PAPERBACK printing, 1977

Preface

THIS is a study of a people in the turmoil of the modern world. The Muslim community in our day, like the rest of mankind, is in serious transition. What distinguishes it is that its members face the perplexities and opportunities of modernity as heirs of a unique tradition. Their society is characterized by a faith, Islam, and a great past. What is happening to the community and to the faith is the attempted subject of this book.

Throughout the Islamic world the processes of contemporary history are so rich and radical that they are, of course, far from easy to understand—whether for the Muslims themselves, precipitately involved in them, or for the outside observer. Yet such understanding is important: for Muslims, in order to participate intelligently in the transformations to which their life is subject; for outsiders, to observe that life intelligently and to relate themselves sanely to it; for both, to communicate. It is the significance of these needs that justifies our present exploratory endeavour to seek such understanding. We are not so fond as to imagine that our treatment of the issues here raised is adequate; but we do insist that those issues are important.

Since the primary characteristic of the Muslim world is that it is Muslim, we introduce our study with an attempt to elucidate what this means: emphasizing that it means a very great deal, including much that is relevant to the currents of modern history. Secondly, illustrating our observation that the present of Islamic society is in significant measure the outgrowth of its immediate past, we turn next to a general survey of the recent background throughout the Muslim world, discerning amidst the numerous diversities something of a common pattern—enough at least to justify the concept that Islamic history continues apace. These basic analyses are followed by a country-by-country examination of the contemporary scene, an investigation that virtually constitutes the remainder of our study. It sets forth the contention that an understanding of current events in the Muslim world involves an understanding of their Islamic quality. By this we do not mean anything formal or prescribed. On the contrary, in arguing that the Islamic factor is persistently significant in the on-going affairs of these nations we are but elaborating the point that the actors

v

in these affairs are persons who are Muslim. History, in our view, is everywhere primarily a human activity, despite its partial conditioning by impersonal forces.

The quality and form of the Muslim's faith ramifies through many segments of his society's development, political, economic, and the rest. Those concerned with the direction of these various factors, then, from within or from without, are in fact dealing with Islam and its current development, whether or not they are effectively aware of this. In one sense, therefore, the present work is offered as some sort of contribution to a politico-economic-social study. In another sense, not contradicting this, it is fundamentally a study in religion, comparative and contemporary. It seeks to discover and to expound the nature and present significance of a community's faith.

The work is proffered, frankly, both to non-Muslim and to Muslim readers. For comparative religion studies in our day, we would suggest, have a function to fulfill in intercommunication. In addition to their academic standards they may adopt as new criterion the capacity to construct religious statements that will be intelligible and cogent in at least two different traditions simultaneously. All books no doubt fall short in various ways of their authors' aspirations. Unquestionably this one will. Yet it seems perhaps significant to note that that aspiration includes this double relevance. The work will fail if it does not enable non-Muslims to understand better the behaviour of Muslims that they observe, books by Muslim authors that they read, and Muslims that they meet. It will fail also if intelligent and honest Muslims are not able to recognize its observations as accurate, its interpretations and analyses as meaningful and enlightening. For both groups it will fail if it does not serve in some small way to further mutual comprehensibility. In such a study, these are tests of validity.

All this might at first sound pretentious. For one thing, has an outsider really any business to delve into the spiritualities of an alien community? To this there are at least two answers. First, a great many Christians besides the author would be deeply delighted if a Muslim writer would undertake a comparable study of contemporary Christianity. Such an inquiry if serious would surely be a step forward in understanding and interrelation, not backward. Secondly, twentieth-century living imposes this responsibility upon us: it is simply a fact that modern conditions, whether we like it or not, oblige us to strive for some apprehension of each other's presuppositions. Isolationism is gone, and with it the kind of world in which it was feasible for one civilization or culture to ignore the values and convictions of another.

Moreover, the hope of proving intelligible also to the Islamic world is itself a kind of discipline towards understanding. There has been too much writing about the Muslim and indeed other communities that those communities would not be expected to acknowledge as apt. The hypothetical study by a Muslim suggested above would surely be a better book if the author explicitly aimed at writing of Christian behaviour and belief in such a way as to be not only enlightening and persuasive to his fellow Muslims but also admissible and therefore presumably illuminating to Christians. In the delicate field of inter-cultural interpretation, a study must first of all strive to meet the requirements of professional scholarship, but in addition it may perhaps also be asked to strive to exemplify that intercommunicability that it implicitly posits.

As we have said, we cannot claim that the present study will satisfy these demands. And we are ready to apologize for our failures; and to hope that where we have fallen short others will do better. Yet we have few qualms about the validity of what is attempted. The alienation between communities in our day is too desperate, and the uncertainty as to where our several developments are taking us is too severe, for any of us to ignore these fundamental questions of faith and history.

In the writing of this book help has been received from many persons, and it is pleasant to acknowledge it. First, of course, and most warmly, thanks are due to numerous Muslim friends and acquaintances in many countries who have unstintingly encouraged me and helped me as slowly over the years I have come to some understanding of Islam. If I have been able at all to gain some valid insight into this faith, this has been due in some part to supplementing my reading with endless conversations with Muslims who generously and patiently have been willing to talk with me—of Islam, of contemporary events, of life in general and in particular. The usefulness of this in clarifying awareness has been great, though often subordinate. I value the experience and friendship in themselves, and am grateful for them. Some of my observations in this study will no doubt prove unpalatable to some Muslims, including some of those with whom I have had the opportunity of discourse. But I am pleased to realize that in the cases where it matters friendship has reached the point where sincerity has long since outdistanced courtesy.

The authorities of McGill University have encouraged my studies and not only tolerated but supported their ramifications; I am truly grateful.

To the Rockefeller Foundation also I am grateful for much assistance. Particularly, the Humanities Division made possible nine years ago a study tour of the Muslim world that enlarged my effective Islamics horizon, especially letting me sense the contemporary problems of Indo-Pakistani Muslims, which I had been studying, as significantly within a wide context of modern Islamic development. The Foundation has also aided McGill University in supporting the Institute of Islamic Studies with which I have been associated for the past five years, and which is working in the realm of study here treated.

I would also thank those at Princeton University where I did my doctoral work, and Professor H. A. R. Gibb under whom I had the privilege of studying while at Cambridge and whose early and constant encouragement has meant more than he knows. And like all teachers I am deeply indebted for criticism, stimulus, and assistance to my colleagues (particularly Professor Berkes, Professor Fazlu-r-Rahman, and Mr. Watson) and to my students.

Since this study represents ten years or more of investigation and reflection, on and off, almost every article I have written, every talk that I have given on an Islamics subject during that time has dealt with some aspect of the present work. Consequently I must thank those editors and publishers who allowed various first approximations to some parts of the present material to appear under their auspices. From the discussions and criticisms and even the silences that were evoked I have learned much. Chapter 1 below, although largely new, synthesizes some ideas and passages that were first adumbrated in *Foreign Policy Report*, Foreign Policy Association, New York (31/2:5-7, October 1, 1951), in an address to the Fifth Annual Conference of the Middle East

Institute (proceedings published in Dorothea Seelye Franck, ed., *Islam in the Modern World*, Middle East Institute, Washington, 1951; cf. pp. 15-30), and in papers presented at conferences held by the Hartford Seminary Foundation, Hartford (abridged proceedings published in *The Muslim World*, Hartford, 42:313-32 [1952]; cf. pp. 321-24) and the Social Science Research Council at Princeton (papers published as Sydney Nettleton Fisher, ed., *Social Forces in the Middle East*, Cornell University Press, Ithaca, 1955; cf. pp. 190-204). Chapter 2 is mostly new, and the first part of Chapter 3; the remainder of Chapter 3 draws heavily on material presented in my doctoral dissertation to Princeton University, Department of Oriental Languages and Literatures (1948). Chapter 4 is a revised version of an article first published in *Islamic Culture*, Hyderabad, 25:155-86 (1951); a "preliminary draft" of Chapter 5 was published by Shaykh Muhammad Ashraf, Lahore, as a pamphlet, *Pakistan as an Islamic State* [1954]. To the editors, publishers, and authorities concerned I am grateful for permission to republish here some of the substance and in some cases some of the wording of these earlier gropings toward this presentation.

For permission to quote from other writers, I am indebted to the following: George Allen & Unwin, London, for the translation of the al-Ghazzali passage (below, p. 116) from W. Montgomery Watt, trans., *The Faith and Practice of al-Ghazālī*, 1953; Longmans, Green and Company, for the passage (below, p. 109) from G. M. Trevelyan, *English Social History*, 1942; *Middle Eastern Affairs*, New York, and *The Christian Science Monitor*, Boston, for the passage (below, p. 151) from an article by the Overseas News Editor for the latter paper, published in both periodicals.

Since the work is offered both to scholars and to the general reader, including those familiar with Islamic languages and those not, the vexatious question of rendering the Arabic script in Latin characters has been handled as follows: in the text, diacriticals have not been used but otherwise the transliteration aims at accuracy; in the footnotes and index the transcription is full, precise, and as unrelenting as feasible. References to the Qur'an cite chapter and verse of the official Egyptian text.

I wonder whether I might be allowed to close as a classical Muslim writer might have done (except that he would hardly have written a work like this): May God forgive me if my book misrepresents a people or its faith, and if on the other hand it may serve as any contribution to truer understanding, then to Him be the praise.

WILFRED CANTWELL SMITH

Institute of Islamic Studies
McGill University, Montreal

Contents

Islam
in Modern History

Chapter 1

INTRODUCTION: ISLAM AND HISTORY

ISLAM today has behind it some thirteen centuries of history. No one knows the future; yet a Muslim might presumably look forward to, let us say, another thirteen centuries still to come. With any unfolding still further ahead, beyond that symmetry, we need not trouble for the moment; such a prospect for Islam is enough to set our perspective. Current situations in the Muslim world lie within a context of a very long-term development of Islam—a development not yet completed.

In the uncertain flux of man's mundane development, and especially now amid the radical transformation already begun in all man's social forms, prophecy is precarious. Yet one prediction would seem not rash: that the history of the next thirteen centuries, or indeed of the next two centuries or one, will for all of us be different. Life on our planet is full of rapid novelty: problems, possibilities, dreams and threats are new.

The present study is in no sense an endeavour—patently absurd —to discern what that future unfolding may be. Our concern is simply to give attention to the fact that the career of Islam on earth, from what it has been, is currently in process of changing into what it will become. One does not know, or need to know, what it will be; but one can actually observe the contemporary process by which some tomorrow or other is being prepared. Islam is today living through that crucial, creative moment in which the heritage of its past is being transformed into the herald of its future. Outsiders may study, analyse, interpret the process; Muslims themselves not only may but must participate in it. For both outsiders and Muslims the most important, most interesting chapter in Islamic history so far is the one that is today in process of being enacted.

If this be true, is it also noteworthy? One might be tempted to cry "platitude," and to protest that such a truth applies to all human affairs, Muslim or other, and to all epochs in history. Life, for both man and his society, has ever been the decisive moment-by-moment creation or emergence of newness on the basis of the cumulative past. Has the meaning of history not always been comprised in the meaningfulness of each "now" as it came along? Has

3

not every personality, every group and institution, every civilization, always existed sandwiched between the pressure of its past and the potentiality of an uncertain future? What is special about the twentieth century, that makes our age so starkly one of critical transition; and what special about Islam, that makes so dramatic its involvement in this crisis?

Our thesis here will be that in both cases a very great deal is special. This aspect of the Muslim's faith—its development, its dynamism—has been little explored. Our exposition of the situation as we discern it will accordingly occupy much of our argument presently. In answer to the former question, on the other hand—the instability of modernity—much has been written on every hand; the point need detain us here but briefly.

Admittedly there has always been change. A language, a mountain range, even the galaxies, we now know, have their life histories; we can document Heracleitos' persuasion that everything we see is, and throughout has been, in flux. Yet our age is distinctive on two scores. First, the pace of change is for us being not merely quantitatively but qualitatively quickened. Secondly, the evolution is for the first time on a large scale becoming self-conscious.

Never before in human history or evolution has change been so swift, so pervasive, so perspicuous as today. Earlier centuries have flirted with transience, or even from time to time become deeply involved; but it remained for our own to contract an overt and indissoluble marriage. From now on, man knows that he must live with change as a permanent partner, in all his activities and all his institutions, for better or for worse.

It is this knowledge that is the second great differentiation. Not only is development, since the Industrial Revolution and the recent strides of science, quick—quick out of all proportion to anything seen before. It is also, and equally fundamental, for the first time recognized, and in part deliberate. This knowledge, like other, brings both power and responsibility. Man both may and must be the architect of mutability.

In the case of Islam, for instance, with the slow dynamics of the past giving way to the swift development of the contemporary scene, consciousness is perforce spreading, amongst Muslims[1] as

[1] It has become so commonplace today for Muslims to speak and write of the fluidity of present-day Islamic cultural and social life, that any choice of

well as outsiders, of how fluid is its present; while, partially, awareness also dawns of how fluid it has always been.[2] With these comes an incipient sense of man's opportunity, now grown inescapable, for directing change.[3]

So much for our twentieth century. Yet in addition to these

illustrative instances can be arbitrary only. One example: Iqbāl speaks of "the enormous rapidity with which the world of Islam is spiritually moving" (Sir Muhammad Iqbal, *The Reconstruction of Religious Thought in Islam,* 1944 ed., Lahore, p. 7). Another: the fact that Muhammad Asad, *Islam at the Crossroads,* has gone through repeated printings in both India and the Arab world (Delhi, 1934; Lahore, 7th rev. ed., 1955; *al-Islām 'alà Muftariq al-Turuq,* trans. 'Umar Farrukh, Beirut, 1946, 1948, 1951). One might also mention the remarkable degree to which such phrases as *tataghayyar al-ahkām bi-taghayyur al-azmān* are increasingly in use.

[2] We refer not merely to the growing tendency to hold that Islām is inherently dynamic, not static. (This point is most strikingly argued by Iqbāl: in English, see *op. cit., passim,* and especially chap. VI, "The Principle of Movement in the Structure of Islam.") The question is rather one of recognizing (but only incipiently so far) an actual evolution of Islamic institutions. As an example of a fairly conservative mind writing a history of the development of Muslim theological interpretations, one might cite Shiblī Nu'mānī, *'Ilmu-l-Kalām,* 1902; reprinted Lahore, 1945 (note the [new?] subtitle). Two contemporary writers seriously treating of Islamic Law as having evinced historical development, are A A 'A Fayzi ("Fyzee") in India and Subhī Mahmasānī in the Arab world. This tendency has, as might be expected, gone furthest in Turkey (see, for instance, the contribution [cüz 36, pp. 608-22] of M. Fuad Köprülü to the article FIKIH in the *Islâm Ansiklopedisi,* Istanbul, 1947, in the form of an addendum to and comment upon the translation into Turkish of the original article FIKH by I. Goldziher, from *The Encyclopaedia of Islâm,* Leiden, 1914; for a less substantial example in English, see Ebül'ulâ Mardin, "Development of the Sharī'a under the Ottoman Empire" in Majid Khadduri and H. J. Liebesny, edd., *Law in the Middle East,* Washington, 1955-   , vol. I, pp. 279-291.) However, perhaps no Muslim has yet asserted a history of the religion of Islām (cf. the present writer's lecture cited at ref. 5 below).

[3] One instance: the move to consider a possible bringing together of the four legal systems of *Sunnī* Islām, or even of various sections of Islām including *Sunnī* and *Shī'ī.* One expression of this is the Cairo *Jumā'at al-Taqrīb bayn al-Madhāhib al-Islāmīyah* (see their monthly journal *Risālat al-Islām,* Cairo, 1368/1949 ff.) Another instance: the move to consider a possible reappraisal of the corpus of *hadīth,* with a view *inter alia* to a possible reformulation of law. See the statement circulated by the Council of the Academy of Islamic Studies, Hyderabad-Deccan, India (founded 1952), *Toward Reorientation of Islamic Thought: a Call for Introspection,* 1954, and the interesting report on the response elicited by this, *Toward Reorientation of Islamic Thought (A Fresh Examination of the Hadith Literature),* 1954. These were reprinted (with minor alterations, and omitting the "List of Correspondents" in the second) in *Islamic Review,* London, 42/4: 3-5 (April 1954) and 43/1: 6-13 and 2: 7-11 (Jan. and Feb. 1955).

new conditions which Islam in its modern context shares with the rest of the present-day world, and which are relatively evident, there are other considerations special to Islam. These help to characterize the particular, intense experience through which the community is currently going. These specifically Islamic factors have received less notice from writers, either eastern or western, and yet they must have careful exposition if the present crisis is to be appreciated. We need a clearer understanding of what kind of thing Islam is, as well as a just discernment of what kind of thing modernity is, if we would gain a sensitive insight into the modern condition of the Muslim world. There has been talk of the "impact" of the West, or of the twentieth century, upon Islam, almost as though the latter were inert, the passive recipient of influence. But Islam, too, is a force, one that has been in motion now for more than thirteen centuries. Upon the modern Muslim and his society there is the powerful impact of Islam, from behind (and, since it is a religion, from above); as well as the impact of modernity from the side. The thrust of Islam in this situation, the stresses and strains generated in its on-going process, the dynamics of its reaction, aggressive or cowering, protective or creative, to the modern world—all this is to be understood, if at all, not only in terms of the crucially new environment, but equally in terms of the nature and drive and inner quality of Islam.

We have suggested that the present is special in Islamic history; it is certainly unique, and is in some ways more significant than any other era. We would suggest also that the historical process in general is special for Islam: the Islamic conception of history is unique, and in some ways history is more significant for Muslims than it is for almost any other group.

So sweeping a suggestion manifestly requires considerable elucidation. This much, at least, may be at once asserted: that the practical rôle of Islam in modern history (or in any other history) cannot be fully understood without an understanding of the theoretical rôle of history in Islam. Much the same applies to the question of social relationships: one cannot adequately understand the rôle of Islam in society until one has appreciated the rôle of society in Islam. It could again seem but platitudinous to stress that the modern Muslim is a member of a community—were it not that his community, like his history, is Islamic; and in both cases this is something quite special. Just how special it is, it becomes our business to inquire. Once more, to grasp aright the present situation in the Muslim world, one must examine Islam. What, then, is Islam?

To begin with, Islam is a religion.

To say this is to say a great deal—more, in fact, than perhaps any one of us can really understand. It is the fundamental fact from which discernment in this field must start. For one thing, all religions, and most clearly the great world faiths, are quite literally infinite. There is no end to their profundity; nor to their ramification, their variety. For each religion is the point at which its adherent is in touch, through the intermediary of an accumulating tradition, with the infinitude of the divine.[4] It is the chief means through which God takes hold of the person, in so far as that person will allow. Whatever it may be as a systematic ideal, and whatever, too, its external details may be sociologically, Islam is also, empirically, the personal religious life, shallow or deep, distorted or magnificent, sinful or saintly, of every individual Muslim.

From the transcendent and deeply personal nature of religion two things follow for the outside observer. One is the fairly obvious point that we falsify any religion if we give attention only to its external form. It is the chief window through which the adherent sees whatever he does see of the meaning and purpose of

---

[4] It has become fashionable in Western academic circles to insist that interpretations of phenomena, including social and human ones, must be in exclusively "objective," positive, non-transcendent terms. Those who adopt this may find the above sentence difficult, because of its final phrase. We believe, however, that any explanation must be inadequate that leaves out of consideration one of the basic and most pertinent of the factors involved; and accordingly that people who deny the reality of God (whether or not they recognize Him by that term) preclude themselves from adequately understanding the history of religion. This does not mean, however, that other factors are not also involved, such as those with which anthropologists, psychologists, and others deal. (Those who believe in God are also precluded from understanding that history, in so far as they deny or are unaware of the reality and relevance of those other factors.) Our position is that religion houses the interplay of these various factors; our attempt to delineate what we understand by it is an attempt to do justice to all these. We hope that even those who disagree with us as to the transcendence of what we call the divine, may nonetheless be able to follow our argument by recognizing that that factor is there, however they may interpret it. The above sentence would presumably be acceptable to, for instance, Durkheim, since he would acknowledge our term, though interpreting it sociologically. He recognizes that the worshipper is in touch with *something*. Compare also the next note.

7

life, the final significance of himself and his fellows and their mutual relations. The student, accordingly, must not only observe the shape and construction of the window, but try also to ascertain what further vision it affords to those who worship at it. In matters of behaviour, the student must descry not only what the religious do, but what they deem worth doing and why. To know Islam, as to know any religion, is not only to be apprised of, even carefully acquainted with, its institutions, patterns, and history, but also to apprehend what these mean to those who have the faith.

Another corollary is the endless diversity of each major faith. To some extent each religion is all things to all men; the import and inner nature of each varies with every member according to his own capacity and response. When we look beyond symbols to their meanings, we cannot but recognize that each world religion has, in the last analysis, as many forms as it has believers. For it is an historical fact, fundamental to religious history and understanding, that even the same materials may mean different things to different persons. Indeed, one could argue that unless the system has lost its vitality, is without religious significance, they must do so. The empirical reality of any faith is what the symbols actually convey, case by individual case.[5] And there is no limit to,

[5] We believe this an important point. And we stress the word "empirical." Yet we are conscious that the position here put forward will probably prove not readily acceptable, or even meaningful, to some other observers, particularly among a certain school of social scientists, especially in North America. We hold that behaviour, institutions, creeds, and other externalities are real and significant, but are not religion. At least they are not all of it, and particularly are not faith. Religion, we suggest, is what these things mean to men. A study of religion, then, to be scientific must deal with meaning, with the personal considered as personal, not as an "object." (One must transcend the facile error that the only alternative to objective study is subjective study.)

For any social scientists to argue that their techniques cannot deal with these is to assert that their techniques are not suited to the study of religion; which may well be true. It is doubtless significant that the sociological work of such men as Weber, Troeltsch, and Durkheim has proven so fruitful for the study of the religions, whereas that of an orientation typified perhaps by Lundberg or Everett Hughes has not. Surely the attempt to interpret religion academically must be an attempt to find a position that will do justice both to intellectual coherence and to all the observed facts. Further, it should not be limited by dogmatic metaphysical presuppositions—such as that of several social scientists that the transcendent is not real; that the universe in which we live is a closed system. (They would phrase this rather as that men's

there can be no definition of, the interpretation that individual spiritual aptitude, circumstance, interest, or vagary may put upon a system, no matter how rigidly prescribed. In Islam this elasticity is particularly true of the protean Sufi movement. Yet it is true also of what even so apparently formal a system as the Law means, not only in each successive century but indeed to each separate Muslim heart.

Manifestly Islam could never have become across the centuries one of the four or five great world religions had it not, like the others, had the quality of having something profound and relevant and personal to say directly to all sorts and conditions of men, of every status, background, capacity, temperament, and aspiration.

Islam, then, is a religion. Like the other world faiths it over-flows all definition both because it is open at one end to the immeasurable greatness of the Divine, and because also it relates itself at the other end to the immeasurable diversity of the human.

Nonetheless, Islam is not merely religion; it is a particular religion. It is distinct; and—like the others—though it cannot be defined, it can be characterized. One need not decide the perplexing issue as to which is more important, that which the great religions have in common, or that in each which distinguishes it from the others. Both, clearly, are integral to an understanding of any. Having insisted on this, we may go on to seek for Islam some approximate description of the latter. We must still avoid the easy error of falling back on the external forms, the shape of the window. These, we have argued, are not the religion itself, which lies rather in the realm of meaning. The reality of Islam is a personal, living faith, new every morning in the heart of individual Muslims. This reality too is distinctive; and this we must attempt to characterize, though we remember that in doing so we cannot but omit many shades of variety, many exceptions, many subtleties. The epitomized "Islam" at which one might hope to arrive is at best a generalized abstraction, the formal aspect of an

---

behaviour is not influenced by unobservable factors.)

Manifestly, the methodological question cannot be fully considered here. The present study is an application rather than an exposition of our position on a question that needs continued critical investigation. For an exploratory statement, not specifically on method, cf. the present writer's preliminary "The Comparative Study of Religion: reflections on the possibility and purpose of a religious science," in *McGill University, Faculty of Divinity, Inaugural Lectures*, Montreal, 1950, pp. 39-60.

impersonal entity of Islam, that will approximate to the inner nature of the religion if it is abstracted not from the outward forms, so much, as from the meaning of these for believing Muslims.

It will be recognized that for an outsider to essay anything in this realm is a hardy venture. The abstraction will be necessarily partial and inadequate, if not actually distorted. Yet, following our conviction already expressed that an understanding of the present condition of the Muslim community is impossible without an understanding of Islam, we have felt that we must make the attempt—with genuine apologies for inevitable failures, but in the hope that this imperfect interpretation might yet be a contribution in the direction of valid exposition. In line with our previous argument, we shall emphasize particularly the question of Islam and history.

To the Muslim, of course, Islam is the religion of God. This means a great many things; among others, that it began not in the seventh century A.D., but at least on the day of creation, if not before. When God created the world, He provided that the forces of nature should operate according to the pattern that He pre-scribed—inevitably, perfectly, and as it were blindly. The world of nature has no choice but to obey His eternal decrees; and in the course of doing so, it at the same time illustrates them, dis-closing, for those who have the wit to discern it, His design and providence, as well as His majesty and might. The patterned behaviour of the natural world is the sign of its Creator.

For man also there is a pattern, which he ought to follow. God from all eternity ordained[6] how men ought to behave, both indi-vidually and in community. There is a proper form of human conduct: *vis-à-vis* the God who made us (and to whom we shall return), and *vis-à-vis* our fellows. *There is a right way to live.* Man, however, differs from the rest of creation in that he was made conscious and free. In his case, there is no inherent compulsion: he, alone in the universe, was given the faculty of choosing to conform or not to conform. There is an eternal righteousness, but it is not compulsory.

---

[6] In the first draft of this sentence, we used the verb "knew." This reflected, no doubt, our predisposition towards the Greek concept of justice. This represents perhaps the essential point that the Mu'tazilah movement in early Islām was trying to make; their overthrow was the victory of the assertion that justice is what God ordains.

Of course, this freedom is a momentous responsibility; and it would be more correct to say that man alone was willing to accept it. There is a passage in the Qur'an (33:72) in which this is magnificently symbolized, in the drama of God's offering the privilege of option to the heavens (the spiritual forces) and to the earth and mountains (the natural world), but these cower from it in abject alarm. Man, on the other hand, accepts; thus taking up the tremendous challenge of consciously ordering his own career. He does not have to live in justice, as the stars have to circle in their spheres. But he will try.

The stakes are high. Only if men live correctly will their society escape disintegration and chaos; yet man has the liberty to choose wrongly, to bring down the whole social order crashing about his ears. More: man is an immortal soul, and his individual destiny throughout eternity as well as his society on earth turn on his willingness to pattern his life here and now on the transcendent norms. God has set up a system of final recompense, whereby those who accept the pattern of "oughtness" will find their reward in an everlasting beatitude, quite beyond this temporal scene, while for those who reject it, who spurn the moral imperative, there is entailed similarly an irretrievable disaster of unlimited punishment. Man is the summit of creation, unique now and for all eternity.

God has not left mankind without guidance on this matter of how it should live. On the contrary: so soon as man was created he was told what the moral law is. In Islamic terms, Adam was the first "prophet" (or "messenger"). That is, God set man in the universe and at once delivered to him the message: thus-and-so he must do, thus-and-so he must avoid doing. This is right; that is wrong. Human history opens with man knowing what he ought to do—but proceeds with him failing to do it. The conception is that Adam proved disobedient and his successors neglected, or forgot, or lost, or falsified, the message; so that a day came when humanity no longer knew the pattern. Man's failure to live justly was no longer simply a refusal of justice, but a groping in the dark as to what justice is. To redeem man out of that uncertainty, God in His mercy thereupon sent down the message again. There was thus another revelation, or disclosure, to humanity of what the eternal demands are; another "prophet," chosen as the instrument for proclaiming anew the ancient truths. But the story repeated itself: again, the community neglected, forgot, distorted, what had been revealed. And so it went—no one knows how many times throughout history persons were chosen to remind mankind of the heavenly norm, and to warn us of the terrors of failing to accept it. This much is known, that they were many, of diverse lands and peoples. Indeed, every community is said to have had its warner. Yet in essentials, despite the wide variety of messengers, the message is always the same.[7]

Amongst the numerous persons whom God has chosen from time to time to convey the message, some names have been preserved, some lost. Of the former, the best known and also the most significant are (apart from Adam) Abraham, Moses, and Jesus. They, like the other "messengers" ("prophets"), were themselves "acceptors" of the divine Command; and to their fellow human beings preached acceptance. In their case the preaching was, while not fully successful, yet effective to a marked degree, with more lasting results than in any previous instance. Indeed, their followers are still with us in vast numbers. They constitute the Jewish and the Christian communities.

Abraham's achievement was the effective proclamation of God's existence and sole supremacy: never since his day has humanity again totally forgotten that it is He, and He alone, who created the universe, He alone who deserves to be worshipped. The doctrine of monotheism, established by Abraham, never again quite lapsed. False gods, man-made idols, spurned by Abraham's vivid fidelity, have remained spurned ever since by at least a section of mankind.

The first step, thus, was taken on the road towards a rehabilitation of history. But other steps remained.

In the case of Moses, his followers preserved the message, and took the second step by setting forth across the centuries to put it into practice. They recognized God's oneness, and also God's law. At least they recognized that God has a law, by which man must be bound. However they were far from whole-hearted in their acceptance of the revelation. And in course of time they allowed (or caused) their copies of the text in which the written record of the message was preserved, to become corrupted. Their "scrip-

---

[7] This sentence is not entirely satisfactory, but we believe that the difficulties inhere in the subject matter rather than in the expression. That is, the relation between Islām and earlier revelations, as it understands them, is somewhat unresolved. (One example: the vexed question of *nāsikh* and *mansūkh*.)

ture" became inaccurate. Moreover, they committed one major blunder: they came to believe that the divine command applied only to themselves—instead of understanding that the prescribed pattern was a universal message, for all mankind.

In due course, to correct this desperate error, God sent another messenger, Jesus. His followers, as well as having certain other special qualities and God-given favours, understood the universalist nature of the faith well; and have been zealous in extending the community to the ends of the earth. But they too made a fundamental, indeed a heinous, mistake: they took to worshipping the messenger, instead of heeding the message. In this Muslim view, Jesus was, like all others in the long line of those whom God chose to proclaim His command, a human being. He was, admittedly, a rather special human being: attested by miracles (e.g., a virgin birth) and of quite exemplary moral character, but a human being for all that. Yet his followers began—to Jesus's own amazement and vigorous disclaiming protest—to deify him, to ascribe to him and his mother wild, even blasphemous and obscene, relations to God Himself. His community of followers, who called themselves "Christians," have through the centuries and across the continents focussed their attention on Christ to the partial neglect on the one hand of God, whose transcendence they thus compromise, and on the other hand of the full moral order, since they have cultivated personal piety but allowed social justice to slide, leaving the conduct of this-worldly affairs to "secular" forces not under the dominion of the eternal norms.[8] Though individually upright, they let history go its own way, unredeemed.

Once more, then, man had demonstrated his perversity or failure, his floundering in the persistent rejection or distortion of the supreme guidance which God kept offering to him, and which alone could save him. Not only were we men incapable by our own efforts of discerning what is right and what is wrong; but even when God tells us and shows us, we refuse to see.

The history of mankind up to this point, then, would seem rather a discouraging story. Progress there had been, certainly. After the first virtually complete neglect of the eternal commands, or rather a series of repeated neglectings, there had come gradually

---

[8] The second half of this sentence is of only relatively modern application, since only recently have Muslims come into touch with the Christian attitude on this matter enough to misunderstand it.

the recognition in principle of God's supremacy, and then the emergence of two communities of men—one, though limited and introverted, yet acknowledging in principle and dedicated to implementing the divine imperative, and the other beginning to understand that God's pleasure involved the bringing of the whole human world into one family in submission to His truth. Yet both these communities, each in its own way, understood very partially and in some respects misunderstood very seriously what God's requirements really are. Would men never grasp aright the everlasting message? And would they never set forth to practise it in full seriousness, to live as from all eternity it was ordained that men should live: preparing themselves personally for that stupendous bliss of deathless communion with God Himself for which the whole drama of creation is the subordinate prelude, and which will continue long after this temporal world has passed into nothingness; and meanwhile on earth constructing and living the perfect society, transforming human history into a record no longer of reiterated failure but at last of divinely guided success?

Had the question rested with man, the answer would doubtless have continued to be a despondent "never." We human beings are a sorry lot, prone to rebelliousness and error. But God's mercy is supreme; and His initiative perennial. In one final and dramatic move He salvaged the ongoing situation, injecting fully and effectively His supernal guidance into human affairs. Once and for all a final, clear statement of His truth and His justice was sent down; a messenger was chosen who would deliver it, interpret it, live it, with undeviating precision; a community was launched on its career that would preserve the message with a scrupulous fidelity, would carry it in triumph to the ends of the earth, and would obey it to the fullest implication of its practical outworking.

This time there was to be no error, no distortion, no neglect. This latest, last, decisive declaration of man's proper function in the universe was no isolated event, was by no means simply the inert statement of a transcendent truth. As we have said, the truth had been disclosed before. What was momentous, superbly creative in this instance, was the event plus its sequel: the application of the truth, its living embodiment in human history from this point. Here was not only a restatement of what God has to say to us, but a society developing around that restatement: a society that, grasping firmly the injunctions which are there revealed, dedicates itself to living according to them, and thereby sets forth on the reconstruction of human life on earth. This society is not exclusive; on the contrary, its welcome to all the world is warm, even insistent, as it earnestly invites others to join in this supremest of all enterprises—setting aright at last what man on his own resources had allowed to go awry. Nor is it quixotic, for it proceeds under divine support and with divine blessing, is led as it were by the divine hand. God Himself has explicitly promised that He will be with the community to sustain and guide it. Besides, the laws that have been entrusted to it and by which its behaviour is patterned are divine and eternal, are objectively valid; to live in accord with them is to live according to the very structure of the universe.

In this way, then, Islam, which had existed from all eternity, came down into history in the seventh century A.D. and began its final, full career among men. The only statement of its message whose text has been accurately preserved, is that in the Arabic recitation ("Qur'an") where it appears in all its fullness, and in language of limpid clarity and surpassing beauty. The only instance of its implementation that has been sustained and fruitful, is that of the group who—banding themselves together under Muhammad's leadership, and then persisting in the enterprise after he was gone—first in Arabia, then in the surrounding lands of the Middle East, and gradually thereafter in successive waves of expanding dominion throughout the world, undertook to organize in accordance with the ordained pattern both their own lives and their social order.

This group consisted at first of inhabitants of but two Arabian cities, later included other Arabs, and presently was joined by men from every nation, language, race, colour, and clime—a group distinguished from the rest of humanity simply in that they accepted, while others did not, the prescription that had been disclosed, and submitted to the divine plan. They are known, therefore, as "acceptors" or "submitters"; in the Arabic (sing.), *muslim*. By the emergence of this group the mundane version of Islam was launched, translating the idea into organized and continuing practice. Thus a new era in human history was born.

The year one of this Islamic era—1 A.H. (622 A.D.)—is not the year of Muhammad's birth (as would parallel the Christian case), or even that in which the revelations began to come to him, but the year when the nascent Muslim community came to political power. Muhammad and his small body of followers, having shifted from Makkah to Madinah, established themselves as an autonomous[9] community; and Islamic history began.

If the above exposition has succeeded at all in its objective of presenting (in interpretive summary) the views of Muslims, we may move on to a presentation also of our own views. To our further exposition we shall add analysis and commentary, and an attempt to explore the implications, as we see them, of these beliefs. We are ready now to justify or elucidate our earlier assertion that for the Muslim, community and history are "special." For him they are, as for no other, religiously significant. The Qur'an, of course, is in Muslim eyes holy, or "sacred." One would be going only slightly too far to say that his society and its history partake of an almost sacred quality also.[10] Here is a community that has explicitly undertaken to live in accordance with God's plan. Since it has been in existence, to become a Muslim means to join that community; and to take part in the enterprise of fulfilling God's good pleasure[11] on earth. The enterprise is hardly

[9] The community was "autonomous" in the sense of being free from non-Muslim control, but not in the precise sense of making its own laws. Rather it was constituted, and has continued, for the adoption and elaboration of the laws of God.

[10] It has sometimes been said that Muslims, at least in theory, do not divide their life, or the world, into spiritual and profane. Yet it would perhaps not be misleading to suggest a certain parallel between the line that discriminates these two spheres and the boundary of Muslim society, the line separating off the *ummah* from the rest of the world. (There are, however, quite other parallels in this realm also, such as between the concepts *barakah* and 'mana'.)

[11] Some of the Muslim theologians distinguish between God's "pleasure" (*riḍwān, riḍā, marḍī*) and His "will" (*mashī'ah, irādah*): the former referring to what ought to happen, the latter to what does happen—on the grounds that God's will cannot be flouted even though His command may be disobeyed. (A classical example: al-Ash'arī, in H. Ritter, ed., *Maqālāt al-Islāmiyīn* . . . , Istanbul, 1929-30, vol. I, p. 294: . . . *lam yarḍi bi al-sharr wa-in kān murīdan lah* [God does not command evil but rather forbids it, and commands what is good; and "is not pleased with evil even though He will it"]; for English translation and context see Walter C. Klein, . . . *al-Aš'arī's al-Ibānah* . . . (. . . Elucidation . . .), *a translation.* . . . New Haven, 1940, p. 33). The point has its counterpart in the discussion on free will and the like in Christian theology. We draw attention to it here only to point out the danger of misunderstanding if Christians use for Islamic matters such phrases as "the will of God" or "the purposes of God" to signify what ought to be. Confusion has arisen here in interpreting the term *Islām* as signifying "resignation," a kind of fatalistic acceptance of God's will, of what happens;

less important than the revelation. The privilege and duty and experience of taking part in it are central to the Muslim's faith.

In this orientation man comes close to God,[12] or human destiny is fulfilled, in so far as his activity approximates to goodness. And goodness, it will be remembered, is here that way of life of which the Qur'an is the revelation and Islamic society the expression. Man approaches God by participating in the Islamic venture, the historical endeavor of the Muslim community to realize the Kingdom of God on Earth.

Every religion designates some element in this world as mediating the other world. It would be going too far to say that for the Muslim, history, even Islamic history, mediates the eternal. However, this much perhaps one may say. For the Greek, the link between finite man and the ultimate scheme of things is rationality. Man, through his intellect, participates in ultimate reality in so far as his ideas are true. For the Christian the link is the person of Christ. For the Muslim (and for the Semitic religious tradition generally), the mediator between man and God is righteousness. It is in moral behaviour that the human and the divine meet. *The eternal Word of God is an imperative.*

Before the time of Muhammad, Islam—or more accurately its principles, the *shar'*, the essential law of Islam, the elaboration of that imperative—existed as a transcendent pattern. The word was with God.[13] Since that time, on the other hand, it is perhaps

---

whereas it originally meant an acceptance of His pleasure, a dynamic readiness to give oneself to carrying out what ought to happen.

[12] This phraseology would perhaps be acceptable as it stands only to the Ṣūfīs. Yet even others speak of man's vision of God (*ru'yà*) in the after-life; and indeed the concept of Paradise itself (*al-jannah*) perhaps justifies our usage. (Yet on this sentence cf. at ref. 17 below.)

[13] For Muslim (and other non-Christian?) readers it is perhaps necessary to indicate that the point that we are trying to make is deliberately, if provocatively, phrased after the fundamental Christian text, the prologue to the Gospel of St. John (*John 1*: 1-14). We use it because we hope that it may help Christians to understand the basic difference between themselves and Muslims. It might also be helpful to Muslims to study that passage in elucidation of the present argument. Muslims and Christians have been alienated partly by the fact that both have misunderstood each other's faith by trying to fit it into their own pattern. The most usual error is to suppose (on both sides) that the roles of Jesus Christ in Christianity and of Muhammad in Islām are comparable. We suggest that much more insight is gained if one realizes that the role of St. Paul in Christianity and that of Muhammad in Islām are much more closely comparable. Both are apostles. St. Paul preached

17

neither blasphemous nor misleading to say that for the Muslim that word has been made incorporate[14] in history, and has "dwelt among us."

Even without going so far, observers have noted the paramount position of the community in Islam. Less thought has been devoted to the significance of Islamic history, which is that community in motion. It is well known that Muslim society has a remarkable solidarity, that the loyalty and cohesion of its members are intense. Many have recognized that the community is not only a social group but a religious body; that "church and state" are one, to use the inappropriate language of the West. We would go much further, as has been said, in interpreting this. Yet to stress these facts, to insist upon the centrality of society, is not to deny but to interpret our initial emphasis on religion as personal. The community is based on, as it is integral to, individual faith.

Not only is Muslim society held together (as are other societies) by common loyalties and traditions, and by a very carefully worked out system of values and of beliefs. Not only is it the product of a superb ideal. It pulsates with the vitality of a profoundly held

a message, as did Muhammad; only his message, and the message of Christianity, is the person of Christ. If one is drawing parallels in terms of the structure of the two religions, what corresponds in the Christian scheme to the Qur'ān is not the Bible but the person of Christ—it is Christ who is for Christians the revelation of (from) God. And what corresponds in the Islamic scheme to the Bible (the record of revelation) is the Tradition (*hadīth*). These analogies are, of course, not perfect. But we suggest that they are closer and more helpful than those usually drawn. (For instance, we believe that the counterpart to Biblical criticism is *hadīth* criticism, which has begun. To look for historical criticism of the Qur'ān is rather like looking for a psychoanalysis of Jesus.)

[14] For this wording compare not only *John 1*: 14, but also perhaps the Christian dogma pertaining to later history, "The Church is the *body* of Christ."

Christians may find it shocking that we have taken the liberty to venture on such bold phraseology as we have resorted to. We do it for the sake of illumination. And perhaps the study of comparative religion can hardly be serious without being shocking. However, it is interesting to note that in Mu'tazilah times there was some sort of awareness on both sides of a parallel between the Muslim doctrine of the Qur'ān and the Christian logos-doctrine of Christ. For one of the Mu'tazilah ('Abbād ibn Sulaymān) accusing another Muslim of sharing the Christian belief about the word of God, see Albīr [Albert] Nasrī Nādir, *Falsafat al-Mu'tazilah*, Alexandria [and Baghdad?], 1950-51, I: 25; and for a Christian answering a Muslim's question as to what was his view about Christ by saying "My view about Him is the view of the *ahl al-sunnah* about the Qur'ān," see *ibid.*, p. 26.

and deeply personal conviction, a religious conviction that is warm and meaningful for the individual member. We may say that this society, this community, is the expression of a religious ideal, using "religious" in the personal[15] sense earlier proposed. As a creed or theological system may be the expression in an intellectual form of a personal faith—as is often the case, particularly with Christians—so a social order and its activities are the expression in a practical form of a Muslim's personal faith. Just as to be a Communist[16] involves being a member of the Party, so the religious conviction of a Muslim implies participation in the group. And there is another parallel, to the different sense in which to be an Anglican or Roman Catholic means to be a member of the Church, in that the religious experience of a Muslim is his experience in the group.

Membership in the community is not something distinct from or added to, is not even simply consequent upon, but is an aspect of a personal Islam.

The social, practical, dynamic character of the faith of Islam—in other words, the involvement of this faith within the processes of history—may be illustrated at many points. Salvation in Islam is, admittedly, by faith; not by works.[17] Yet it is faith in the validity of works. It is faith in God, and in the obligatoriness of what He has enjoined.[18] A Muslim is saved not in the final analysis by doing

[15] Above, pp. 7-9.

[16] Compare the party-member's disdain for the "arm-chair socialist," or for the "mere intellectual" who thinks but does not join in acting.

[17] See, for instance, the accepted al-'Aqā'id al-Nasafīyah of Abū Ḥafṣ 'Umar al-Nasafī, the section on al-Kabīrah ("great [sin]"). In the London edition of this text (Wm. Cureton, ed., Pillar of the Creed of the Sunnites, 1843), this is p. 3 (second series), lines 9-12. An English translation may be found in D. B. Macdonald, Development of Muslim Theology, Jurisprudence and Constitutional Theory, New York, 1903, p. 311. For elaboration, see the 'Īsà al-Bābī al-Ḥalabī edition of the text, with commentaries, Cairo, 1335 [1917] pp. 117-124 and the English translation of one of these latter, E. E. Elder (trans.), A Commentary on the Creed of Islam, New York, 1950, chap. 12 (pp. 107-15).

[18] This is the significance of the kalimah, the famous two-clause "creed" of Islām. To say "and Muhammad is the apostle of God" is to commit oneself to a belief, not about the person of Muhammad, but about the validity of what he brought. The personality of Muhammad is essentially irrelevant. To declare that he is a prophet is to accept the Qur'ān as binding (and therefore the community that lives according to it as embodying on earth what is of divine prescription).

good works; but by recognizing that they are good, that he *ought* to do them.

Differences that have arisen within Islam, therefore, have concerned themselves less with what is true than with what is good.[19] The sects of Islam have differed amongst themselves not on matters of theology so much as on questions of practice. There would seem to be no word in Arabic, or indeed in any Islamic language, meaning "orthodox." The word usually translated "orthodox," *sunnī*, actually means rather "orthoprax," if we may use the term.[20] A good Muslim is not one whose belief conforms to a given pattern, whose commitment may be expressed in intellectual terms that are congruent with an accepted statement (as is the case generally in Protestant Christianity), but one whose commitment may be expressed in practical terms that conform to an accepted code. The counterpart to the Christians' intellectualist concept of "heresy" is the Muslims' procedural *bid'ah* (which might be translated "deviation").

Sectarian differences exemplify our point most readily in the case of the legal *madhāhib*. At this level divergencies are relatively minor. One comes nearer the heart of the matter with the great Sunni-Shi'ah dichotomy in Islam, which arose from a dispute as to how society should be organized, what sort of leadership it should have. The fundamental religious debates in Islam have been concerned essentially with what shall be the direction in which the on-going historical enterprise is to proceed.[21]

The underlying notion is of a society in motion. In relation to this, the individual must not get out of step, must not turn deviationist; while group leadership is responsible for seeing that the whole venture knows and follows the right direction. In order

[19] It could be argued that a closer approximation to the Muslim view might be obtained by using the adjective "right" rather than "good" (cf. W. D. Ross, *The Right and the Good*, Oxford, 1930). We retain "good," since we are deliberately attempting to transpose to terms closer to our Greek intellectuality what it is that the Muslim believes.

[20] Even *sunnī* may be regarded as a popular term; the technical phrase is *ahl al-sunnah wa al-jamā'ah*, which stresses again the community aspect.

[21] We do not mean that Islām knew no theological discussion. It did not begin as early as moral-sociological (the Khawārij), but presently genuine creedal issues were debated, as between the Mu'tazilah and the Ashā'irah. When we say that these debates were not "fundamental," we mean that they did not affect the community so basically as in Christian history, or as the other issues affected Islām.

that it know, there is the body of *'ulamā*, the *muftī* (the religious scholars); in order that it follow, there is, ideally, the *khilāfah* (*imāmah*) ("caliphate"). Usually, points at issue are minor; but in principle and in final analysis, although the matter has never been phrased in these terms, yet there is a sense in which the basic Islamic question is what form Islamic history shall take.

Finally, perspective and illumination on the relation of Islam to history may be won by sketching a comparison with the positions of three other major *Weltanschauungen*: the Hindu, Christian, Marxist. Of course, the matter is in each of these cases elaborate and subtle; only a highly simplified, schematic indication of general type is here attempted. By ignoring complexities, one might arrange representatives of these faiths in a graded series as follows: the Hindu, for whom ultimately history is not significant; the Christian, for whom it is significant but not decisive; the Muslim, for whom it is decisive but not final; the Marxist, for whom it is all in all.

Hindu teaching especially is manifold, but for our illustration we may single out characteristic doctrines. A religious, or anyway moral, significance is given to history in the concept of *karma*; yet salvation lies in extrication from this. For the Hindu, history, *saṃsāra*, is to be transcended. Indeed, this world and all its activity are *māyā*. Protests have been lodged against translating this simply as "illusion"; yet the tangible world and its transient development remain but a veil that religious insight pierces to the motionless truth beyond.

For the Christian, history paradoxically both is and is not fundamental. It is ceaselessly significant, but never final and decisive. God's activity in history was crucial; human activity in history thereafter must be the result, not the criterion and not even the theatre, of faith. Morality flows out of, not into, salvation. History accordingly is the field of Christian endeavour, and it has a purpose that is divine. Yet it is also the field of human sinfulness, so that that purpose is relentlessly frustrated. The Christian, therefore, in his historical endeavour, hopes for forgiveness rather than utopia.

In this connection we may draw attention to the significant and startling fact that the concept "Islamic history" exists at all. In the strict sense there is no such thing as Christian history; certainly there is no Hindu history. There is the history of Hindus and of Christendom, there is even the history of the Christian Church; but these are not quite the same thing. As Reinhold Niebuhr and others have been vigorously reminding us of late, history can never be fully Christian. Man's attempt to build a Kingdom of God on Earth, a just and harmonious and ever more prosperous social order, imagining that finally history itself can be redeemed, is, they have been preaching, an aberration—as it will, inevitably, be a failure. And even those who do believe that to Christianize history is a feasible proposition, a legitimate goal, admit that it has not yet been done. At the most it is an ideal to be striven for, something for the future. Even for the optimist, a Christian history has not yet begun.

Nonetheless, Christianity takes very seriously the all too human history that has long since begun; in which the Christian like others is and ought to be involved. The Cross illuminates both the heights and the depths of human nature, laying bare at once the love and the wickedness of which history is intrinsically compounded. It symbolizes the lengths to which we are called upon to go, as well as the frustration which we are warned to expect, because of our own perversity which we are taught to recognize. Accordingly the significance of the historical process lies not in how much we accomplish, but in how devotedly we love. It is the Christian's duty, because he is a Christian, to try to save and to improve civilization, consecrating his life to and if the need arise sacrificing it in the relentless struggle to make history approximate to justice, and to make a fuller, better life available to all mankind. Yet it is also the Christian's duty, because he is a Christian, to contemplate with equanimity the possibility of failure. American jitteriness at the present menace to Western civilization is a disconcerting measure of the extent to which there has been substituted for the Christian faith a faith in the American way of life.

Not that Islam, of course, even in its most legalist form, ever became fully idolatrous. Attention was never *confined* to the this-worldly manifestation of value. For the Muslims, involvement in history, though absorbing, is at the most only the obverse of their coin; the reverse of which, polished, brilliant, and pure gold, is in the other world. Islam begins with God, and to Him it well knows we shall return. Its endeavour to redeem history, though total, is derived; it is an endeavour to integrate temporal righteousness in this world with a timeless salvation in the next.

The deep significance of this is in part made clear in the stark unlikeness here to our fourth example: Marxism. In other aspects of their orientation to history, Islam and Marxism—the world's two chief large-scale endeavours to implement a social ideal—have much in common, more than any other religion has in common with Marxism, with the partial exception of Islam's prototype, Judaism. The disparity in this one aspect is therefore telling. Indeed, in this contrast one can find illumination on the general question of the crucial difference that is made in history by a concern for the extra-historical.

The Marxist movement we may take as the largest, most resolute, organized, explicit attempt in man's development thus far to construct a good society, to control historical development and to realize within it a dream of what life for the human community should be.[22] It is distinguished from the religions, of course, by its exclusive concern with this mundane world. It is distinguished also from Western humanism, from the impulsion instanced in secular liberalism and in the American and French revolutions, by its intense and all-inclusive articulation, its total concentration on this one ambition. It puts every last egg in the historical basket: nothing whatever matters but the kind of history that it is sure will, and is determined shall, evolve. In its view there is no meaning, no value, and in the end no reality,[23] to human life other than its meaning as an item in the on-going historical process, as a contributor or obstacle to the kind of history that is to obtain tomorrow. It is as a means to an end, or in any case in relation to that end, an end that is given within and by history, that in

[22] The use of the terms "good" and "should" is not quite justified, nor yet quite invalid. The Kremlin subsequently repudiated the moral aspect of Communism's goal, in a trend that culminated in the Great Purge of the mid-1930's. Yet there was a strong moral element in the original impulse of the movement, and it has remained powerful for fellow-travellers and for novices in the party. It is our view that the later repudiation of morality was not unrelated to the original metaphysical position that history is self-sufficient, and a closed system; see below in the present discussion. We hold, accordingly, that the Marxist movement began, and is still sustained from the outside, particularly in Asia, as a movement toward a good society; and that its failure to maintain this objective internally has been due at least in part to the false metaphysics of its *Weltanschauung*.

[23] *Manifesto of the Communist Party*, 1848: "Human nature, . . . man in general, who belongs to no class, has no reality, . . . exists only in the misty realm of philosophical fantasy." From the Authorized Indian Edition, People's Publishing House, Bombay, 1944, p. 52.

Marxism the human person has significance; and this is his only significance, for himself and for others.

There follows logically what in observable fact has followed historically; namely, that for Marxism there is no reason (literally no reason: our universe, the movement posits, is the kind of universe where there cannot conceivably be any reason) for not killing or torturing or exploiting a human person if his liquidation or torture or slave labour will advance the historical process.

This is, indeed, the logical outcome of any repudiation of transcendence. The non-Marxist movements of repudiation in the West have, so far, avoided these frightening historical consequences by being less relentlessly logical, and by being less consistently comprehensive. They have not taken themselves quite so seriously, nor imposed themselves so exclusively. Dewey and the social scientists, too, reject metaphysics and the Other World. Yet there is an important "cultural lag" that fortunately saves the West from the worst consequences of its own technological pragmatism. Further, the non-Marxist secularists lay stress on individualism. This is a stress on the part rather than on the whole, from the viewpoint of historical development; and also, if our own view of the nature of the individual and of the universe be at all valid, it is despite themselves a stress on transcendence. The kind of reason inhibiting us from killing or torturing or exploiting our neighbours, even for a worthy cause, the Marxists assert is based on reasoning from metaphysical or religious or other non-historical reality. They are correct in this assertion. To insist that there is a timeless quality in human personality, an intrinsic value or disvalue in certain means, whatever the ends, and in certain moments today, whatever come tomorrow, is to insist that the whole meaning and nature of existence are not subsumed within the historical process.

We have emphasized that for the Muslim history is important. But for the Marxist it alone is important, and the difference here is vast. For the Muslim, like the Marxist but unlike the Hindu, what happens here below is of inescapable and lasting significance. The building up of a proper community life on earth is a supreme imperative. Surely the Islamic enterprise has been the most serious and sustained endeavour ever put forward to implement Justice among men; and until the rise of Marxism was also the largest and most ambitious. Yet it differs from the Marxist in that for Islam every mundane event has two references, is seen in two contexts. Every move that a man makes has an eternal as well as a temporal relevance. The on-going march of mundane affairs is a great collective drama of group achievement; at the same time it is a series of discrete items, of which each human individual will at the Day of Judgement be accountable for his personal share. That is, every deed has consequences of one kind in this world, and consequences of another kind in the world to come. In other words, each action must be assessed in itself, as well as in its relation to historical development.

This sort of judgment, it can be argued by the metaphysician, comes closer to the objective reality of the kind of world in which we live, the kind of being that human beings are, and the kind of life that history consists in our living, than does any one-sided view that denies a morality transcending the temporal flux. History has meaning, ultimate meaning; but its meaning is not exhausted within itself. Rather there are norms and standards, standing above the historical process, according to which that process may and must be and indeed is being judged.

Whatever the metaphysical position, the empirical historian may note the mundane, historical counterpart of this logical argument. In practice, as well as in theory, they who start by denying transcendence end by denying value. The Marxist doctrine has in fact let itself be embodied in a movement wherein not only are the means amoral and indeed by any known criteria immoral, but also the end itself has been lost. "Social justice" which the Marxist first set out to achieve has become in the hands of the actual Soviet organization but one more historical concept, an ideological weapon to serve the purposes of nihilistic mundane power. The Marxist movement, repudiating external norms by which it may be judged, has eventuated rather quickly in an enterprise with no norms at all. Man's one utterly this-worldly venture after Justice has rapidly turned sour.

Our point is simply to illuminate the quality of the Islamic attitude to history that emerges from its insistence on the transcendent reference of each step in the historical process. This has been a guarantee both of whatever ability to avoid going sour the movement has maintained in the course of its persistence through history, and of that persistence itself over now many centuries. By Islam this insistence on the transcendent reference has been symbolized in the notion of Heaven and Hell, of another world "after" the end of history. This colourful, dramatic metaphor has impinged with a fluctuating but never negligible urgency on the whole course of the Muslims' historical development. Collectively and singly they have sought both Paradise beyond this world and, within history, a kind of society which, they believe, is proper to personal preparation for that Paradise and at the same time proper to the mundane scene itself, correct both for the individual for the next world and for the community for this. With the Christians, they have shared the conviction that the former is, in the final analysis, more important. That is, they have believed that the course of history in its total sweep is ultimately less significant than the quality of one's personal life. Yet they have approximated also to the Marxists in their conviction that the course of history and the social shape that it may assume are profoundly relevant to the quality of personal life within it; that there is inherent in the structure of this world and its development a proper course, a right social shape; that the meaning of history lies in the degree to which these become actualized; and finally that they who understand the essential laws for these, and accept the responsibility involved, are entrusted with the task of executing that actualization, of guiding history to its inevitable and resplendent fulfillment.[24]

So much for the Islamic theory of history.[25] Let us turn for a

[24] It behoves us perhaps to add a word in regard to Judaism. Much attention has recently been given by scholars to the question of the religious significance of history, particularly in Old Testament times, for that faith. In many ways the Jewish and the Muslim attitudes to the historical process are similar. As throughout, Islām may be seen as in part a kind of fulfillment of the Jewish development. There is, however, an important distinction. In the Old Testament attitude, history itself is continuingly revelatory. History is to revelation as subject to predicate, rather than *vice versa*. Classical Hebrew thought learned from history, and—so the modern interpretation runs—put what it learned into its scripture. Islamic thought learned from scripture, and put what it learned into history. Ideally, for Islām, history ought to be subordinated to revelation—which is final. For the Old Testament, revelation itself is a long-term process.

[25] It is perhaps incumbent to refer to the two studies on what might seem ostensibly this topic: the article by H. A. R. Gibb, TA'RĪKH, in *The Encyclopaedia of Islām*, Supplement, Leiden, 1938 (there are three articles under this heading: one in vol. IV and two in the Supplement; Gibb's is the second of the latter two); and Franz Rosenthal, *A History of Muslim Historiography*, Leiden, 1952. However, what we mean by "history" is not just *ta'rīkh*; the

moment to consider practice: the history of the Muslims as it has worked out empirically. The two things are, of course, intertwined. The actual course of the Muslims' historical development, especially in its early centuries, greatly affected the conception that they elaborated of this world and of Islam's role in it. The germ of this conception is found in the Qur'an; but the full doctrine is the product of men who studied the Qur'an from the vantage point of the particular historical situation in which they found themselves, and in the light of as much of Islamic history as already lay behind them. Certainly the idea of history implicit in their religion has vitally affected the course of their mundane career (and as we shall presently be contending at length, continues to affect it). Equally certainly the latter has affected that idea.

So much, indeed, have fact and ideology interacted, that once again we must stress the fluidity and comprehensiveness of this idea of history, its varying from century to century and even from person to person. We must stress again too the concomitant fact that our or any presentation of that idea is at best a generalized abstraction, an approximation to a classical type. Nonetheless ideas, although they ever bear marks of the environment in which they are born, and are understood in ways related to the environment in which they are interpreted, yet have a life and power of their own. This is supremely true of religious ideas, whose persistence and persuasiveness far outstretch in space and time the original milieu to which they are, as it were, naturally correlated. The later history of any religious community, accordingly, is to be construed only in terms jointly of its contemporary situation and of its inherited ideals.

In the case of the Muslims, it is our thesis, to be elaborated in due course, that both their religious condition today and their potentialities, mundane and other, for tomorrow have to do with a tension between these two—between their sense on the one hand of what Islamic history is essentially, and their awareness on the other hand of what their actual history is today observably.

Arabic for our concept is rather al-dunyā, or better, al-dunyā al-mutaṭawwirah. We would suggest as a translation of the title of our present chapter, "al-Islām wa al-taṭawwur." In older, slower days, however, the concern for society (so conspicuous in Islām) was not consciously a concern for the process of development of that society in time. We should mention also, as relevant to our discussion, the seminal work of H. Butterfield, Christianity and History, London, 1949.

That tension in its present degree is new. In the past, particularly the classical past, the Muslim could look out upon a world in which the essence and the existence of Islam more nearly converged. The religious reality in which his faith taught him to believe, and the historical reality by which he saw himself surrounded, seemed in reasonable equilibrium.[26]

Of the early history of Islam on earth, a salient characteristic is overt success. This is in sharp contrast with the early Christian counterpart as well as with the late Islamic. The first, formative centuries of Islam were centuries of temporal as well as spiritual achievement, an age of conquest and brilliance. The Muslims burst forth in triumph into the surrounding lands. The Persian empire and much of the Roman fell before them. The new community expanded, it prospered; it became both powerful, effecting large-scale operational control, and great. Islam quickly established and took responsibility for a new order stretching from the Pyrenees to the Himalayas, an empire larger than the Roman at its height; and followed up political dominion with wealth and with social and cultural advance.

The success was comprehensive as well as striking. As we have said, the enterprise gained not only power but greatness. In addition to quickly attaining political and economic mastery, Muslim society carried forward into new accomplishments both art and science. Its armies won battles, its decrees were obeyed, its letters of credit were honoured, its architecture was magnificent, its poetry charming, its scholarship imposing, its mathematics bold, its technology effective.

The success, furthermore, was of an Islam creative and responsible. The conquerors of Jerusalem and Damascus, of the Nile valley and the Tigris-Euphrates, of North Africa and Spain on the one hand and of Central Asia into India on the other, proved not only prosperous but original and constructive. They brought into being a new civilization. On a new linguistic and legal as well as administrative and commercial basis, a great new society arose—

[26] This is the substance of the classical Sunnī position. The Khārijī and Shī'ī were those minorities for whom the *status quo* was an inadequate social expression of the Islamic ideal. Yet their outlook too was not radically different, in that their movements were motivated by a confidence that *they* could realize in practice true Islām once they came to power. The divinely ordained pattern of society was either achieved or certainly achievable.

under their endeavour and guidance, the product of their powerful spirit.

The success, moreover, was religious. The Muslim achievement
was seen as intrinsic to their faith. They were not only victorious
on the battlefield and effective in many diverse departments of
living, but they succeeded also, and again in a relatively short
period of time, in integrating life into that wholeness that constitutes a culture. Many elements went into the making of Islamic
civilization: elements from Arabia, from Hellenism, from the
Semitic cultures of the ancient Near East, from Sasani Iran, from
India. The achievement of the Muslims was that they welded these
into a homogeneous way of life, and also carried it forward into
new development. And it was Islam that provided the integration,
as it provided too the drive and power to sustain it. Islamic form
was given to almost every aspect of life, whatever its content. And
it was an Islamic pattern that gave the society cohesion as well as
vitality. The centre of this unifying force was religious law, which
regulated within its powerful and precise sweep everything from
prayer rites to property rights. The law gave unity to Islamic
society, from Cordoba to Multan. It gave unity also to the individual Muslim, his entire life activity being organized into a meaningful whole by this divine pattern. It gave unity also in time,
providing the community with continuity, as dynasties rose and
fell and could be regarded as episodes in the persisting enterprise
of Islam's endeavour to build on earth the kind of social order
that the divine imperative prescribes.

The satisfying success of this enterprise, and even the enterprise
itself, contrast with the corresponding earthly career of the early
Christians. *Their* religion was launched upon a world already
organized, and their formative centuries were spent under some-
one else's rule. Christianity for a time served in significant measure
as the faith of the proletariat of the Roman empire; whereas
nascent Islam was the faith, and indeed the *raison d'être*, of an
entrepreneurial ruling class. The Christian religion advened in a
world that was already a going concern, with its laws and its languages, its government and its economic structure. While Christians concerned themselves with their personal moral lives, the
task of organizing a social order had long since been accomplished,
and the task of carrying it on rested on other people's shoulders.

Indeed, early Christianity was persecuted. For it, the superlative virtue was the moral stamina of martyrdom, the ability of the person by inner resources to stand against the course of history.[27] Even in group life the ideal was to stand apart from the course. And in practice the social community of the Church had for three centuries little say as to how history at large should proceed. The ordering of the historical process was no part of the Christian programme.

It is worth our while to digress for a further moment from the historical progress of Islam itself, since it is instructive to follow the later development of the Christian-Western situation. The oppression that marked the early stages of the Christians' historical experience was in time outgrown. They did not always remain a minority, on the defensive or *distrait*. Yet even when they came to constitute society rather than to protect themselves against it, and when in the historical flux they themselves reached positions of responsibility and power, they took over the social order as an extant and functioning process. They retained it; yet as something extrinsic to their faith. As Christians they might see their duty as at most to improve it, but not to replace it with something new.

Accordingly, modern Western civilization (alone among the great cultures of man) is dual. It is explicitly a civilization composed of two traditions, which it has never integrated: one from Greece and Rome, one from Palestine. Throughout, these two have existed and developed side by side: sometimes in conflict, sometimes in uneasy tension, sometimes in harmony, but never fused. Though they have influenced each other profoundly, they have remained distinct. For the West it is axiomatic that such things as grammar, and hygiene, and politics (which it derives from its Greco-Roman background) are to be distinguished from matters of the spiritual life (from the Palestinian, Biblical heritage). And in both its traditions it is deeply persuaded that the distinction is important and ought to be retained—the discrimina-

[27] Contrast the classical Muslim conception of "martyr" (*shahīd*), who gave his life fighting not against history but with it. His death was seen as *fī sabīl Allāh*, "in the path of God," i.e. in the furtherance of the Islamic cause in the world. He died in a battle that was thought of as extending the *dār al-Islām*: that is, extending the mundane area of Islamic control. The Christian Church, on the other hand, had at this time no thought of historical, earthly success. It saw the martyr as allowing himself to be overwhelmed by history but not vanquished by it. He was winning a spiritual victory in the face of a this-worldly defeat.

tion between the secular (the word originally means, in effect, the "historical") and the religious.

Even when Christians, therefore, have in their turn become successful on the worldly plane, this has not been regarded as a success for them as Christians, as an achievement of or for their faith. That the course of history should prove favorable is no particular spiritual triumph.[28] Conversely, a disintegration in temporal affairs is not, for Christians, a religious failure.

Indeed, Christianity has been in some ways supremely a religion of adversity. Admittedly, as a great world religion it has like Islam and the others been meaningful in divergent ways to different kinds of people in many different situations. Yet not far from its centre has almost always been a note of wistfulness. It has in a sense been at its best in times of distress. The cross, at the core of its faith, is a symbol of suffering. Christianity is a religion of triumph out of sorrow, of salvation in the midst of defeat. Islam is equally multi-faceted: it too in its worldwideness has had something significant and personal and direct to say to different men in very diverse circumstances, and in its Sufi version has stressed quite other interpretations. To the individual it has certainly given a superb self control in the face of adversity. Yet its emphasis is on moral choice,[29] on the individual and society doing the right, and therefore the effective, thing. In some ways, at least for the community, it has been characteristically a religion of triumph in success, of salvation through victory and achievement and power.

[28] We do not deny that some Christians have taken pride, even a spiritual pride, in worldly success. They have regarded power, wealth, productivity, as an indication of their own or their society's moral excellence. But this is contrary to the central genius of Christianity, and has almost never been seriously advanced by outstanding exponents of church doctrine. For every leader who has argued in this sense, there have been more than one taking the opposite position: that worldly success is a temptation, and satisfaction in it is a sin. Even when, as with the Puritans, mundane prosperity was taken as a proof of virtue, it was seen as the reward for, rather than the application of, faith; and usually as an individual, rather than a community, achievement. Muslim piety, too, even before the fall of Baghdad, warned the individual against self-righteousness and a pride in riches, but thought it right and proper that Muslim society should flourish. The Christian movement recently approaching most nearly the Muslim position has been that of "The Social Gospel." One may perhaps compare also earlier heresies throughout Christian history: the Waldensian, Anabaptist, etc.

[29] For an elaboration of this point, see Marshall G. S. Hodgson, "A comparison of Islam and Christianity," a paper read before a seminar at the University of Chicago, 1955.

Let us return, then, to our consideration of the actual development of Islamic society on earth, having gained this clarification of the significance of its first success and homogeneity. We saw the early Muslims taking on the whole burden, and opportunity, of government—and more than government, of cultural creation in the widest sense. We saw that they executed this assignment with remarkable distinction, so that presently they could look out upon the society that they had constructed with the gratifying sense that it led the world. God had told men how to live; those who accepted this and set out to live so were visibly receiving His blessing.

They were therein also illustrating the soundness of the plan. In Islam God had spoken; through it He was acting. The brilliant success of the enterprise confirmed the validity of the whole conception. History confirmed faith.

History, however, moves.

If one truth of earthly Islam is that its programme worked for a time well, another is that it was only for a time. As others of man's civilizations have done across the centuries, the Arab civilization rose, flourished for a period—and declined. The fall of Baghdad in 1258 marks the formal end of the once tremendously successful Arab empire. The Mongol invasions that that fall epitomizes certainly dealt the Arab world a devastating blow. Many millions were killed; whole areas were laid utterly waste; and political rule in the centre of the Muslim world passed into the hands of barbarian infidels. Yet the date is but a symbol. On the one hand, Arab culture flourished for another two centuries and more in areas unravaged by the Mongols, notably Cairo and Spain. On the other hand, it can be argued that the conquest in the thirteenth century gave the *coup de grâce* to a civilization already past its prime. There had already been vicissitudes, especially political. It is not to our purpose here to trace the course or to investigate the causes of the disintegration of the Islamic achievement in its first, Arab phase. We simply observe that the disaster happened. The classical period of Islamic history came to an end.

This constituted in a sense the first great crisis of Islamic history[30] (as we shall presently urge that the modern period con-

[30] An argument could be made, but it would take us too far afield here to elaborate it, that the eventual failure of the Arab venture was the second rather than the first great crisis: that the first was rather the death of Mu-

stitutes the second). Islamic history seemed to have bogged down. It could be felt that the great endeavour to realize God's purpose was petering out, if it had not actually failed.

Islam on earth survived this crisis. It survived, but not inertly; rather, it responded creatively to the challenge. For it presently emerged into new and rather different, and in some ways fuller expression. As the European "Middle Ages" drew to their close, Islam's mediaeval period—between its classical and its modern eras—got under way. To historians of Islam, whether Muslim or Western, this mediaeval phase of Islamic development has been the subject of much less concern than the classical. Yet there was much that was new, and much that is significant. Islam produced

---

hammad. This came so close to the beginnings of things—before any of the Muslims' records, for instance, were compiled, let alone their theories formulated—that it has received little attention. The solution to the crisis is presupposed in all subsequent Islamic thinking; that is, in virtually all Islamic thinking. The point at issue when the Prophet died, however, was in fact whether there should be any Islamic history at all. Some of the members of the then community felt (e.g., the Badū) that the affair was now over: they had given their allegiance to a leader, he had died, and that was that. Others felt that socially the *status quo ante* should now be restored: tribal and urban realities should once more be recognized, while religious faith presumably would take its individual course on those bases. The proposal that finally prevailed, however (not without struggle, and indeed even armed struggle), was to reject these possibilities and instead to keep the community of Muhammad's followers intact, as a socio-political-economic unit and as one that would sally forth into the world to implement as a unit the new revelation. The immense significance of this decision, and indeed the fact that it *was* a decision, which conceivably might not have been taken, seem to have received less attention than they deserve. It is surely one of the most sweepingly consequential decisions in all human development. Those (including, of course, practically all Muslims since) who take for granted that, given Muhammad's career, it was the only logical or an inevitable decision, forget how little in man's history is either logical or inevitable.

That the community should remain and should choose a leader for itself in the Prophet's place, can be seen as a more basic matter than the question—which has received untold attention—of who that leader should be. Those (all but the Shī'ī Muslims) who note that the Prophet left no guidance on the latter question, usually tacitly presume that the former decision he nonetheless took for granted. To the present writer this is not clear. It would be interesting to investigate what evidence there may be that he foresaw the problem. In our view, it is the subsequent rather than the preceding history of the community that makes the course finally chosen at the *saqīfat* Banī Sā'idah seem so natural.

(One may note further the not unimportant view that the onslaught of Greek thought was the real great crisis of classical Islam.)

in this second major phase various constructive answers to the problems posed.

Religiously, the fundamental innovation was the spread of Sufism. The Sufi or mystic interpretation of Islam goes back to, and even through, the classical period. Yet at that time it was the treasure of a small minority, an élite of the pious withdrawn from the main stream of Islamic advance. As the Arab period began to weaken, more and more in Muslim society turned to this somewhat precious version of the faith. The mediaeval period expanded it widely. For instance, it developed the organized Sufi order, which gradually spread throughout the length and breadth of the Islamic world. The movement was institutionalized and popularized. There was development also in interpretations. For example, the greatest of the Sufis, Jalalu-d-Din Rumi, produced his poem *Masnavi* a few years after the fall of Baghdad (it is not too fanciful to compare the appearance of Augustine's *City of God* following the fall of Rome?). Non-Arab Islam is steeped in Sufism; and even the Arabs, in post-classical times, infused much that is Sufi in their understanding of the faith.[31]

Secondly, Islam converted the conquerors. Within fifty years the Mongol dynasty that had subjugated so much of the Islamic world and set up over it an alien dominion, itself became Muslim—itself took on the role of champion of the Islamic cause. The new rulers undertook with conviction, energy, and brilliance to promote again the very enterprise that they had recently seemed to overthrow.

This may be seen as one instance of the third great development: of Islam finding for itself in this new period new peoples and new cultures to carry forward its advance. If the Arab spirit had spent itself, historical Islam soon began to flower afresh in Persian and in Turkish forms. These forms were different from any previously

[31] The Arabs did not have the creativity, or the good fortune, to produce Ṣūfī poets of the Persian quality and depth, and had to be content to have their greatest expressions of the mystical view of God and the world in prose. It is interesting to speculate whether this may have played any part in the Arab world's adopting Sufism less fully than the Persians, Turks, and Indians have done—in addition, of course, to more obvious and straightforward reasons such as the Arabs' greater closeness to classical Islam. It is at least questionable whether the intellectual expression even of a Ghazzālī or an Ibn al-'Arabī can in the nature of the case be as adequate an expression of the truth that the mystics have grasped, as the artistic expression of a Rūmī.

known—different in governmental framework and political theory, in economic structure and social organization, in cultural and aesthetic values. With these differences, doubtless because of them, the Muslims again marched forward to historical achievement. After the nadir of the thirteenth century came fairly soon a re-rising culminating in a new zenith in the sixteenth. The latter in some ways could be represented as the Muslims' greatest century to date: with the Ottoman empire at its mightiest and most re-splendent, Europe quaking before its seemingly inexorable drive; the Safavis in Iran, combining imperial power with artistic exquisiteness; the Mughuls in India, composing of power, wealth, and sophisticated beauty the greatest rule the subcontinent had seen for many a long day.

Nor was Islam's second earthly efflorescence confined to the building of empires. There was expansion also in geographical and in spiritual senses. The second great wave both of military conquest and of missionary zeal carried the world of Islam north into Asia Minor and the Balkans and Central Asia, south into Negro Africa, east into Indonesia. Mediaeval Islam at least doubled classical Islam's extension in space and numbers. Once again the historical enterprise of the Muslims seemed in full swing.

Nevertheless, with the partial and certainly significant exception of the Turks, this second, mediaeval outburst of historical creativity has not been generally regarded by the Muslims as fully intrinsic to Islam. This period has not been seen as a major instance of "Islamic" history in quite the same sense as the first, classical period. What the Muslims effected in it is not so keenly felt to be another example of Islam at work in the world, organizing into a divine pattern the flux of historical development. We shall be investigating the Turkish exception presently, in its bearing on the modern situation in Turkey, and investigating also other particular interpretations. The general reasons for the difference in attitude are not entirely clear. Tentatively, three such reasons may be suggested, though doubtless there are others, and the whole subject needs exploration.

First, the early phase of Islamic history takes precedence over all others simply because it came first. The original becomes the normative; the classical period becomes "classical" in the sense of exemplary, standard. Later periods, which differ from it (and it is of the nature of history that each period necessarily differs from what went before), are thought of as deviating from it.[32] The first historical expression of the movement is felt to be the "right" expression—or not even as an expression at all, but as the movement in its pure form. (For example: the Law, which both as a developed concept and as an actual system is in fact an historical product of the second and third centuries *hijrī*, has come to be regarded as part of the transcendent essence of Islam. This comes from taking history seriously, but not quite seriously enough.)

Moreover, the mediaeval Muslims themselves felt a much less close link than did classical Muslims between the temporal and the eternal; between their own history and true Islam. The historical leaders and the religious leaders came to feel that they were leading two different things. Politically, the *khalifah* gave place to the *sultan*; that is, a religious executive was replaced by an explicitly independent mundane power. It would be an exaggeration to regard the Sultan as a "secular" ruler. Yet he comes much closer to this Western concept than his predecessor had done, at least in theory. In the concept of the state and of society that came to be accepted among mediaeval Muslims, religion was seen almost as coordinate with other aspects of the world's life, rather than as their coordinator. Classical Islamic political theory had seen the faith as ideally the regulator of life and society, assigning each his due place, with the temporal ruler's function that of carrying out religion's decrees. Mediaeval Muslim political theory, on the other hand, saw it as the emperor's task to maintain the balance of mundane society, giving each group within the social order its due place and function: the army, the bureaucracy, the peasantry, etc., and also the *'ulamā'*.[33]

[32] An illustrative instance: "The earlier past of Islām represents its basic principles, true essence and immortal teachings," Sobḥī Maḥmaṣṣānī, in "Muslims: Decadence and Renaissance. Adaptation of Islamic Jurisprudence to Modern Social Needs," *The Muslim World*, Hartford, 44: 186 (1954). This chance quotation is not particularly authoritative, but is apt; and the idea expressed is representative of an almost unlimited number of Muslim writers.

[33] This point has been brought to my attention by my colleague Prof. Niyazi Berkes in one of his seminars. He hopes to investigate it in some detail and write on the matter for future publication. In the meantime, others are incipiently turning attention to the same sort of point: cf. Ann K. S. Lambton, "The Theory of Kingship in the *Naṣīḥat ul-Mulūk* of Ghazālī," in *The Islamic Quarterly*, London, I: 47-55 (1954); and Leonard Binder, "Al-Ghazālī's Theory of Islamic Government," in *The Muslim World*, Hartford, 45:229-41 (1955).

Thirdly, this incipient sense of separateness between mundane history and spiritual life is manifested on the spiritual side as well as on the political. It is not merely that even the formal religious leaders accepted the new political theory.[34] More basic in this connection is the new religious interpretation of the mystics that was, as we have said, gaining ground—even though it never fully usurped the official classical view.

Sufism differs from the classical Sunni *Weltanschauung* radically; and not least in its attitude to history, the temporal mundane. It stresses the individual rather than society, the eternal rather than the historical, God's love rather than His power, and the state of man's heart rather than behaviour. It is more concerned that one's soul be pure than that one's actions be correct. Some Sufis thought the Law unimportant. Most regarded it as a private discipline guiding the person towards transcendent fulfilment, and paid little heed to its function in ordering society, in marshalling history into a prescribed pattern.

Clearly, then, the Sufi, little interested in the historical process[35] and conceiving a God who is little interested, had a faith well suited to cope with earthly turmoil and distress; and enabling him to stand undismayed before external disaster. By the same token, however, his faith was less suited to political guidance. Like the Christians', it needed supplementing by a secular political acumen for the man in office whose responsibility was to guide society rather than himself. The Sufi could become indifferent also to historical success. Just as the world's calamities could not affright him, neither could its triumphs elate. To be specific, an Islam that, impregnated with Sufism, had learned to survive the misfortunes of the thirteenth and fourteenth centuries, was not so concerned to appropriate to itself the earthly glories of the fifteenth and sixteenth.

[34] The great example is the famous Osmanlı Şeyh-ul-İslam, Ebüssu'ûd Efendi (1490-1574). See *Encyclopaedia of Islām*, new ed., Leiden, 1954-   , s.v. Abū 'l-Su'ûd (article by J. Schacht), and the reff. there cited.

[35] Perhaps a certain caution should be evinced here, lest we fall into a too easy overestimation of the unqualified other-worldliness of the mystics. Certainly they calculatedly avoided involvement in political processes. And in general we believe that our position as stated may stand. Nonetheless there was an important Ṣūfī temper according to which the welfare of man on earth is best served by the spiritual influence of saintliness (and not that the welfare of man on earth is of no significance). The position is perhaps not too distant in many cases from the standard Christian one.

37

One must not overemphasize this tendency. The classical version of Islam remained official, and has always remained socially important. And there was many a Muslim throughout the world who saw in the conquest of Constantinople in 1453 an illustration of God's power as well as of Sultan Mehmet's.

In any case, the fact is that in the sixteenth century the Muslim world was once again powerful, wealthy, and touched with splendour. Whatever view he might take of it, the Muslim of this period—in Morocco, Istanbul, Isfahan, Agra, Acheh—was participant in a history expansive and successful.

A further fact is that this success did not long persist. The second wave of Islamic upsurge was more short-lived than the first. Muslim society presently ceased to advance. And by the eighteenth century it was in serious decline.

Very serious decline indeed. There was a disintegration of military and political power. There was enfeeblement of commercial and other economic life. Intellectual effort stagnated. An effete decadence infected art. Religious vitality ebbed. The writings of the great masters elicited commentaries rather than enthusiasm; and the classical systems were used to delimit the road that one must travel rather than to provide the impetus for one's journey. On the Sufi side, the orders degenerated from mystic perception to gullible superstition; from the serene insight of the saint to the anxious abracadabra of the charlatan.

The Muslim world seemed to have lost the capacity to order its life effectively; Muslim society was losing its once firm, proud grip on the world.

Moreover, it so happened that this degeneration coincided with the exuberance of Europe. At about this time Western civilization was launching forth on the greatest upsurge of expansive energy that human history has ever seen. Vitality, skill, and power vastly accumulated. With them the West was presently reshaping its own life and soon the life of all the world.

This new giant, striding forth in exploratory restlessness, met the Muslim world and found its own growing might confronted with growing infirmity. By 1800 the West was pressing hard on such centres of indigenous power as remained, and in many areas had imposed its domination. During most of the nineteenth century the pressure and the domination increased. The Dutch in Indonesia, the British in India and elsewhere, the Russians in

Central Asia, the French in Africa, ruled Muslim society in full formality. Iran and the Ottoman Empire retained political sovereignty but were independent without being free. Apart from the matter of political control, Muslim society, once august, forceful, and alert, was now everywhere in drooping spirit, and subject both in initiative and destiny to forces outside Islam.

The modern period of Islamic history, then, begins with decadence within, intrusion and menace from without; and the worldly glory that reputedly went with obedience to God's law only a distant memory of a happier past.

We are now ready to recapitulate our argument thus far, as preface to our presentation of the modern Muslim situation. Our thesis has been that Islam is essentially a religion, and as such profoundly personal and also finally transcending all particularities and the confines of this mundane world and all its affairs; nonetheless that it has been distinctively characterized by a deep concern for these affairs. It has had a central conviction that the true Muslim life includes the carrying out in this world of the divine injunction as to how mankind, individually and corporately, should live. It has been characterized equally, therefore, by an intense loyalty towards its own community. At its fullest, this conviction has risen to the vision of building the ideal society. Or, if one looks at the same thing from another viewpoint, stressing God's initiative rather than human response, one may say, of seeing the ideal society built. Still more passively, one may say that the true Muslim lives in the ideal society; and to its corporate life has a cosmic loyalty.

In essence Islamic history, therefore, is the fulfillment, under divine guidance, of the purpose of human history. It is the Kingdom of God on earth, to use the Christian phrase;[36] the good society, to use the Greek.

We have seen, further, that in fact actual Islamic history was for some centuries a more or less acceptable approximation in practice to this ideal. We have seen that in its subsequent stages

[36] Attention was called, in the West, to the incipient Muslim usage of this phrase, by Murray T. Titus, "Islām and the Kingdom of God," in the *Macdonald Presentation Volume*, Princeton and London, 1933; pp. 391-402 (article reprinted from Calcutta, 1932). The usage has grown greatly in contemporary times.

that actual history had its ups and downs, but enough "ups" to corroborate the theory, and enough flexibility to cope with and for a time even to negate the "downs." We noted that the mediaeval period ends, however, in disorder.

This gives us the background and perspective with which to come to our central question: the condition and the dynamics of Islam in the modern world.

Chapter 2

ISLAM IN RECENT HISTORY

THE fundamental *malaise* of modern Islam is a sense that something has gone wrong with Islamic history. The fundamental problem of modern Muslims is how to rehabilitate that history: to set it going again in full vigour, so that Islamic society may once again flourish as a divinely guided society should and must. The fundamental spiritual crisis of Islam in the twentieth century stems from an awareness that something is awry between the religion which God has appointed and the historical development of the world which He controls.

It is with the contemporary manifestation of this problem and crisis that we are chiefly concerned. Our later chapters are devoted to an analysis of the Islamic situation in major areas of the Muslim world today (in general, since World War II). First, however, there is value in glancing quickly at the over-all history of Islam in the earlier modern phase, from the decline of the great mediaeval period until yesterday. This can be only the sketchiest of outlines.[1] Yet it is hoped that it may serve two purposes: first, to illustrate the bearing of Islam's spiritual quality, as we have discerned it, on the historical developments that have in fact occurred; and secondly, to interpret the bearing of these events on the contemporary spiritual evolution of Islam.

Arabia. The Wahhabis

The first Islamic movements in the modern period were protests against the internal deterioration. They would call a halt to decadence, summoning Muslim society back to its first purity and order. One of the earliest of these, and the most major, still reverberatingly influential, was the Wahhabiyah[2] in eighteenth-

---

[1] For the period surveyed in this chapter, cf. the treatment of other writers; most notably Gibb and Faẓlu-r-Raḥmān. H. A. R. Gibb, *Modern Trends in Islam*, Chicago, 1947, reprinted 1950; and F. Raḥmān, "Internal Religious Developments in the Present Century Islam," *Cahiers d'histoire mondiale/Journal of World History*, Paris, 2: 862-79. See also G. E. von Grunebaum, "Attempts at Self-Interpretation in Contemporary Islam," in his *Islam: essays in the nature and growth of a cultural tradition*, n.p. (also London), 1955, pp. 185-236.

[2] For an analytical and critical bibliography of the Wahhābī movement,

century Arabia. It was puritanical, vigorous, simple. Its message was straightforward: a return to classical Islam.

It rejected the corruption and laxity of the contemporary decline. It rejected too the accommodations and cultural richness of the mediaeval empire. It rejected the introvert warmth and other-worldly piety of the mystic way. It rejected also the alien intellectualism not only of philosophy but of theology. It rejected all dissensions, even the now well-established Shi'ah. It insisted solely on the Law. The classical Law, said the Wahhabis, is the sum and substance of the faith—and that in its straitest, most rigid, Hanbali version, stripped of all innovation developed through the intervening centuries. Obey the pristine Law, fully, strictly, singly; and establish a society where that Law obtains. This, they preached, is Islam; all else is superfluous and wrong. Apart from preaching, they set to to establish that society—to bend earthly life once more to the classical purposes of God. The founder (Ibn 'Abd al-Wahhab: 1703-1787) effected an alliance with a local ruling prince (Ibn Su'ud: -1765) so that theory and practice should go hand in hand. Their interpretation of Islam was as a vivid and strict idea, strictly and seriously to be implemented.

By dint of their geographical remoteness in central Arabia, they were able, not without difficulty, to abstract themselves from the mediaeval environment (Ottoman Empire) from which they were by conviction resiling. Presently they were able to hew for themselves in the desert a community that should carry forward the divine programme from where the earlier Muslims, succumbing to distortions, had left off. Not until the 1930's, with the discovery of oil on their borders, was the career of their reversionary social

---

see the master's thesis in the library of the Institute of Islamic Studies, McGill University, Montreal: Hisham A. Nashshabah, "Islam and Nationalism in the Arab World: a selected and annotated bibliography," 1955, pp. 7-26. To this should be added the original works of Muḥammad ibn 'Abd al-Wahhāb, published by the Maktabat al-Nahḍah al-'Ilmīyah al-Su'ūdīyah, Makkah.

It may legitimately be asked whether the Wahhābīyah is significantly to be classed as 'modern'; whether it is not rather an essentially mediaeval movement (cf. earlier Ottoman parallels, such as the movement of Birgivi, q.v. in *Islam Ansiklopedisi*, Ankara, 1943). Our defence for beginning our study of the modern period with it is that, whatever the original intention of its proponents (who were not aware of modern problems), a large and perhaps still growing number of Muslims in the world, confronting those problems, turn to the Wahhābīyah for inspiration and even solution.

42

oil = evil ?

order seriously interrupted: by the intrusion not again of the mediaeval world but now of the fully modern. But that sudden intrusion has been peripheral, and cautiously guarded; the results are not yet. In the meantime the Wahhabis' example had become widely famous, at first for the ferocity of their iconoclasm, later for the stringent purity of their faith. Their isolation has allowed them to execute their experiment relatively undistracted, but has not precluded their influence from becoming both widespread and strong. From the Holy Cities came provocative reports of a lean and stark Islam once again being seriously and exactly lived.

These reports were the more stimulating in that the Wahhabi proclamation was strongly transcendentalist. Their condemnation of the present was narrow yet profound; essentially, the criterion was not past history but graphic moral apprehension. Their rejections were vehement. Yet their movement was not purely negative; the positive kernel of their faith was mighty and compelling.

Theirs was not a pure idealism in the Western sense: devotion to a transcendent concept, of which all human implementations are necessarily partial and inadequate. This is too Platonic, too Christian. The Wahhabi reform named as authoritative, as the source of inspiration, not just the Qur'an, but the Qur'an and pure *sunnah*. We would interpret this as signifying in part that they were advocating allegiance not to the Qur'an as pure idea but to the Qur'an as implemented; yet as implemented originally, correctly—as Westerners might say, ideally. The interpretation of Islam against which they were fighting was that which had become dominant, that Islam is the purposes of God for mankind as expressed in the Qur'an and as at work in the on-going community. As we have tried to stress throughout, Islam for Muslims is not an abstract idea but an idea in operative practice. The Wahhabis rejected the actual practice, but not the conception that Islam is a practice, is essentially a divine pattern in this-worldly, historical motion. Their message was a way of proclaiming that what is ultimately right and imperative is not the actual embodiment of Islam in history but the ideal embodiment.

We have said that they summoned to the Law. Their own interpretation of this was rigid and narrow. Yet it might be more precise to say that their summons was to obedience—to God, in

His overwhelming majesty and power; and to a society that would embody His decrees. Their shift from the existent to the essential, from the actual to the ideal, from what the Muslims had made of Islam to what they *ought* to make of it, was and has remained cogent and vitalizing, even liberating. The waves of their expanding influence have extended far beyond the domain of their immediate community and practical power. And while there have been fundamentalist conservatives among those inspired by their orientation, others crying "Back to the Qur'an!" and "Back to the Sunnah!" have meant, "Back to the God of the Qur'an and His commands; back to the spirit of the Sunnah and its exhilaration."

To many Muslims committed to their faith yet perplexed by the inadequacy of their community and its history in the modern world, eager to act yet uncertain what to do, the enthusiastic voice of the Wahhabis has proven penetrating and powerful. And although an actual embodiment of their programme has proven feasible only in the desert, there has been a wide appeal in the spirit of their fervently rejecting the immediate past and of starting all over again to work out the practice of Islam from scratch. Like the Wahhabis, other men have thought to renounce the Muslims' current history, and to construct again in this world the kind of history that original Islam taught and inspired.

India. Waliyullah

Other purificationist movements rejected the degeneration of post-classical Islam but not so indiscriminately its achievements. The chief instance is the movement in India stemming from the reformer Shah Waliyullah of Delhi (1703-1762).[3] He grew up watching the Mughul empire crumble. Unlike Ibn 'Abd al-Wahhab, therefore, he thought and worked from within one of

---

[3] For a bibliography of this important but inadequately studied figure, see the master's thesis in the library of the Institute of Islamic Studies, McGill University: Mu'inu-d-Din Ahmad Khan, "A Bibliographical Introduction to Modern Islamic Developments in India and Pakistan," 1955; pp. 13-50. For a list of 28 of his own writings, with a description of each, see the introduction by Mawlānā 'Abdu-r-Rahmān to his Urdū translation of Shāh Walīyullāh's greatest work, *Ḥujjatullāh al-Bālighah*, Lahore, 2 voll., 1953, I: 76-83. (This list does not include the letters recently discovered and edited that are noted at ref. 6 just below.) Walīyullāh was a contemporary of Ibn 'Abd al-Wahhāb, and studied in Makkah; but there seems no evidence of any mutual influence.

the passing mediaeval empires, rather than outside. He would refashion and revive rather than reject.

Waliyullah's vision of a purified Islam retained a marked Sufi colouring. He repudiated the degeneration of the corrupted Sufi practice of his time, and the aberration of extreme Sufi views. He attacked the latitudinarian nonchalance that religiously tolerated a decadent society. Yet he was a Sufi.[4] His significance as a thinker is not least in his striving to postulate an interpretation of Islam that would coalesce a purified Sufism with a purified Sunnah. His Islam is therefore more comprehensive and richer than the Wahhabi; also more flexible. He would, for instance, embrace and enliven[5] all the schools of law in his new amalgam. That is, he accepted more Islamic development. He was more mediaeval than classical.

Yet he insisted no less that the true Muslim must not accept the contemporary decline. His political ambition was to restore Muslim power in India more or less on the Mughul pattern.[6] Pure Islam must be reenacted, a regenerated Muslim society must again be mighty.

It was the next century before some of his reform ideas were organized into socio-political movements, in the time and to some extent under the leadership of his son 'Abdu-l-'Aziz (1746-1824) and his grandson Isma'il (1781-1831). By this time the decline of Indo-Muslim society had gone still further, conspicuously in political power, where the weakness was of course attracting aggressive outside powers. Specifically, in northwest India an expansive and vigorous Sikh régime had supplanted what was left of the decadent Mughul one. In Bengal the British were becoming

[4] He succeeded his father as local leader of the Naqshbandī Order, 1719. In addition to this practice, his expounding of Ṣūfī theory is evident in much of his writing; perhaps especially *Ham'āt*, of which the original Persian is not available to the present writer and was not to 'Abdu-r-Raḥmān (cf. preceding note), but the following Urdū translation has appeared: Muḥammad Sarwar (trans.), *Taṣawwuf kī Ḥaqīqat awr us kā Falsafah'-i Tārīkh*, Lahore, 1946.

[5] For his positive attitude to *ijtihād*, see his *'Iqd al-jīd fī Aḥkām al-Ijtihād wa al-Taqlīd*, (the ed. available to the present writer is Delhi, 1344 [1925-26]). For an English translation, cf. M. D. Rahbar, "Shāh Walī Ullāh and Ijtihād," *The Muslim World*, Hartford, 44: 346-58 (1955).

[6] See Khalīq Aḥmad Niẓāmī, ed., *Shāh Walīyullāh ke Siyāsī Maktūbāt*, Aligarh [1951]. On these letters, see the same writer's "Shah Waliullah Dihlavi and Indian Politics in the 18th Century," *Islamic Culture*, Hyderabad, 25: 133-45 (1951).

solidly established. In western India there was a revival of Hindu power.

Accordingly one finds this movement for Islamic regeneration expressing itself in two directions: against internal decay, and against external threat or domination. Some of those inspired by the new emphasis on a revived and purified Islam wrote and wrought against the abuses in Muslim society. Others preached and fought against its new infidel rulers. This latter aspect came to coordinated and vigorous life particularly under the militant and able Sayyid Ahmad Barelawi (1782-1831).[7] Many Muslims answered his call to rise against the Sikhs in the Panjab, and to reimpose an "Islamic," or anyway Muslim, rule on themselves (and others) in these parts. The campaign was well organized and some of the battles were successful; Sayyid Ahmad was proclaimed *khalifah* ("caliph") in Peshawar for a time (1830-31). The eventual failure of these martial exploits gained the renown of "martyr" for the leaders and for a good while the movement persisted in underground endeavour to recreate Muslim ascendancy. One may compare the Fara'iziyah[8] of Bengal, also in the early part of the century. There was later some connection perhaps also with the 1857 Mutiny, the last great upheaval in the struggle to reinstate the old Muslim dominance.

Even more lasting and more widespread was the persistence of the movement's impetus and ideal. The attempts to oust the infidel could be, and were, suppressed. The attempts to refine and renew Muslim society and to restore its glory must continue, and incidentally keep it reminded of its more proper destiny on both scores. The dream of revived Indo-Muslim power remained into the twentieth century, to haunt or incite the community.[9]

[7] See Ghulām Rasūl Mihr, *Sayyid Ahmad Shahīd, ya'nī Mujāhid-i Kabīr Hazrat Sayyid Ahmad Barelawī ke mufassal sawānih-i hayāt awr un ki tahrīk-i ihyā'-i dīn kī mukammal sar-guzasht*, Lahore, 2 voll., n.d. [1953-54], an impressive work which seems to mark a new stage in Urdū historiography.

[8] See the article M. Hidayet Hosain, FARĀ'IDĪ[YA] in *The Encyclopaedia of Islâm*, Leiden, 1913 (slightly revised in the *Shorter Encyclopaedia of Islam*, Leiden, 1953). This group's activity seems to have been devoted chiefly to defending Islamic society (or the empirical Muslim community) against outsiders. The counterpart, the society's peaceful internal reform from corruption, was carried out in Bihar and Bengal chiefly by a development of the Walīyullāh-Barelawī movement, led by Karāmat 'Alī (q.v. in *Shorter Encyclopaedia of Islam*, article by A. Yusuf Ali).

[9] An example is the celebration in Lahore, 1941, of a "Shāh Ismā'īl Shahīd Day," organized by the All-Punjab Muslim Students' Federation. See 'Ab-

Although the leaders for a time looked elsewhere, the masses retained the ideal of rebuilding a great and a truly Islamic society in India.

This double orientation has introduced us to the second great *motif* of modern Islam. To the protest against internal deterioration was linked the protest against external encroachment. However local these nineteenth-century Indian movements might be in the details of their particular development, in this they were typical of the whole Muslim world, recognizing and trying to reject corrosion within and aggression without. The latter has remained through a hundred and fifty years a dominating threat to Islamic society: pressing on different areas with differing force, in varying forms, but in its essence constant. Almost every Islamic movement, in almost every part of the Muslim world, throughout that period has been in some way a variation on this double theme.

In this early modern period Turkey was not an exception. The Turks were beginning to evolve also other trends, which in the end made their handling of the problem quite distinctive. Yet there were among them as well at this time, and indeed from the beginning of the eighteenth century, major developments inquiring how to arrest the un-Islamic decadence of their society, and how to resist the infidel encroachment on their domain. From Ibrahim Müteferrika (1674-1745) to Namik Kemal (1840-1888) there have been representatives of the movement to proclaim that a true Islam demands a restored glory for the empire.[10]

Afghani

These two tendencies—internal reform, external defence—are typified and fused in a person whose outstanding figure is central to the nineteenth-century Muslim world, Jamalu-d-Din Afghani (1839-97).[11] In him are to be seen also other facets of the develop-

---

dullāh Baṭ, ed., *Maqālāt-i Yawm-i Shāh Ismāʿīl Shahīd*, Lahore, 1943; and Abdullah Butt, *Aspects of Shah Ismail Shaheed: essays on his literary, political and religious activities*, Lahore, 1943.

[10] Cf. ref. 38 below.

[11] An adequate study of Afghānī is still awaited. For a partial bibliography, dealing with Arabic and Western sources, see the Nashshābah thesis noted at ref. 2 above. For a study with particular regard to his work in India, and with supplementary bibliographical reference to the otherwise little exploited Urdū sources, see the further thesis in the library of the Institute of Islamic Studies, McGill University: Sharif al-Mujahid, "Sayyid Jamāl al-Dīn al-Afghānī: His Role in the Nineteenth Century Muslim Awakening," 1954. This latter is to be published presently in Karachi.

ing situation, for he both represents the new trends and carried them vigorously forward. Since he was reputed also for his classical Islamic learning, he may be said to represent the traditional Islam as well. In fact he is supremely comprehensive, the complete Muslim of his time.

Geographically, his career encompassed Iran, India, the Arab World, and Turkey, as well as the European West. He was both Sufi and Sunni. He preached a reconciliation with the Shi'ah. He united with traditional Islamic scholarship a familiarity with Europe and an acquaintance with its modern thought. And as we have said, he was himself active in both internal reform and external defence. He inspired political revolutionaries and venerable scholars. He advocated both local nationalisms and pan-Islam. A very great deal of subsequent Islamic development is adumbrated in his personality and career. In fact, there is very little in twentieth-century Islam not foreshadowed in Afghani.

Yet his contribution was not as a thinker, either creative or systematizing; nor even on the practical side, as an organizer and planner. It was not what he introduced into the development of the Islamic world that gives him significance, so much as what he brought into focus—focus so sharp that it was able to ignite. He is important because he summed up in himself so wide a sweep of the contemporary Muslim world in difficulties, and then reacted against those difficulties with a prodigious energy. He was embracingly catholic: in his concern for the community's new problems, impinging impartially on its various elements, he transcended its traditional divisions and would turn attention from them. He was the firebrand agitator; taking deeply to heart the then condition of Islam, he sensed with a passionate poignancy the plight of his fellow Muslims, and in his rebounding zest stimulated them to a keen consciousness of their situation and to a determination to redress it.

The previous movements on which we have touched, except in Turkey, had assessed the internal decline of Muslim society only on a criterion of classical Islamic prescriptions, and had opposed its non-Muslim rulers or enemies only in immediate and local terms, more or less *ad hoc*. In Afghani both problems came to a more sophisticated self-consciousness. By this time the internal inadequacies were more pronounced, and the inner penetration and outer pressure of Europe had both proceeded much further.

It was his genius to see the situation in comprehensive terms and in perspective. He realized that the entire Islamic world, not just this or that part of it, was threatened; and by the West as a powerful, dynamic entity. He saw that in comparison with that entity—that is, on a European criterion—the entire Islamic world was weak. He realized that in a sense that world was threatened by its own weakness. The earlier reformers had preached that the Muslims' social condition was wrong. Afghani insisted that it was feeble.

We cannot follow the detail, but must give due weight to the substance of the quite considerable direct political agitation against European imperialism, particularly British, to which Afghani devoted himself in London, Paris, and at home. It was zealous and telling. Moreover he seems to have been the first Muslim revivalist to use the concepts "Islam" and "the West" as connoting correlative—and of course antagonistic—historical phenomena. This antinomy, as is well known, has since become quite standard in virtually all Islamic thinking. It would be fruitful and revealing to explore the growth in the Muslim consciousness (outside Turkey) of the spectre of the West as an accusing, menacing power. It was in Afghani that this became explicit; and that the response to it became active.

Also beyond the scope of our study are the details of the direct activities and intrigues with which Afghani took part in internal Islamic political affairs, particularly Irani. We may incidentally note his connection with and almost instigation of the Tobacco Monopoly affair in Iran, beginning in 1891, when the traditional Shi'i religious leaders were inspired to lead the mass of the people in an effective and striking protest—against the Shah's further weakening of Muslim society by handing over more of the nation's resources to the "enemies of Islam," European financial interests. Afghani was also involved in the activities that led to the assassination of the Shah in 1896. Moreover, he was not without influence in the Egyptian uprising against internal misrule, under 'Arabi in 1882. In other Muslim areas also, often less directly, his vigour stirred discontent into active reform.

Of great significance, further, for the development that we are trying to trace, is the first conspicuous appearance in Afghani of another developing aspect of modern Islamic consciousness: an explicit nostalgia for the departed earthly glory of pristine Islam.

With his ebullient rhetoric and tireless repetition, Afghani fired audiences in one Muslim country after another to a reawakened consciousness of how they had once been mighty, but now were weak. That memory was not far below the surface, but it was below and was generally without delineation, a feeling rather than a picture of past greatness. His vivid evocations elicited a spirited response that has since ramified. Indeed, in addition to internal reform and external defence, this recalling of erstwhile Muslim grandeur has become a third dominant trait of modern Islam. It has been vastly developed, as we shall return to consider.

There are further elements to be noted in Afghani's position, typifying aspects of the evolving situation that subsequently developed importantly. We have already noted his encouraging of local nationalisms—Irani, Arab, Indian, etc.—and also of pan-Islamic sentiment.

Further, Afghani exhibited a partial appreciation of intellectualism and of Western values and particularly Western science and techniques. He saw the West as something primarily to be resisted, because it threatened Islam and the community, but secondly, in part to be imitated. He was vigorous in inciting his Muslim hearers to develop reason and technology as the West was doing, in order to be strong.

Another salient and effective element was his ardent insistence that the resurgence of Islam on earth was the responsibility of the Muslims themselves. They must be up and doing; their future would be great if they made it so. He incited them to discard resignation, or wonderment, in favour of plunging excitedly into the exuberant task of themselves creating the kind of Islamic world that ought to be. The Qur'an verse "Verily, God does not change the condition of a people until they change their own condition" (13:11), which had for some centuries lain unemphasized if not almost dormant, he singled out for enthusiastic employ. On this text he built many a sermon, in a fashion that has since come widely to prevail. The citing of this verse in particular, and the general resolve of Muslims to take into their own hands the refurbishing of their community's earthly history, are today standard. Indeed, no Muslim transformation of the past hundred years is more striking than that from the quiescent passivity that led nineteenth-century observers to speak of the Islamic world (and even of Islam) as static and fatalist if not moribund, to the exuberant ferment of the present day.

Indeed, this urging to action, the transition from a non-responsible quietude to a self-directing determination, was carried further; into an almost irresponsible or effervescent dynamism. Afghani himself had no clear programme, no ordered philosophy. But he did have abounding energy and the knack of inspiring others to busy enthusiasm. The vitalistic activism that characterized him has been a marked quality of Islamic development since. It was given more or less explicit formulation by the poet Iqbal[12] and practical embodiment in numerous movements (the Ikhwan in the Arab world, the Khaksar in India, the Kashani in Iran, the Daru-l-Islam in Indonesia, for instance; we shall return to this point[13]). In fact, it has coloured a very great deal of modern Islam, whose renascence has been more ebullient than thoughtful, and indeed has been aimed more at recapturing the vitality than at redefining the content or even the methods of faith.

As we have said, Afghani is important for typifying and vitalizing these several trends. It is the trends themselves that demand attention; their development by other men and groups through the subsequent decades has almost constituted the recent story of the faith. Particularly, he is illustrative as a man passionately concerned to defend and to reactivate the mundane aspect of Islam. It was his vision and his determination (as it has become the aspiration providing the clue to most subsequent Muslim 'modernism') that Islamic history shall once again march forward in full truth and full splendour.

Later Developments

The later development of those trends, of that defence and that reactivation, was vigorous and widespread. Much of it was directly or indirectly related to the Wahhabis, Waliyullah, or Afghani. Some was more or less parallel and independent. All, of course, was complex. It would be false to oversimplify recent Islamic

---

[12] Shaykh Sir Muḥammad Iqbāl, 1876-1938. For literature, see Abdul Ghani and Khwaja Nur Ilahi, *Bibliography of Iqbal*, Lahore, n.d. [sc. 1954?].

[13] In our concluding section "Dynamism" below, pp. 89-91. For the Ikhwān, see our next chapter, below, pp. 156-60 with ref. 196; for the Khāksārs, see the present writer's *Modern Islām in India*, Lahore, 1943, pp. 270-83 and bibliography; London, "1946" [sc. 1947], pp. 235-45.

moves, constraining them into too neat a common pattern. At the same time it is misleading to omit from the particularities of each the generalized Islamic form and impulse which relate them to the still living past and to each other.

Of overt expressions in active group endeavor, one might mention the Sanusi movement in Libya (beginning in 1842);[14] the Mahdi movement in the Sudan (from 1881);[15] the Irani movements of the 1890's already referred to, and Constitutionalism (culminating 1906);[16] the Sarekat Islam and the Muhammadiyah in Indonesia (from 1911);[17] and so on. Each local manifestation has had its own immediate causes, in the economic, political, and other factors of the particular area. Each inevitably fits into the local history and may be so studied. Yet each also fits into a total pattern such as we have already discerned—as aspiration towards

[14] The two basic works on this movement are E. E. Evans-Pritchard, *The Sanusi of Cyrenaica*, Oxford, 1949; and Muḥammad Fu'ād Shukrī, *Al-Sanūsiyah Dīn wa Dawlah*, Cairo, 1948. For full bibliography, see these works, and more especially the Nashshābah thesis (cf. above, ref. 2), pp. 27-43.

[15] In English the most recent work is A. B. Theobald, *The Mahdīya: a history of the Anglo-Egyptian Sudan, 1881-1899*, London, 1951, with bibliography. To it should be added the relevant parts, brief but careful, in Mekki Shibeika, *British Policy in the Sudan 1882-1902*, London and New York, 1952; and a forthcoming study by P. M. Holt, London. In Arabic, Tawfīq Aḥmad al-Bakrī, *Muḥammad Aḥmad al-Mahdī*, in the series *A'lām al-Islām*, Cairo, 1944, with bibliography; add the relevant parts of Sa'd Muḥammad Ḥasan, *al-Mahdīyah fī al-Islām*, Cairo, 1373/1953, and the important documentation, Ḥusayn Mu'nis (ed.), *Wathā'iq 'an Mahdī al-Sūdān*, Cairo, 1953.

[16] The basic foreign work here is E. G. Browne, *The Persian Revolution of 1905-1909*, Cambridge, 1910; for further outside observations cf. L. P. Elwell-Sutton, *A Guide to Iranian Area Study*, Ann Arbor, 1952, esp. p. 52. In Persian, see Mahdī Malikzādah, *Tārīkh-i Inqilāb-i Mashrūṭīyat-i Īrān*, Tihrān, 6 voll., 1328-1332 [1949-53]; [Aḥmad] Kasravī Tabrīzī, *Tārīkh Mashrūṭah'-i Īrān*, Tihrān, 3rd ed., 1330 [1951]; and Maliku-s-Shu'arā' Bahār, *Tārīkh-i Mukhtaṣar-i Aḥzāb-i Siyāsī: jild-i awwal: Inqirāż-i Qājārīyah*, Tihrān, 1321 [1942].

[17] For bibliography, see the compilation, Hedwig Schlieffer, "Islam in Indonesia," section VI of "Selective Bibliography on the Economic and Political Development of Indonesia" (mimeographed), Cambridge, Mass., Center for International Studies, Massachusetts Institute of Technology, 1955; s.vv. in index, and generally. To be added to this list are the following more recent items: Harry J. Benda, "Indonesian Islam under the Japanese Occupation, 1942-45," *Pacific Affairs*, 28: 350-62 (1955); and G. W. J. Drewes, "Indonesia: mysticism and activism," in Gustave E. von Grunebaum, ed., *Unity and Variety in Muslim Civilization*, Chicago, 1955, pp. 284-307 (cf. further pp. 307-10).

a reflorescence, and more particularly as aspects of the vast protest against internal decline and external encroachment.

The Indian Khilafat movement also (1918-1924),[18] whose form has puzzled outsiders, testifies to the degree of emotional tension with which Muslims have sensed the earthly disintegration of traditional Islamic power, and responded to its symbolization. It illustrates further the willingness to struggle for a restoration, even without any clear programme. An incident such as the 1948 Hyderabad fiasco in India, moreover, is illuminated also when understood in terms of such a pattern. Here again is the fierce endeavour to resist, psychologically and practically, the further disintegration of Islam's seemingly evanescent earthly greatness.[19]

These are political, organizational, or mass movements. Artistic and imaginative expression also has been given to the modern Muslim's mood. We noted Afghani evoking in his rhetoric that historical nostalgia, the dream of ancient glory. This trait has been much developed throughout the Muslim world since. In India the

[18] A survey of previously published literature on this movement, and also perhaps the only study that takes into account the subsequent and manifestly related emergence of Pakistan, are to be found in a master's thesis in the library of the Institute of Islamic Studies, McGill University, Montreal: W. J. Watson, "Muḥammad ʿAlī and the Khilāfat Movement," 1955. This may be published presently in Karachi. Cf. also the following note.

[19] See "Hyderabad: Muslim Tragedy" by the present writer, in *The Middle East Journal*, Washington, 4: 27-51 (Jan. 1950). The study of this particular incident, written up in that article, was one, but only one, step whereby we gradually came to the general interpretation and analysis of Islam's contemporary development that are presented in this book. The article does not, accordingly, set the Hyderabad situation in so wide a context as is here suggested. Particularly, toward the end of the article we indicated our then failure fully to understand the religious quality of the sense of loss of worldly power. This understanding now seems possible in the light of the thesis advanced in Chapter 1 of this book.

Of the Indian Khilāfat movement, just above, our much earlier study (*Modern Islam in India*, Lahore, 1943, London, "1946" [*sc.* 1947]; s.v. in index) is one example (cf. previous paragraph in the text just above) of a study concerned with the ". . . immediate causes, . . . the economic, political, and other factors of the particular area" and "the local history." This is legitimate, but does not go far enough; the substance was explained, but "the form puzzled" this particular outsider. We admitted in our then delineation that the ideological structure of the movement seemed unrelated to the immediate issues at hand. It is hoped that the analysis here presented, alongside of the factors there studied, combine to make the movement intelligible. Cf. similarly on the later but comparable Pakistan movement, below, chap. 5, ref. 5.

most eloquent instance is the superbly moving lament of the poet Hali: his *Musaddas* (1886),[20] brilliantly recalling vanished Islamic grandeur, and penetrating deeply into the whole community's heart. Later examples are Iqbal's superlatively significant *Shikwah* ("Complaint") (1912);[21] his *Masjid-i Qurtubah* ("The Mosque of Cordoba") (1935);[22] and the like. In prose, Amir 'Ali's substantial *Short History of the Saracens* (1899),[23] though written as much for Western apologetic as for internal edification, is illustrative. In the Arab world, Jurji Zaydan's *History of Islamic Civilization* (1902-06) might almost be instanced.[24] Certainly Shakib Arslan's *Why have the Muslims become Backward?* (1930)[25] may serve as an example. This stirring essay was elicited by an Indonesian inquiry, which (as Afghani had done) quoted the Qur'an verse "Power belongs to God, and to His Apostle, and to The Believers" (63:8), and asked where, today, had this last power gone. These are outstanding instances, each of them reprinted repeatedly, translated, and still today widely read and widely

[20] *Madd-o Jazr-i Islām* ("The Flow and Ebb of Islam"), popularly known as *Musaddas-i Ḥālī*. It was published first in Delhi.

[21] The poem is in the collection *Bāng-i Darā* (1924). In the edition available to us, the 12th, Lahore, 1948, it is pp. 177-87. There is an English translation in Altaf Husain, trans., *The Complaint and the Answer*, Lahore, 1943.

[22] In the collection *Bāl-i Jibrīl* (1935); 7th ed., Lahore, 1947, pp. 126-36. English version in V. G. Kiernan, trans., *Poems from Iqbal*, Bombay, 1947, pp. 68-71; London, 1955, pp. 37-42.

[23] This was published originally in London; there was a New York ed. the following year. The work is still in print; the 4th ed., 1924, is currently in its 5th impression, 1951.

[24] *Ta'rīkh al-Tamaddun al-Islāmī*, 5 vols., Cairo. We say "almost" because the author (Jurjī or Jirjī Zaydān, 1861-1914) was Christian; though the wide success of his work was due in great part, of course, to its Muslim readership. The complex involvement of Arab Islam in Arabism, in which Christian Arabs are then also involved, is illustrated here. Compare chap. 3 below, especially ref. 2.

[25] Al-Amīr Shakīb Arslān, *Li-mādhā ta'akhkhar al-Muslimūn wa li-mādhā taqaddam ghayruhum?*, Cairo, 1349 [1930-31]. This work appeared first as a series of articles in the Cairo journal *al-Manār*; and subsequently in book form in Arabic and other languages. It is interesting that the English version published in India (1944; itself reprinted in Pakistan, 1952), was translated from the Malayalam, which version, first in newspaper serial and later reprinted as a book, "sent a wave of national fervour and kindled Islamic fire in the hearts of the Mopplahs" (translator's preface to the English edition, Lahore, 1944: Amir Shakib Arsalan, *Our Decline and its Causes; a diagnosis of the symptoms of the downfall of Muslims*, translated by M. A. Shakoor, p. x).

effective. The trend has come to expression also in hundreds of lesser books and thousands of poems, articles, and speeches.

It would be too ambitious to attempt here to trace further, however briefly, the story of these Islamic developments area by area or instance by instance.[26] When that full story comes to be written, it will be possible to revise and amplify the observations that, rather, are here essayed. These relate to some of the chief over-all trends that have appeared. For our understanding of the contemporary situation, to which we shall turn in subsequent chapters, it will be instructive if we can clarify as background the further principal elements that were introduced or evolved in the next stage of development. The two major matters here are liberalism and nationalism. These deserve relatively extended examination, partly because of the degree of their impingement on the historical evolution of recent Islam, partly because of their proneness to being misunderstood through false Western parallels. More recently elaborated phenomena, particularly apologetics and dynamism, we shall treat but briefly, leaving more detailed consideration for illustration and study in one or other of the present-day portrayals.

Liberalism

A trend flourished in the next phase of Islamic evolution, about the turn of the present century, that we may, perhaps not ineptly, designate Islamic liberalism.

There are two major elements from within the past Islamic tradition from which a contribution to liberalism could be drawn: philosophy and Sufism. The intellectualism of the former and the humanism of the latter could provide important bases for reinterpretation. This was precisely the reason, of course, for which the conservatives had throughout distrusted them—and still distrust them today. The resurgence of classical Islam involves, in fact, a newly invigorated repudiation of these two liberating forces. We have already noted that the modern period in Islamic history begins with such a resurgence.

Mysticism was repudiated by the Wahhabi movement, and this

[26] The Institute of Islamic Studies, McGill University, is planning to prepare over the next five or ten years monograph volumes on at least some of the areas: modern Islam in Turkey (cf. below, ref. 38); modern Islam in Indonesia; etc.

rejection has been markedly influential in the Arab world.[27] Nevertheless, the founder, Ibn 'Abd al-Wahhab, was himself a Sufi in his thirties.[28] That is, he—despite his movement—is no exception to the generalization that every major Islamic reformer of the modern age shows deep Sufi influence. Other instances are Afghani, 'Abduh,[29] Gökalp,[30] Iqbal. In a world in which the extant Law as a formal system could seem a somewhat obsolescent method of bringing persons vividly face to face with the divine, some might argue that Sufism provides an inescapable factor in any refreshened version of the faith. (However, it is also strikingly true that the very flexibility of Sufism has meant that in the post-mediaeval decline its institutional degeneration has been outstanding, far outstripping that of other aspects of Muslim society. Sufism itself has sorely needed purgation.)

Rationalism was repudiated by both the Wahhabi movement and the Waliyullahi. Indeed, this has been seen as a major explanation for the persistent weakness of the intellectual side of modern

[27] For a modern instance of the rejection of Sufism on the grounds that it weakens the toughness of Islām under attack, see the almost rabid work of 'Umar Farrukh, *al-Taṣawwuf fī al-Islām*, Beirut, 1366/1947.

[28] Ibn 'Abd al-Wahhāb "went to Iṣfahān at the commencement of Nādir Shāh's reign (1148/1736); here he is said to have studied for a period of four years peripatetic philosophy, the *Iṣhrāḳīya* and the Ṣūfī systems; for a year he attracted students as an exponent of Ṣūfīsm, then went to Ḳumm, after which he became an advocate of Ibn Ḥanbal's school."—*Shorter Encyclopaedia of Islam*, Leiden, 1953, s.v. WAHHĀBĪYA, reprint of an article by D. S. Margoliouth.

[29] On Muḥammad 'Abduh (1849?-1905) the standard works are Rashīd Riḍā, *Ta'rīkh al-Ustādh al-Imām*, 3 vols., Cairo, 1326-50/[1908]-1931; and Charles C. Adams, *Islam and Modernism in Egypt*, London, 1933. See the article MUḤAMMAD 'ABDUH by J. Schacht in *Shorter Encyclopaedia of Islam*, Leiden, 1953; to the bibliography there given add the following: (1) Osman Amin, *Muhammad 'Abduh, essai sur ses idées philosophiques et religieuses*, Cairo, 1944 (this work is appreciably fuller than the Arabic pamphlet in the series "A'lām al-Islām," 'Uthmān Amīn, *Muḥammad 'Abduh*, Cairo, 1944, which was translated into English as Osman Amin, *Muhammad 'Abduh*, Washington, 1953); and (2) Muḥammed El-Bahay, *Muhammed 'Abduh, Eine Untersuchung seiner Erziehungsmethode zum Nationalbewusstsein und zur nationalen Erhebung in Ägypten*, Hamburg, 1936. On 'Abduh's early Sufism see Adams, *op. cit.*, pp. 23ff.

[30] On Ziya Gökalp (1875-1924), see Uriel Heyd, *The Foundations of Turkish Nationalism*, London, 1950; and Niyazi Berkes, "Ziya Gökalp: his contribution to Turkish nationalism," *The Middle East Journal*, Washington, 8: 375-90 (1954). An edition in English of his collected writings is to be published shortly by the latter. On his Sufism, cf. Heyd, pp. 23, 26, 83.

Islam.[81] As a matter of fact, the repudiation goes further back, and deeper. If mysticism was never quite fully acceptable to the religious leaders, intellectualism was not acceptable at all. Some Muslims have seen the introduction of Greek thought into the Islamic world as a greater threat to the religion than the Crusades or the Mongol invasions. Even theology was suspect. As we have previously argued, the Islamic counterpart to the Christian theologian has been the legist: the Muslim's supreme duty has been less to know the truth than to do the right. Further, whereas mysticism, as we have seen, even if unstandard, in the pre-modern period became popular, philosophy was even in its Arab heyday the preserve of but an élite handful. Nonetheless, the tradition thinly endured. In the very recent past, rationalism has again seemed feeble, overwhelmed in the contemporary revival of conservative Islam. But around the turn of the century there was a brief flowering, which has left its mark—and which, some hope, may yet again come into its own.

A third factor in Islamic liberalism was the penetration of the West. From the late nineteenth century to the First World War, European liberalism was at its height. So also was European ascendancy. Many Muslims went to the West and came to know, even in part to admire, its spirit and values. This was true especially of some of those students who in increasing numbers were seeking training in its universities. Much of the West came to the Muslim world—again, not least its educational institutions, rearing indigenously a generation deeply exposed to Western modernity. Many new ideas, and at least equally important the subtle presuppositions of ideas, and new evaluations, new orientations, were inculcated in these formally educational ways. In addition, there was increasing penetration of other Western and modern institutions: legal, political, social, and many others. To some extent these were imposed, to some extent sought after. Some Muslims resisted, some welcomed them, or were brought up to or gradually came to welcome them; eventually many came to take them for granted. The process has continued apace.

We have seen that the West was first seen as essentially an external threat to Muslim society. The newer penetration, this internal 'Westernizing' of the Islamic community, could be regarded as a subtler and more dangerous version of the same threat:

[81] See F. Rahman, *op. cit.* p. 864.

a 'fifth column' disruption from within. Its potential devastation to *Islamic* history and society could understandably alarm those who conceived these as the implementation and embodiment of the classically known divine precepts. We shall presently see that this attitude to Westernization has in recent decades reasserted itself into prominence. At the moment our concern is to note that for a time a different attitude found expression alongside the other: one that welcomed Western liberalism in fact if not in name, and sought to incorporate it into or harmonize it with Islam.

In many instances the harmonizing was permissive rather than creative. It allowed a person to be both a Muslim and a Westernized liberal without conflict; but also without generating a new synthesis that might incite to constructive new dreams and new adventures. This is true also of the more indigenous movements that would re-embrace for Islam the rationalist strand in the historical tradition. These would prove revealed Islam and reason compatible, a proof the need for which had not been felt so pressing for some centuries. Yet they hardly expected reason to generate new religious truth; nor looked upon it as in essence divine. Nonetheless some serious and original work was done, of constructive value not yet exhausted.

Liberalism—and we are using the term here in a deliberately broad sense—is inherently not an established system nor of fixed content or even intention. Islamic liberalism too has evinced many forms, taking on, as it should, the individual quality of various persons who have given expression to it, have accepted its loyalties. Hajji Agus Salim (1884-1955) and others in Indonesia; Sir Sayyid Ahmad Khan (1817-98) and the 'Aligarh movement in India, and such a notable modernist as Amir 'Ali (1849-1928) on the one hand, and such theologians as Shibli (1857-1914) and Abu-l-Kalam Azad (1888-   ) on the other; Shaykh Muhammad 'Abduh (1849-1905) in the Arab world, followed by such a rationalist as Taha Husayn (1891-   ); Sangulaji (1890-1943) and others in Iran;[32] Shinasi (1824-1871), Namik Kemal (1840-1888), Abdulhak Hâmid (1851-1937), Tevfik Fikret (1870-1915), among many

[32] See the master's thesis in the library of the Institute of Islamic Studies, McGill University, Montreal: Amir Abbas Haydari "Some Aspects of Islam in Modern Iran, with special reference to the work of Sangalajī and Rāshid," 1954.

others in Turkey; these illustrate some though not all aspects of this wide-ranging development.[33]

Certainly, a Muslim growing up today in a world in which these men have thought and written is in a very different position, religiously, from his predecessors a hundred years ago. He has access to interpretations of Islam, and therefore of God, the world, and himself, very different from those to which he would find himself confined if the religion were somehow deprived of their work and were available only in its earlier versions. Singly, their achievement has been major; taken together their contribution can be seen as constituting an impressive, even exciting, step in the intellectual and spiritual adventure of Islam.

However, it can also be seen, perhaps more justly, as a contribution of which the significance has as yet been far from fully worked out. The next step in Islamic evolution may quite possibly be a matter of more wide-reaching influence and much deeper import. It may affect the central groups and institutions and formulations of the religious community; whereas liberalism so far, however striking, has been religiously peripheral. The quality of such a new development will in large part turn on whether the community decides, or certain sections of it decide, for or against taking seriously the liberals' contribution and expanding it, pursuing the lines of inquiry that it opened up and consolidating the results firmly and sincerely within the faith.

That, however, is a matter for the future; and for the Muslims. Not only do we leave that aside; we shall not here, in our hastening survey, even examine closely what has observably been effected in the past. It would take us too far afield to study even a few illustrative instances of liberal Muslim accomplishment, or to trace its general development as a movement. This has in part already been done. We ourselves have previously had occasion to treat, although inadequately, the Indian aspect;[34] more important, Professor Gibb has given both outsiders and Muslims a descriptive analysis of modernism in wide range with emphasis on the Arab

[33] Apart from the preceding reference, specifications for persons named in this paragraph, or for the movements that they served, will be found as follows: above, reff. 17 and 29, and below, reff. 34, 36, 38, 39, 47, and 48.

[34] *Modern Islām in India*, Lahore, 1943; London, "1946" (sc. 1947). See especially chap. 2; and s.v. in index.

scene.[35] The Irani[36] and Indonesian[37] developments remain to be studied. So does the Turkish, which in a way has been the most successful.[38]

The comprehensive history of Islamic liberalism we must leave to other investigators or another time. Here we must content our-selves with certain observations on its relation to the main stream of Islamic resurgence, and then endeavour to deal with the basic problem in regard to liberalism that must confront a student of the contemporary Muslim world, namely its recent decline. For Islam today, what requires elucidation is that the liberalism of the period just before World War I seems everywhere except in Turkey and perhaps Indonesia to have weakened as the century progressed.

We must discriminate among persons, formulated values (and ideas and systems), and formally religious values (ideas, systems). Among liberals, liberalism, and Islam the interrelationships have been often subtle, and sometimes but not always close. There have been and are a great many Muslim liberals. There has been a con-siderable amount of liberal exposition of Islam. There has been relatively little Islamic, or even Muslim, exposition of liberalism.

Let us examine this a little more fully.

For some generations now a very sizable and probably grow-ing number of Muslims have lived individual lives, have nursed aspirations for themselves and their societies, and have exercised their minds, on quite recognizably liberal patterns. They have as

[35] H. A. R. Gibb, *op. cit.*

[36] For literature on modern Islām in Īrān, cf. above, reff. 16 and 32, and below, chap. 7, ref. 6.

[37] Cf. above, ref. 17. Note also below, chap. 7, ref. 7, where it is indicated that the significance of Indonesia in Islamic liberalism is partly that that unique country has the Muslim world's apparently only indigenous liberal tradition, pre-Islamic and still vigorously alive.

[38] The basic study here will be the forthcoming monograph of Niyazi Berkes, *The Development of Secularism in Modern Turkey*. In the meantime, see his chapter "Historical Background of Turkish Secularism" in Richard N. Frye, ed., *Islam and the West*, 's-Gravenhage, 1957, pp. 41-68. Note also the brief but important article Abdulhak Adnan-Adivar, "Interaction of Islamic and Western Thought in Turkey," in T. Cuyler Young, ed., *Near Eastern Culture and Society: a symposium on the meeting of East and West*, Princeton, 1951, pp. 119-29 (this appears also, in substantially the same form, in *The Middle East Journal*, Washington, 1: 270-80 [1947]). For the recent period, cf. also ref. 30 above; and the reff. of Chap. 4 below, esp. 16, 20, 25.

individuals met and mingled with liberals of other faiths, on terms of personal equality and ease and mutual understanding.

Such men have been not only numerous but greatly significant. They have supplied the recent leadership of their societies in almost all spheres of activity (except the religious). Not only have they staffed most of the educational institutions, virtually constituted the major professions, written a great many of the books, and edited the major newspapers. At the present time also they man the governments of almost every Muslim state.

It is only partially untrue to remark that in this century the higher a Muslim's position in leadership, the more liberal he has generally been. Though a minority, the liberals have come close to being a dominant minority more or less throughout the modern Muslim world.

If the liberals are so strong, why is liberalism weak? Whence has come about the gradual weakening in Muslim society of the ideas and attitudes, the convictions and loyalties that have expressed and sustained the distinctive outlook of this liberal group? Some elucidation of this is gained if we revert to our Islamic theme. For the rise and present decline of this ideology may significantly be viewed as almost episodic to the gradual resurgence in modern times of Islam itself as a force and a community. At least we must inquire how far the ideology was independent of Islam, how far and wherein related to it. And we shall observe that, however frequently and closely related, it does not seem to have been much integrated with the faith.

Before we proceed, a further discrimination is in order: between ideas on the purely theoretical level, and operative ideas charged with power and commanding personal allegiance. This distinction, we shall see, is not quite the same as that between an extraneous liberalism and one related to Islam. Yet the two lie close.

Early, and to some degree this has persisted throughout, there was a Muslim liberals' non-indigenous liberalism. It was their personalization of a position of which the formulation was the work of Westerners. Thus Amir 'Ali,[39] in some ways the greatest of them, states that he had been "enthralled" by Gibbon before he was twelve, and by the age of twenty had read most of Shake-

[39] On Sayyid Amīr 'Alī of India see the article s.v. (by the present writer) in *The Encyclopaedia of Islam*, new ed., Leiden, 1956.

speare, Milton, Keats, Byron, Longfellow, and other poets, along with the novels of Thackeray and Scott, and "knew Shelley almost by heart."[40] Similarly Tawfiq al-Hakim's novels read almost like translations from the French. Neither its enemies nor its friends would think to deny that the liberal movement in Islam in the last sixty years owes an enormous debt to that in Europe.

In many instances the values so absorbed have been genuine and fruitful. The inspiration has been effective, generating a true and creative liberality of individual temperament, thought, and act. In certain other instances this Western-derived ideology has been accepted but not appropriated; has elicited no enthusiasm, and has carried its passive adherents along on a tide that flowed around but not within the personality.

In both cases the persons remained explicitly Muslims. In the latter case no doubt the religious loyalty was for a time like the liberal, lukewarm, though it could later be re-aroused. The former, dynamic participants gave their movement intellectual expression in a liberalized Islam. Again our best example is Amir 'Ali, whose monumental *Spirit of Islam*[41] is probably the greatest single work of this whole trend. In the Arab world the several lives of the Prophet in the 1930's—by Taha Husayn, Haykal, 'Aqqad, and others[42]—are illustrative. Thus an indigenous Islamic formulation was given to the new viewpoint of this group. It related their liberalism to their Muslim-ness not merely by juxta-

[40] "Memoirs of the late Rt. Hon'ble Syed Ameer Ali," *Islamic Culture*, Hyderabad, 5: 520, 526 (1931).

[41] A first version of this was published in 1873 as: Syed Ameer Ali, *A Critical Examination of the Life and Teachings of Mohammed*, London & Edinburgh (Williams & Norgate). In 1891 W. H. Allen of London published *The Life and Teachings of Mohammed, or The Spirit of Islâm*. A third edition of this came out in 1899. An "amplified and revised" edition was published by Christophers, London, 1922, and by Doran, New York, 1923: Syed Ameer Ali, *The Spirit of Islâm: a history of the evolution and ideals of Islâm, with a life of the Prophet*. This was reprinted in London 1923, and in a further revised edition posthumously in 1935; reprints of this have appeared in 1946, 1949, 1952, and 1953. There was an abridged Turkish translation, by Umer Riza, *Ruh-u İslâm*, Istanbul, 1341 [1922-23?]. The present writer has been told of, but has not seen, sections translated into Arabic and published in *al-Bayān*, Cairo.

[42] Cf. Ṭāhā Ḥusayn, *'Alà Hāmish al-Sīrah*, Cairo, 3 vols., n.d. [sc. 1934?], and subsequent edd.; Muḥammad Ḥusayn Haykal, *Ḥayāt Muḥammad*, Cairo, 1354 [1935] and subsequent edd.; Tawfīq al-Ḥakīm, *Muḥammad*, Cairo, 1354/-1936 and subsequent ed.; 'Abbās Maḥmūd al-'Aqqād, *'Abqarīyat Muḥammad*, Cairo, n.d. [sc. 1942?].

position but as content and form. Surely here, it would seem, was a creative synthesis.

Yet this ideology, though impressive, has in fact proven neither contagious and inspiring, nor even sustained. It was admirable, and was admired.[43] But it was not cogent. And if one examines it more closely, one discovers that this is after all not really Islamic liberalism. One can hardly think, perhaps, of a major or significant work by a Muslim setting forth liberalism as an independent or even as an inspiring attitude, a set of intrinsically compelling values.[44] Yet one can point to many setting forth Islam as a liberal force, thereby eliciting applause but not devotion. The interpretation of the heritage incorporated the conclusions rather than the premises of liberalism. For those who had already adopted liberal values from other sources, it was satisfying. But it was not contrived to instill those values in a reader from scratch. The movement has not served to instigate a creative reform, nor to nourish the integrity of committed loyalties.

There was another liberal Muslim development, which touched more closely the dynamic centre of Islamic impulses, and more deeply the hearts of its devotees. The generalization seems historically valid that those who drew their chief inspiration for liberalism from the West achieved results that were greatly more liberal, while those who drew it from the Islamic past achieved results that have been greatly more lasting, penetrating, and seminal. 'Abduh's has been a less elegant, less thorough, less winsome[45] modernism than Amir 'Ali's or Khalifah 'Abdu l Hakim's (1894-   ),[46] but immensely more energizing. 'Ubaydullah Sindhi

---

[43] Cf. the present writer on Amir 'Ali; *Modern Islam in India*, Lahore p. 56 (London ed., p. 55).

[44] Is Iqbal, especially perhaps in his earlier work, an exception? And Sayyidayn (cf. K. G. Saiyidain, *Iqbal's Educational Philosophy*, Lahore, 1938; rev. ed., 1945; the same, *Iqbal: The Man and the Message*, London, 1949)? Yet Iqbal is so contradictory and unsystematic that it is difficult to assess him. He is the Ṣūfī who attacked Sufism, and perhaps the liberal who attacked liberalism. The historical consequence of his impact seems on the whole to have served to weaken liberalism among Indian Muslims and to help replace it (cf. the later part of this present section, below) with an illiberal nationalistic and apologist dynamism.

[45] Cf. Gibb, *op. cit.*, p. 43.

[46] Author of *Islamic Ideology: the fundamental beliefs and principles of Islam and their application to practical life*, Lahore, 1951 (2nd ed., *ibid.*, 1953); and editor of the monthly journal *Saqāfat*, Lahore (1955-   ). He is Director of the Institute of Islamic Culture, Lahore (1950-   ).

and Abu-l-Kalam Azad in India, Rashid of Tehran, Rashid Rida of Cairo, produced less sophisticated books than Khuda Bakhsh and Yusuf 'Ali, or 'Abbas Iqbal, or Ahmad Amin; but they provoked much more excitement and action.[47]

One might, indeed, almost question the validity of lumping together these diverse developments under one heading. Might one not better separate at least a Westernized liberalism from an indigenous modernist reform? Yet one is justified, if not forced, to treat them unitedly by at least two considerations. The first has to do with the nature of the liberal values themselves, such as the concern for every man in his individual personality, with its own distinctive capacity for growth, its superlative freedom and inner responsibility, and for the rational consent of his mind, over against all systems and overt authority. These values, we believe, are in fact universal; however particular certain liberal "move-

[47] On 'Ubaydullāh Sindhī (1872-1944) the chief works are in Urdū: Muḥammad Sarwar, *Mawlānā 'Ubaydullāh Sindhī*, Lahore, 1943, and Sa'īd Aḥmad Akbarābādī, *Mawlānā 'Ubaydullāh Sindhī awr un-ke Nāqid*, Lahore, 1946. The former writer has edited 'Ubaydullāh's own writings. In English, see M. Mazheruddin Siddiqi, "Obaid-ullah Sindhi" in *The Islamic Literature*, Lahore, 8:379-89 (1956).

Abū-l-Kalām Āzād (1888-   ), venerable religious scholar and at present Education Minister in the Government of India, has long been an important Muslim political and intellectual leader in Indian nationalism, and a great writer in Urdū. One may mention the influential paper *al-Hilāl*, Calcutta, 1912-14, which he edited, and of his many books perhaps *Tarjumānu-l-Qur'ān*, Calcutta, 1931-   (2 voll. have appeared so far) and *Ghubār-i Khāṭir* (numerous edd.; that available to us, Lahore, 1946). See further the Mu'īn bibliography noted at ref. 3 above.

Ḥusayn 'Alī Rāshid (1902-   ) is not a writer of books but a preacher; he has become very popular over the Tihrān radio. There is a 5-volume collection of his talks: *Sukhanrānīhā-yi Rāshid*, Tihrān, 1322-24/1943-45. See Ḥaydarī, *op. cit.* at ref. 32 above.

On Rashīd Riḍā (1865-1935) see Adams, *op. cit.*, s.v. in index; al-Amīr Shakīb Arslān, *al-Sayyid Rashīd Riḍā, aw ikhā' arba'īn sanah*, Damascus, 1356/1937; and Henri Laoust in his introduction to his translation *Le Califat dans la doctrine de Rašīd Riḍā*, Beyrouth, 1938. On Khudā Bakhsh (1877-1931) and Yūsuf 'Alī (1872-1953), see W. C. Smith, *op. cit.*, s.vv. in index. 'Abbās Iqbāl (1899-1956) was an Īrānī literary historian.

On Aḥmad Amīn (1886-1954) see his autobiography *Ḥayātī*, Cairo, 1950; cf. M. Perlmann, "The Autobiography of Ahmad Amin," *Middle Eastern Affairs*, New York, 5: 17-24 (1954) and Kenneth Cragg, "Then and Now in Egypt. The Reflections of Ahmad Amin," in *The Middle East Journal*, Washington, 9: 28-40 (1955). He is known chiefly as an historian (cf. below, chap. 4, ref. 5) and as a littérateur; see the article of H.A.R. Gibb s.v. in *The Encyclopaedia of Islam*, new ed., Leiden, 1956.

ments," Victorian or other, may have been. Formal patterns of liberal ideas have definable histories, but liberal attitudes must be acknowledged as such wherever they occur.

Secondly, the two strands in recent Muslim history have in fact intertwined; not only in their ramifying results in the community, but in individual cases. The influence of both types on the rising generations has been widespread and on the whole undiscriminating. Indeed, the leaders themselves have not kept them distinct. The Westernizing liberal Taha Husayn was, before his Paris education, a student of the rationalizing orthodox 'Abduh. Conversely, the Indian orthodox rationalizer Shibli was first a disciple of the pro-Westernist Sir Sayyid. In both cases the early influence was clearly significant.

Indeed, if one tried to dichotomize, it would be difficult in the case of a great leader such as Sir Sayyid[48] to decide into which category he would fall. In some ways strikingly a Muslim gentleman of the old school, hardly knowing English and willingly dubbed a Wahhabi, yet perhaps his major contribution was his insistent introduction into the community of explicitly Western liberal ways.

Moreover, the more indigenous, practical tendency of liberalized Muslim reform is for our purposes to be compared with the Westernized intellectualist tendency also on one further score. This is the negative but significant point that it too fell short of producing an effective, transmissible synthesis of Islamic and liberal loyalties. As in the other case, individual leaders achieved such a synthesis for themselves. Yet they could not give it an expression that would spur others to continuing their creative achievement.

Sir Sayyid exemplified liberal Islam more forcefully than he formulated it. He was a Muslim acting on the liberal values with sincerity and effectiveness. Yet he did not succeed in getting across to his generation or its successors an interpretation of Islam into which the liberal values were integrated.

This is true also of Muhammad 'Abduh. The spirit of the man and of his teachings is inherently liberal, deeply and greatly so.

---

[48] On Sir Sayyid Aḥmad Khān (1817-98) see the article AḤMAD KHĀN by J. M. S. Baljon, Jr. in *The Encyclopaedia of Islam*, new edition, Leiden, 1956. To the bibliography there given, add the important Special Aligarh Number (" 'Alīgaḍh Nambar"), 1953-54—1954-55, of the *'Alīgaḍh Maygazīn*, Aligarh, 1955; and Nūru-r-Raḥmān, *Ḥayāt-i Sar Sayyid*, Aligarh, n.d. [1956?].

Yet the finished product of his work transmitted to others incorporates this only very partially. We have seen that the intellectual exposition of the Westernizers lacked power and drive. The forceful work of the reformers lacked effective systematic exposition.

In sum, then, we would attribute the decline of liberalism in recent Islam in significant part to the fact that such liberalism as has been achieved—whether primarily of external or internal source, whether primarily in ideas or in activity—has not yet been formulated in such a way as to envisage its dynamic truth as within the central structure of the Islamic faith.[49]

This means that it has not been set forth in such a way as to be theoretically compelling to a Muslim as such; nor incorporated in practice—specifically, related to worship—in such a way as to give religious power to those intellectually persuaded. The liberal leaders of society have been but little provided with a religious base appropriate to their life and thought; the paraphernalia of Islam have failed to keep pace with them, while they kept pace with modernity. The consequence has been not only their inability to communicate their vision to others, but also that in times of stress they have not had the necessary courage and integrity to fight for it themselves.

Our analysis so far has been on matters of principle, dealing with the relation of the ideology that was elaborated to Islam primarily as a system. We believe this important for our understanding. Yet the development is richly illustrated and further clarified when one then turns to treat the new patterns in relation to the actual movement of Islam in recent history—the drive towards mundane resurgence. We shall see that the use in fact

[49] That there has been as yet virtually no explicit reconsideration of the central issues of the faith is attested both by Muslims themselves and by outside students. "The few main fundamentals of Islam were not subject to any serious revolution or evolution caused by modern Western secular or any other Western influence. . . . The modern Muslims never touched the main theological concepts in their reforms. . . . The theological aspect has not been subject to any substantial evolution," Mohammad Hassan El-Zayyat, "Islam Confronted by Western Secularism: Evolutionary Reaction," in D. S. Franck, ed., *Islam in the Modern World*, Washington, 1951, p. 32. Cf. similarly F. Rahman, *op. cit.* The most attentive observer in the West of modern Arab religious thought: "Few, if any, of the basic theological and orthodox doctrines of Islam have been directly involved in the intellectual debates of twentieth-century Arab Islam"—Kenneth Cragg, "The Modernist Movement in Egypt," in Richard N. Frye, ed., *Islam and the West*, 's-Gravenhage, 1957, p. 151.

made by the community of the ideas and tendencies introduced, has been in terms less of liberalism's inherent qualities than of the community's felt needs and goals. Its handling of this as of other modernities has been largely in relation to its own intrinsic development.

If we revert to our central theme, seeing Islam's fundamental modern problem as that of rehabilitating its earthly self, we may consider its development of liberalism also as an activity with a practical purpose. This is only in part true of the liberal leaders. These, as we have seen, in some cases evolved for themselves a loyal and genuine commitment to the new values. Those who followed them more generally saw liberalism, or some particular aspect of it, as at least in part a useful instrument in the refurbishing of Islamic society. We have already noted that some Muslims regarded rationalism, humanism, Westernizing, and the like as further disruptive threats to the on-going process of actualizing the Islamic ideal on earth. Others disagreed. These felt or argued, consciously or by implication, that to employ one or other of these would, rather, prove effective expedients in the task. Some took the position even that it was necessary to adopt them in order that Muslim society might once again be strong.

In a sense something similar has been partly characteristic even of Islamic liberalism in Turkey.[50] Certainly in most of the Islamic world the liberal movement hardly obscured and sometimes illuminated the *motif* of endeavouring to redress the internal decline of Muslim society, to stand against external encroachment, and to recapture a former greatness.

The community's attitude is shown in the selectivity it exercised and the development it accorded to such work as was accomplished. For example, the Indian Muslim community accepted (not un-

[50] Here, too, the appropriation of Western values, the rigorous rationalizing of social processes, and even religious reform have in significant measure been in the service of the regeneration of the community. We shall explore this situation somewhat in chap. 4 below. We shall presently be considering also as an aspect of nationalism the question whether the Turks gave the whole matter a distinctive and indeed crucial twist, by making the fundamental shift of its being Turkish rather than Muslim society whose cause they were serving, as it has seemed to some Muslims as well as to some Western observers. Their revolution is accordingly seen as on a nationalistic rather than a religious basis. This is, of course, up to a point true. However, we shall presently argue that the difference here between them and other Muslim groups is not in fact quite so great as either they or others have supposed.

reluctantly) Sir Sayyid's introduction of English education. But it insisted that in his College neither his ideas nor the English language should be applied to the study of Islam.[51] It gave serious attention to his appeal for liberal social reform,[52] but has neglected his venture into liberal Qur'an interpretation.[53] 'Abduh's sincere and moving appeal for an Islam unbound by inhibiting traditional interpretation (*taqlid*) has led to a few remarkable individual advances in the realm of intellectual insight. Yet it has much more effectively led, in the *Salafiyah* or *Manar* movement, willingly accepting Wahhabi influence, to a reinvigorated fundamentalist activism.

Indeed, one can generalize these matters further. The liberalism that appeared in the Muslim world, chiefly before the First World War, in so far as it was unrelated to Islam tended to be weak, uncreative, inert. In so far as it was related to Islam, and has been absorbed or utilized by the community, it has tended to become subordinated to prior Islamic purposes. Liberalism has modified Islam much less than it has been modified by it. The movement, particularly in its humanism, has served to strengthen the this-worldly emphasis of the Islamic outlook. It has assisted in concentrating religious aspiration on temporal programmes—such as nationalism, which is our next topic. But in this process of subordination it has been adapted, even transformed. The reason on which the liberals insisted has been employed to defend the faith. The freedom from constraint that they exalted has been turned to activate without discipline the community's self-assertion. In

---

[51] Cf. J. M. S. Baljon, Jr., *The Reforms and Religious Ideas of Sir Sayyid Aḥmad Khān*, Leiden, 1949, p. 41, and the reff. there cited. Cf. also the present writer's brief article "Ek Sawāl," '*Aligaḍh Maygazīn*, Aligarh, 1955, pp. 81-83.

[52] Expressed most markedly in the journal *Tahẓibu-l-Akhlāq*, (1870-76), which he edited, and the organization Mohammedan Educational Conference (1886-   ), which he established.

[53] *Tafsīru-l-Qur'ān, wa huwa al-Hudà wa al-Furqān*, 6 voll., Lahore, n.d. [1880-95?]. This work has long been out of print, and was never influential (except to call down upon its author the vituperation and wrath of the religious). A study of it, with partial translation into English and full translation of the prolegomena *Taḥrīr fī Uṣūl al-Tafsīr* (ed. available to us, Lahore, 1913) is under preparation by our colleague Muḥammad Da'ūd Rahbar. A part of this last has been published as "Sir Sayyid Aḥmad Khān's Principles of Exegesis," *The Muslim World*, Hartford, 46: 104-12 (1956). On the general question of opposition to Sir Sayyid's religious views, cf. Baljon, *op. cit.*, pp. 68-76, and the reff. there cited.

short, the intellectualist aspect of liberalism has been merged into apologetics, and its practical aspect into vitalistic dynamism.

Nationalism, apologetics, and dynamism, as we have already indicated, are the three outstanding new tendencies of modern Islam. We shall be taking them up presently. In the meantime, before closing our discussion of liberalism's decline, we must note one final major factor: the West. We have said that the ascendancy of Europe, with its liberalism, was at the end of the nineteenth century clearly significant in the rise of Islamic liberalism. Equally, in the latter's more recent decline it is not difficult to discern Western influence.

For one thing, there has been in the West itself after the First World War a great enfeeblement of the liberal tradition. The reasons for this are subtle and complex; we cannot go into them here. Yet it is worth our noting that many throughout the world have deemed that liberalism has proven unable in severe crisis to hold the rein of man's passion, or to bear the weight of his anguish.

Secondly, there has been also the marked decline in the West's prestige as a whole. The ascendancy was first successfully challenged by the Japanese victory over imperialist Russia in 1905. The moral authority of Europe suffered a serious blow in the First World War. It virtually crumbled in the Second.[54] There has been, of course, much misinterpretation, even misrepresentation; other civilizations have been hardly more successful in understanding the real values or inner springs of the West than the West has with them. However that may be, very few Westerners have any inkling of how little esteem their culture has today in the Orient.

Indeed, a situation has been reached where the Western connection of liberalism—or of any trend—is itself a strong argument against it. The West used to be resisted for its economic and political domination, its overt power threat to Muslim (and other Eastern) society. But the inner quality of its life, and especially its liberalism, was considerably admired. And it was generally believed that Western liberalism was in conflict with Western imperialism, was the friend and ally of Oriental and subject peoples.

[54] This language is perhaps too gentle, too self-righteous. Some would claim that the West's "moral authority" never existed among but a tiny minority, and such as it was had been shattered long before mid-century; by the time of the First World War, not the Second.

Nowadays this is widely changed. The West today is not only feared but disliked. The antipathy is to its spirit, not only to its arms. And the shift in Western leadership after the Second World War has exacerbated this. In power, arrogance, and insensitive uncouthness, America has seemed to many Easterners almost to have enhanced the failings and moderated the virtues of the European tradition.

If the dominating feature of global affairs today is the question of Communist expansionism, surely of rival long-range significance for tomorrow is the depth and bitterness and increase of anti-Westernism throughout most of the world.

Thirdly, there has been disappointment in the specific relations between Islam and Western liberalism itself. We have seen that many Muslims approached liberalism in a spirit of hope or conviction that the West, or reason, or Western liberalism would prove of assistance in the basic enterprise of reconstructing Islamic society, of setting Islamic history once again on the road to fulfillment. These hopes have on the whole proven deceptive. In the 1890's Muslim liberals, though a minority in their own communities, could believe that cooperation with the (even more optimistic) liberals of Europe could bring about fairly quickly a brave new world. Such cooperation or assistance did not appear to be effectively forthcoming. The advance of liberalism at home did not seem to be reflected in a corresponding fulfillment of its promise for the outside world, specifically in this case Islam.

With the exception of a few individuals, the West was seen as continuing to act as either indifferent to or even still the opponent of the Muslim peoples, or at least of their corporate personality. Politically, the West seemed resolute to maintain imperial domination. Economically, its pressures remained forceful.[55] Culturally, its arrogance persisted. While a few scholars and expositors were slowly and with great labour striving to understand more accurately and to interpret more appreciatively the Islamic tradition,

[55] In the second half of the twentieth century began the new policy of Western economic assistance to "underdeveloped" countries. It is too early yet to assess the psychological and spiritual results of this. One thing is certain: that these are vastly less favourable for human understanding and rapprochement and mutual friendship than they would have been had the policy been less explicitly linked to ulterior political purposes, and less sharply divorced from humane sympathy and cultural insight. There has been a sad ineptness, on the whole, in the giving of assistance.

their work could not begin to keep pace with the growing contact; Muslim discovery of the West was in large part a pained discovery of Western antipathy to Islam. It is in the Arab world that a pained awareness of being rejected has been most acute, symbolized of late in Zionism; and we shall consider the very instructive Arab situation with some attention in our next chapter. In general it gradually became the conviction of even the Westernized Muslims that any reconstruction of their society to which they might aspire they must undertake themselves, without the help and even against the weight of Christendom.

This betrays a tendency to look upon liberalism as a force that might help them, rather than as an attitude by which they might help themselves. Perhaps the former must come first. In any case, conviction was inhibited not only by Western liberalism's general insouciance for Islam. Where there was overt application, here too it became increasingly felt in the Muslim world that what little was being offered was of small actual value for stopping the erosion increasingly threatening the Islamic community. Western secular leaders presumed (and still tend to insist) that Muslim liberals should be secular, playing down the Islamic element in their society. Western religious liberals, even if not still in an exclusivist sense Christian (as most of the missionaries still tend to be: Christian liberalism has hardly yet come to the point of recognizing a religious value in serving Islam as such), presumed that Muslims should be individualist, playing down the social element in their faith.[56] Western liberalism did not seem to orient itself to Islam in a way that would contribute to solving Islam's central modern problem.

Something similar is true of Orientalism, in a sense the West's application of reason to the data of Islam. Some have recognized a large debt that Muslim learning owes to Western scholarship in this field. Many have found selected parts of its results useful for their apologetic purposes, especially in glorifying the Islamic past. Some helpful work has been deeply appreciated. Yet on the whole the work of Occidental Islamics scholarship, not always

[56] An illustration: a Muslim friend remarked to us (Karachi, May 1949): "I attended a mission college in the South. I was very happy there. The teachers met us at the personal level, and they were extremely good to us. They took a personal interest in our future, would do anything to help us as individuals. But it never crossed their minds to help us as a community, to help us find the self-realization of our culture."

reverent or constructive, has appeared to many Muslims as in basic tendency disintegrative of Islam in its central formulations, as one more attack upon and threat to the faith.[57]

Finally there remains a basic fact: the indifferent performance in Muslim countries of imported liberal institutions, from parliamentary democracy to mixed swimming. Even the functioning of "liberal" educational systems was open to serious indictment. Western observers would attribute this failure to the societies' very imperfect understanding of and commitment to the principles on which these institutions rest, the inevitable failure of operating external forms without the inner loyalties of spirit. They would infer a need for more and deeper liberalism, rather than less. But many in the Muslim societies themselves come to a contrary conclusion, feeling rather that these un-Islamic ways have been tried and found wanting. Their recent history, it is not difficult for the return-to-Islam school to argue, has conspicuously demonstrated the ineptness of liberalism, its inability to lead the Muslims in practice to social justice or the good life. Few, whether Communist or Western, religious or secular, liberal or other, would disagree that something new is needed for that regeneration of which Islamic society, as the rest of us today, stands in need.

Whatever the interpretation—and we shall pursue and illustrate our analysis later in the particular cases of the Arab world and Pakistan—the general fact is that during the past quarter century or so, liberalism in Islam has markedly waned. In some areas one might be tempted to say, evaporated.

There are exceptions to the general trend, or apparent exceptions. The chief is, as so often, Turkey. We cannot trace historically the highly special and highly significant Turkish case, though we shall devote a chapter presently to some aspects of the present Turkish situation. In post-partition India, also, as we shall explore later, something significant may be developing. The Muslim com-

[57] Even in its more recent, more sympathetic, orientalism, Western studies are widely misunderstood and rejected. The attempt to be analytic is regarded as merely destructive. Western books on Islam are often read not in order to see how illuminating they may be, but how laudatory. One recent minor instance illustrating the present mood is afforded by the way in which a petulant attack upon *The Encyclopaedia of Islam* elicited an emotional response from a wide circle of Muslims, as evidenced by its repeated use: we have chanced to see it in *The Islamic Literature*, Lahore, 7: 581-83 (1955); *Yaqeen*, Karachi, 4: 52 (1375/1955); and elsewhere.

munity in India was in 1947 suddenly and shatteringly bereft of alternatives that until recently it had ardently espoused; and it is showing signs in some sections of perhaps taking up again, though reluctantly, the liberal course. In Indonesia, neither the rise of an Islamic liberalism nor its decline seems to have gone so far as in other Muslim countries. The special quality there is that many of the values of liberalism—especially tolerance, and the status of women as full persons—are indigenous, particularly Javanese (pre-Islamic). The great question is whether the contemporary resurgence of Islam in Indonesia will lead to a synthesis or a conflict with the local tradition.

Common to these instances is that the strength and persistence, and perhaps even the content, of liberalism are due to explicitly non-Islamic factors. And in no case has the relation to Islam been worked out, or even much attempted. Hence our qualification that they may be only apparent exceptions. It has yet to be seen whether these communities will develop liberalism as a force within Islam; and in any case even these exceptions have put the emphasis elsewhere. By and large one may say that throughout the Muslim world liberal interpretation has been giving way in Islamic development to other methods of reconstruction, to which we must now turn. These are chiefly three: nationalism, apologetics, dynamism.

Nationalism

It is obvious that the nationalist movements in the various Muslim areas have become strenuous and almost overriding. A great deal of the energy of the entire Islamic world has been devoted to the long struggle to ward off or oust foreign domination. Such nationalism, of course, here as elsewhere, is highly complex. It is related to nationalism in Europe: both the ideas and institutions of the West affected deeply the Westernized minority who led the movement. It is related to nationalism in the rest of Asia: there is clearly much in common between the Muslim nationalist movements and those of India, China, and the like. It is related to nationalism in past Islamic history. For instance, Iran has a continuous nationalist tradition culturally from the time of Firdawsi at least, in the eleventh century, and politically from that of the Safavis, who in 1500 set up one of the world's early nationalist states. And so on. It can obviously be no part of our purpose here to treat Muslim nationalist movements in any sort of full analysis or comprehensive outline. We consider them in one aspect only, their relation to the religion of Islam.

This in itself is complex enough. It is complex not only in the obvious and important sense that each nationalism is of course distinctive, with its own geographic, historical, economic and other particularities, individual characteristics that it is the nature of nationalism to stress. The nationalism of Indonesia is Indonesian in the way that Arabs cannot share and indeed mostly cannot understand. The role of Islam in Turkish and that of Islam in Iranian nationalism are necessarily and inherently divergent.

The complexity lies, further, in the fact that there has developed in each case and in general an ambivalence within the religio-nationalist relation which has as yet not at all been resolved.

The first and altogether fundamental consideration here concerns nationalism regarded in its overriding negative quality as the drive to eject alien control. This is not only compatible with Islam in its traditional and its religious and its social and every other sense. More: it is part and parcel of Islam's modern resurgence. The endeavour of the Indonesian Muslims to get rid of the Dutch, of the Syrian and Maghribi Muslims to get rid of the French, of the Indian Muslims to get rid of the British, has been an inherent and indeed basic element in the overall endeavour of Muslims in general to reassert their community in the contemporary world. Similarly, the Turkish thrust to throw back the Greeks (1922) or the Iranian to frustrate Anglo-Russian "spheres of influence" (1890's, 1940's) have also been direct steps in the revitalization of mundane Islam.

It would be palpably false to aver that the Islamic was the only element in these movements. Clearly there were others, from economics to language and more. Yet it would equally be false to suppose that the Islamic note was either absent or in any way discordant.

Within the task of rehabilitating Islamic history from the decline into which it had sunk, the need was imperative and crucial and of top priority to end the subjection of the community to infidel power. In general, those who have wanted to see Islam once again "a going concern" have naturally and emphatically supported the several attempts to free its peoples. In the leadership of such movements, especially in their early stages, primarily religious figures have in some cases been prominent and even decisive. We have already noted Jamalu-d-Din Afghani's inciting of local nationalisms. Examples in individual countries are Muhammad 'Abduh in Egypt,[58] the Deobandis and Abu-l-Kalam Azad in India,[59] Ahmad Dakhlan in Indonesia.[60]

Furthermore, the driving force of nationalism has become more and more religious the more the movement has penetrated the masses. Even where the leaders and the form and the ideas of the movement have been nationalist on a more or less Western pattern, the followers and the substance and the emotions were significantly Islamic. (The Westernizing leaders have frequently been surprised to discover the degree to which they have let loose an Islamic upsurge.) In the realm of opposition to outsiders, there was decidedly no conflict between the two. On the contrary, they have been mutually helpful, each contributing an important and even essential element to the other's success. As we have said, this is the fundamental fact regarding nationalism in the modern Islamic world.

Some Muslims[61] and some Westerners have contended, nonetheless, that there is inherently a very much less harmonious relationship between Islam and nationalism as basic ideas. They have had in mind nationalism in its positive rather than negative aspect, as a constructive loyalty to a national group. This is a different matter. It is true that nationalism in this form would seem in theory less assimilable to Islam. Also it is true, in practice, that this form of nationalism has been very much less in evidence in the Islamic world.

[58] For 'Abduh as a nationalist leader, cf. Adams, *op. cit.*, pp. 52-57.

[59] The Dāru-l-'Ulūm (1876-   ) at Deoband, U.P., India, has played a distinguished part in the political and religious life of the Indo-Muslim community. Yet no careful published study of it seems to be available. A small amount of information is to be found in W. C. Smith, *op. cit.*, pp. 320-21 (London ed., pp. 295-96), and see s.v. in index. See further the Mu'in bibliography noted at ref. 3 above.

[60] On Kiyai Hajji Ahmad Dakhlan (1868-1923) see s.v. Dachlan in *Ensiklopedia Indonesia*, Bandung/'s Gravenhage, vol. 1, n.d. [sc. 1954].

[61] E.g., "Islam and nationalism in any form are two incompatible modes of thought and life"—[Maẓharu-d-Dīn Ṣiddīqī, Editor] *The Islamic Literature,* Lahore, 8: 435 (1956). "In their spirit and in their aims Islam and nationalism are diametrically opposed to each other"—Sayyed Abulala Maudoodi, *Nationalism and India* (trans.), Pathankot, 1947; 2nd ed., Karachi, 1947, p. 10. Cf. also the pungent poem of Iqbāl, "Waṭanīyat," *Bāng-i Darā,* Lahore, 1924; 12th imp., 1948, p. 173.

It is important to distinguish the two. To resist aliens, to work against their domination, even to hate or despise them, is one thing. To respect all members of one's own nation, to envisage its welfare, to evolve an effective loyalty to that welfare, and to work constructively so as to bring it about, is quite another. It is easier to see what one is or should be fighting against, than to imagine what one is or should be fighting for. For a religion also, opposition is easier than construction. And it is sometimes not appreciated how negative until now have been the nationalisms of the Islamic world. Turkey is, as ever, the exception; the Turks are the one Muslim people in modern times who have generated a positive conception of what they want, and an operative loyalty towards attaining it. The particular relation of this goal and this loyalty to Islam will later occupy our attention. Of the other Muslim peoples, the nationalist programmes so far have either been purely negative, aimed at getting rid of something; or else they have proven unable to engender enough devotion to get themselves implemented.

Indian nationalism, like Turkish, has evolved a positive ambition: to be a secular welfare state. But from it most Muslims chose to withdraw; and those who could not in the end do so have far from worked out their own, let alone their religion's, relation to this objective. To their situation also we shall be returning. Pakistan, Syria, and to some extent Indonesia are examples of movements where recent success in throwing off foreign rule after long and persistent struggle has been followed by a vast and serious uncertainty as to what to do next. And there has been a disconcerting inability to elicit on any wide scale that constructive allegiance that is needed for a nation to survive a deep crisis and to build for itself an effective life in the modern world. Iran and Egypt also are examples of Muslim countries where nationalism, with a longer opportunity to develop both a positive programme and a loyal commitment to it, again has evinced strength only on the negative, anti-foreign score. Whether the military régime of 'Abd al-Nasir ("Nasser") will succeed where the Wafd failed remains to be seen.

One may ardently hope so. One may, and indeed must, hope also that the other areas too will quickly discover, or create, a positive content for their national existence.[62] This is contemporary history, and we shall return to its deep problem later. Our present concern is simply to stress that the relation between this positive nationalism and Islam has remained almost purely a theoretical problem, since acceptance of it by Muslims has remained so slight. This much at least would seem valid: that some writers have been too hasty in assuming or concluding that a Western-type nationalism in this positive sense could be or has been adopted fairly easily or effectively into the Islamic world. They would seem to have overestimated the readiness of that world with its different tradition of loyalties and emotions to incorporate this alien phenomenon. Negative nationalism, yes; the desire and determination to be on one's own. But, once one's group is free, the discipline to get up early in the morning, to work long hours, to turn down bribes, the inspiration to dream and the energy to actualize one's dreaming, all for national welfare and for national rewards, these have been less obvious. In the past, only Islam has provided for these peoples this type of discipline, inspiration, and energy.

A third basic point in this matter is that wherever nationalism has been adopted in the Muslim world, and in whatever form, the 'nation' concerned has been a Muslim group. No Muslim people has evolved a national feeling that has meant a loyalty to or even concern for a community transcending the bounds of Islam.[63]

[62] Or else a new form of existence. This seems less likely, but is advocated by a few voices; e.g., Khalīqu-z-Zamān in Pakistan (cf. below, ref. 69). In the Arab world, Sāṭi' al-Ḥuṣarī has advocated that the individual nationalisms of the Arab states, at least, should be superseded by a more encompassing common life, even though this would still be but Arab. Of his some twenty books and pamphlets, see perhaps especially his *Ārā' wa Aḥādīth fī al-Qawmīyah al-'Arabīyah*, Cairo, 1951; and his inaugural lecture to the Arab League's new Institute of Higher Arab Studies, *al-Muḥāḍarah al-Iftitāḥiyah*, Cairo, 1954.

[63] Indeed, on this score also Western nationalisms are hardly an exception. In theory, nationalism in the West has posited the nation as the unit of loyalty, ignoring religious differences. This theory has been successful in practice chiefly where the differences were sectarian, intra-religious. Even the United States, which is justly proud of having assimilated many diverse types of peoples, has never included significant numbers of Hindus, Buddhists, or Taoists. Indeed, no Western nation has ever included non-Christian groups of any size—except Jews; and the treatment of Jews by the West, though it has at times been good, at other times has been a matter of indescribable shame. It is true that non-Muslim minorities feel insecure throughout the Muslim world, and in some instances are very deeply frightened. But it is

The striking test has been India. The Indian nationalism, Hindu, Muslim, Sikh, to which some Muslims once gave themselves with zeal, presently collapsed in shreds so far as the general Muslim group was concerned. In fact, that group turned against it with a terrifying violence. There were, of course, as always, other reasons for this collapse: economic, political, Hindu, and the like.[64] But the relevant fact here is that those other reasons prevailed. A non-Islamic nationalism could not, for Muslims, stand against them. The appeal to the Muslim group for loyalty to a society other than its own religious one, failed.

Elsewhere, Muslim groups differ as to the degree to which the Islamic interplay with nationalism is overt and explicit. They do not differ in the fact that everywhere their nationalisms are enthusiasms for Muslim nations.

Indonesia provides the apparently clearest example of nationalist and Muslim movements working not merely side by side but interpenetratingly in the period of anti-foreign struggle, and then separating out once independence is achieved. Thereupon, too, the Islamic groups have further divided, into those whose goal is

---

also probably true, in varying degrees, that throughout the world (except pre-Communist China?) hardly any religious minority feels secure.

[64] Of the rise and reverberating fall of Muslim participation in Indian nationalism, there is no monographic study, and perhaps no adequate study investigating this matter as a problem in itself. For tangential treatment from various points of view, see B. R. Ambedkar, *Pakistan*, Bombay, 1947; Shaukatullah Ansari, *Pakistan: the problem of India*, Lahore, 1944; W. Norman Brown, "Hindu-Muslim Communalism" and "The Creation of Pakistan," chapp. VII and VIII of his *The United States and India and Pakistan*, Cambridge, Mass., 1953, pp. 112-43; Sir Reginald Coupland, "Hindu-Moslem Antagonism" and "The Moslem Reaction," Part 1, chap. III and Part 2, chap. XVIII of his [*Report on*] *the Constitutional Problem in India*, London, 3 voll., 1942-44 (Bombay, one vol., and New York, one vol., 1944; abridgement: *India: a restatement*, London and New York, 1945) (1: 28-36 and 2: 179-207 of the full Indian ed., 1945 reprint; see further s.v. "Moslems" in the indexes); Jawaharlal Nehru, "The Question of Minorities. The Moslem League. Mr. M. A. Jinnah," chap. VIII, §5 of his *The Discovery of India*, New York, 1946, pp. 384-99; Mohammad Noman, *Muslim India: rise and growth of the All India Muslim League*, Allahabad, 1942; Richard Symonds, "The Muslims and Indian Nationalism," chap. III of his *The Making of Pakistan*, London, 1950, pp. 38-48. These are written, respectively, by a non-Muslim non-Congress Indian, a Muslim Indian-nationalist, an India-oriented Westerner, a British official, a non-Muslim Congressman, a Muslim Leaguer, a Pakistan-oriented Westerner. See also Smith, *op. cit.*, Part II *passim* and esp. the 2nd (London) ed., pp. 231-34 and chap. 5; cf. further below, chapp. 5 and 6 of the present work.

an Islamic state, and those whose nationalism is explicitly Muslim but rather in content than in form. It would, however, be an over-simplification to identify these major trends simply with the three major parties: Nationalist, Nahdat al-Ulama, and Mashumi. The existence of these illuminates rather than defines what is developing. In fact, as in other areas, most nationalists are Muslims, and vice versa. Most Muslims are Muslims socio-politically. Within the Muslim divergencies, and between the Muslim groups and the Nationalists, there is difference rather than conflict—a difference, most Indonesians sense, to be resolved rather than a conflict to be fought out. The fact that the parties worked against each other in the first elections (1955), and with each other in the first government (1956), is significant.

In other areas, one or other of these differences of degree but similarity of substance is also to be seen. Irani nationalism is significantly Shi'i, sectarian. In Arab nationalism one striking element is the identification of Arabism with Islam. And so on. Nationalism, for Muslims, is everywhere a Muslim nationalism. As within Indonesia, so across the Muslim world, one could arrange the groups in a series according to the degree of formality and emotion with which this relationship is recognized and emphasized. At its most explicit, the community is not only Muslim in composition but becomes also Islamic in form, or at least in name: the nation is identified by its Muslim members as itself religiously significant. This is the case with the Islamic Republic of Pakistan. Yet even when the nation is not a group symbol of the faith, it is still the home of the faithful. To this, even Turkey is no exception. It would stand at the other end, but not outside the series.

Turkish nationalism is explicitly lay. Nonetheless, only a Muslim group is involved; the few Christians or Jews in the country are not considered Turks. Loyalty to the group is still to an exclusively Muslim group, as it has always and elsewhere been. The flare-ups in 1955 have illustrated the fact that Turks too can be bitter in their repudiation of non-Muslim elements.[65]

It is true that the Nationalist Party in Indonesia, as also Egyptian nationalism of the al-Liwa' type, has made a point of including Christians; and the speeches of numerous political leaders have

[65] For the anti-Greek rioting in Turkey of September 6-7, 1955, see "Riots in Turkey," *The Middle East Journal*, Washington, 9:435 (1955).

recognized the minorities' role. But this is a type of nationalism that has everywhere waned, if not failed. Nowhere in the Muslim world (except perhaps in Indonesia?) do Muslims feel that a non-Muslim member of their nation is "one of us." And nowhere do the minorities feel accepted.

Indeed, in many instances there is very serious trepidation. A great many Muslims are genuinely unaware of the insecurity and apprehension of their non-Muslim minorities. Many do not see the problem: it simply does not occur to them that non-Muslims would expect to be included in the group along with them.[66] Others content themselves, though they do not content the minorities, by a serene assurance that "Islam treats minorities well."[67] In any case, no Muslim group has cut across a Muslim society for a nationalist one; has substituted nationalism for Islam. The Turks have perhaps come closest to apparently doing this. Yet even their extreme case illustrates rather than contradicts the argument. For in abandoning a wider Muslim loyalty for Turkish allegiance, they have not replaced Islam with a quite new grouping. Rather, they have taken a part for the whole—as in effect, though less explicitly, the Pakistanis and Arabs and Iranis and Indonesians have also come close to doing.

The fourth consideration regarding Muslim nationalisms, then, is their relation to pan-Islam. The Muslim's feeling for his total community is well-known. We have previously noted the deep religious base on which this rests—how the central concepts of Islam give spiritual significance to the group, and strengthen the human tendencies to stress a closed society and to identify it with the religious one.[68] It is a negative aspect of this that we have just

---

[66] Cf. Pierre Rondot, "Islam, Christianity, and the Modern State," *Middle Eastern Affairs*, New York, 5: 341-45 (1954), esp. p. 342.

[67] E.g., at the Annual Session of the All India Muslim League, Delhi, April 1943, at a time when there was major confusion as to what would be the situation of non-Muslims if a Pakistan were established, Jinnāḥ simply assured them that a resolution ensuring them safeguards had been passed, and that the history and Prophet of Islam gave "the clearest proof that non-Muslims have been treated not only justly and fairly but generously"—cf. Smith, *op. cit.*, 2nd (London) ed., p. 287 at ref. 104. This sort of remark is repeated widely.

[68] Cf. above, chap. 1, pp. 18-19. The tendency towards a closed society, and that towards a religious society, and even the tendency to identify the two, are universal; as the sociology of religion and general sociology carefully attest (cf. Émil Durkheim, *Les Formes élémentaires de la vie religieuse*, Paris, 1912; Henri Bergson, *Les Deux sources de la morale et de la religion*, Paris,

been noting, the virtual absence among Muslims of any "we-feeling" that includes men not of the faith. On its positive side it has two expressions: one, to give added intensity to any social grouping of Muslims, strikingly operative in producing Pakistan; secondly, to reach out in aspiration towards a social grouping of *all* Muslims. The former strengthens every Muslim nationalism. The latter is pan-Islam.

The two are different. But they are not essentially in conflict. They can become on occasion practical alternatives, as when any Muslim or a body of Muslims must choose whether to give prior loyalty to one particular section of the Islamic world, or to the whole. They can even come temporarily into conflict, if the interests or apparent interests of the part conflict with the whole. Equally, they can be or seem to be complementary, or stages in one larger process, or aspects of one whole; the regeneration of Islam throughout the world may be seen as something to be practically attained in manageable sections. The chief or first contribution to the mundane resurgence of Islamic society as a whole that Indo-

---

1932; Joachim Wach, *The Sociology of Religion*, London, 1947; etc.). In the West a large number of competing tendencies have developed. Probably Islam stresses the identification more than any other world religion, though not more perhaps than the Hindu in some of its aspects, but for precisely this reason "Hinduism" is not usually regarded as a world religion.

On the level of pure religious thought, the Hindus are the group who have gone furthest in interpreting religious diversity, in making room in their religious philosophy for the fact that other peoples have other faiths. The Semitic group, Jewish, Christian, Muslim, have gone least far; that is, Western civilization and Islamic are the two most intolerant on the religious plane. But the Hindus, with their caste system, negate their intellectual breadth by a social intolerance that is the most rigid in the world. Christians and Muslims may officially believe that the outsider is going to Hell after he dies (an insolent doctrine, which they will have to abandon), yet they are both quite happy to shake hands with him, entertain him at a meal, and treat him on a level of social equality. Official Hindu teaching may accord him equal status in the next world, but in this world treats him as "unclean," with a contempt and distance that are equally insolent, and can be more obtrusive. All of us have a great deal to learn in this matter.

The Chinese, who in the past have attained the greatest degree of both theoretical and practical compatibility in religious matters (though at the cost of taking religion much less seriously), have recently become Communist, thereby joining the ranks of those who damn the rest of the world, and insist—in their case with armed violence—that every society must conform to their one pattern.

'Co-existence' is a matter not only of political but religious and cultural necessity.

nesians can make is, they feel, the strengthening of that society in Indonesia, that is the strengthening of Indonesia. Also, other Muslims can in fact help Indonesia in this in so far as they have first succeeded in regenerating and strengthening their own societies. It is only a few Muslims here and there[69] who disagree with the modern consensus that the rehabilitation of Islam throughout the world is taking place and ought to take place in terms of local rehabilitations. The pan-Islamic vision today is essentially the envisaging of each of the Muslim nations or communities—the Arab world, Turkey, Iran, Pakistan, Indonesia, etc.—individually regenerated, revitalized, prosperous, and strong. Such a vision adds to the particular nationalisms of each region only the hope—or the presupposition—that these would all cooperate in friendly mutuality.[70]

Europe, composite of many nationalisms which virtually disrupted the erstwhile unity of Christendom, may perhaps be in process today of transcending them in some new kind of larger loyalty—under the pressure of the external threat of Russia, and the growing awareness of Asia and Africa (and perhaps America?) as differentiation. Similarly the Islamic world may transcend but not negate a multi-national vitality in a supra-national brotherhood. At least, such is the dream.

Pan-Islam is, and always has been, primarily a sentiment of cohesion. It is not cohesion itself; or any institutional or practical expression of it. The unity of the Muslim world is a unity of

[69] One of the few significant Muslims advocating a political unity of the Islamic world, and even he somewhat obliquely, has been Chawdhrī Khalīqu-z-Zamān, president for a time (1949-50) of the Pakistan Muslim League. He made a tour of other Muslim countries during that time to urge his view; perhaps the rather discouraging reception that he received led him to relax his thesis somewhat. He held that an 'Islamic state' could not be established in Pakistan as but one segment of the Muslim world; it must by definition be pan-Islamic. Cf. his brief pamphlet, *Conception of a Quranic or Islamic State*, Karachi, n.d. [c. 1950?].

[70] The *locus classicus* for this view is now the expression of Iqbāl: "For the present every Muslim nation must sink into her own deeper self, temporarily focus her vision on herself alone, until all are strong and powerful to form a living family of republics" (Sir Mohammad Iqbal, *The Reconstruction of Religious Thought in Islam*, 1944 ed., Lahore, p. 159). A comparable conception was formulated by Jamālu-d-Dīn Afghānī, despite the prevalent view that his concern was political unity; see his "al-Waḥdah al-Islāmīyah" in *al-'Urwah al-Wuthqà*, the collected ed. of Muḥammad Jamāl, Beirut, 3rd ed., 1351/1933, pp. 146-57, esp. the paragraph beginning "*Lā altamis . . .*" pp. 155-56.

sentiment. Attempts to activate it into concrete form, to express the unity on political or other levels, have in modern as in earlier history broken on the rocks of restive actuality. Jamalu-d-Din Afghani reasserted it, but the political expression that it found, in Ottoman plans of Abdul Hamid, was, to say the least, unfortunate; and the failure was stark. The Khilafat movement in India also proved perilously romantic. Nonetheless, except in Turkey, the sentiment persists. Though it has been dormant, it remains strong.[71]

It is worth noting that this ideal of an integrated Muslim brotherhood, comprehending all the faithful in a united social grouping, has from the first been a compelling but an unrealized dream. It was deep in the religious consciousness of pristine Islam, and has retained its force. But it was the first major Islamic ideal to be in fact shattered by history. Within a very few years of the Prophet's death, the unity of the group was broken, and parties of Muslims went to war with each other. The Muslim religious consciousness was shocked profoundly by this; the rift opened at the Battle of the Camel (36 A.H.) has never yet been healed. And from the intellectual problem posed in the recalcitrant fact that the integrity of the faith was thus being negated by fissiparous behaviour of the faithful, Muslim theology arises.[72] Subsequent history did not remedy but rather elaborated and ramified this disunity. In classical times there was a brief period of what has been looked back upon later as not too unreasonable an approximation in practice to the ideal; but presently that too disinte-

[71] The sentiment finds expression, for example, in the 1956 Constitution of Pakistan, where we find among its "Directive Principles of State Policy" a clause 24 that reads, "The State shall endeavour to strengthen the bonds of unity among Muslim countries" (as well as to promote peace, goodwill, etc., "among all nations"). More concretely, the Government of Pakistan sponsored an International Islamic Economic Conference, which convened first in Karachi, 1949, and has remained in being; the Government of Egypt sponsors an Islamic Congress, Cairo, 1953-   ; etc. One may note also such private moves as the organizing of the Mu'tamar-i 'Ālam-i Islāmī/World Muslim Conference, Karachi, 1949-   . Its energetic secretary, Mr. In'āmullāh Khān, was also Chief Organizer of the International Assembly of Muslim Youth, Karachi, 1955-

[72] Theology ('ilm al-kalām) was inaugurated in Islām by the Mu'tazilah. For the view that this group originated in a political issue, and that their famous position regarding the "manzilah bayn al-manzilatayn" was originally a political solution, see the fundamental article of H. S. Nyberg, al-MU'TAZILA, in The Encyclopaedia of Islām, Leiden, 1934.

grated. Through most of its centuries the Muslim community has in fact been fragmented. Nevertheless the ideal has remained, and has retained its warm attractiveness until today.

The Turks in our day have abandoned the sentiment because it has seemed sentimentality: an emotion that could not be acted upon, and indeed that interfered with the practical task of making their own segment of Muslim society strong.

The real problem, for Muslims, of pan-Islam is not that it conflicts with nationalism. As a sentiment it does not in practice conflict with the sentiment of nationalism, as we have seen; the two loyalties can corroborate each other. What it conflicts with is tangible reality. It is one more instance of the divergence between theory and practice in modern Islam.

It is not, however, an instance to which much attention has been given; except by the Turks, who rejected rather than solved it. Their rejection shocked the Muslim world; the explicit repudiation of the theory and sentiment of unity was much more drastic than the actual repudiation in practice in many instances, such as the previous Arab revolt against the Ottomans, the present Afghani-Pakistani friction, and so on. Other Muslims, unwilling to accept or to countenance the Turkish decision, have not themselves seriously come to grips with the issues involved; have not attempted a theory that would do equal justice to the facts but more justice to the sentiment.

This is one more instance of the Turks' boldness in being ready to modify even the central convictions and feelings of traditional Islam in their severe adjustment to the realities of modern history, their practical grappling with the task of how to make their society strong. Their honesty is more important than other Muslims have recognized; though perhaps those others' dream of a wider brotherhood is, for all its current romanticism, also more important than the Turks have grasped. The issue between them has not been formulated on either side, let alone a solution essayed. Unfortunately there has been no religious discussion between Turkish and other Islam since the divergence.

This fact in itself, and the entire matter of Turkish Islam's new orientations, raise questions for pan-Islam, religious and other, that have not yet been faced.

To summarize, the modern Muslim world has accepted and

espoused with fervour those aspects of nationalism that are relevant or contributory to the historical rehabilitation of Islamic
society, and compatible with Islam's central precepts. It has accepted only superficially, or briefly, or not at all, those aspects
that would interfere with or distract from the practical task of that
rehabilitation. And except for the Turks, and then to only a
limited degree, it has not accepted those aspects that would run
counter to traditional Islamic loyalties.

Apologetics

The next matter for our consideration is apologetics: the
endeavour to prove, to oneself or others, that Islam is sound. An
appreciation of this is altogether basic to any understanding of
recent Muslim interpretation. For an almost overwhelming proportion of current Muslim religious thinking comes under this
heading. Most books and speeches on the faith by those within it
today are defensive.

They try to champion rather than to understand, to buttress
rather than to elucidate.

This fact in its far-reaching ramifications is fundamental in
Muslim-Western misunderstanding, and also in the internal de
velopment (or lack of it) of modern Islamic thought. Neither
Muslims themselves nor Western observers of the Muslim world
have usually understood the situation at all fully. A great many
Muslims simply take apologetics for granted and do not understand the alternative, let alone the need for an alternative. A great
many Westerners simply take intellectual analysis for granted and
do not understand apologetics, let alone the Muslims' need for
apologetics.

Much of the apologist literature is addressed, at least formally,
to the West. Further, much of it would appear, at least on the
surface, to treat Islam's relation with modern problems. Yet it is
precisely the apologist quality of this writing that most effectively
frustrates Western appreciation of modern Islam; and, more
serious, most effectively stands in the way of a genuine Muslim
wrestling with modern religious difficulties.

For the Indian scene, the content of the liberal apologetic has
been examined by the present writer, in its defence of Islam in
relation to science, civilization, progress, feminism, peace and the

liberal values generally.[73] The situation has been remarkably parallel in other countries.

The "defence" of Islam may be analysed roughly into a three-fold orientation: against attack, against unbelief, against Westernization.[74] The three, of course, overlap: the differentiation is purely interpretive. The apologetes have set themselves to answering the direct assaults on Islam of Western critics, which especially before the First World War were numerous and often caustic—attacks in the name of Christianity, rationalism, liberal progress, or the like. The West today has little inkling of how mordant and sustained was its earlier denigration of Islam. Secondly, the apologetes have endeavoured to check a tendency to disloyalty among their own community, especially its educated youth. These, like educated youth throughout the world, have seemed liable to abandon their faith under the pressure of modern living and modern thought, and simply to drift. Thirdly, they have felt the need to ward off the tendency of the same Muslims to adopt new and un-Islamic ways and even values (chiefly "Western," or "modern," according to one's interpretation; latterly also, but much less, Communist).

It is this into which liberal thought, after its first promise, chiefly was transformed. Not to re-think Islam, but to re-think its defences. Even in Amir 'Ali, the most effective illustration of Islamic liberalism, the defensive note is clear. He was primarily the advocate defending the cause of Islam before the bar of Western opinion. His work, and that of lesser men, have served equally to defend it in the minds of Westernized Muslims who showed signs of losing their religious faith.

The output of the apologetes has not been creative or dynamic. Yet it was satisfying. It served to soothe the conscience of those many thousands who chose to live or found themselves living Westernized lives, and yet would have been unhappy at "abandoning Islam." Or it aimed at making them unhappy at the thought of abandoning it. This served an important secondary function, for it called back to Islam those members of the Westernizing party who might otherwise have drifted from the faith.

We have already remarked that Islamic liberalism was "per-

[73] Smith, *op. cit.*, part I, chap. 2.
[74] The paragraph that follows presents ideas some of which show an indebtedness to F. Rahman, *op. cit.* above at ref. 1.

missive," allowing a Muslim to be liberal. It also allowed a liberal to be Muslim, to stay within the fold.

Indeed, this increasingly became the primary and avowed objective of ostensibly liberal Islamic thought and writing. It not only allowed a liberal to be Muslim; it more and more invited, insisted. A growing number of Muslims, appropriating the new outlook less fully than the liberal leaders and at times only superficially, and moving much less far from the inherited tradition, let loose a spate of writing devised to corral allegiance to that tradition in a swiftly modernizing world. Work after work has appeared in the vast effort to convince apparently vacillating semi-skeptics that their loyalty to Islam must remain intact.

Socially and historically all this has been of great immediate significance. Intellectually, however, the price paid has been enormous. And the indirect social and historical consequences accordingly are vast. We have had occasion elsewhere to consider some of the metaphysical and pragmatic issues arising from the question of intellectualism in modern Islam.[75] The basic disruption of apologetics is that it has diverted the attention of contemporary Islamic thinkers from their central task—the central task of all thinkers: to pursue truth and to solve problems. A lack of integrity always leads to disintegration; and any failure of intellectual integrity in a society raises the threat of disastrous intellectual disintegration. The Muslim world, including its intelligentsia, has hardly recognized what a responsible, crucial role its intellectual class plays in the present crisis; and how far the future of Islam and of the Muslim community depends on the ability of the intellectual to face, understand, analyse, and solve the new issues that confront them.

In so far, accordingly, as thinkers and writers have succumbed to the apologist tendency, there is very serious danger. For the function of reason has then not been seen as that of ascertaining new truth and solving new problems—and particularly, not religious truth or religious problems. They have turned to an interpretation of Islam, presumed or explicit, according to which the solving of problems, spiritual, moral and social is the function of revelation, of Islam. In classical Islam the intellect was considered an instru-

[75] "The Intellectuals in the Modern Development of the Islamic World," in Sydney Nettleton Fisher, ed., *Social Forces in the Middle East*, Ithaca, 1955, pp. 190-204.

ment to explicate what is revealed. In modern times, this rational system has seemed obsolete to some; and the intellectuals' only duty is seen as that of proving the faith (unexplicated, even undefined) to be valid. This attitude would be less damaging to a community in less strenuous times, with fewer new and stringent problems desperately needing solution.

Yet at any time there is danger in a tendency to view Islam—or any religion—not as an imperative that places on man the responsibility to strive, but rather as a system that relieves him of that responsibility. And many an apologist's exposition of Islam aims at inviting not implementation but applause.

For apologetics has quickly turned romantic and self-indulgent. Defence becomes pretence. Dissemblance is professionalized, and is confused with service to Islam. For those who have lost touch with transcendence, apologetics becomes the intellectualized self-righteousness of one's community and its past, its convictions and predilections. Even at a higher level it regards intellect as subordinate, truth as ultimately conformity with and confirmation of one's revelation. It has forgotten that truth is conformity to fact, with revelation reminding man of truth's overwhelming, indeed sacred, value, and making vivid something of the appalling consequences of any human willfulness in tampering with it.

These are serious and rather sweeping observations. For we believe the matter to be, as we have said, of far-ranging ramification, and altogether basic in modern Muslim thought. For both Muslims and outsiders, then, an awareness of what is at issue would seem of prime importance. Nonetheless we shall postpone a full analysis of it for later consideration. The prevalence of apologetics is widespread. From Durban to Lahore, from Tehran to Jakarta, it has for fifty or more years been appearing in steady stream: book after book, pamphlet after pamphlet, address after address, on Islam in general and on every aspect of it, its history and its achievements. However, it is in the Arab world, particularly Cairo, that it has been at its height. And it is in Arab "modernism" that it has played perhaps the most integral role. Certainly insight into the modern Arab situation of Islam waits on a firm reckoning with apologetics. Accordingly we shall endeavour to come to terms with it in our next chapter, on the Arab crisis.

Here, then, we must content ourselves with the generalization that throughout the Muslim world a great deal of the energy of thinking Muslims has been devoted to the intellectual defence of their traditional faith in the modern world. At this theoretical level also, as on the practical, the task has been conceived as essentially that of warding off attack. Islam is seen as having reached its modern period weakened and threatened, and the function of reason has been understood as that of bolstering it.

We shall see, in the Arab case, how terribly significant is this use of the mind not to solve problems but to prove that really they do not arise.

Dynamism

The third new element in modern Islam to which we have referred is dynamism: the appreciation of activity for its own sake, and at the level of feeling a stirring of intense, even violent, emotionalism. The need and value of this kind of dynamic in a Muslim world that had become passive and inert are apparent. The transmutation of Muslim society from its early nineteenth-century stolidity to its twentieth-century ebullience is no mean achievement. The change has been everywhere in evidence. It was given poetic expression by the Indo-Muslim Iqbal with an eloquence and inspirational fieriness that are artistically superb.

But the modern situation can be understood aright only if one recognizes how often this dynamic quality has been associated with no pattern of control or directional rationale. It can then become nothing more than the froth of frenzied ecstasy, or even the irrational fury of the mob. Iqbal himself lauded passion (*'ishq*) as excellent in itself, and attacked the intellect (*'aql*), which might not only have checked but guided it. It is a deeply disconcerting experience to reread his throbbing poems of uninhibited Islamic drive in the light of Muslim violence in the subsequent 1947 massacres.[76]

Under the impact of this kind of rousing enthusiasm, not only does activity become furious but blind; also faith becomes intense but contentless.[77] The work of the apologetes that we have just mentioned, was successful in keeping many loyal to "Islam," as a somewhat unidentified concept, who would otherwise have dis-

[76] On the point that in the massacres of 1947 the Muslims were not only victims, cf. below chap. 6, ref. 14. Of course, non-Muslims were equally violent.

[77] Cf. Fazlu-r-Rahmān, "Modern Muslim Thought," *The Muslim World,* Hartford, 45: 16-25 (1955); also *op. cit.* (above, ref. 1), esp. p. 867.

carded the faith altogether; but it was not constructive enough to give any framework of solid theology or ethics to that Islam, in the place of the old doctrines and the Law which they had abandoned. Their faith was like a balloon, buoyant but empty, and liable to explosion.

In some cases this exuberant but undefined loyalty was given to the local Muslim nationalism. This meant that the devotion to God that Islam had once inspired and that the 'modernists' had transferred to Islam, was now offered to the regional Muslim community, excitedly but without programme.

Of late this fervent dynamism has combined with other elements in the modern Islamic situation. Although at times it went into Muslim nationalism, it could also unite with the zeal to 'defend Islam'; and most of all with the dream and drive of reviving Islamic glory and reinstating once again on earth the proud society of Islam's divine prescription. It has taken advantage of the withdrawal of European control, achieved at long last; political independence gives the opportunity for this enthusiastic culmination of Islam's resurgence, and is seen as simply a step towards it. The dynamism is combined also with frustration: the growing and bitter disillusionment over the desperate inability, except in Turkey, of liberalism and secularism in the practical realm to state a programme and to effect it—and in the realm of thought to come to grips with an increasingly disconcerting world.

The result has been that a growing number of Muslims have been turning of late to a series of movements, remarkably widespread throughout the Muslim world, in some cases of fanatical outburst. Even in Turkey this has found expression on a small scale, otherwise not significant, in the Ticani. In other countries it has not been so negligible: in Iran the Kashani party, in Pakistan the Khatm-i Nubuwat frenzy, in Indonesia the Daru-l-Islam movement. One may add the Rizakar in Hyderabad. And one may add perhaps also, in some degree, the Ikhwan al-Muslimun ("Muslim Brethren") of the Arab world and the Jama'at-i Islami of Pakistan;[78] or at least, if not these movements themselves, then the new atmosphere that their self-assertion has encouraged. Among these dynamist elements there has been growing at times a violent fury that almost rejoices in destruction, a bitter vehe-

[78] See below, chap. 3 pp. 156-60 and chap. 5 pp. 233-36 respectively.

mence in opposition to the West, to local non-Muslims, to Muslims who disagree with them, and to all outsiders; and a telling combination of self-righteousness with lust and power-hungry ambition. At their disciplined best these movements are, of course, not without positive value; and we shall have occasion to analyse one or two in particular regions in our later chapters, searching out also the strength of their appeal. Yet for their violence and fury, of unlimited potential disaster, their own Muslim governments have had to suppress them.

In striking respects they are sorry representatives of the faith. Their emergence is symptomatic of that fundamental malaise of Islam in the modern world that we designated in opening this chapter. It is symptomatic, further, of the fact that the malaise is still unresolved, and indeed is growing. They are reacting against the failure of Islamic liberals to satisfy either the spiritual sensibilities or the practical needs of the modern Muslim world. Yet in doing so they represent even more starkly the failure of Islamic conservatives. They emphasize rather than overcome the fact that Islam has yet to define, let alone take up, its position in modernity.

The spiritual crisis is aggravated. The development over the past century has been very great; changes have been deep. But though some problems have been solved, other new ones, more baffling, have arisen. We shall study some of them in detail in individual areas of the Muslim world, to which we now must turn.

It is time, then, to bring this introductory survey to a close. We have seen Islam entering on the modern period of its earthly history at a low ebb in its external fortunes and its internal development, and menaced by outside attack. We have seen its people turning to remedy the state of lapse: by purifying their implementation of Islam, by thrusting back its outside enemies, by rousing themselves to a vivid remembrance of its early glory. We have seen them undertaking to refashion their societies, borrowing from the West or introducing from modernity new ways and new ideas, and from their own past the inspiration and determination to succeed. We have seen them welcoming as much of these newnesses as would seem to serve their task. We have seen them successfully reasserting their independence in national movements, and vigorously defending their faith in intellectual endeavour. They have moved far towards acquiring freedom not only politically but internally, by substituting activism for passivity, their destiny now in significant degree in their own hands.

Yet this is also the very measure of their dilemma. For in seeking to reaffirm Islam in theory but especially in practice, modern Muslims have had sufficient success that they now face more squarely, and more inwardly, the very problem of their religious quest: the relation of Islam to the actual problems and prospects of the modern world.

The question before the Muslim today is no longer simply that of why there is a gap between his convictions and the world in which he finds himself. It is rather the still more searching one as to how, or indeed whether, he himself will or can or should close that gap (or bridge it)—between his faith and the world which he has now to construct.

Chapter 3

THE ARABS: ISLAMIC CRISIS

THE Arabs are a proud and sensitive people.

No adequate understanding of their situation today is possible unless due weight is given to both these factors. Further, some appreciation is needed of how much they have in their past of which to be proud, and how much in their present about which to be sensitive.

Moreover the Arabs are, of course, a Muslim people.[1] Their Islam interweaves with their pride and their sensitivity—as it does with all their Arabness; to give the distinctive pattern of their current living. Not only is Islam integral to that pattern; also the distinctive quality of their modern Arabism is integral to their particular version or instance of present-day Islam. Insight into the Arab's contemporary crisis, and insight into the characteristic Arab form of the faith today, cannot go but hand in hand.

In order, therefore, to attain some discernment of the latter, to understand religious developments in the current Arab scene, we must see these in the full context of Arab glory and frustration. History and Islam are here as elsewhere interpenetrant. We do not mean that Arab Islam is atypical; on the contrary, the Arabs sum up in concentrated intensity the modern crisis of the whole Islamic world. Yet they do so in a specifically Arab fashion. It is their Arabness that gives poignancy and pith to their Islam.

The Arab's pride in being Arab is profound. There are many elements in this, some going as far back as the pre-Islamic ideal of manly virtue (*muru'ah*), of which the true Arab is the paragon; and the Arabic language, which has always held its people entranced. To these have been added the great pride in Arabic literature; and in the glories of Arab history, the earthly triumph of the classic age.

On this last the emphasis has of late been growing, until it has

[1] Statistically, this is not fully true. In the nation-states that today constitute the political existence of the Arab world, 90 per cent of the population is Muslim (calculation based on the figures in Harry W. Hazard, *Atlas of Islamic History*, 2nd ed., Princeton, 1952). In the case of Lebanon, the Christians claim an official majority. In general, however, the existence of the Christian (and the few Jewish) Arabs plays but a small part in Muslim Arab self-consciousness. Cf. also at the next ref.

become a supreme mark of modern Arab self-consciousness. The Arabs once produced one of the world's great cultures. The cultivated remembrance of this is fundamental to their condition today.

With most of these matters the religion of Islam is closely intertwined. The Arab Muslim is, like other Muslims, proud of his faith: no other religion in the world has been so successful as Islam in eliciting a confessional pride in its adherents. However, in the Arab's case this pride in Islam is not separate from his national enthusiasm, but infuses it and gives it added point.

On the personal level, it is Islam that has undergirded and given a cosmic context to the individual human dignity that is the Arab's honour. It was the Arabic language which God chose for His supreme revelation to mankind; and which anyone must study who would clearly know God's will. It was the Islamic impetus that carried the Arabs from their obscure home into historic greatness, in conquest and creativity. Islam gave the Arabs earthly greatness; and *vice versa*, it was the Arabs who gave Islam its earthly success.

The synthesis is close: an identification, at times unconscious, of Islam and Arabism. On the one hand, an Arab need not be pious or spiritually concerned in order to be proud of Islam's historic achievements. Indeed, he need not even be a Muslim; Christian Arabs have taken a share in that pride.[2] On the other hand, Muslim Arabs have never quite acknowledged, have never fully incorporated into their thinking and especially their feeling, either that a non-Muslim is really a complete Arab, or that a non-Arab is really a complete Muslim. Arab Islam has never given much serious thought to either group. It is uninterested in and virtually unaware of Islamic greatness after the Arab downfall.

[2] Striking examples are Jurjī Zaydān (cf. above, chap. 2, ref. 24), and an interesting article in a Christian missionary quarterly, Charles Issawi, "The Historical Role of Muhammad," *The Muslim World*, Hartford, 40:83-95 (1950). One should perhaps mention also the champion in America of Arab nationalism and Arab history, Philip K. Hitti (most noted for his *History of the Arabs*, London, 1937, of which subsequent editions, revisions, abridgements, and translations have appeared in a steady stream), even though he has explicitly seen the Arab past as Arab rather than Islamic, and as a result has even been criticized of late by petulant Muslims. The Christian participation in Arabism is increasingly complex and difficult.

For it, in 1258 (the fall of Baghdad), or for Egypt in 1517 (the Turkish conquest), Islamic history virtually came to an end.[3]

We have seen that this memory of past greatness is characteristic of virtually the entire Muslim world in modern times. In the Arab case it is typified and concentrated. For them it is heightened by nationalism, and intensified by Arab sensibility. The Arabs feel more intimately the early glory than do any other Muslim group; and feel more tautly the nostalgia. The Arab sense of bygone splendour is superb.

One cannot begin to understand the modern Arab if one lacks a perceptive feeling for this. In the gulf between him and, for instance, the modern American, a matter of prime significance has been precisely the deep difference between a society with a memory of past greatness, and one with a sense of present greatness. The one, imaginative and romantic, dreams of the future in terms of a reconstructed vision of the haunting past; the other, realistic and programmatic, plans for it, in terms of the practice of the satisfying present.

If insight requires an appreciation of this basis of Arab dignity, it is utterly incomplete without a further comprehension of how severe also has been the modern assault upon it. The second great point in today's Arabism is the degree to which the modern world has conspired to undermine its confidence. The attack has been relentless upon the very citadels of Arab life.

The most overt instance of this attack is the sheer and massive onslaught of Western imperialism. The guns of British warships in Alexandria harbour, 1882, shelling into suppressed submission the first major Egyptian attempt, under 'Arabi Pasha, to redress internal misrule; the bombing planes of French colonialism, wrecking Damascus in 1925 in vindictive overpowering of the Syrian aspiration for self-rule; the tanks of British armies crushing the gates of 'Abidin Palace, Cairo, 1942, to buttress a "suggestion" that would force upon the country a government agreeable to the Allies; these and many another such display of naked, brutal, and

[3] Cf., below, chap. 4, at reff. 3-8. Egyptian writers, if they note at all the period in Egyptian history from 1517, think and feel of it as part of the history of Egypt, not of Islam. One exception is the brilliant historian Shafīq Ghurbāl, who is an exception to most of our generalizations on historiography. See his study of Muḥammad 'Alī (1769-1849) as a figure in Islamic history.

utterly unanswerable might have burned deep into the Arab soul. These have been categorical illuminations of the ponderous fact usually more hidden, but constantly operative as a heavy threat waiting to be implemented whenever need might arise: the fact that rule, the control of destiny, lay with outsiders because with them lay power.

Demonstration of this power has been most vivid in the case of military bludgeoning; it has been institutionalized and enduring in the case of political control. Both are still in painful evidence in the instance of French domination in North Africa, where the administration rules, and when it cannot rule, shoots. In most other Arab areas, the authoritarian political structure has recently at last been broken; but the presence or proposal or at least possibility of troops persists. For seventy-five years the Arab has got up in the morning, has lived his life, has pursued his pleasures and his dreams, always under the shadow of guns—guns in alien, unfriendly hands, ready to fire, ready to call in from across the sea more guns, ships, tanks, planes, might. Whether this power was used (as from time to time it shatteringly was), or was merely threatened (as often it cogently could be), or was merely there, always the shadow, the shame, the oppression remained. Whether terror or insult, provocation or opiate, this bitter foreign power has stood, an abiding fact. Any thought about the Arab world uncoloured by the vivid imagination of this dominating reality is unfruitful, misleading, false.

Apart even from military and political domination, Western power has had other manners of imposing its weight. The most pervasive is the economic. The middle class, particularly, is brought face to face with reiterated instances of Western economic puissance, to which it may, perhaps very comfortably, accommodate itself but which it cannot withstand. Both individually and in groups, even at governmental level of allegedly 'independent' national existence, the Arabs are still subject to political and economic pressures from the outside. Such pressures are of varying intensity but are often onerous, at times exacting. Perpetually adumbrated is the threat of their being potentially overwhelming.[4]

[4] The Arab world is entwined in an economic net of which outsiders pull the strings. During World War II, a situation developed where the ability of the Middle East area to eat depended not on its inhabitants but on the great powers, who controlled trade, transport, and international supplies

There is even an extended sense in which the concept, or at least the feeling, of imperialism or colonialism is carried over from enforced control to more subtle influence. This is almost as ineluctable. It is what the French with witty symbolism call 'Coca-Cola-nisation'; and if Europe resents it from the New World, how much more the Arabs in large doses from them both. At this level, objects and manners and ideas are involved, of alien origin and penetrating impetus. And if the power of the foreigner in this realm is less compacted and peremptory than in the military, political, and economic, yet it is no less intrusive. And some feel that it is in the long run no less subversive. It is the insidious power, in sphere after sphere of living, of what is non-Arab—infidel, unintegrated—to dominate, oust, or suppress the distinctively or traditionally Arab.

The Arab increasingly lives in a world that he feels is not his own; that he can only partially understand, and certainly cannot control.

(Actually, the whole of humanity lives in this kind of world in the twentieth century; all of us are faced with a modernity that undermines our past and challenges our survival. But few Arabs realize this; most see the novelty as alien, a disruption from outside, and see other human beings—particularly the West—not as sharing their distress but as inflicting it.[5])

---

generally and whose armies consumed great quantities of whatever could be handled by local facilities. If these outsiders had not set up and administered an organization to meet this problem, a major disruption of the rural economy and a total collapse of the urban would presumably have occurred. The psychological, moral, cultural, and perhaps even religious implications of facts like these have not been as carefully thought out as the economic. (For the latter, cf. Guy Hunter, "Economic Problems: The Middle East Supply Centre," in George Kirk, *The Middle East in the War*, Survey of International Affairs, 1939-1946, London & New York, 1952, pp. 169-93; and Martin W. Wilmington, "The Middle East Supply Center: a reappraisal," *The Middle East Journal*, Washington, 6:144-66 [1952].)

5 Our argument in the present chapter endeavours to illuminate that sense of being battered by the world, and of being alienated from their fellows, that we regard as basic to the modern Arab mind and behaviour. Yet in our effort to portray the historical situations that have helped to produce this effect (or anyway that live within the Arab consciousness as psychologically responsible for it), we do not mean to externalize their plight. In enumerating felt difficulties, we are struggling for sympathy with the Arabs not in the degenerate and impertinent sense of "feeling sorry for," but the true one of appreciation and understanding. The special quality of the Arabs today lies less in the problems with which the world has confronted them than in the

The West, or the modern world, not only attacks; it accuses. Here again there is both an overt external assault and an interior subverting of integrity. On the former score, the West has evinced at times a criticism of Arab-Muslim life that is severe, rising on occasion to a scorn that is bitter. There has been the standard arrogance with which the West confronts all other peoples—the 'natives.' There has been the detailed criticism, whether explicit or implied, of social life and personal mores: the assessment of 'backward' peoples, evident even in offers to help. In matters such as the shocked reaction to polygamy, this was at its most acute half a century ago; today there is more emphasis on low economic levels; throughout there has been an indictment of failure to measure up to educational, medical, and many other norms. The West none too suavely reminds the Arab world of all its short-comings.

Indeed it goes beyond calling attention to those that it can all too easily notice. Through its inability to achieve an understanding by the majority on the cultural place of intangibles, it not only fails to appreciate what are the real values, but distorts the actual situation to invent shortcomings that are spurious.

All this, and much else, came to expression in the Zionist issue. Here the Arabs were dismayed not only by the West's generally turning against them (we shall return to this) with guns, votes, money, methods, and the whole might of modernity. They were dismayed also by the reasons that it gave itself for doing so. The image of the Arab as an uncouth bedouin, unkempt, uncivilized, and essentially unimportant, that was conjured up in order for the West to push aside his claims in favour of the Jew's—this was galling.

However, the arraignment by the West of Arab modernity need not be distorted in order to be painful. It need not even be expressed. It is not only ill-will or misunderstanding, or even honest appraisal, that at times is biting. The accusation is in part the sheer fact that the West is there. The Jones's by simply existing

---

attitude with which they confront the world and respond to those problems, and most seriously in their attitude to other people. It is perhaps helpful, however, to remember that it has been the distinction of the Arabs for centuries to be one of the most sensitively imaginative of peoples on earth. (On the possible relation of Arabic literature to Western chivalry and romanticism, for instance, cf. H. A. R. Gibb, "Literature," in Thomas Arnold and Alfred Guillaume, edd., *The Legacy of Islam*, London &c., 1931, reprinted 1943, pp. 180-209.)

engender the distress of not being able to keep up with them.

The Arab world, then, suffers from external aggression, at the level both of deed and thought. It suffers also from internal, subjective incrimination. The attack is interiorized; and thereby gains its anguish.

It is by Western standards that the Arabs are weak, by imported criteria that their self-esteem is undermined. A defeat by superior power not only curtails one's freedom; it also demonstrates or reminds one of one's impotence. Incident after incident seems almost contrived to press home upon the Arab consciousness the modern world's insistence in practice and in theory that Arab greatness is over.

The West not only accuses; it betrays. At least, so the Arabs feel. One of the crucial elements in contemporary Arab psychology is the ravaging sense amongst its Westernizers of having been let down. This, too, came to culmination over Zionism and the establishment of Israel. The modern West for seventy-five years had been bearing down upon the Arab world with what appeared increasingly to be irresistible pressure, saying in effect: "Give up those antiquated ways, those superstitions, those inhibitions; be modern with us, be prosperous, sophisticated. Emancipate your women, your societies, yourselves!" The theme re-echoed, sometimes with siren beguilement, sometimes with haughty disdain. Many Arabs (like other Easterners) succumbed, or saw their children succumb. Yet those who chose this path found that when a crisis arose the modern West did not effectively care for its converts. It had seduced them from their indigenous loyalties, but took no responsibility for them when they needed it most. The protégé of the West proved void of protection.

As a result, the leaders of liberalism found not only their position in society razed, their following gone, but their own confidence sapped. As a leading intellectual of Damascus said to the present writer in 1948, while the Palestine war was in progress: "Against the wishes of my family I broke with our tradition, our environment, and took up Western culture. I went to Paris and for six years I studied and lived there. I adopted Western ways— of life, of thought; and Western values. Our old-fashioned critics used to say to people like me, 'You are letting down the Arab cause and are betraying us.' We used to think that they just did not understand. Now we wonder if they weren't right. The way it is turning out, we feel that we have backed the wrong horse. We sided with the West; and the West has let us down."

In our preceding chapter we have already observed how this betrayal by liberalism has for the whole Muslim world except Turkey been internalized as well in the failure of incorporated liberal institutions. The Arabs are representative also of this, and have intensified it to the point where for some the institutions are regarded as not merely ineffectual but disruptive. In April 1954 the streets of Cairo resounded to demonstrations vehemently voicing popular protest against reaction, corruption, and parliamentarianism. The present government was swinging the populace against its former hero, Najib ("Naguib"), by manoeuvring him into the untenable position of apparently championing the processes of institutional democracy, which were made symbolic of all the infirmity, dishonesty, and degradation of the old régime.[6]

The bitterness of Arab disillusionment has gone very, very deep. It is illustrated in a charge[7] that at 'Aka (Acre) during the fighting in 1948 the Red Cross—symbol and summit, as it were, of Western liberal humanitarianism or modern Christian goodwill—discriminated in its succour in favour of Jews against Muslims. Not only on the battlefield but in the hospital ward, the Arabs saw themselves repudiated as of no account. Whether this particular charge is justified or not is essentially irrelevant; in a sense its use would be the more revealing of Arab attitudes if it were a misinterpretation of the facts. Whether or not the symbol is intrinsically accurate, what it symbolizes is, unfortunately, all too valid. And what it illustrates of the conviction and inner feelings of at least one section of the modernists throughout the Arab world is widespread. It is one example among many of what was perhaps the essential shock of the whole Palestine affair: the terrible discovery that the Arabs were not accepted by the West, were not regarded as members of the civilized community. If not more important

[6] March 26, 1954. The present writer was in Cairo at the time, and had the somewhat eerie experience of seeing come into sharp focus the usually vague but persistent Arab tendency to identify the ills of its own society with its imported (Western) institutions, in this case elections and the whole formal democratic process. The demonstrations were not altogether spontaneous, but neither were they ineffective; the fact that such slogans could be launched at all was revealing.

[7] Muṣṭafà Khālidī and 'Umar Farrukh, al-Tabshīr wa al-Istiʿmār fī al-Bilād al-ʿArabīyah, Beirut, 1372/1953, pp. 24-26; quoting al-Diyār, Beirut, issue of July 7, 1948.

than the unveiling of their own weakness, at least more wide-spread and more deeply grasped, this was a fundamental blow: the realization that, as they interpret it, they have no friends.

The Arab is Muslim. We must consider more closely the bearing of this equation on his recent development. We have already spoken of the ambivalence of the relation. This continues. Though Arabism and Islam are ultimately different things, yet the Arab tends as ever to identify them, at least within himself. He is the one or the other as the case arises; or what amounts to much the same thing, he is the one and the other at once. However, recently there has come to evidence a trend towards greater prominence of the Islamic element in Arab consciousness. In the sense of being under attack and criticism, of being rejected, the Islamic aspect has throughout been present. Lately, his awareness of and attention to its presence have grown. In recent literature, in conversation, and in practical response, there seems a more marked disposition for Arabs to think of the attack to which they see and feel themselves subject as an attack upon their religion. The world is against them, they have felt; the world, or at least the West, they latterly increasingly add, is engaged on a deliberate vast enterprise to disrupt Islam.[8]

[8] As one stray example of an increasing trend, see under the editorial caption *Yawmīyāt al Akhbār* in the Cairo newspaper *Al-Akhbār* for Sept. 16, 1955: "al-Ta'aṣṣub al-Dīnī!", by Muḥammad al-Tābi'ī. See also the Introduction to the 3rd Arabic edition (Cairo, 1952) of 'Abd Allāh 'Inān, *Mawāqif ḥāsimah fī ta'rīkh al-Islām* (first published Cairo, 1934; English translation, *Decisive Moments in the History of Islam*, Lahore, 1940, 1943, 1949). Indeed, one can see in the successive Arabic introductions (1934, 1943, 1952) an increasing firmness of the sense of Western antagonism. However, as the author states in the latest, "the basic idea of this book . . . remains the same: . . . the perpetual struggle between East and West, Islam and Christianity. The reader will see how the Crusading idea has remained for centuries the axis of this struggle, and how it has blazed the more vigorously whenever a new Islamic outburst of power or revival has appeared. . . ." (p. 4). He goes on to make the point that modern colonialism is a new guise of the Crusading spirit to crush Islam; an idea that is more and more coming into prominence also elsewhere. For example, Muḥammad Quṭb, *Shubuhāt Ḥawl al-Islām*, Cairo, 1954, uses the term ṣalībī ("Crusader") for Christian, *passim*; and even al-ṣalībiyah for Christianity, Christendom, and the modern West. See specifically pp. 4ff. where the idea is pressed that the Crusades are still on. This writer even insists, regarding the prevalent belief among the educated that Islam, and religion in general, are things of the past (cf. below, at ref. 15) that this belief has been planted by British imperialism to weaken the Muslims (*e.g.* pp. 4-5). This is not as atypical as one might think.

The situation that the Arabs have faced has not, in fact, been essentially different from that of other Muslim peoples in the modern world. It is in the response to the challenge that the basic dissimilarity of the Turks has lain. Their reaction, psychological and practical, to virtually the same kind of development has been radically other; as we shall explore in our next chapter. Of the rest of the Muslim world the various sections have reacted in ways that are, of course, in each case individual and distinctive; yet in significant measure all evince a shared family likeness. So far as psychological reception of the situation is concerned, the Arabs have differed chiefly, as we suggested earlier, in experiencing it all the more intensely.

If the Arab instance of Islam, then, continues to be, as it has always been, an important instance, it is also true that the Islamic element in Arabism continues to be, as it has always been, an important factor. It is an aspect in the total situation to which the Arabs have good reason to be giving their currently increased attention; and to which also outsiders must give their careful heed if they are to understand aright.

It is certainly true that Islam is central within the Arabs' present difficulty. It is even somewhat true that Islam has been a factor in the gulf between the West and themselves.[9] This is not at all to subscribe to their interpretation of any malicious intent on the non-Muslim side: the growing Arab conviction that the West is out to crush Islam. On the contrary, the Muslim world in general, and the Arabs in particular, have no grasp of the serious and strenuous efforts that the West has been making to try to understand Islam. Certainly they have utterly no inkling of how extremely difficult such understanding is. For it is a fact that differences between the great civilizations of the world are both subtle and deep. Neither Western culture, on any scale wide

---

[9] For instance, the gulf has been less deep for Arabs who are not Muslims. While it is true that many Christian Arabs have participated deeply in Arab nationalism (and even in Islam-tinged Arab nationalism) (cf. above, ref. 2), it is also true that individual Christian Arabs have been able to understand the West in ways that Muslim Arabs have never been able (or indeed tried?) to do. Also, Westerners, Western institutions, etc., have usually found—often without preconception, and indeed in the American case usually without awareness and often with astonishment—that the Arabs with whom they can best 'get along' prove to be, in fact, of the Christian minority. (This has, indeed, sometimes misled Westerners in their dealings with or orientation to the Arab world.)

enough to be as yet effective, nor Islamic, has recognized of just what dimensions the intercultural gulfs are.

It is one of the novelties of modernity that these gulfs must be bridged, that communication and understanding be created. In the past, civilizations have got along without such understanding of their neighbours; either ignoring other civilizations, or fighting them. The unprecedented task of our day, of learning to live in close touch and even collaboration and indeed even large-scale interpenetration with them, demands a creative effort. Such an achievement cannot be taken for granted, nor the way to it learned without difficulty.

On the Western side, especially the New World, politicians, journalists, tourists, and others have yet to grasp how significant and ramified are the differences; and how they can subtly pervade every aspect of interrelationship. On the Muslim side there has been an inability to realize and even to admit how hard it is for an outsider to understand Islamic culture and specifically the religion that underlies it. To a Muslim, Islam is completely straightforward, clear-cut, logical, and obvious. Misunderstanding seems to him appalling and perverse. He does not discriminate, and has never formulated, the presuppositions on which the system silently rests, and which he takes for granted; the *Weltanschauung* within which the specific doctrines take on meaning. He does not know how divergent these presuppositions are from the fundamental postulates of other civilizations. Both he and the Westerner have in general still to learn that the great religions of mankind differ among themselves in their orientation to the universe not simply in giving different answers, but in asking different questions.

It is, of course, a major thesis of this book that an understanding of Islam is requisite insight to an appreciation of what is going on in contemporary Muslim society. And if, grossly or at all, this study fails in that understanding, then this but illustrates our further contention that understanding is no facile attainment.[10]

If differences between civilizations are difficult, those in religion are superlatively so. Indeed, it is rather novel even as a concept

[10] However, if it fails—or doubtless we should say, in so far as it fails— one may confidently presume that it will be taken by many Arabs (and to a much less extent by other Muslims outside Turkey) rather to illustrate once again the Western attempt 'to subvert'.

that a person, let alone a society, should understand a religion other than his own. Yet that is part of the task with which modernity confronts mankind. That in the Muslim case such religious discernment is required not only for spiritual matters but also for understanding at the lower level simply of mundane culture is not a private conviction of our own. That Islam as a religion is relevant to all aspects of life and society, permeating the civilization in a way that religion in the West does not attempt (or indeed understand), is a basic and insistent claim of the Muslims themselves.

Yet the difficulties in the way of such interreligious comprehension, though they might seem obvious enough in any case, are partially exemplified in the fact not merely that Muslims do not at all understand the faith of Christians, but that in general they do not even know that they do not understand.[11]

The Arabs, then, are justified in their feeling, though unjustified in their complaint, that Islam has been a significant element in the alienation between themselves and the West. In the first place the West, like other civilizations, has in general still very far to go in evolving the new ingredient of compatibility, which may well prove indispensable to any group's survival in the coming

[11] "There isn't a single Moslem scholar in all history, so far as I know, who has written an authentic essay on Christianity"—Charles Malik, "The Near East: The Search for Truth," in *Foreign Affairs*, 30:258 (1952).

The present writer also knows no book by a Muslim showing any "feel" for the Christian position; nor indeed any clear endeavour to deal with, let alone understand, the central doctrines. The usual Muslim attitude is not to take the central doctrines seriously at all. That is, they do not recognize that Christians take them seriously; and that however absurd they might seem to outsiders (to Muslims they appear both stupid and blasphemous), the Trinity, the Deity and Sonship and Crucifixion of Christ, and the like are affirmations deeply meaningful and precious and utterly integral to the Christian's faith. The immediate reasons for this failure are the Islamic doctrines on the same topics; we have endeavoured to present as sympathetically as possible the Muslim position on Jesus and Christianity in chapter 1 above. Muslims therefore have religious convictions for genuinely imagining that they know real Christianity better than Christians do themselves. And in what then appears to them as the "pseudo-Christianity" of historical and personal existence, the faith by which Christians actually live, they have not been intellectually interested.

For a recent and most perceptive discussion of the need for, and possibility of, mutual conversation on the religious level by the most appreciative of modern Protestant missionaries, see Kenneth Cragg: "Each Other's Face," in *The Muslim World*, Hartford, 45:172-82 (1955).

age. In the second place, in the particular case of Islam the West has most of all to learn—and to unlearn. History has been such that the West's relations with the Islamic world have from the first been radically different from those with any other civilization. These two have throughout shared a common frontier—which has meant that they have been constantly in contact and often in open conflict. China and India were remote, fabulous, virtually unknown until the eighteenth century (by which time the Enlightenment and cosmopolitanism were replacing religious zeal; and anyway the West was much too powerful to be in danger from them). On the other hand, Europe has known Islam for thirteen centuries, mostly as an enemy and a threat. It is no wonder that Muhammad more than any other of the world's religious leaders has had "a poor press" in the West, and that Islam is the least appreciated there of any of the world's outside faiths. Until Karl Marx and the rise of communism, the Prophet organized and launched the only serious challenge to Western civilization that it has faced in the whole course of its history. How serious a challenge, how menacing a threat it once seemed is worth recalling.

The attack was direct, both military and ideological. And it was very powerful. To the Muslims, of course, it seems only right and proper, something altogether natural and inevitable, that Islam should have expanded as it did. Rather different is the attitude of the outsider, for whom it was none of these things, and at whose expense the expansion took place. It was greatly at the expense of the West. At once Christendom lost to the new power "the fairest provinces of the Roman Empire," and was in danger of losing that empire *in toto*. Although Constantinople did not, quite, fall to the Arab armies as had Egypt and Syria, the pressure was long maintained. And in the second great wave of Islamic expansion, Constantinople did fall, in 1453; and in the very heart of frightened Europe siege was laid to Vienna in 1529 as the seemingly inexorable drive continued—and again as recently as 1683. The fall of Czechoslovakia to communism in 1948 was hardly as alarming in modern times to an apprehensive Western world as was for century after century the steady westward push of this massive, relentless, and repeatedly victorious challenge.

Again, as in the case of communism, the challenge and the victories were also in the realm of values and ideas. The Muslim attack was at the level of theory as well as of practice. The new religion based itself firmly on a strident repudiation of the central affirmation of the Christian faith, the sublime conviction around which Europe was at that time slowly building up its civilization.[12] The Muslim challenge was flung with vigour, and was sweepingly successful in almost half of Christendom. Islam is the only positive force that has won converts away from Christianity—by the tens of millions. It is the only force that has proclaimed that Christian doctrine is not only false but repulsive.

It is doubtful whether Westerners, even those quite unaware that they are involved in such things, have ever quite got over the effects of this prolonged fundamental strife—or of the Crusades: two centuries of bitter ideological aggressive warfare.[13]

We recall here this long history of conflict not, of course, in any sense to rekindle or at all to justify recriminations. On the contrary we simply suggest that the success of those who today are hoping or working for reconciliation and understanding should not be expected to come either easily or soon. It is possible to trace a steady movement over the centuries: this legacy of antagonism in the West began in mediaeval Europe with fear and hatred and bitterness, and has gradually given way to mere misunderstanding and failure of appreciation. In recent times improvement has rather swiftly gathered momentum. Nonetheless, it will clearly be some time yet, and will involve continued effort, before the estrangement is on any but a small scale transcended in friendly collaboration.[14] Nor is it difficult to understand that in a situation such as the Zionist crisis, the sympathies of the Christian West

[12] Christians have proclaimed, and believed, that Jesus Christ is the Crucified Son of God. It is on this that the whole religion turns. See, for instance, Qur'ān 4:157 for a specific denial that Jesus was crucified; 4:171 and 5:72, 73 specifically rejecting as derogatory to God the Trinity and Sonship (the former passage in particular suggesting the blasphemy of the idea).

[13] Cf. above, ref. 8. In the Arab world, the memory of the Crusades is still alive, and has been rekindled by recent developments and is growing. In the West the effects have not yet been outlived, though we believe that they are palpably dwindling.

[14] It is too early yet to say whether the recent Christian-Muslim Conference (Bhamdun, 1954) and its ensuing Continuing Committee on Christian-Muslim Co-operation (offices in Alexandria and Washington), are significant, let alone effective. Other quieter, perhaps deeper, perhaps more long-range signs are not to be ignored.

were more effectively won on behalf of the Jews, whose culture had been appropriated over millennia within Western civilization, than of the Arabs, whose extraneous case had to contend with a thirteen-century tradition of conflict.

Islam, then, as a religion and an historical civilization, has played its role in the external aspects of the development that we are trying to understand, the plight in which the modern Arab world has increasingly found itself. Islam plays a role also in the internal course of that development. This is subtle but significant, contributing powerfully to the inner crisis of the Arabs. For they find Islam under attack in and by the modern world not only overtly. The attack is also interiorized, within individual Arab minds. It is here that the agony is greatest; and perhaps also the danger.

First, there is the well-known but not simple fashion wherein all religion is under attack by modernity. The West is well acquainted with this phenomenon and has finally learned to take it more or less in stride, or believes that it has learned. In the nineteenth century, however, the struggle was keen. The notion that modern science by its ideas or its prowess, and modern life by its enchantment, have made all religious faith untenable or unnecessary, would seem universal. Yet at first glance Western observers, so intimately schooled in this matter with regard to Christianity, have tended to be surprised at how little evidence appears, on the surface, of a similar disenchantment with religion on the Arab scene; or indeed throughout the Muslim world. There is in every Arab city ample illustration of the insouciant life of non-belief in practice. Yet the literature of scepticism is sparse. There would seem little theoretical expression of secularism; so little that one is left wondering whether the practice of it rests on insincerity. (In that case, it carries with it a guilty conscience.)

However, documentary evidence of a widespread belief that religion is *passé* is in fact afforded and in quantity, by the apologetic literature for Islam (which we shall be considering presently). Book after book, pamphlet after pamphlet, written in defence of the faith, begin by noting how general in the Arab world is the drift from religion. They deplore how facilely Arab youth have adopted Western rationalist or other arguments against the validity of faith.[15] One may assume that these complaints are exaggerated (else they would suggest a situation in which religion is less popular than in, say, modern America). Yet the very existence of this defence literature indicates that the problem exists and is acute.

It exists and is acute not only for society but for the individual. If there are many who have drifted from the faith, there are many others in the no-man's land of uncertainty where the drift is in their own spirit, with the currents of belief and unbelief in indecisive swirl.

This is more significant and more damaging, both personally and socially, than was the similar situation in the West for two reasons. First, the secularist attack is foreign. It is a great deal easier for a person, and a great deal healthier for a society, to find an inherited tradition questioned by new values that his or its own people have evolved, than by values insinuated by one's supposed enemies. To admit, even to oneself, that one has been wrong always takes courage. The sense of insecurity is vastly greater if the criterion is alien. The Westerner who finds his religion no longer tenable is being challenged to adopt a different set of his society's values. The Arab in a similar condition is being challenged to abandon his society's values. In a civilization as singly religious, Islamic, as the Arab's has been, to abandon Islam is seen as betraying one's community.

The second reason is related—is, in fact, another facet of the same. The absence already noted of positive secularist statement, in the midst of much secularist behaviour, is significant. It means that life is lived on an un-Islamic basis not on principle, but on absence of principle. The Arab world has had no Tom Paine and no Voltaire. The West has had a non-religious tradition of solid substance, cherished by some of its noblest spirits, and expounded with coherence, conviction, and force. We are thinking here not of the secularism that breeds cynicism or corruption, but philo-

---

[15] Some illustrative examples: "The 'educated' [or 'cultured'] in their crisis are bewildered, and have thought that this Islām has come to an end, its purposes are exhausted"—Muḥammad Quṭb, *op. cit.* p. 1; cf. ref. 8 above. "That cultured skepticism, born of caustic modern knowledge, that has found its way into men's hearts"—Farīd Wajdī, *Majallat al-Azhar*, 18:3; cf. at ref. 187 below. "The materialist school of thought, which has spread with the speed of fire in dry twigs. . . ."—*id., op. cit.*, 9:419; cf. at ref. 119 below. And so on, again and again.

sophic secularism at its best—the development of the Graeco-Roman side of Western culture, rather than the Palestinian-Biblical. Western secularism at its noblest is a positive system of values, based ultimately on Greek ideas of justice, order, reason, and humanity. Or it is simply the positive concept that values should be independent, not tied to religious faith. The Turks, alone among the Muslim peoples, have acquired such a positive secularism. It was given intellectual expression in the work of a Ziya Gökalp,[16] and given operative expression in the formal decision of the community to proceed on this basis. Arab secularism, by contrast, lacking the Greek or any philosophic basis, and lacking the Turkish practical commitment, tends to be simply an absence of all values, of life unsupported by conviction.

Both personally and socially, then, the attack on Islam is a thrust pushing the Arab into the void.[17]

[16] Cf. above, chap. 2, ref. 30.

[17] We believe it difficult to exaggerate the importance of this, even though so little attention has been paid to it. On the contrary situation in Victorian England, Trevelyan has the following passage, which will perhaps be of interest in connection with the above two paragraphs:

"The older and more definite religious beliefs that meant so much to these men were being successfully attacked by the 'Agnostics' of the same period [1870's and 1880's]. Yet even the 'Agnostics' were Puritan in feeling and outlook. . . . The fame and authority enjoyed by George Eliot's novels were largely due to the fact that they were taken by many as 're-stating the moral law and process of soul-making, in terms acceptable to the nationalist agnostic conscience.' Carlyle's prophetic utterance in Sartor supplied a vague but emphatic creed to many, including Darwin's militant champion Huxley, who defied the clergy at the famous meeting of the British Association in Oxford in the spirit of Luther at Worms. Leslie Stephen's and John Morley's passionate refusal to compromise with dogmas they had come to disbelieve, breathed the unyielding spirit of Seventeenth Century Puritanism. Leslie Stephen had once been a clergyman, and so had J. R. Green, the popular liberal historian. In literature and thought it was a period of quasi-religious movement away from religion."

Trevelyan then goes on to cite G. M. Young: "In its many-sided curiosity and competence, its self-confidence and alertness, the Late Mid-Victorian culture is Greek. In its blend of intellectual adventure and moral conservativism, it was really Athenian." See G. M. Trevelyan, *English Social History*, New York and London, 1942, pp. 563-64; the illustrated edition of Ruth C. Wright, vol. 4, p. 104.

One may note further that the Christian missionary onslaught, for instance, though severely felt and resented, is deemed to have the tendency to undermine the Muslims' own religious convictions—but there is no suggestion that Christian ones are being imparted in their place. This point could be illustrated also from the modernist editor of the *Azhar Journal*, studied below,

Still there is more. The more basic threat to Islam is not the challenge of ideas, from whatever source. It is the challenge of history. We have said that Islam is a faith expressed not primarily in a system of ideas, but in a system of life, a community and its ways. Islamic society is endangered not only from without but from within, and not only its existence but its essence. There is an attack upon Islam by events, considered not from outside but from within its own development; the subversion of Islam, as it were, by Islam's .own contemporary history. One may blame the British or Americans for their injustice. One may inveigh against the ideas that they impose.[18] But how comes it that they can wreak such injustice, can get away with their ideas? How comes it that the Islamic world is impotent, and backward? These things ought not to be! But—far back in one's mind, quite unformulated; repressed, yet felt—is the question: if they ought not to be how comes it that they are? That "the Muslims are backward" (the phrase is freely used in current Arab writing)[19] is ultimately a contradiction in terms, if *Islam* means what it purports to mean. The British army in the Canal Zone was resented by the Egyptians not only as a remnant of foreign domination (though we must never get too far away from the realization of that crushing power), not only because it reminded them of their own decline. It was rejected also because it symbolized the dilemma of their souls.

---

who makes no distinction between the attack specifically on Islam and the drift from all sense of spiritual values (cf. below, ref. 121). Nor in the materialism that he so much deplores is the dialectical variety in evidence. Lately this has changed somewhat. In general, however, the profound feeling of a tendency on the part of modern Muslims to desert Islam is an awareness not of a people's substituting new persuasions for old, but of a drift into a worldly unbelief.

[18] Of course ideas are not imposed, but accepted. So also tastes. The present writer has observed—for instance, in Damascus, November 1948—editorial tirades against the obscene and disruptive West for producing the salacious cinema that crowds of young (and not-so-young) Damascenes were paying their admission fee to see in a local cinema-house. We also deprecate with scorn the generally execrable taste and degenerate morality of Hollywood. But what is really sorrowful is not that Hollywood produces such films, but that our society likes them. The Damascus editors did not ask why Damascenes chose to see these shows. Imported immorality can corrupt only those whose sense of values is already weak.

[19] Cf. the famous essay of Shakīb Arslān, noted above, chap. 2, ref. 25. Another instance, in a minor pamphlet picked up on the streets of Cairo: Muḥammad 'Abd Allāh al-Sammān, *al-Ma'ānī al-Ḥayyah fī al-Islām*, Cairo, 1372/1953, opening sentence.

It was not only that their country was oppressed, but that their ideals were negated. Similarly, especially for the Asian Arabs, the Palestine war. For a proud and sensitive people who are Muslim, it is intolerable to see Islam the plaything of infidels.

The Islamic tradition was formed on the principle that destiny is in the hands of God. It is Allah who controls events. The Mu'tazilah and others argued the point: some Muslims have felt that, under God, destiny was in their own hands. The recent bitterness was that it seemed to be neither God nor the Muslims who controlled events but the British or Americans—the domineering, discourteous, brash infidels who suddenly pushed themselves noisily on the scene.

Scientific discoveries in the nineteenth century were of crucial significance for the Christian. Theological and interpretive questions of fundamental and at first ravaging import were raised, questions that worried and teased the church, shattered the faith of many and set others to a radical rethinking of their affirmations. Christians have been surprised that Muslims have not seemed to face the same kind of problem. There has been no great 'evolution controversy'; no T. H. Huxley debate; no large crisis in theology. Yet the Muslim disarray and turmoil have been no less. Only, the spiritual crisis has taken its own Islamic form. The question has reached the heart of the faith along a practical rather than a theoretical route. The battle has been not of ideas but of politics; relief of distress is sought not in a revision of doctrine but in a redressing of history.

The Christian saw emerging out of science new thoughts and concepts—which seemed in conflict with his previous ideas and doctrines. The truth of science seemed different from, and in some ways truer than, the truth that he had from God. For the believer the collision was painful; the problem posed, acute. In the case of Islam the significance has been different. The Muslim has been troubled not by questions of truth so much, as by questions of power. He saw emerging out of science a new technology and industrial might, new social processes and patterns among an alien people. These seemed in conflict with his previous patterns and institutions. The power of science, of the West, seemed different from and in some ways more powerful than the power that his community had from God.

In accord with God's command and with His blessing, Muslim

society once erected a great civilization; but now this is seen as being attacked, without and within, and perhaps superseded, by a new power based not on God's ordinance or on any divine sanction. A new society has come to birth before which the society of God seemingly cannot stand; a new society more successful, and perhaps in some aspects even more attractive. Islamic backwardness implies that something has gone wrong not only with the Muslim's own development but with the governance of the universe.

For many Arabs the problem is no longer that the Islamic dream is unrealized. Religions can live with their dreams unrealized; this is part of the religious genius. With its dream unrealized, the Muslim world has been living for long; the Arabs, throughout the centuries of their Middle Ages and until now. One may live a straitened life and feel that in His good time God will actualize the ideal community, will make the dream come true. One may awake to a strenuous life and with one's fellows strive to actualize it, with God's favour to make it come true oneself. But it is harsh to wake to the fact that aliens, without that favour, have in some ways actualized it while one slept.

The challenge is no longer simply that the dream is unrealized. The new challenge to the Arab world is in the fear of the recognition that the dream may be invalid.

By this we do not mean a questioning that it may not be true. This would be un-Islamic, in every sense; not least, in the important sense that Muslims do not generally approach religion in such intellectualist terms. The spectre is rather that it may not be efficacious. The problem is theological not in a dogmatic sense but because in Muslim conviction power comes from God, and yet here were the British empire, the Dutch empire, the French empire growing daily more powerful than Islamic society. In this view, the recent disquiet has been not only that the Muslims were too weak or too erring to implement the aspirations of their faith. It has been rather the fear that Islam itself even in its ideal form, even if implemented, would—the very idea is blasphemous—be too weak in the world of today.

Here, then, is the Islamic plight of modernity, as deeply felt by the educated Arab. A century and more ago awareness spread of the need to defend the faith against external encroachment and internal decline. Today, despite progress in many directions, the attack upon Islam is seen as more rather than less severe: an attack from without and from within; not only from outside the society by foreign enemies and inside it by subversion and betrayal, not only in one's outer environment and within the recesses of one's own mind, but also an attack on the external, historical phenomenon of Islam as an existential reality and as well upon the inner power of its essential truth.

Response to Attack

This sense of attack illuminates much of the Arabs' recent Islamic development. It would doubtless be going too far to see all their activities even on the religious plane wholly as reactions to this attack or to this feeling. Of course other factors have entered in. Nonetheless, in almost every facet of those activities such reaction can be discerned. In many it is very powerful indeed. There would seem to be very little Islamic history in the modern Arab case that cannot be better understood if this aspect of it is firmly borne in mind.

The modern Arab is first and foremost a person defending himself and his society against onslaught.

This is obvious enough and need not detain us in the case of nationalism, which has been in large measure quite simply a reaction against attack, the "negative" nationalism of our previous chapter.[20] It is exceedingly powerful. Its fierceness and intensity, though they have surprised some observers, are readily understandable in terms of the massive and overbearing and penetrating quality of the assault.

Any growth in Arab strength that is not accompanied by a growth in confidence and trust has been used and must be used in self-assertion, in rejecting outside control or influence. Any failure of outsiders to recognize the profundity and momentum of this drive, the supreme need to push back encroachment, is bound to lead to miscalculation and deception. Any move that further weakens any Arab sense that the outside world is reliable and friendly is bound to increase defiant antagonism.[21]

[20] Above, pp. 74-76.
[21] Such as the apparently calculated and certainly flamboyant rebuff of July 1956 over the Aswan dam project. Washington (19/7/56) and London (20/-7/56) abruptly pulled out from under 'Abd al-Nāṣir ("Nasser")'s feet the carpet that they had invitingly spread out for him, as soon as he had finally agreed to take a rather spectacular stance upon it. The present chapter was

Similarly understandable is the marked xenophobia which has been especially strident in Arab cities, particularly Damascus and Cairo, since World War II. This came into an outburst of overt expression in the "burning of Cairo" in 1952, particularly in the burning of Shepheard's Hotel, symbol of foreign arrogance. This was one activist and extreme expression of the isolationism that widely obtains, not simply as a policy but as a mood. The Arabs, like most other Muslims, are today's isolationists *par excellence;* they wish to high heaven that the world would leave them alone.

The reaction to attack is visible also in other developments. We wish to consider particularly two: in the realm of thought, and the realm of action—apologetics, and the Ikhwan.

First, however, in the realm of emotion, one must note that the experience of hostility and disruption has in some cases been so crushing as to lead not to positive reaction at all but here and there to a sort of paralysis of the will, or a distortion of awareness. This kind of thing is so familiar in the modern West that it should not be difficult to understand. The chief difference in the two cases is between a predominantly social and a predominantly individualist orientation of the person, in responsibility, in triumph, and in sorrow. The modern West has laid stress on individualism, the Islamic World on the identification of the individual with his society. Further, in the Arab world it is the social personality that has been wounded by outside attack and inner conflict. In the West the total society is expansive and by outward standards successful. It is rather the individual within it, caught in its maze of competitive struggle, and in modernity's subversion of meaning and of patterns of value, who feels isolated, rejected, and helpless before a hostile environment. Unable to cope with the overwhelming perplexity and aggression of contemporary life, he (by now a standard and recognized type) is driven by anxiety and a loss of inner values to a suspecting of others' hypocrisy and yet a desperate craving for their approval. He weaves between himself and the world a defensive pattern of concepts which inhibits an objective viewing of reality and inhibits also a constructive effort towards genuine goals.[22] This

written before that disastrous event and the Suez Canal crisis that ensued, but in the meantime nothing has happened to suggest modification. (Cf. at ref. 204 below.)

[22] The above is sincerely based on personal observation, yet in part also

type of person is increasingly prevalent in the modern West; it would be surprising if a comparable phenomenon were quite unknown in the Arab world. It would be going perhaps too far to insist that this sort of defensive anxiety is constantly characteristic of that world's modernism. Yet it would seem unsympathetic not to understand it when it appears.

The onslaught against which Arab society is defending itself has not seemed so minor as to have failed in every case to affect the emotional foundations of its life; to influence not only behaviour but the central predispositions to behaviour, and even to perception. It is the total Arab personality that is involved—and deeply so.

An ability to understand what the Arab thinks and does turns on an ability to understand how he feels about the modern world.

Apologetics

Apologetics is the ideological expression of the reaction against attack. With Arabism and Islam both threatened, its aim is to prove that they are both Good Things. It is the attempt to develop a system of ideas that will serve as protection against insecurity. The literature cannot be adequately understood except in terms of the function that it performs, and of the overpowering psychological need for this type of defensive thinking. In a world of uncertainty and aggression, it is written, and is read, to meet a very deep demand.

So far as the Arab aspect is concerned, it is chiefly a question of historiography: to demonstrate the brilliance of one's past. On the Islamic side, there is both this historical glory and an almost unlimited range of other examples of its excellence.

In a sense, therefore, the literature of defence would seem almost straightforward. One might be tempted to suppose that something so obvious would call for little comment. What could be more natural than that a people under attack should justify itself, and that those whose faith is questioned should rally to its defence? What more carping than to seem to indict this reaction; as it were, to begrudge an almost overwhelmed society its legitimate defence?

summarizes sections of Karen Horney, *Our Inner Conflicts*, New York, 1945. A book of this kind, the present writer has found, helps him both to understand himself as an individual and to understand the modern Arabs as a group.

Indictment or begrudging would indeed be intolerable. Our point is rather a recognition of the difficulties that ensue. For on further examination it becomes apparent that this defensive literature, and the intellectual and psychological attitude that it involves, in fact raise some of the deepest questions of Islam's place in the modern world. Here again, as in other instances, the Arabs, out of the emotional depth of their concentrated experience, speak at an enhanced level of intensity for all the Muslim world (except the Turks, one section of whose society also passed through this stage, but who seem now decisively beyond it).

In our previous chapter we have already briefly commented on apologetics generally, seeing it as a part of the recent world-wide attempt to defend Islam. We suggested there that both Muslims themselves and Western observers would find it rewarding to give the issue more attention than it has customarily received. For this defensive device turns out to aggravate difficulties rather than to solve them. Despite appearances, the drive to interpret the world in ways emotionally satisfying is inherently disruptive. As the psychologists well know, and in a slightly different fashion, also the classical Muslims,[23] it cannot satisfy, but rather betrays those whom it ensnares. Some of the deepest distress of the present

[23] Cf. al-Ghazzālī, cogent as usual: "People who seek knowledge are of three types. There is the man who seeks knowledge . . . for the life to come; he seeks thereby only the Countenance of God [as we might say, seeks knowledge for its own sake, seeks Truth]; . . . such a man is saved. Then there is the man who seeks it for the help it gives in his transitory life . . . and at the same time is aware of that ultimate truth. . . . Such a man is in jeopardy . . . ; yet, if he is given grace to repent . . . and [if he] adds practice to theory, . . . he will join the ranks of the saved. . . . A third man has been overcome by Satan. He has taken his knowledge as a means to increase his wealth, to boast of his influence and to pride himself on his numerous following. By his knowledge he explores every avenue which offers a prospect of realizing what he hopes for from this world. Moreover he believes in himself that he has an important place in God's eyes because with his garb and jargon he bears the brand and stamp of the scholar despite his mad desire of this world both openly and in secret. Such men will perish, being stupid and easily deceived, for there is no hope of their repentance since they fancy that they are acting well. They are unmindful of the words of God most high, 'O ye who have believed, why do ye say what ye do not do'? (Q. [sc. Qur'ān] 61, 2)." (The translation is that of W. Montgomery Watt, *The Faith and Practice of al-Ghazālī*, London, 1953, pp. 88-89. The original will be found in Abū Ḥāmid Muḥammad al-Ghazzālī, *Bidāyat al-Hidāyah*; text available to us, the ʿĪsà al-Bābī al-Ḥalabī ed., on the margin of *id.*, *Minhāj al-ʿĀbidīn*, Cairo, n.d., pp. 5-6.)
Between Karen Horney (cf. previous ref.) and this, what is there to choose?

situation is for those who have trusted themselves too exclusively to this apologetics. Their difficulties cannot be understood, let alone overcome, without an appreciation of the insidious distraction.

Let us consider first the question of history. It appears at first disarmingly innocuous. We have said that the Arabs are proud— and of course have good reason to be proud—of their classical history. It has been one of the achievements of the Arab world in the modern period to revive among its people the sense of the past, to bring into some delineated awareness the previously almost subconscious memory of historical achievement. It has revived or reinvigorated the historian's craft among a people who once practiced it with critical capacity. Vis-à-vis the West, the neglect of the Arab participation in the total movement of the Mediterranean world from Greece to modernity has in part been righted. The sheer uncovering of new data has also been important.

All this has been creditable, and the emphasis upon positive qualities of the classical period has been understandable enough. It is understandable even in universal human terms whereby each of us tends to see his own past in a somewhat favourable light. It is all the more natural in the specifically Arab case with the cruel sense of modern decline. Present "backwardness" is offset by past achievement.

The process turns disruptive only when, as has sometimes happened, the grip of the need to defend is tightened to the point where this delight in greatness, this compensatory self-satisfaction, becomes the compulsive cause rather than the honest result of historical reconstruction. Historiography is then designed almost explicitly to nourish and to support one's predilections. It seeks not to analyse or to understand the past, but to glorify it; that is, to glorify oneself. The purpose is not investigation but aggrandizement, not intellectual accuracy but emotional satisfaction.

As we have said, this is understandable in terms of the mordant feeling of contemporary decline. The more acutely is felt the inadequacy of one's present, the more one insists on the splendour of one's past. In the Muslim case, the crucially important religious factor is added. For those dubious of Islam as a sufficient or effective ideal today of the good life in community, the endeavour is pushed hard to show that in the past it was spectacularly so. The more insecure one's faith, the more imperious the drive to argue for this. It becomes seemingly indispensable to one's relation both to the modern world and to eternal destiny that this conclusion be maintained—and even that any adverse evidence be repressed.[24]

This treatment of history plays its practitioners false in two ways. The attempt to glorify rather than to understand of course fails to understand. Further, it succeeds in glorifying only temporarily and on very costly terms. Both matters have serious consequences in perpetuating the situation out of which they arise.

The glorifying is of necessity self-defeating; it leads to a closed circle. For in the end it rests the case for confidence not on history but on an interpretation of history. One's self-esteem which the world of reality threatens to undermine is made to rest increasingly on what is in effect the work of one's imagination. Accordingly, inner assurance is further weakened, since it is more than ever cut off from outer support. Any failure of courage to face the historical picture in full and critical frankness, "warts and all," means a further, more imperative drive to construct and to defend idealizations. The more one writes and reads books in order to bolster a conclusion predetermined by one's desires, the more one has to write and read books so designed. The more Arab greatness is simply something proven by modern Arab books about the past, the less possible it becomes to read criticism for the sake of what illumination it may purvey—let alone to produce self-criticism for the sake of realistic constructive action. For any adverse material in the actual situation that might be allowed into consciousness would seem a further attack upon one's position, a further threat to one's confidence or faith. One therefore becomes afraid of the facts, since they have the power to undermine one's version of the facts. The very endeavour to overcome

---

[24] To anyone familiar with modern Arabic historical literature, illustrative examples will come easily to mind. One fairly innocuous one which is by no means extreme and indeed might be said to be almost commonplace: an article entitled (characteristically) "The Achievements of the Arabs in the Science of Geography," *Majallat al-Azhar*, Cairo, 5:567-73 (1934). This purports to be a translation of the German orientalist Brockelmann. Although it is, in fact, based rather squarely on that scholar's information (Cf. Carl Brockelmann, *Geschichte der arabischen Litteratur*, 1st ed., Weimar, 1898-1902, I. 225-30, 475-77), it is rather an essay paraphrasing and treating the original with freedom, adding a few eulogistic paragraphs by way of introduction (5:567, the two opening paragraphs; it is not indicated that these are not from the original), and omitting remarks such as the original's opening one that Arab geography grew out of Greek (Brockelmann, *op. cit.*, I, 225).

one's insecurity in the objective world by glorification, ends by making one the more insecure.

Secondly, the neglect of sheer historical understanding is in itself costly. A careful and realistic historical analysis of any situation may well prove an important element for ameliorative action. To recognize a problem clearly, and to see how it came about, are two manifestly major steps towards solving it. To grasp an ideal clearly, and to have an analytic awareness of the objective conditions in and by and against which it must be or has in the past been realized, is an important step towards putting it now into practice. Any attitude or trend, therefore, that neglects or stands in the way of such clear recognition and understanding is a significant obstacle to progress.

Those Arabs whose intellectual realism is starkly honest are accordingly in a much stronger position for constructive advance and real greatness than those many whose enmeshment in historical apologetics has diverted them from present issues or past inquiries to past utopias. The psychological need for historical idealization is, as we have seen, great. The practical as well as intellectual need for historical understanding is even greater, but has been receiving scant attention.

As one illustration among many one might take the case of science. The market abounds with treatises exhibiting, sometimes glibly, sometimes as a result of great labour and research, the Arab (or Muslim) contribution to science in general or to this or that particular branch. At a more superficial level of factual knowledge, the case is emphatically urged that Western science is essentially a borrowing from the Arab (Islamic) world. At a more abstract level, the thesis is ardently presented that Islam as a religion, far from being in conflict with science, encourages and nourishes it.

Much of this, though complex, is true. More important, all of it is satisfying. Yet equally important, little of it is effective. For there has been, along with this voluminous output of applause, extremely little investigation by Arab minds of the actual factors leading to the development of early science in Arab classical culture, the role that it played in the society, and the objective relations, either social or intellectual, over the various centuries between the scientists and the religious authorities.[25] Great atten-

[25] One can hardly document an absence of writing; but perhaps there is

tion is called to the fact that Arab science existed. Little thought
is given as to just how it arose, or what it implied. And so far as
the present writer is aware, there has been virtually no study at all
of the obviously crucial question as to how or why Arab science
declined.[26]

The Arab writing of history has been functioning, then, less as
a genuine inquiry than as a psychological defence. Most of it[27] is
to be explained primarily in terms of the emotional needs that it
fulfills (and is designed to fulfill). This is further illustrated by
the avidity with which Western praise of past Arab greatness is
culled and exploited. Professor Gibb speaks for all Western students acquainted with the literature (and some Muslims[28]), when
he calls it "disconcerting" to find "modernists in Egypt eagerly
seizing on any pronouncements by Western writers, no matter how
ill founded, uncritical, or partisan, which chime in with their own
sentiments or flatter their pride," and speaks of the general "imma-
turity" of modernist historical perspective.[29]

However, these do not show simply poor judgement. They are
evidence, rather, of a judgement held captive by the emotions,
and of the desperate search for approval into which these writers

---

value in citing a typical instance of what is produced in this realm, indeed a
work that is representative of the Arab attitude at its best, one might say.
This is 'Umar Farrukh, *'Abqarīyat al-'Arab fī al-'Ilm wa al-Falsafah*, Beirut,
1945; 2nd ed., 1952. This has recently been made available in English:
Omar A. Farrukh, *The Arab Genius in Science and Philosophy*, trans. by
John B. Hardie, Washington, 1954. Dr. Farrukh holds a Ph.D. degree from a
German university.

[26] If this last question were treated, one might expect that in the hands of
most writers it would be *a priori* in order to prove that the decline was not
really the Arab's or Islam's fault, rather than genuinely to inquire as to its
true causes or its course.

[27] Not all of it, of course. We trust that our study will not give the impression that we are impervious to such excellence as some historical work
has undoubtedly displayed. We have already mentioned Shafīq Ghurbāl (cf.
above, ref. 3); it is invidious to single out names, but such historians also as
Ḥusayn Mu'nis in Egypt, 'Abd al-'Azīz al-Dūrī in Iraq, and others must be
mentioned with respect. These men themselves would probably recognize
the general point that we are endeavouring to make. For a documented indictment of modern Arab historiography by an Arab writer who is not a
Muslim, see Nabih Amin. Faris, "The Arabs and their History," in *The
Middle East Journal*, Washington, 8:155-62 (1954).

[28] Among the present writer's Turkish and Indian friends are some who
have themselves noted and commented on the kind of point to which Gibb
here refers.

[29] H. A. R. Gibb, *Modern Trends in Islam*, Chicago, 1947, p. 127.

and their readers have been impelled. Western writing on the Arabs, as on Islam, is customarily read by modern Arabs and appraised, not in terms of whether its statements are accurate or its contributions illuminating, but whether they are laudatory or adverse. Western writers thus suffer for the aggression of their society, since anything they say is first suspected to be part of the attack. The price paid for long-standing hostility is the inability to communicate.

Gibb relates the failure of objective historiography to certain developments within the classical and especially mediaeval Islamic tradition itself;[30] but stresses that the 'modernists' have made the situation seriously worse.[31] He concludes the most authoritative and perceptive analysis of Islam's (primarily Arab) modern trends that has appeared, with the suggestion that the single most significant step that could be taken by the intellectual leaders of the religion today is the attainment of a true coming-to-terms with historical thinking.[32]

Let us turn, then, from this question of historical apologetics. The next matter, the apologetics of Islam, is still more serious. It is of deep consequence both for the Arabs (and other Muslims throughout the world who widely resort to it) and to Islam itself. In some ways the defensive interpretation is the most serious intellectual development within the religion in recent times. It is serious because it involves what men of faith, Muslim or other, have always known to be deeply irreverent and also essentially

---

[30] *Ibid.*, pp. 124ff.

[31] *Ibid.*, p. 127.

[32] *Op. cit.*, concluding pages. He makes the point that "The way to the reconciliation of Islamic orthodoxy with the modern movement of thought lies not, as is so often supposed, through compromise with the hypotheses of modern science. The scientific habit of thought has never been lost for Muslim scholars, though they may very likely need to revise their scientific method and to broaden out as well as deepen their grasp of it. The way is to be found rather in revaluation of the data of thought through the cultivation of historical thinking" (p. 126). We also, above, have urged that science does not pose for Islam intellectualist problems in a way comparable to what has happened in Christendom. In a sense this present essay is but an elaboration and amplification of Gibb's observations. In another sense, with our stress on the psychological and the historical elements, it involves a shift of emphasis, from what we would regard as Gibb's still slightly too theological and intellectualist interpretation. However, all of us working in this field find, as R. Mitchell has indicated, that the more closely we study the modern Islamic world, the more we find ourselves simply "writing footnotes on Professor Gibb's survey."

destructive: the attempt to make use of religion for human purposes. Islam, ideally, in its central nature has been the personality's and society's sincere dedication of itself to what it knows of the purposes of God. Islam for the apologetes is in danger of becoming rather an instrument in the personality's or society's pursuit of its own purposes—in this case, of self-esteem and emotional security and of position in the world.

If Professor Gibb feels that the way to advance for Muslims lies through the '*ulama*', the custodians of religious thought, taking history seriously, one might venture also to feel that that for the modernists lies essentially in their taking Islam seriously. There can surely be no progress in Muslim society, no real solution of its modern problems, unless the leaders. of thought and action show a truer understanding and more genuine reverence for the essentially religious message of their faith.

These statements might at first seem presumptuous, or odd. We must therefore elucidate rather carefully what we have in mind, and especially what we mean by apologetics. It is our observation that understanding and reverence for Islam, as for history, have been inhibited by the turn of mind that seeks primarily to defend, that is impelled by a desire to shield either the religion or oneself. We contend, further, that this losing touch with the heart of the faith has worked to the grievous detriment of both persons and society. Yet this losing touch has been in large part unconscious; it is in the name of Islam that the apologetes have disrupted their own and others' faith.

To clarify our position we must take some pains to illuminate apologetic modernism, and make clear the radical difference between this and the more truly religious Islam of traditional piety. Fortunately, an effective illustration of both is provided by the journal of the Azhar, the great Islamic centre in Cairo. This journal was edited first (1930-33) by one of the Azhari '*ulama*' (classical scholars), and subsequently by a vigorous representative 'modernist.'[33] The nobility of the former's position, the essential

---

[33] The journal, published monthly in Cairo from al-Muḥarram 1349/May-June 1930, first bore the title *Nūr al-Islām*; from vol. 6 no. 6 this was changed to *Majallat al-Azhar*. The first editor was al-Sayyid Muḥammad al-Khiḍr (al-Khaḍir?) Ḥusayn.

Muḥammad Farīd Wajdī (1875-1954) assumed editorship with vol. 4 no. 5, Jumādà al-Ūlà, 1352/August-September 1933, and held the office until 1952. The present study is based on an examination of the journal from the be-

vacuity of the latter's work, exemplify all too cogently the grave loss involved in the drift from an integral Islam.

Our choice of this particular work is, we repeat, for illustrative purposes. The journal has an importance of its own, certainly; and the second editor, Muhammad Farid Wajdi, has been also a writer of independent significance.[34] However, our point is not to discuss individual interpretations but to consider them in so far as they are instances of general trends. It is clear enough that the first editor and his school represent the classical Islamic tradition in the modern Arab world.[35] Wajdi's particular ideas[36] are a little out of date, but not his attitude. His interpretation of Islam and his general approach to the world will, we believe, be readily recognized by modern Arabs and by their friends as a fair example of the orientation of modernist ideology. And the contrast afforded with the previous editor's position serves so strikingly to clarify the basic points at issue that it seems rewarding to give the matter extended examination. All this is in addition to the fact that, although no voice can be said to speak officially for Islam whether traditional or modernist, the official organ of the Azhar[37] can hardly be dismissed as insignificant.

ginning through vol. 18 (November 1947). For a full descriptive and analytic study of the journal, see the present writer's doctoral dissertation, "The Azhar Journal, Survey and Critique," 1948, in the library of Princeton University, Princeton. In the remainder of this chapter, references to the journal are made by volume number and page, without further identification.

[34] See Carl Brockelmann, *Geschichte der arabischen Litteratur*, Supplementband III, Leiden, 1942, pp. 324-25. Some of his writings have also been translated into Urdū, by no less a person than Mawlānā Abū-l-Kalām Āzād: *Musalmān 'Awrat*, 6th ed., Lahore, 1953.

[35] We do not mean representative of that tradition in the average, but rather at its best. Also, there is the disturbing possibility to be kept in mind that, just as Wajdī (cf. next ref.) is an old man formed by and reflecting an earlier atmosphere, so al-Khiḍr Ḥusayn, also an old man, may at heart represent a type of traditional piety that is somewhat dying out (in the Muslim world as it has in the West). The present writer does not know how many young men nowadays are coming up with the same essential honesty, dignity, humility, and grace.

[36] Especially his replies to scientific materialism, and his interest in spiritism, indicate his era, and have a turn-of-the-century flavour. In the light of this and the preceding reference it should be noted that the argument built on this journal here presented reflects essentially the situation fifteen years ago more accurately than that today. However, the situation today is understandable only in terms of that which produced it, and this has not, so far as we are aware, been depicted or analysed previously as is here attempted.

[37] That it is official appears from the statement of each cover and title-page:

Islam, in the conception of al-Khidr Husayn, the first editor, is a true and right religion which has been posited, once for all, complete and fixed. But that religion is a transcendent Idea. Man's knowledge of what it really is, is both progressive and fallible; and man's implementation of it is always imperfect. Consequently, authority and worth pertain to Islam *per se*; not, in the form of an authoritarianism or an idealization, to any particular Muslim's pronouncements, either past or present, nor to any particular mundane embodiment. What has been handed down, therefore, is not inviolable. What has been so far achieved is not sacrosanct.[38] He exhibits no nostalgia. His interest is not in the past but in the timeless, and its relation to the present; in the vision of an ideal Islam and in the practical implications of this for today.

That he is an idealist runs throughout his writing, an idealist both philosophically and morally. Truth is for him a supramundane form. The problem is to ascertain and expound it; all else then follows. The ideals are to him so clear and so compelling that he takes idealism for granted. It is undeclared throughout, yet he unconsciously assumes it also on the part of his readers. This colours all his endeavours, and gives the very words he uses a meaning different from what they have from the pen of another type of thinker. Moreover, he pays his readers the Socratic compliment of assuming that they can recognize goodness when they see it.

The idealism is, as we have said, not only metaphysical but moral, pragmatic. To him, exposition is instruction; both are exhortation. He asserts it as the primary duty of himself, of the

---

"Issued by the rectorate of the Azhar" (vols. 1-17; beginning with vol. 18, the statement reads, "Issued by the rectorate of the Azhar Mosque"). The fact is given also as a reason for changing the name to *Majallat al-Azhar*: the old title "did not distinguish it from journals issued by private persons" (6:440). The status is also mentioned editorially: "The journal *Nūr al-Islām*, which is the official mouthpiece of the Azhar" (6:102—cf. Gibb, *op. cit.*, p. 136, note 3).

[38] He expressly rejects any claim of infallibility for the journal (3:3). It is written, he points out, by human beings who are liable to error; even the great *'ulamā'* of old were not inevitably right (*loc. cit.*). He does not appeal for a presentation of or return to the past. His vision for the journal upon this score is that it "accepts of what is new whatever is a good idea or a good practice, and rejects of what is old whatever is a wrong idea or bad practice; so that when people hasten to a novelty that is unprofitable, it is preserved by its inherent stability; and when they congeal around something that is not advantageous, it is content that they be no longer on its side" (*loc. cit.*).

journal, of the Azhar, of the *'ulama'* generally, to expound: to make Islam accurately known. In practice, his own writing, on issues large and small, is to instruct. This takes the form of endeavouring to delineate a matter in such a way that the reader will be enabled to see for himself what in it is good and what bad —that is, what ought to be done and what avoided.[39]

Because of this dynamic idealism, then, instruction is not separable from exhortation. To elucidate a moral ideal is with him the essential element of advocating it—on the unformulated premise that goodness is inherently attractive; or at least that the Muslim is committed to the will of God once he knows what it is. The proportion of his contributions that fulfill a moral purpose is large; and their moral tone extraordinarily high. This is far from being a superior moralizing, a preaching in any offensive sense. It is saved from that by many things, perhaps the chief being that he is holding up moral ideals under whose judgement he himself is the first to stand, and to realize which his sincerity is clearly drawing him also. The "we must's" abound. The ideals of active participation and the fight for social betterment;[40] of personal politeness, even to enemies, but carefully kept free from the nearby vice of flattery and pretence[41]; of scrupulous intellectual integrity,[42] of self-respect and modesty, to be discriminated from the nearby vices of, respectively, pride and self-abasement[43] —these and other ideals are portrayed with genuine reverence and an obvious response of his own to their moral pressure.[44]

[39] An example is his discussion entitled "Muslims' Copying of Foreigners" (3:375-82). This, after an acute, sensitive, dignified and essentially liberal analysis, ends by saying that the article is for those who will listen, "—perhaps they may find in it the true difference ascertained between imitation of foreigners that is commendable and that that is to be rejected" (3:382). Similarly his lucid, probing studies on *al-sunnah wa al-bid'ah* (2:539-46, 611-18): these expound these terms, show where the ambiguities lie and where the *'ulamā'* have not "ascertained" (this recurs as one of his favourite idealist expressions) the presence or degree of reliability; and indicate the moral obligation.
[40] *Passim.* Specific examples: 1:163-68; 1:243-48; 3:663-69.
[41] 2:147-54.
[42] 2:235-43 (cf. below at ref. 79).
[43] 2:467-73.
[44] He relates the obligation of morality not only to himself but to his group. He writes as one of the *'ulamā'*; and writes with colleagues of that profession in mind. Just as with almost every subject that he takes up he draws practical moral inferences as to what can and should be done about it, so almost every problem he relates practically to teaching. "It is, therefore, the duty of him to whom the upbringing of youth is entrusted, to strive . . ." (2:473) is a

Regarding the extant religion of the community—the tangible Islam of contemporary history—he recognizes a need to purify, not merely to defend. One must combat internal deviations and apathy as well as external criticism.[45] The deviations from (true) Islam which his writings would serve to combat include both those to the right and those to the left. Not only the secularism of the educated,[46] who feel that they have gone beyond Islam, is under fire; but also the superstitions and degenerate Sufi practices of the masses, who have not caught up with it.[47]

We have mentioned his frequent use of "we must." Indeed it is in our judgement crucial that one of the things that differentiate him from the later editor is the extent to which the verbs "should," "ought," "must" occur throughout his writings. In modernism, on the other hand, there is no imperative. Al-Khidr Husayn's social concern is keen and persistent. He repeatedly calls attention to the low standard of living—economic,[48] political,[49] educational[50] and other—in Muslim countries, for which he shows a genuine

---

typical way for him to start the concluding sentence of an article. Again, when he writes against living as a recluse (3:663-69), the recluse that he has in mind is the scholar.

It is clear from these and other indications that he is writing principally for the 'ulamā'. One of his editorials (1:163-68) is on the part that the 'ulamā' must play in social reform. Another (1:723-33) is on the role of the Azhar: a vigorous article showing concern felt not only for the religious heritage, which it must mediate, but also, and deeply, for the condition of men and women (including their political freedom), whom it must serve—so that Azharīs may be regarded as "men created to strive for social reform to the utmost of their wisdom and power" (1:733) [italics ours]. "If the Azhar has in the past devoted itself exclusively to scholarly research and ignored the ills that were afflicting Muslims in their religious and civil life, certainly now it is aroused from such negligence. It remembers its past, and is conscious of the loftiness of its position; and has become confident that it has it within its power to remedy those ills, and to raise the East to a pinnacle of well-being" (1:732).

[45] 1:5; 3:3; etc.

[46] 1:85ff. (on the pagination, cf. the footnote to the page of errata following 1:160).

[47] E.g., his discussion of al-bid'ah, 2:539-46, 611-18; especially 2:612ff. He mentions both modernist and superstitious deviations, but the latter predominate. The two are, for him, not unrelated: he puts the masses' distortions of Islam at the head of a list of reasons why the former fail to appreciate the religion's true worth (1:83ff; on pagination cf. preceding ref.).

[48] E.g., 1:247; 1:324-25.

[49] E.g., 1:733; 1:382-87 [second series; lege 442-47]; 2:69.

[50] E.g., 1:323.

concern, and with his usual moral ardour holds up ideals of practical betterment that demand implementation.[51] Man must *strive* to make real society approximate more closely to the ideal one (which Islam proclaims).

His self-criticism is remarkable. There is not only his personal and professional self-criticism in the light of his moral ideals, leading on to criticism of the Azhar, and even, in a sense, of the extant Law. He brings to bear also a national self-criticism,[52] and criticism even of Islamic history. This last is incidental, unpretentious; he finds it natural to use the history of the community[53] to provide illustrations of what not to do, as well as of what to imitate. The Islam to which he is committed is, in effect, a celestial vision, of which the earthly history is but an imperfect expression (and in recent times, he admits, a sorry one).[54] He can therefore afford to keep his eyes open to defects in that expression—though by and large he is, of course, proud of the Muslim past.[55] It is the man whose devotion is to the Islam of history who must romanticize that history.

There are other instances where he makes use of Islamic history to point a moral or to incite emulation.[56] On the whole, however, throughout his writing and his editing[57] he does not appear particularly concerned with the past. His interest is in the actualities of today, and in the potentialities of and responsibility for tomorrow.

Defence of Islam is not absent from this editor's conception of today's needs, and of the functions of the journal. Actually, he puts it next after instruction in his opening statement of the journal's objective.[58] However, writing specifically setting out to

[51] *Passim.* See especially his articles "The Ideal Society in Islam" (1:243-48); "The Bases of Community Welfare" (1:323-27).

[52] An example is that he often has the confidence and integrity (both wanting under Wajdī) to contrast certain conditions in his own country unfavourably with those that he had seen in Germany (1:324-25; 3:377-78) by way of inciting his fellow-countrymen to emulation. A linguistic discussion too, entitled "The Excellence of Arabic" (3:231-44), while it upholds, naturally, the preeminence of that language, admits that it has latterly fallen behind and suggests practical steps for rehabilitating it.

[53] An instance (on honesty) is cited below, at ref. 79.

[54] Examples: the Azhar, 1:724; the community generally, 3:668.

[55] E.g., 2:14; 3:377.

[56] E.g., 2:5-14; 2:683-89; 3:83-91.

[57] See ref. 59 below.

[58] 1:4.

be on the defensive in the usual sense proves in fact rare.[59] And when it does appear, it is usually[60] transformed by the distinctive orientation into something quite different from apologetics of the sentimental type. For this writer's dynamic idealism is operative also here, and makes a basic difference between his meaning for the concept and that of the modernists.

One illustration is provided even in his major series to justify the Law.[61] This defends not an historical entity handed down by tradition, but a transcendent Idea. Indeed, it includes a careful discussion of the principles of legal reform. It makes considerable difference whether one is defending a moral ideal or a social institution—the difference, in fact, between a reformer and a conservative.[62]

Constantly he makes clear his conviction that to defend Islam what is needed is to make it effectively known. That is, accurately

[59] By al-Khiḍr Ḥusayn himself, and by others under his editorship. There is one bald instance of an apologetic contribution by another hand, laudatory rather than practical, and specifically looking for "the things in Islam, in its first period, of which one may be proud" (1:707; cf. 708, line 10, etc.). This is an article entitled "The Role of Islamic Culture in Intellectual Development" (1:700-09, 790-800). It is by the only writer in vol. 1, 'Urjūn, who is still a contributor to the journal in vol. 18. Also, significantly, it is the only article on Islamic history contributed during the first editor's régime. (Apart from his casual use of history, mentioned above, the editor himself devotes one article to the theologian al-Ash'arī, 3:303-16.)

[60] There is one long article by the editor himself, "Islam's Clemency in the Treatment of Non-Muslims" (2:683-89), which is designed to show that the religion enjoins the greatest kindness in dealing with outsiders, both in war and peace. A reader who wished to take this simply as apologetic, rather than as an appeal for clemency, would not in this one case be prevented by anything within the article itself from doing so.

[61] "The Sharī'ah of Islām Valid for All Times and Places," series, voll. 1 (36ff.)-3. The object is explicitly to refute "the illusion that the Canon Law is not suitable to conditions of the modern age" (1:36). Cf. Wajdī's editorial, "The Teachings of Islām Meet the Needs of All Men at Every Time and Place" (17:12-15). The two treatments differ importantly. Al-Khiḍr in his idealism ascribes the "illusion" to persons who do not know what (true) Islām is; and goes on at once to make as his first point that ijtihād is basic to the Law and therefore one must begin with a study of that. There follow quite an elaborate presentation and discussion of the principles on which this (ideal) law is (imperfectly) apprehended—including the today crucial ijmā'.

[62] Cf. John Dewey (of all people!), in his discussion of Plato's idealism as revolutionary over against the conservative realism of Aristotle; see his article "Philosophy" in Encyclopaedia of the Social Sciences, New York and London, 1930-35, 12:124b.

discernible. Moreover, and this is crucial, the Islam that he is defending is not, as with the later editor, an earthly society or a given system of practice or belief. It is, rather, a moral imperative.

In one sense, therefore, this editor might be said in all his expository and exhortative writing to be "defending" the Islam to which he is committed. Wherever he is advocating a virtue or elucidating a truth, he is defending the divine in human life.

This, for him, is the essential task of the journal, and indeed of the Azhar. In his "Introduction," giving the initial declaration of the journal's policy and *raison d'être*, he begins by declaring that Islam is a sound guidance and the source of a flourishing life, but that it is corrupted by groups who, out of ignorance and error, attack it.[63] Thus for him the danger is corruption (of earthly Islam, presumably primarily by its own people). And the attack, which he too senses, is the product of ignorance of the true faith. The need, therefore, is instruction and a summons to righteousness.[64] Throughout his work, he lives up to his promise to provide these.

The position that we are endeavouring to clarify is not exclusively, of course, that of the editor as an individual person. He represents it at a particularly high level, but others of his school exemplify the same general orientation. In the traditional departments of the journal (under the classical rubrics *tafsir, sunnah,* etc.) the viewpoint persists even into the later editor's régime. It would be sociologically inept to underestimate the significance of the quiet nourishment of homely virtues.[65] Sermonettes, for instance, are provided month by month by a scholar who chooses a *hadith* as his text, explains its literal meaning, and then goes on,

[63] 1:3.

[64] "The summons to good" (1:4); variously, "the summons to the truth" (4:4); and many similar expressions, *passim*. The later editor's summons is more for an institution. The ease with which the first can use *shari'ah* and "Islām" as almost interchangeable terms is also not found under Wajdī.

[65] Cf. Butterfield on the chief role of the Church in the history of the West: "Those who preach the Gospel, nurse the pieties, spread New Testament Love, and affirm the spiritual nature of man are guarding the very fountain, dealing with the problems of civilization at its very source, and keeping open the spring from which new things will still arise. Compared with this contribution it is unimportant if they themselves make mistaken judgements on mundane issues in history"—Herbert Butterfield, *Christianity in European History*, London &c, 1951 (University of Durham: Riddell Memorial Lectures), p. 55.

at greater or less length, to point a moral. These men's concern is not to argue that Islam has lofty principles. Taking this for granted, they rather strive to urge Muslims to live up to them. Subjects are brotherhood,[66] good upbringing for children,[67] discipline,[68] initiative,[69] the mean between extravagance and parsimony,[70] and the like.[71]

There is a distinctive element in contributions even of lesser writers in the classical tradition, an element that is still prominent even when their discussions combine with an exposition and advocacy of their position a certain explicit defence of it. This element differentiates their defensive writings from more modernist types. It is the religious and other sensitivity with which their work is executed.

Yusuf al-Dijwi, for example, in urging the teleological argument for God, describes in intense and vivid style the marvels of nature

[66] Often; e.g., 3:605-08; 4:535-38; 5:179-85.

[67] 1:507-13, 592-97, 667-71; 2:497-505.

[68] E.g., 5:316-23.

[69] 5:466-73.

[70] 3:679-84.

[71] However, this too rather peters out gradually. The first editor lists al-Sunnah among the chief sections of the journal (1:6), while the second makes it and other classical departments secondary to apologetics (9:3-4). After the first two scholars who handle this rubric (Ḥasan Manṣūr, and after his death, Ibrāhīm al-Jibālī—to vol. 5 through no. 9), there are three articles (by Yūsuf al-Dijwī: 6:30-38 and 92-101, 164-70, 235-42) that preserve somewhat the ḥadīth pattern, though without the regular heading; then a gap of two years, after which 'Abd al-Raḥmān al-Jazīrī takes up the department (from vol. 8 no. 2) and handles it month by month until his death five years later (12:640). His treatment is characterized by a greater diversity of subject matter, and a greater attention to the specific details of the moral, or the canon, law. He too deals with the general virtues ("Sincerity," 8:121-25, 223-28; "Justice," 11:458-62; etc.) but devotes several of his articles to questions such as divorce (8:540-47), mortgages (10:251-55), and the manner and the occasion of reading the Qur'ān (9:369-76; 11:520-23). He discusses also points of theology, from revelation (10:573-78) to the intercession of local departed spirits (12:583-86). There is then a year-and-a-half's further interval; after which the feature reappears under Ṭāhā al-Sākit, who is still handling it at the end of our period, five years later. He too takes up personal moral questions, and treats both of human virtue and of moral theology. He insistently inculcates, both in general and in detail, a sense of high ethical responsibility and of sincere piety; it is clear that he writes with a genuine religious feeling. There is, however, a tone of asceticism and of formalism which at times would lay him open to a charge of mechanism (one example, taken more or less at random from many that might be cited: 14:475-77). His conservatism extends to the incidentals, and one misses the moral discrimination and warm humanity of the early writers.

and its majesty and splendour, and wonders at the insensitivity of atheism: at times the argument in fact, whatever it may be formally, is less from design to Designer than from beauty and sublimity to reverence.[72] Similarly, in Qur'an exegesis there is on the whole[73] a skirting of modern intellectual problems and an avoidance of argumentation but a considerable level of moral intensity and numinous response. The moral and intellectual plane is highest when this form is handled by the Rectors of the Azhar.

One should mention also the small quantity of material that is primarily of a devotional nature. In one instance it is confided that the endeavour has been "to write a brief article that would arouse love of God in men's hearts."[74] The article, appropriately, makes extensive use of poetry.[75] In the writings, too, of one or two other contributors,[76] the reverential overtones are usually clear and not seldom carry the main melody.[77] Much of the chief example in this devotional area, the most beautifully done, are some of the addresses of the Rector al-Maraghi: the language brilliant, the spirit deep, the feeling limpid and sincere.[78]

To return to the editor himself, we may conclude by noting his editorial on "Fidelity in Scholarship."[79] This is a forceful essay on the intellectual honesty required of a scholar, with illustrative stories of both honesty and dishonesty from Islamic history. It demands a punctilious faithfulness in reporting, a total lack of pretence in a ready admission of ignorance, a willingness to con-

---

[72] E.g., 1:14-23.

[73] One exception: the rather laboured defence in the series on *Sūrat al-Mulk* (2:15ff.) of the arrangement of chapters and verses. Also to be excepted are the several studies *about* Qur'ān studies and about the Qur'ān, not in exegesis of it.

[74] 8:84.

[75] See also 'Alī Manṣūr, "Evidence in the Natural World for the Existence of the Great Creator," 15:265-67, which is ostensibly the teleological argument again, but is unusually naïve logically. The reader's sense that this is less a process of argumentation than a statement of feeling is satisfied three times when the author breaks into poetry.

[76] E.g., the young and able al-Sharbāṣī, whom one can watch in the journal's pages graduating from the Azhar as a student and later joining its staff. Cf. 15:64, 128; 16:439.

[77] E.g., 16:187-89; 17:39-42. For another devotional writer, cf. 6:508-09.

[78] An example: his New Year's address at the Azhar convocation, vol. 14, prefix to no. 1, pp. a-d.

[79] 2:235-43.

fess past mistakes and to correct them, honest criticism even of the work of friends, and so on. The conclusion, significantly, relates it at once personally: since honesty among scholars is a source of a community's life and greatness, in addition to being a personal quality of the scholar himself, it is up to us, he says, to instill it in our students by pursuing it ourselves in all our studies, and by answering their questions when we do not know by frankly saying that we do not know, never putting them off with a reply that we know within ourselves to be not really adequate. Having acquired a rigorous honesty himself, the teacher should then take care that the student not get careless, and should teach him that knowledge without honesty is worse than ignorance.

We have elaborated our presentation of this position not merely for its intrinsic interest. The intellectual and emotional sincerity here evinced are indeed precious, as are the moral discernment and commitment. These virtues are rare in our modern world, and of vital practical significance for both man and society. Our purpose, however, is rather to induce the contrast between this traditional Islam and the modernist version. If one can grasp the fundamental distinction between this general attitude and that of the liberals, one has gone far towards understanding a major element in the transition that has been coming over Islam in recent times. The journal in the successive phases of its publication exemplifies the critical shift from the traditional faith to the modern ideology.

We stated above that for al-Khidr Husayn, Islam "is a true and right religion." This applies equally to the second editor, Farid Wajdi. In introducing editorially two of his fifteen years of editorship, he speaks of expounding Islam and offering arguments in its defence,[80] rather in his predecessor's fashion but with more suggestion that he regards the two as discrete. And in the very first editorial he promises to strive to make the journal now under his charge "a lighthouse of guidance, a standard for the truth, a pure source of religious science and exposition."[81] Furthermore, he once states that his intention with regard to studies to be published embraces "all that will result in awakening the religious feeling within men's souls, and in directing the human personality

[80] 6:3; 8:4. On the general tone of the latter foreword, cf. just below at ref. 83.
[81] 4:297.

towards its perfection and true happiness."[82] Moreover, his fore-word to a later volume,[83] both in the preliminary ascription of praise to God[84] and in the subsequent purport, stands out as suggestive of appreciative sensitivity on his part of an inner, personal significance of Islam. Here for once Wajdi betrays a genuine subjective feeling, not unlike that of the former editor.

Yet these are isolated instances. In general the contrast between the spirit of the two men is sharp; and the sentence cited above from the first editor is one of the very few in our analysis of his position that could be applied to the second. On virtually every other point some antithesis rather than a comparison would be in order. In his understanding of and attitude to Islam, in his conception of the function of the journal and of the need of modern Muslim society, in the spirit, form, and substance of his thought, the second editor strikes a new note.

He himself realizes this, and speaks of his predecessor's failure to reach the heart of modern man because of his old-fashioned approach.[85]

As we have said, the policy statements cited above are rather exceptional. Their stand is in danger of being submerged in the flood of protestations that the purpose of the journal is to serve Islam. "The object at which the journal is aiming (is) the service of Islam";[86] "the various studies all . . . have one object: the service of Islam";[87] and so on. This principle is repeated again and again. Wajdi indicates this purpose as also his personal ideal for himself. He remarks, for instance, "Ever since we devoted ourselves to the service of Islam. . . ."[88]

Furthermore, it is usually clear that for him Islam is an institution. It is what an idealist would call the earthly expression of Islam's transcendent reality. Islam for him is a set of ideas in men's minds, a heritage, a society. It is not a moral imperative but something tangible, an historical reality. To the first editor, there would be little meaning in "serving" Islam, since Islam is an idea

---

[82] 12:3. [83] 8:3.

[84] "Praise be to God, for guiding us to the right religion and setting us on the straight path, and bestowing on us His counsel that gives life to the heart . . . ," etc. Usually he praises God for enabling him to work hard for Islām; e.g., 6:3; 7:3; . . . 17:3.

[85] Cf. below, at ref. 187. [86] 7:3. [87] 14:3.

[88] 12:3; cf. also just above, latter part of ref. 84.

in the mind of God. It is hardly something to which to lend a helping hand in the time of its difficulties.

Sometimes Wajdi expands his conception. "The Azhar Journal has two great objectives. The first is to serve Islam. . . . The second objective is to serve the cause of religion in general" (by attacking materialist philosophy).[89] More often, he adds a social objective: "The Journal [is] devoted wholly to the service of Islam and its community";[90] "its basis is the service of Islam and its people";[91] "all the effort expended is simply for the service of Islam and the Muslims; and also for general culture."[92] However, it is not evident that the service to be rendered to the Muslims as a people is over and above or distinct from the service of rehabilitating their religion. It is presumably this latter of which the Muslim world stands "in the direst need."[93]

Where al-Khidr Husayn would have spoken of serving God, by elucidating the foundations of Islam, instilling its principles, and exhorting men to observe its teachings, Wajdi writes that the journal aims at "the service of Islam, by demonstrating the firmness of its foundations, the loftiness of its principles, the validity of its teachings."[94]

Similarly, his hopes are of spreading not Islam so much as "the excellencies of Islam, and its irrefutable arguments."[95] Virtually his entire endeavour is to convince or to reassure his public that Islam is all right. His declarations of purpose reveal his belief that they want such conviction or reassurance.

For the first editor Islam was a transcendent idea, which it is man's duty to ascertain and to follow. For the second it comes close to being an historical phenomenon which it is man's duty to defend. For Wajdi makes clear his conception of the service that Islam today requires. It is defence.

To the defence of Islam[96] all else is admittedly secondary.[97] This

---

[89] 15:3.   [90] 10:3.   [91] 17:3.   [92] 15:3.   [93] 14:3.
[94] 7:3.   [95] 6:3.

[96] *al-difāʿ ʿan al-Islām*; also, *al-difāʿ ʿan al-dīn*. Such phrases are ubiquitous in modern Arabic religious literature. Cf. also W. C. Smith, *Modern Islām in India*, Lahore, 1943, p. 92; London, "1946" (sc. 1947), p. 84.

[97] Wajdī writes of his practice of publishing proofs of the soundness and universal validity of Islam, "proofs taken from tangible things and supported by the new sociological studies. And we stand up to the doubts that some religious propagandists excite in Muslims, and refute them with a refutation that leaves them no longer standing. And *along with this* we do not neglect to publish chapters of *al-tafsīr, al-sunnah al-nabawīyah*, and articles on philos-

is reiterated and emphasized relentlessly in his annual forewords. It is recapitulated and formalized in the official regulations for the journal drawn up for a new period beginning with a later volume.[98] These in their opening paragraph, "The Objects of the Journal," proclaim as the first object the defence of Islam; with this is linked the setting forth of Islam's excellences. The second paragraph, commenting on the subjects to be published, lists first "studies that support the belief and practices of Islam."

Further, if Wajdi promises in his editorials that he will use his best endeavour in the journal to defend Islam, certainly in his abundant writings he carries out this promise. Virtually the whole of his massive output serves this one purpose. Whatever subject he touches, whether it be poetry[99] or the concern for health,[100] naval battles[101] or democracy,[102] the treatment of children[103] or George Bernard Shaw,[104] he deals with it not in and for itself but in its relation to Islam. Each is made to serve in one way or another to build a case in favour of the religion and "to ward off doubts."[105]

The point is illustrated, further, in the monthly (as distinct from annual) editorials. Al-Khidr Husayn, as we have noted, often contributed a sermonette advocating some point of individual virtue, with his rare moral discrimination and forceful sincerity. He also commented keenly on contemporary social problems,[106] with his active sensitivity as to what should be done about them. At times he uses the occasion to discuss theological matters[107] or to argue against modern heresies.[108] Wajdi uses the same form but

---

ophy, history, literature, and everything that an Islamic journal published by the Azhar must inevitably include" (9:3; emphasis ours). On another occasion, after several paragraphs on the journal's defending of Islām against doubts (quoted in part below, at ref. 120), he goes on, "and besides this, it publishes enjoyable articles on al-tafsīr and al-sunnah, undertaken by two great Azhari scholars; and other studies on philosophy, literature, history, and scholarship" (10:4).

[98] 18:93-95.

[99] 9:480-83 (this article is unsigned; but the Table of Contents and Index ascribe it to Wajdī, of whose style it is indeed characteristic).

[100] 5:404-10.   [101] 6:198-202.   [102] 10:36-38.   [103] 5:196-201.

[104] 4:720-24.

[105] This phrase occurs throughout his writings, as throughout his announcements of policy. Examples: as title, 9:498; 14:54; in the body of articles, 9:505; etc.

[106] E.g., 1:83-89, 243-48, 323-27; 3:375-82.

[107] E.g., 2:539-46, 611-18; 3:303-16.

[108] The Bahā'ī, 2:75-96. The Qādiyānī, 3:447-63; 4:5-17, 110-19. Against Farīd Wajdī, 3:7-20.

exploits it rather differently. He favours the continuity of series, delighting to display facet after facet of a chosen subject—which throughout remains, essentially, the excellence of Islam. He begins with the series entitled "The Mission of the Religion of Islam in the World," one or other aspect of which provides him with an editorial each month through three volumes.[109] This is followed by "The Spirit of Islam and the Extent of its Influence on the Soul of Man."[110] Finally, "The Life of Muhammad in the Light of Science and Philosophy" is the generic heading under which for seven years he rings the changes in his unceasing argument on the validity of the Prophet's message.[111] The point for our consideration lies in the fact that, for instance, the fifty-nine articles of this last series do not urge the reader to implement that message, to feel it binding upon himself, but simply to admire it. It is a search for applause, not for action.

Again, we have noted that he treats everything with which he deals not for its intrinsic value or interest but for its relevance to apologetics. This may be illustrated further in the attitude to science. Under the first editor's direction science hardly figures; but in so far as it does, it is presented for its inherent interest. The journal has a section on "Translations" from English, French, and German. Under al-Khidr Husayn's editorship, this is devoted in part to "articles of scientific research and modern inventions"[112] that will be useful and instructive, and will serve to keep the reader in touch with Western as well as Eastern currents of thought.[113] The subjects range from "new ways of preserving eggs,"[114] and "pearl culture in Japan,"[115] to spontaneous combustion,[116] and half a hundred more. Some articles are considerably longer, including three from the German on child psychology.[117] No need is felt to interpret philosophically or religiously the scientific information presented; it is assumed that the reader is

---

[109] From vol. 4 no. 5 (when he took over as editor) to vol. 6 no. 10, twenty-six articles in all. The first twelve of this series are published in translation in the English supplement to voll. 4-5.

[110] Fifteen articles in all, sporadically in voll. 7, 8, 9.

[111] Fifty-nine articles, voll. 10-17, vol. 13 excepted.

[112] 2:3.   [113] 4:3.   [114] 2:391.   [115] 1:331.

[116] 1:373.

[117] A series, 1:226ff. (translated and compiled by the administrative editor; the matter would appear to be one in which he shows considerable interest); 1:396-400 (second series; lege 456-60); 2:676-79.

interested, not perplexed.[118] Under Wajdi, on the other hand, scientific information is pressed into service in so far as, by judicious selection, it can serve to bolster the case for Islam.

So much defence implies an enemy against which to defend. The enemy is clear: the drift away from religion. To judge from these writings, one would get the firm impression that the educated Muslim world is abandoning Islam *en masse*, that the Azhar is one of the few outposts still standing against the onrush of secularism.

As we have already noted, Wajdi calls for resistance to

the materialist school of thought, which has spread, with the speed of fire in dry twigs, among the classes who study the natural sciences, and has fixed firmly in their minds that whatever spiritual manifestations there may be apart from these physical sciences are illusions, on which one must not rely—are, in fact, superstitions of which the mind ought to be cleansed.[119]

Again:

We have realized ever since we first concerned ourselves with speaking of Islam that the chief obstacle in its way are the doubts expressed by those who hastily acquire a tinge of learning   They hold in their terror that these doubts confute the teaching of religion and shake it to its foundations, and that when in modern civilized lands it was exposed to such assault, many forward spirits gave themselves over to these doubts.

Such scepticism is today sowing its seeds among us . . . and doing to us what it has done to others, on the illusion that to get rid of faith is a precondition of cultural advance and intellectual freedom. . . .

The Azhar Journal therefore spends its effort in tracking down this scepticism that has worked its way into learning, and in analysing it, exposing its strong and weak points, and showing that it does not militate against Islam or touch its essence, but confirms and supports it and makes it the universal religion from which there is no deviating;[120]

and similarly, time and again.

These passages illustrate also his equating irreligion with philosophic materialism, a recurrent motif throughout his contributions.[121] He does not leave his adversaries' position undefined;

[118] Cf. the box on the place of science in the journal, 2:384.
[119] 9:419.
[120] 10:3. Many similar quotations could be adduced. 9:3-4; 14:3; etc.
[121] Actually, there are two types of assault that his writings are seen to be

there are repeatedly descriptions of what it is that he is combating.
For example:

The materialists are at great pains to establish that the universe is
material and that man is material; matter with them being first and
last, form and substance, that from which all that is arose and to which
it will return. In their view, what is said about a creator for the universe and a spirit for man, and a life after this life, is all airy nonsense
—something engendered by the imagination, in which men came to
believe, and handed down century after century until they took to
regarding it as part of the natural order; when in fact it is nothing
but the product of the exuberant, boundless imaginative faculty.[122]

At other times he quotes directly from the (Western) sources
that he is striving to refute, placing fairly before his readers the
antagonist's statement and then replying to the points one by one.
An example is his article entitled "Scientific Doubts about Religions,"[123] which treats a book called *The Irreligion of the Future*
by "the great [*sic*] French philosopher Guyo" (*sic: lege* Guyau.)[124]
An example of "refuting doubts about Islam"[125] is his rebuttal
of allusions to a supposedly aggressive belligerence in Islam, re-
produced from a petulant chapter on the Muslim bloc in a Western geographical text.[126] These and many other instances of the

---

resisting: this against religion in general, and criticism specifically of Islām.
Articles to meet the latter are considerably less numerous, though they form
a group in themselves sizeable enough. The distinction between the two is not
made vivid. Nor is it functionally important, since the attack on Islām,
whether missionary, orientalist, or general, is evidently considered as having
essentially the same effect as the other: namely, an increased atheism, a cynical
and worldly unbelief. Cf. above, ref. 17. On Christian missions, cf. 10:154,
where the sentiment is expressed that adult Muslims are impervious to evan-
gelism; more eloquent is the silence on the subject that the editor elsewhere
observes. Similarly there is a lone discussion of communism (11:39-42, 98-101);
its criticism is social rather than philosophic.

[122] 9:635.

[123] 9:505-09.

[124] Jean-Marie Guyau (1854-88), *L'Irreligion de l'avenir*, Paris, 1887.

[125] This phrase is used as title for a number of articles; including the one
here noted, 6:337-43.

[126] Isaiah Bowman, *The New World: Problems in Political Geography*. The
edition accessible to the present writer is the 4th, New York and Chicago,
1928. Chapter III, "The Mohammedan World," uses such language as "the
Moslem menace," "appalling" and "ruthlessness" (p. 126); reassures its readers
against the "disaster to modern civilization" (p. 125) that the Muslims might
be expected to perpetrate, and discusses how the West may best control their
countries.

sort indicate that the function of the journal, in both types of case, is to deal with doubts on Islam existing in Arab minds but coming from the reading of Western books.

The defence is against modern materialistic scepticism, and the instruments of defence are sound learning and sound philosophy to prove that Islam is indeed a good thing. The method used in combatting modern intellectual doubt must itself be intellectually modern, he avers.[127] This demands, for one thing, the philosophic approach.[128] He is convinced that the fight must be conducted "with the very weapons"[129] on which the opponents rely: the pronouncements of science.[130]

So far so good. Yet this reliance on selections from Western learning to defend Islam has its dangers. One is that only those aspects of Islam be considered to which the West's secular intellectualities are relevant; and it is at least questionable whether the heart of religion will not be missed in this process. As we shall see as we proceed, this seems indeed to have happened. It may be asked whether Wajdi has not in fact sold out to the West's materialism in the very act of supposedly defending Islam against it. The other danger, also more demonstrable as we proceed, is that of deliberately choosing evidence with a view to substantiating an already held thesis, rather than following where the evidence itself may lead.[131]

[127] The journal must "serve Islam in a way suitable to contemporary ideology" (14:3); again, its object is "to serve Islam in a way that is in harmony with the culture of the present age, and acceptable to the intellectual climate of modern man" (15:3).

[128] He more than once defends himself against criticism for introducing so many philosophic articles into the journal: "Is it desired that we should leave hearts exposed to the invasion and conquest of secular philosophy, while we devote all our energies to the purely religious side? . . . Philosophies today have a dominion over men's minds that they have not had in any other age" (17:4).

[129] 14:3.

[130] "Ever since we devoted ourselves to the service of Islām, it has been our custom to familiarize ourselves with the natural sciences and with Western philosophy, realizing that the relation between our culture and that of the West imposes on us the duty of understanding the stages upon which the latter culture has entered . . . ; without hesitating to cite the scepticism of its materialists and to bring them to the bar of basic science and the established propositions of sound philosophy. This method has, in fact, succeeded in directing attention to the lofty wisdom that is in Islām, and the unshakeable inviolability" (12:3; cf. 9:3-4 for a paragraph in similar vein).

[131] E.g., 4:297; 11:3.

The content of Wajdi's apologetic, against materialism and against objections to Islam, is, we have already suggested, particular to himself. He has his own views on these matters, and his own special interests, which he has developed at great length. Other writers in the Arab world and elsewhere present different arguments; here we confess that he cannot be taken as widely representative. However, on the method of defence he remains typical, and his treatment significantly reveals the general tendency of modernism. We may, therefore, profitably make certain further observations on trends that have a validity and importance far beyond his individual ideas.

First, in all his defence, the relation to the West is intimate. Half the journal's articles are written under the shadow of the West, answering criticisms that Westerners, or Muslims under their influence, have levelled against the religion on the theoretical plane, or pondering practical problems that the West, or so it is alleged, engenders. Yet a separate category also is constituted by articles in series, and for a time virtually an explicit department,[132] devoted specifically to Islam and the modern West. The bulk of this material is by Wajdi and much of it is cast in the form characteristic of his writings: translations from the French, with comments.

Virtually all the contributions fall into one of two well-defined but disparate groups. There are those setting forth instances of good opinion of Islam in the West, and those pointing out and replying to criticisms. The one group holds up Western approval for admiration, and uses it to answer indigenous critics or doubters. For instance, Muslims who are slack about the ritual prayer are confronted with a foreign acknowledgement of its value.[133] The second type, on the other hand, holds up for ridicule or rebuttal Westerners', particularly Orientalists', depreciation; the point, often explicit, being that they do not understand Islam.

On the laudatory side, the articles include testimony of "the

[132] "The World's Views on Islam and the Muslims" (the wording of the heading varies slightly), 9:324, 554; 10:76 etc.; 11:123 etc. The series includes one note (10:792-93) on a Shanghai newspaper report of Chiang Kai-shek's testifying to Muslims' valour and patriotism. Otherwise the entire department is concerned with European (occasionally American) "views," as are all the other articles of this type. The theosophist Annie Besant is also called a "leader of thought in Europe" (Wajdī, 7:644; 8:290).

[133] 3:253-54.

great philosophers and historians"[134] of the West, as well as stray newspaper references[135] and extracts from other minor sources[136] alluding to Muhammad,[137] woman's status in Islam,[138] Muslim law,[139] the early Muslim conquests,[140] the Azhar,[141] etc. There are also a few notices of the spread of Islamic studies in Europe.[142]

The protests have targets ranging from an article in the academic *Encyclopaedia of Islam*[143] and a judgement passed on Islam by H. G. Wells[144] to casual remarks in, for instance, a London daily newspaper.[145]

It is important to note how strikingly the spirit of the defence is Westernizing. Islam is defended not only against Western disparagement. It is defended also by means of Western approval. Herein is betrayed again the ambivalence to European civilization. It comes into focus in the chance fact that H. G. Wells' judgement of Islam is held up for rebuttal, as we have seen; whereas from the same writer, same book, a quotation is elsewhere given as a tribute to the religion.[146] Again, in the defence against criticism the criteria employed are often Western.

This simultaneous repulsion and attraction in relation to the modern West is profound, and can be seen to underlie and to explain much of Wajdī's writing. It indicates that he and his readers are sufficiently involved in a community lack of self-confidence that the good opinion of Europe is a matter of deep concern to them.[147] Yet that very lack of self-confidence is nourished by, or even stems from, an apparent adoption of the standards on which Europe supposedly forms opinions. At a more basic level, it stems from an inability to form, and live by, genuine value judgements of one's own.

[134] This phrase occurs in the title of more than one of Wajdī's contributions; e.g., 4:531, 720; cf. 5:259 It is used pretty indiscriminately.

[135] E.g., 10:154-58, 236-40.   [136] E.g., individual letters: 10:234-36.

[137] E.g., 8:95-98.   [138] E.g., 8:290-93.   [139] E.g., 13:420-22.

[140] 9:423-25.   [141] 9:407-12.

[142] In post-war Arabic writing, it is the rapid growth of Near and Middle Eastern and Islamic studies in America that is advertised.

[143] 5:556-66, 639-46.   [144] 10:305-10.   [145] 10:630.

[146] Cf. 10:305-10 with 1:610-12. The latter is before Wajdī's time, but we think the point is not invalidated.

[147] Again one is reminded of the individual personality whom somewhat comparable conditions have produced in great numbers in the West: athirst for outsiders' approval, defiant of their rejections, he is mercilessly buffeted by life in so far as his self-esteem is dependent on the opinion of others.

Something similar obtains in the philosophic realm. There it is less overt; but more far-reaching, for all its subtlety. Wajdi is proudly explicit that he uses Western science itself, and the evidence of the senses, to confute the materialists.[148] It is doubtful, however, whether it is to the heart of the faith that these premisses and this logic lead. By calling in the aid of psychic research, hypnotism, and the like,[149] and some fundamental physics,[150] he is able to sustain, to his own and presumably his readers' satisfaction, the view that the objective universe consists of spirit as well as of matter. It may be inferred that by and large his readers are not of that group who would question whether the evidence, even if valid, does indeed prove this contention, and not rather the alternative one, now widespread among scientists, that the matter of which the objective universe consists is more ethereal or complex than was once supposed.

For example, he quotes from Le Bon facts and theories on the non-solidity and kinesis of matter,[151] without realizing that this dynamic etherealization of matter makes it more, not less, capable of sustaining the universe without the help of an extrinsic second principle. This is, in fact, the conclusion that Le Bon himself

[148] Cf. above, at ref. 130. The titles of many of Wajdi's articles include the same point; e.g., "Scientific Doubts about the Religions: Their Analysis and Refutation by the Method of Science Itself" (19:505); "Tangibly Proving the Human Spirit: New Demonstrations Based on the Requirements of the Scientific Method" (series 11:625ff.-12); etc. In the body of his writings, *passim*; e.g., 14:290, opening paragraph.

[149] References for this luxuriate. Spiritualist phenomena figure in much of his prolific writing on nature and science generally (an example: his series on "The Battlefield of the Two Philosophies," voll. 9, 10, 13-15). The following are examples of articles devoted specifically to the psychic: 7:205-09; 8:105-14; 9:193-99; 9:345-50; 11:625-29 and 12:285-87, 375-77, 433-37; etc. Note his article, "The 'Isawī Group [of dervishes] in Europe, performing Preternatural Feats to which Investigators Attribute a Spiritual Cause," 9:117-20, as an interesting example of traditional Islamic wonder-working now tied in with Western science.

[150] E.g., 4:649-52; largely a translation from a 1907 lecture on the planetary theory of the atom by Gustave le Bon (whom he astonishingly calls "the discoverer of this important matter"—4:649). Wajdi's repetitiousness, apparently unconscious, is brought out by his giving ten years later (14:348-52) a fresh translation of the same lectures, with new comments. In the latter instance he also quotes Henri Poincaré on the supersession of materialism now that "it is established that matter is not a solid body" (14:348). Cf. also his article, "What Ether Is," 8:46-48.

[151] See the preceding ref.

draws[152] and for which Wajdi has to take him to task.[153] Actually, what Wajdi is unwittingly accomplishing is the overthrow of naive materialism by means of a more refined and modern materialism.

This on the physical plane is less important than its counterpart on the human. Here he makes, for instance, great play with the scientific establishment of the fact that man has a subconscious mind. He calls this "higher than the ordinary mind."[154] That it is "higher," he repeats,[155] though many of his illustrations are from morbid[156] psychology. He goes on to quote one Gustave Geley on the subconscious as the explanation of genius, intuition, and artistic and literary creation,[157] and concludes that the new scientific studies—of delirium, schizophrenia, etc.—are uncovering "a reality of the utmost splendour,"[158] namely that man has a spirit independent of the body and belonging to "a higher world."[159]

The splendour might surely be questioned, and the evaluation that the "spirit" evinced is "higher." Those directly acquainted with the Western material might find it rather pitiful that Wajdi should be resting his case for the divine in human affairs on phenomena that his source calls instances of "a throng of troubles"[160] in the mind. Again, the Gustave Geley from whom

[152] " 'These cosmic forces were brought into existence by existence (the universe: al-wujūd) itself, which is the spirit of everything within it, and is sustained by the forces that are the cause of the existence of the world and things in it. Each of these things that exist is a microcosm of marvellous complexity, sustained by forces that were unknown, forces whose magnitude exceeds to an indefinite degree any known in the past' " (14:352).

[153] Wajdī inserts a parenthetic question mark after the phrase al-wujūd nafsuh in the preceding; and then adds two concluding paragraphs of comment protesting against this "strange" and "meaningless" position (loc. cit.). Cf. also his rejection of Büchner's vitalist interpretation of matter, 14:518-20.

[154] 14:82, line 15.   [155] Ibid., line 18.   [156] E.g., see 14:85.

[157] 14:82-85; the same point is often made elsewhere, quoting various other Westerners, e.g., 15:53.

[158] 14:85.   [159] Loc. cit.

[160] Wajdī, 14:140, in an article on the subconscious memory, cites the account by T. Flournoy (1854-1920) of an alleged Sanskrit-speaking girl as an instance proving "the permanence of spirit" (the subtitle of the article, 14:139). Flournoy's own account is as follows: "Au point de vue physiologique, on a vu que Mlle. Smith, comme sans doute tous les médiums, présente pendant ses visions et somnambulismes une foule de troubles de la motilité et de la sensibilité, dont elle paraît tout à fait indemne dans son état normal" —T. Flournoy, Des Indes à la planète Mars, Paris, 1890, p. 412. Similarly, Flournoy calls mediumship one of "les affections fonctionelles du système nerveux" (loc. cit.).

he repeatedly quotes[161] was a French spiritualist whose original works[162] set forth a philosophy that is a kind of scientific idealist rationalism. It would probably not be unfair to call him an atheist. Certainly in any meaning of terms that Wajdi could accept he would have to be classed as an atheist. In fact, many Westerners, and presumably some Westernized circles in Islam other than those whom the journal reaches, feel quite able to accommodate the adduced phenomena within an irreligious ideology. Paralleling the development in physics, their neo-materialism is, by these advances, actually the better armed to interpret the world.

The purpose here is not to dispute the philosophic validity of Wajdi's arguments. The point, rather, is to draw attention to the fact that, whatever their philosophic validity, the moral, aesthetic, and numinous content is small. The amorality of psychic phenomena is striking, both in general and of those that crowd the pages of this editor's writing. The journal evidently catered to a group other than those who feel that a religion reduced to supporting itself on hypnotism and spiritism is in a parlous state.

Nor are this triviality and axiological tenuousness confined to his treatment of science. So keen is Wajdi to satisfy doubters by using Western criteria that, paradoxically, a marked irreligiousness permeates almost all his defence.

An important aspect of this is his contention, enormously typical of the modern Arab intellectual scene, that Islam first taught what Europe now teaches. "See, then," he concludes one of his earliest articles in a vein that runs through almost to the latest, "how philosophy in the twentieth century comes establishing what the Qur'an laid down some fourteen centuries ago."[163] Again, he writes about "democracy, whose edifice Muslims pride themselves on their religion's having first set up in the world."[164] He states that "European scholars have discovered that our forefathers had been working on the evolution theory, the latest of all scientific theories."[165] And so on. Many of his monthly editorials, more or less explicitly, are designed to show that the teachings nowadays

[161] E.g., 14:35-39, 82-85, 140-41.

[162] The following was available to us: G. Geley, *From the Unconscious to the Conscious*, trans. by S. De Brath, New York & London, 1920. This is a version of the French work cited often by Wajdi; cf. his articles noted in the preceding ref.

[163] 4:411.   [164] 10:36.

[165] Supplement to vol. 14, no. 8, p. 3.

esteemed in the West and by Westerners were long since pro-
claimed by Islam. The subtitle of one illustrates this: "Islam Was
Ahead of its Time, Establishing for its People Principles which
They had not Attained in the Course of their Development, and
Some of which the Entire World Attained only after many Cen-
turies."[166]

Apologetic of this sort, common enough in all religions, would
hardly call for comment[167] were it supplemented by positive teaching. The significance of its place in Wajdi's writing has to do with
the fact that there is so little else. In his endeavour to lift Islam to
the standard that the West accepts, he forgets that unless Islam
not only reaches but surpasses such a standard, unless the religion
is not only as good as but better than secular requirements, there
is presumably no case against those who abandon Islam and go
over to Westernism. If Islam originally taught the essence of
modernity, then presumably they are not really abandoning Islam
after all. In extolling Islam's achievements, Wajdi does on occasion
speak apologetically of its success in bringing men near to God,
and in inspiring them morally.[168] Such occasions are, however,
noticeably rare; they are almost overborne by the emphasis on
social success, scholarly attainments, and material progress.

If Islam centuries ago taught the moral, social, and even scientific principles with which only recently Europe has caught up,
if it established on earth in its golden age a good society, then
fairness demands that it be admired as an historical phenomenon.
And this is approximately the position that Wajdi in fact puts
forward. The Islam that emerges from a close study of his articles
is indeed primarily an historical phenomenon, chiefly to be seen
in the fairly distant past, and deserving to be admired. Unlike
al-Khidr Husayn, who constantly measures existing conditions
against the high ideal before his eyes, Wajdi compares them to
Islam of the first centuries.[169] Accordingly, there is his great interest in Muslim history, and his oft-repeated sentiment that
"Islam produced in the world a transformation such as mankind
has not witnessed at any other stage in history."[170] (This unique-

---

[166] 15:424.

[167] Yet on the seriousness of Islamic antagonism to Europe, cf. Arthur J.
Arberry, in his Preface to his translation of Sir Muhammad Iqbal, *The
Mysteries of Selflessness*, London, 1953, pp. xiii-xvii.

[168] E.g., 5:156-61, 231-34.   [169] E.g., 14:54.   [170] 5:191.

ness of Muslim history is advanced rather glibly. This too is standard.)

Yet if all that is claimed for Islam is a past greatness—whether in its own historical concrete achievements or as a precursor of modern science and philosophy's achievements—then if one is sincere it should be accorded appropriate applause, and let gradually die out like other historical phenomena. Wajdi's writing skirts the fact that no amount of emphasizing this claim will logically do more than increase the applause. This would at most summon it back for a final curtain call.

The claim being essentially secular, the applause is due more or less equally from Muslims and non-Muslims. Wajdi realizes this. For instance, he speaks of a small English-language appendix to the journal, at a time when it was publishing *inter alia* his own articles, as "spreading the excellences of Islam among Muslims and non-Muslims"[171] indiscriminately. And practically all his writings would serve equally well for either group. In a strict sense, even, such apologetic is more appropriate for non-Muslim consumption.

In fact, a fanciful case could be made out that these writings are really functioning for readers who in the most profound, most religious sense are not Muslim; rather are men who, religiously ex-Muslim, are (or want to be) proud of their heritage, and desperately need reassurance in a hostile world. They believe (or want to believe) ardently in Islam and delight to see it defended. A true Muslim, however, is not a man who believes in Islam—especially Islam in history; but one who believes in God and is committed to the revelation through His Prophet. The latter is here sufficiently admired. But commitment is missing. And God appears remarkably seldom throughout these pages.

The political and social implications of these attitudes are far-reaching. Most apparent is that profoundly emotional belief in the Islamic community that characterizes the modern Muslim "communalist" variation upon secular nationalism.

The materialism that surreptitiously colours Wajdi's presentation, as well as the pressure of European censure with its distorting effect, under which he and his readers feel themselves to be labouring, are revealed in his brief report on the visit to Cairo of 'Uthman Wu, official delegate of the Islamic Union of China: "We

[171] 6:4.

spoke with him and inquired about the conditions of the Chinese, and learned several valuable things from him. One was that the number of Muslim Chinese comes to fifty million as shown by the official census—which means a correction in the view of many Western writers, who estimate the number of China's Muslims at twenty million souls."[172] Among the "several valuable things," this is the only one that he deems worth mentioning.

The moral poverty of these writings is most evident in the absence of exhortation. In striking contrast to al-Khidr Husayn's constant appeal to follow ideals, his constant presentation of Islam in such a way as to incite moral striving, his constant use of the verbs "must" and "ought" and "should," the second editor makes almost no demands. The Islam that he presents is content to be admired. When he mentions moral values, it is more often to prove that Islam has them than to instigate their practice.

The point is illustrated in many articles—not least, in that ironically entitled "Islam Urges Action."[173] With a presentation of this article we may draw to a close our consideration of this writer. His discussion here too is apologetic. The opening paragraph states that it is superficial not to realize that one draws near to God not only in quietist worship but also through an activity for good; "and this is a characteristic of Islam, making it a religion of civilization, valid for all times and places and for every people." "The first Muslims," it goes on, "conquered the earth by unceasing activity; and kept it under their control by great and constant striving." There follow three pages on the outstanding achievements of these first Muslims, incited as they were to tireless activity by their religion and putting forth great effort in commerce, industry, scholarship, and other fields, so that "their scholars were the most learned scholars on earth. Their physicians were the most honoured physicians on earth. Those engaged in other fields of learning were the leaders to whom problems were referred for solution. And their craftsmen and artificers were the most gifted and most skilled of all their fellows on earth." Some modern scholars, Wajdi continues, try to explain these superb accomplishments in terms of what the Muslims borrowed from other cultures, but it was clearly Islam that gave them the impetus

[172] 14:208 (the second of the two contiguous pages so numbered). There had, in fact, been no official census.

[173] 5:311-15.

and unity. Similarly today, he ends by saying, "the conservatives and men of religion, far from preventing the new renascence, have like their predecessors of old become among its leading advocates." The conclusion is, "There is then no question but that the doubts of Islam's enemies are confuted, and their explanation of the Muslims' first florescence falls. Praise be to God."

Except for a few lines, this not atypical essay transports the reader to the golden age of the past. The object, as the conclusion shows, was to confute doubts. A great deal of this defensive writing betrays rather pitifully the intellectual insincerity of its writer; but the present essay is a sad example of the emotional insincerity inculcated in its readers. For, despite the title, it contains very little urging to action. It seeks not to instigate, but to comfort and console. The reader is left in his armchair, with a glow of warmth in his heart.

This poses the fundamental weakness of the whole modernist position. Wajdi is right that Islam urges to action. One might, then, without too great presumption be tempted to suggest that Muslim modernism is not really Islamic.

Its essential tragedy is that it has lost touch with the heart of faith.

The same kind of apologetic is amply illustrated in many articles from other hands in the latter years of the journal. They range unevenly from greater or less sincerity to less or greater sentimentality. It would be tedious to press investigation of these. We shall conclude our attempt to give an exposition of the two divergent trends by offering one final instance, exhibiting both at once. It is provided by a translator preparing material for the sporadic English supplement.[174] The difference between positive and defensive[175] preaching is again illustrated in what happens to one of al-Khidr Husayn's own articles. He has an editorial which he entitles "Kindness to Animals"[176] in which he arrays materials from the Qur'an and from the *hadith* and abundant stories from the Muslim past to prove that Islam requires and used successfully to inculcate a lively consideration for animals; and pleads for it

[174] Voll. 2 to 14 carry sporadically an "English Supplement," of a few pages, appended at the end of some of the monthly issues. The pagination is rather erratic.
[175] *al-duʿā* and *al-difāʿ*.
[176] 3:83-91.

now. The English version[177] is a plea less for animals than for Islam. It quietly changes the title to "Islam and Kindness to Animals." And while most of the translation is straightforward enough, the following comparison from the concluding paragraphs is revealing:[178]

ARABIC ORIGINAL

The heart bleeds in sorrow that societies for kindness to animals have been founded in Europe for about a hundred years and the appeal for merciful treatment of animals is louder there than in Muslim countries. So much so, that many of our young men and the common people, who judge between religions by the behaviour of their adherents, suppose that Islam has not given attention to the duty of treating animals with compassion, and that it is Europe to whom the credit goes for appealing for this compassion.

The Royal Society for Kindness to Animals in England was founded in 1824; and it is a matter of shame that that society should have a branch in a Muslim city like Cairo but that no group of Muslims has undertaken the same sort of task—when the true religion awakened in the hearts of their predecessors the emotion of mercifulness to animals 1350 years ago.

ENGLISH TRANSLATION

It is significant that societies of prevention of cruelties to animals were founded in Europe a little over a century. Many ignorant people who are wont to judge religions rather by the conduct of those who profess it than by the intrinsic value of its precepts, have deemed Islam oblivious of the claims of animals to kindness and wrongly accord the honour to Europe for the institution of those humane codes. Suffice it to say that the first society of prevention of cruelty to animals was founded in England in 1824 while Islam has urged a kind and merciful treatment of animals thirteen and a half centuries ago.

There has apparently been a widespread inability to see the difference between these two; or, if one has seen it, a feeling that

[177] Supplement to vol. 3, nos. 7 and 8. It could perhaps be argued that, since it was to appear in English, the translation is addressed primarily to non-Muslims and therefore the moral exhortation might be dropped legitimately (cf. also the next ref.). This would obviate the charge of emotional insincerity, leaving only intellectual. However, the English version of this piece is so thoroughly typical in spirit of a vast amount of literature in Arabic written by and for Muslims, that such an argument is really not at all cogent. Again, our point in reproducing this here is not at all to cavil at this particular item, but to illustrate by it an extremely common characteristic of "modernism."

[178] Arabic, 3:91; English, Supplement to vol. 3 no. 8, p. 31. Another example of similar treatment is in the English version (Supplement to vol. 3, nos. 5-6) of

the defensive version is to be preferred. Any such inability, any such preference, is surely an important explanation for much of the difficulty into which the modern Muslim world has fallen. Our extended treatment of the modernist position has been proffered not simply as a perhaps interesting piece of literary criticism; but rather because it illuminates, we believe, a great deal of Arab behaviour and frustration, in fields from national development to the crises of international affairs.

Indeed, the appalling price always exacted by a loss of intellectual and emotional integrity ramifies from this type of Islamic modernism into religious, intellectual, and practical life. The sorrow of much Arab and other Muslim modernity is the extent to which that loss, of which the analysis of one illustration has here been attempted, colours the whole intellectual and emotional climate of sophisticated society.

Material written, even explicitly, as apologetic may also or instead serve some other function. The history of Islam, Christianity, and other religions gives evidence suggesting that apologetic has an inherent tendency to transform itself into dogma. What begins as defence, even insincere, may end as idealism. Articles in the journal that are designed to honour or to defend Islam by showing that it has certain virtues, certainly by some readers may be taken rather as honouring those virtues. And by praising Islam's classical history, while some readers may only be made comfortable, others may be incited to emulation.

Secondly, even if the apologetic serves only the function for which it is intended, it may, of course, be supplemented from other sources. Muslim leaders might, from many of the writings here considered, derive only reassurance and "the warding off of doubts." Yet the moral discernment and dynamic, the sensing of the holy and the experience of communion, that Islam has traditionally offered and without which a religion is hardly significant and certainly not complete, they might be deriving from other literature or, most appropriately, from worship.

The point here is simply that the literature here studied in itself largely lacks these other qualities. And in this it is representative.

---

al-Khiḍr Ḥusayn, "Just Judging in Islam" (2:5-14); where the concluding sentence, which applies the moral to the present day, is omitted.

By its emphases and methods it suggests that it may be catering for at least some readers who have themselves lost contact with those values, and are in consequence bewildered and afraid, almost cringing before or driven by hatred of a disdainful alien civilization, and beset by doubt lest the one thing that they have on which to rely be also somehow failing. In their apprehension they would buttress their refuge by ascribing to it not values in which they themselves believe but those, as best they can estimate them, of their critics and adversaries—until this unconscious insincerity undermines their own values and they are left not really knowing in what they themselves believe, or no longer really believing in anything. And if they cling for salvation to a sentimentalized version of their erstwhile religion, they are at heart almost *mushrikūn*: revering Islam in history along with, or even instead of, God.

There would surely seem more to admire in, more to hope from, a religion that produces a man of the moral stature of the first editor, than one that is defended with the forensic skill of the second.

It seems to us,[179] then, that the "modernist" position of Islam

[179] Also to Gibb; cf. the by now almost famous clause with which he concludes his chapter on Law and Society: ". . . the intellectual confusions and the paralyzing romanticism which cloud the minds of the modernists of today" (*op. cit.*, p. 105; cf. p. 106). Cf. also the next ref. Cf. further the significant article, ably expressing an assessment of the situation that would be accepted by most outside observers, Joseph G. Harrison, "Middle East Instability," *Middle Eastern Affairs*, New York, 5:73-80 (1954); e.g., pp. 76f. ". . . While it takes no great degree of insight to recognize that the Middle East today is an area in which the former way of life is falling apart without a satisfactory substitute having yet made its appearance, it is more difficult to draw positive conclusions as to the cause of this deterioration. Perhaps all that can be said in a limited amount of space is that it has become abundantly apparent that the intellectual foundations of Arab life have been found almost wholly wanting in this period of grave crisis. Faced with the necessity of quickly and decisively evolving a new social, economic and political pattern, the educated classes in the Middle East have so far shown themselves almost totally inadequate to the task. Accustomed to believe that their way of life was inherently superior to that of any other religious or racial group, they have been unable to grasp the fact that this way of life has failed them. . . . Refusing to acknowledge where they themselves have failed, they have fallen into the pitfall of blaming others, in this case the West." This article was reprinted under the title "The Riddle of Arab Unrest" in *The Christian Science Monitor*, Boston, April 29, 1954, the author being Overseas News Editor of that paper.

has developed severe weaknesses in comparison with the classical tradition. The latter preserves a dignity and nobility that are surely of the utmost significance, and that cannot be lost without disaster to society. However, it would be unrealistic not to recognize that its position too in the modern world is characterized by a fundamental weakness of serious import. This is its failure adequately to relate itself to modernity. It does not itself effectively grasp modern problems; nor is it able to communicate, to get itself across to those who do. The very weakness of modernism is itself an indication of the failure of classicism to make intelligible or accessible to modern minds and hearts the inner reality of the faith.

It is profoundly true that the problems of the Muslim world cannot be adequately met unless men have an intellectual honesty, self-critical humility, and some kind of effective faith. Yet it is also true that they cannot be solved unless men are aware of what the problems are. Our study here would suggest that Gibb is right at least for the Arab world in stating that "the future of Islam rests where it has rested in the past"—on the orthodox *'ulama'*.[180] But as he goes on to say, they have yet to come to grips with the modern world.

The first editor and his group themselves partially sensed this failure to communicate with modern men. Their insistence that the drift from religion is due to a lack of awareness of what true religion really means, is in a sense valid—but in a sense much more profound than they themselves realize. They have no inkling of the real gulf that separates their exposition from modern mentality and modern life. Al-Khidr Husayn's firm idealist persuasion is both his strength, as we have seen, and his weakness. The weakness has to do with the fact that, his own conviction being so positive and clear, he is seriously out of touch with those who do not share it.[181] He expresses the point himself—referring to an accusation that the community's material backwardness is due to the religion—using terminology that is meant to be rhetorical, but is in fact revealing: "I do not know how anyone can imagine" such

---

[180] *Op. cit.*, p. 122.

[181] Even, not being able to conceive that anyone who really apprehends it departs from true (orthoprax) Islām except from a base motive, he is occasionally led to insinuations against opponents. An example: 3:4-6. This article is below the usual humane and high moral level of this writer.

things.[182] It is true that he does not know. He cannot conceive what it is that the modernizers have in mind, nor grasp their point of view. He reiterates his certitude that ignorance is the cause of men's belittling or deserting Islam.[183] This may be true in the platonic sense. The problem is that modern men are not platonists. He evinces no recognition that the truth that he so clearly sees may need restating in modern terms; the steps of his arguments are not so much in question as the old logic itself.

His writings can hardly function for men who use quite different categories of thought, who unconsciously attach different meanings to the same words. There is what might be mistaken for almost a touch of complacency in his assurance that the spread of (classical) knowledge is the answer to the drift away from religion: "If the authorities take good care of religious instruction throughout the schools; if the *'ulama'* sharpen their pens in defence of the *shari'ah* against those who attack and misrepresent it; if fathers follow God's guidance and preserve their children from schools established to shut them off from the right way;"[184] all will be well. In investigating the Baha'i heresy he feels that it would get nowhere if religious instruction in schools were compulsory.[185]

To list as the *'ulama'* 's prime duty the setting forth of the basic tenets and ordinances of Islam convincingly[186] is really to beg the question. For the problem is how to do this. The entire journal bears its testimony to the need in which men today are floundering: need for leadership, need for a way of life and an attitude to life that will satisfy; specifically, the need for an interpretation of Islam that can be embraced. This kind of writing hardly recognizes that need in all its profundity, nor begins to grasp how vast a transformation is required in the forms and paraphernalia of religion if it is to cross effectively the appalling chasm that separates modern man from it today.

He does not cater to nor at all envisage that epitome of the contemporary religious problem, the modern man who wants to believe but cannot.

[182] 1:247.
[183] E.g., in his careful discussion, "Turning Away from Religion: its Causes, its Results, and its Cure," vol. 1, no. 2, pp. 3-9 (*sic; lege* 83-89. Cf. footnote to the page of errata following 1:160); and elsewhere frequently.
[184] 1:89 (on pagination, cf. the preceding ref.).
[185] 1:369-70 (first series).
[186] 1:88 (on pagination, cf. ref. 183 just above).

The remark levelled at al-Khidr by his successor in the editorial chair shows how large is the group who fail to appreciate what the former is driving at. Wajdi in a late volume looks back over the journal's history and says that when it first appeared it was heartily welcomed by the Muslim world "even though" it was confined to the traditional religious pattern. It did not, in its first period, he avers, "plunge into that cultured scepticism, borne of caustic modern knowledge, that has found its way into men's hearts"; though "the readers were aware of the pressing need."[187] The accusation is not without justice. And apparently the circulation of the journal did double soon after the new editor took charge;[188] by 1937 he was able to claim that the journal had "reached a degree of circulation never before attained by any monthly journal in the East."[189] Even though he may have less to offer it, he is not wrong in thinking that he is more closely attuned to the new age.

Whenever the classical group deals, as it often does, with religious questions nowadays in dispute, these are given serious and sincere consideration. Nonetheless, while the orthodox Islamic position is ably expounded, an inability to appreciate the questioning modernist's approach is apparent.[190] We have earlier cited a presentation of the teleological argument for God that is striking for the reverential quality and sensitive perception of its overtones.[191] This, however, goes with an intellectual argument that has long since been answered.[192]

A similar dichotomy prevails through much of this writing: between an excellence on the emotional, aesthetic, and moral side on the one hand, and on the other an inadequacy from the point of view of those of the journal's readers who are familiar with the modern world. The inadequacy, indeed, is both intellectual and social.

For example, one of the Azhar scholars, in an article[193] on the

[187] 18:3.   [188] Cf. 18:3-4.   [189] 8:3.

[190] E.g., al-Dijwī, 1:14, opening paragraphs; and 1:43-53.

[191] Above, at ref. 72.

[192] Through this, and many more of the numerous articles contending that nature is marvellous and therefore is created by God, one hears the persistent ticking of Paley's watch.

[193] 1:116-21. The article's subtitle, "It is the Effective Remedy for the Worst Ills of Human Society," and the conclusion (1:121, last paragraph) read as apologetics. Yet the function otherwise is to argue for the zakāh so that it will be practised and its benefits enjoyed, rather than to vindicate it theo-

Islamic alms tax, *zakah*, mentions the institution as such only rather casually; the thesis is addressed almost entirely directly (in the second person) to those who have wealth, and is a vigorous plea for generosity, as essential to both individual and social well-being. There is an unusually accurate sensitivity to the plight of the poor, for whom the writer exhibits a genuine and immediate concern. Though economic assistance is deemed the chief it is not the only point at which for him social solidarity is requisite. Brotherhood and understanding amongst men are in themselves effectively urged. This makes much better reading than the ubiquitous attempts to prove that *zakah* solves all modern problems of economic justice. Nonetheless, that there are rich and poor, and a great gulf fixed between them, is accepted as presumably inevitable and even as ordained of God. Socialist-minded readers, therefore, would dismiss the article as worthless or reactionary; readers sensitive to a need for both human sympathy and economic reorganization would admire its power in the one regard but miss modernity in the other. There is simply no awareness that modern applied science has revolutionized the possibilities before human society in this respect, entirely transmuting the objective situation from what it was when the classical version of Islam was formed. Even less is there any wrestling with the theological and legal problem that this fact involves. Those who know that the modern world is fundamentally new are left perplexed and without guidance.

Furthermore, the emotional vigour and sincerity and the devotion to envisioned ideals of these writers operate, of course, also in their conservativisms. Here, too, their defence is not sentimental but dynamic.[194]

---

retically. (There is also, in passing, a concern lest poverty lead to "the ugly demon of bolshevism," 1:118).

[194] This comes out, for instance, in an anonymous denunciation ("A Book that Rejects God's Revelation," 1:598-606) of a proposal to reform the legal status of women. Apparently a book on this subject, by a lower graduate of the famous Zaytūnah Mosque, Tunis, attracted some favourable attention in both Tunis and Cairo, though condemned by the orthodox. Its thesis was that a distinction should be made between the nucleus of the Islamic revelation, that for the purpose of which it came, on the one hand, and on the other the less central parts of historical Islām that show the influence of conditions of the Prophet's time and that can be altered with temporal development. It would put monotheism and high morals in the former category; but polygamy, discrimination in women's inheritance, and such in

But we need not belabour the point. It is well known, in the Muslim world as elsewhere, that the traditional religionists have lost the power to speak intelligibly and convincingly to or about the modern world.[195]

The Ikhwan

The reaction to attack is visible also in the new activist movements, chiefly the Ikhwan al-Muslimun ("Muslim Brethren," The Muslim Brotherhood).[196] It does not constitute the whole explanation of these, but contributes a very significant part. To regard the Ikhwan as purely reactionary would, in our judgement, be false. For there is at work in it also a praiseworthy constructive endeavour to build a modern society on a basis of justice and humanity, as an extrapolation from the best values that have been enshrined in the tradition from the past. It represents in part a determination to sweep aside the degeneration into which Arab society has fallen, the essentially unprincipled social opportunism interlaced with individual corruption; to get back to a basis for society of accepted moral standards and integrated vision, and to go forward to a programme of active implementation of popular goals by an effectively organized corps of disciplined and devoted idealists. It represents in part a determination to sweep aside the

---

the latter. It states that this second division " 'cannot even be considered a part of Islām' " (1:601, quoting the book). Islām " 'in its essence is aiming at complete justice and the spirit of what is supremely right' " (1:602, *id.*), and accordingly should accept monogamy and the principle of social equality of the sexes now that the time for these is ripe.

This position is rigorously rejected. It is rejected partly on the basis of indignation at one man's discarding Islamic ordinances on subjective grounds; and partly, of course, because the writer's fervid feeling is that the proposed reform would not be for the better. "The author," he writes, refusing the principle of conscience, "has invented this opinion, to use it as a ground for rejecting every injunction in Islām . . . that does not suit his taste" (1:602). (Cf. below, chap. 4, ref. 24.) There is also a statement emphasizing how the orthodox practice is good and right.

[195] Cf. Gibb, *op. cit.*, p. 122.

[196] For a very full bibliography on this movement, see the master's thesis of H. A. Nashshābah (ref. 2, chap. 2 above). To it (1955) should now be added the English translation, Beirut, 1956 (not yet available to the present writer) of Isḥāq Mūsà al-Ḥusaynī's Arabic study there listed; also, Werner Caskel, "Western Impact and Islamic Civilization," in Gustave E. von Grunebaum, ed., *Unity and Variety in Muslim Civilization*, Chicago, 1955, pp. 335-348. A forthcoming doctoral dissertation of R. Mitchell, to be submitted to Princeton University, will presumably supersede other studies.

inactive reverence for an irrelevant, static, purely transcendental ideal; and to transform Islam from the sentimental enthusiasm of purely inert admirers or the antiquated preserve of professional traditionalists tied in thought and practice to a bygone age, into an operative force actively at work on modern problems.

These are important developments. Without them, or something to take their place, Arab society in our judgement cannot in fact proceed. Without some accepted *morale* and driving force, some effective inspiration directed to concrete opportunities, even the best social or national programme will remain on paper, and Arab life will continue a romantic débâcle. It is in the cogency of this answer to some of the community's most fundamental problems that part of the Ikhwan's appeal has lain. Until some other group has emerged with a comparably effective willingness to deal with these issues, one may be sure that the Ikhwan may, despite suppression, endure. So far, apart from the Communists, they are the only party to produce an ideal able to call forth on any effective scale more than mere lip-service.[197]

Nonetheless, the Ikhwan have combined with these virtues two major failings. To these their progressive adherents have been blind, their opponents exclusively attentive. The first is a lamentable lack of a realistic awareness of the actual problems of the modern state or its society, let alone solutions to them.

The Ikhwan are not purely conservative: they have constructed modern industries for themselves, which they own and operate, and have organized trade unions. However, their published literature shows no grappling with the more intricate responsibilities of modernity.[198] This is not too important in itself, since technical experts can be hired or trained, even if not cheaply or quickly. It is a failing that could in principle be remedied, though it must first be admitted. What is serious is the Ikhwan's failure to recognize that they do not know the answers to modern politico-socio-economic questions in detail. So is the assumption that adequate answers are available from the past or from the Azhar. And al-

[197] Whether the nationalist Liberation Rally of the 1952 revolution, first under Muḥammad Najīb ("Naguib") and now led by Jamāl 'Abd al-Nāṣir ("Nasser"), will be able to do this, it is too early for the present writer to discern.

[198] The English-knowing reader has available as illustration the translation Sayed Kotb, *Social Justice in Islam*, Washington, 1953. Cf. the review by the present writer, *Middle Eastern Affairs*, New York, 5:392-94 (1954).

though their policy is not fully clear on this, they have certainly suggested that their programme rests on the conviction that Islam in history already has extant and precise answers to all problems. Other Muslims,[199] closer to realities, see that in the modern world this is both morally arrogant and practically disastrous.

The second failing is related to this. In a certain sense it is not a failure of the Ikhwan as a movement so much as of the society in which it operates. That society has deteriorated to a point where violence is almost inevitable. The Ikhwan's attempt at cure may only provide an opportunity for that violence. The reaffirmation of Islam endeavours to counter the failure of modern life but may not succeed in transcending it. Unfortunately, for some of the members of the Ikhwan and even more for many of their sympathizers and fellow-travellers the reaffirmation is not a constructive programme based on cogent plans and known objectives, or even felt ideals; but is rather an outlet for emotion. It is the expression of the hatred, frustration, vanity, and destructive frenzy of a people who for long have been the prey of poverty, impotence, and fear. All the discontent of men who find the modern world too much for them can in movements such as the Ikhwan find action and satisfaction. It is the Muslim Arab's aggressive reaction to the attack on his world which we have already found to be almost overwhelming—the reaction of those who, tired of being overwhelmed, have leapt with frantic sadistic joy to burn and kill. The burning of Cairo,[200] the assassination of Prime Ministers,[201]

[199] This is based on personal conversations in Cairo. However, one may refer to the published work, Ṭāhā Ḥusayn and others, Ha'ulā' hum al-Ikhwān, n.p., n.d. (Cairo, c. 1954). Very recently one or two Ikhwān publishing trends have indicated a greater readiness to recognize that some modern social and other problems are not easy of solution. Nonetheless a fundamental reassessment of the meaning of revelation is perhaps involved before this matter can be seriously tackled.

[200] January 26, 1952. We do not suggest that the Ikhwan as an organization or individually were responsible for the rioting. Neither do we underestimate the emotional provocation for the outburst. Our thesis is rather that there has been an emotional relation between such explosive violence ("dynamism") and the Ikhwan's reassertion of Islam when that reassertion has not been accompanied with a rigorous intellectual and numinous reawakening. Similarly in the next two references, the Ikhwan officially disapproved the involvement of individuals from its membership ranks.

[201] Maḥmūd Fahmī al-Nuqrāshī, assassinated Dec. 28, 1948. Cf. J. Heyworth-Dunne, Religious and Political Trends in Modern Egypt, Washington, 1950, p. 69; George Kirk, The Middle East 1945-1950, London, Survey of International Affairs, 1954, p. 292.

the intimidating of Christians,[202] the vehemence and hatred in their literature[203]—all this is to be understood in terms of a people who have lost their way, whose heritage has proven unequal to modernity, whose leaders have been dishonest, whose ideals have failed. In this aspect, the new Islamic upsurge is a force not to solve problems but to intoxicate those who cannot longer abide the failure to solve them.

The leaders of the Ikhwan and to a considerable degree the movement's official literature are not directly responsible for this emotionalism and violence, and indeed have on occasion taken steps to restrain it. It is still perhaps too early yet to make a pronouncement on the Ikhwan, to discriminate between good and bad factors apparently working together in its upsurge and still to sort themselves out: real religion and neurotic fascism, honest idealism and destructive frenzy. It would be wrong to deny the former, and perhaps dangerous to ignore the potentiality of the latter.

In our discussion of "dynamism" in recent Islam above we were tentative in including under that heading this movement and its Pakistan counterpart the Jama'at group, to which we shall return. The announced programme of these organizations and the temper of their better leaders are rationalist (formalist, legalist) rather than vitalistic. Yet it would seem to an outside observer that those programmes nevertheless function for many who applaud them not as rational policies genuinely accepted as deliberate solutions to problems responsibly faced, but rather as symbols around which cluster "Islamic" emotions irrationally stirred. In a disintegrating social situation the vigorous assertion of a revolutionary principle, in this case a revitalized Islam, may

---

[202] Based on personal conversations with Egyptian Christians and Church authorities.

[203] One example, among many: Muḥammad Quṭb, *Shubuhāt hawl al-Islām*, Cairo, 1954. This book is bitter, blind, furious; see especially its longest chapter, "Islam—and Woman," pp. 94-133. Most Westerners have simply no inkling of how deep and fierce is the hate, especially of the West, that has gripped the modernizing Arab. (The "Conclusion" of the book is also noteworthy. How are we to achieve this dream?—it asks; and answers, By faith. We do not need arms, tanks, planes, to regain our past glory. A handful of men, with faith, troubled the impotent British empire at the canal. They did not need heavy arms for that. If we can regain our disciplined faith, we shall, as did the early Muslims, defeat the great empires of the world. We can hold the balance between the great powers of East and West.)

be either constructive or, as Communism has shown, desperately misleading.

We leave the Arabs, then: still under attack, still reacting to an insecurity almost greater than they can bear. Islam is still expressed for many, especially outside the cities and amongst the best at al-Azhar, in the classical tradition: an alive and great and ancient force. For the more modern world, it is still struggling to find an expression for itself: in modernism, but vapidly; in the intelligentsia, but casually; in the Ikhwan, but explosively.

The crisis of the Arabs is acute. And within it, the crisis of Islam is acute. Its greatest problem is the degree to which those who in the fullest sense know the religion have largely lost contact with the modern world, and those genuinely oriented to modernity have largely lost contact with their religion.

Meanwhile, the attack continues. The West, immense factor in Arab life, continues to bully, to disparage, to accuse, and to betray.[204]

The humour and charm of the Arab heart, the finesse of the Arab mind, the warmth and sensitivity and brilliant imagination of the Arab spirit, are under a cloud.

[204] This sentence is of general relevance, but was induced by the appalling international developments of the summer of 1956.

Chapter 4

TURKEY: ISLAMIC REFORMATION?

THE people of Turkey are Muslims.

This fact is well enough known. That it is a deeply significant fact has been less widely appreciated. An understanding of the modern Turks as Muslims has of late been little cultivated, either by Western students or by the other Islamic peoples. Yet it is essential for any valid appreciation not only of post-revolutionary Turkey, but even more of what is our basic interest throughout this study: the present-day development of Islam. Any Muslim, or any outside observer, who would come to grips with the question of Islam in the modern world, must take very seriously the Islam of the twentieth-century Turks.

The people of Turkey not only are Muslims, but for many centuries now have been of all Muslims the chief. It is they who for long have primarily carried Islam and given it greatness and vitality in the world of men. Continuous with this historic fact is a present potentiality. In the new religious formulation to which the modern world, in Islam as in other faiths, is struggling to give birth, the Turks may still be Muslim protagonists.

Our concern here is to present and to investigate those aspects of the religious situation in modern Turkey on which the latter possibility rests—in sum, the possibility of a Turkish reformation in Islam.

Certainly, we shall argue, the Turks have not renounced Islam but re-viewed it.

Both in theory and in practice, the Turks' version of Islam today is different from other Muslim peoples'. It is, we believe, of major significance in itself; as we shall presently try carefully to understand. Also, its very differentiation from the others is significant; and this too needs clarification. It is, of course, not unrelated to the fact that the historical context is different, both present and past. Quite apart from religious interpretation, the Turks stand out from among other Muslims both for their current activity and development, their revolutionary prosecution of modern life, and for their past role in Islamic history, especially in recent centuries. As with other Muslims, their understanding of Islam is enmeshed with their understanding of Islamic history, and their participation in it. These have been markedly distinctive.

In our second chapter, in our swift survey of Islam in recent history, many generalizations about trends had to be qualified with the caveat, "except for the Turks." It is not that the Turks have stood outside modern Muslim development. Rather, with a unique orientation they have in many ways outpaced it. Much of what characterizes other Muslims in the nineteenth and twentieth centuries, the Turks underwent in the eighteenth and nineteenth. Other developments, however, have been strikingly their own. We cannot here examine the course by which Turkey has reached its present religious position.[1] One may, however, point out that it included much that is typical but also much that is distinctive. Modern Turks studying contemporary Islamic developments elsewhere recognize a great deal as recalling aspects of their own now outgrown history. To a considerable extent, however, the characteristic quality of the Turks in the modern Muslim world seems to rest on the uniqueness of their immediate past. (The prime matter here is continuity: the unbroken sequence from their mediaeval grandeur, including a persisting independence—and therefore active responsibility.)

We cannot follow, therefore, those who forecast that other Muslim countries will necessarily follow where the Turks have led. Other Muslim peoples are free to work out their own development, Islamic and other; and are responsible for it. Or, in so far as they are not free, they are bound by the particularities of their individual situation and their local heritage. 'To go the way of the Turks' in modernization is a solution being canvassed by some in Cairo, Karachi, and Jakarta. But it is only one possibility—and is not even easy, let alone inevitable. It would, for instance, be presumptuous to predict that there will prevail a decision such as that of the Turks, to abandon the whole concept of a specific Islamic prescription of social pattern, and to accept a separation of religious and politico-economic institutions. Even those deeply convinced that in the modern world any alternative endeavour is bound to fail cannot infer that therefore this solution will be chosen.

Neither can we follow those at the other extreme, who feel that

[1] See chap. 2, ref. 38 above.

since the Turkish interpretation of Islam is new and distinctive, it is therefore false.

Our contention is much simpler, and indeed more obvious: that however the rest of the Islamic world may or may not develop, the fact that one section of it, a section of major importance, is developing in this way is and will remain a matter of prime significance. The significance is religious as well as social. If other Muslim societies imitate or approximate the Turkish handling of the faith, clearly this will be notable. If they do not, the very variety introduced into modern Islam by this radical development will be ineluctable and striking. Already the Turkish interpretation of religion, implicit if not overt, is an emergence of real moment in Islam.

This much can hardly be gainsaid: that the Turks are the only Muslim people in the modern world who know what they want. Theirs is the only Muslim nation that has evolved intellectual and social foundations that in the main they can and do regard as substantially adequate to modernity. We have argued that Islam as a religion takes history very seriously. The Turkish segment of Islamic history is the only one in the contemporary period that those involved in it can look upon without misgiving. The Turks are the only Muslims who can regard their participation in modern Islamic history as reasonably effective.

This is of not only temporal interest. The Islamic tie between religion and history, which we have stressed, makes religiously significant the historical success of the Turkish revolution. For Muslims, it renders theologically precarious if not intolerable any glib judgement that such success has been the historical, mundane counterpart of a Turkish weakening or distorting of true Islam. For any student, if the tension between faith and history lies, as we have suggested, close to the heart of the modern Muslim dilemma, then the success of the Turks' coming to terms with modern history must impel a rather heedful study also of their relation to the faith.

Such a study must be in two parts. For as we have already suggested, the role of Islam in Turkish history today has something to do with the role of the Turks in Islamic history yesterday. If we consider first the modern Turkish orientation to Islamic history, we gain some helpful clarification for our examination then of their present salient interpretation of religion. Indeed, a failure to appreciate this last, and in the extreme case a rejecting of the modern Turkish version of Islam altogether as negligible or false, have often reflected a failing in historical as well as religious viewpoint.

Two illusions then go hand in hand. Stated summarily, these are: first, the idea that Islam went through its 'golden age' at the beginning of its career, the significant period of its history coming to an end in what is now the fairly distant past—in effect, before the Turks came substantially on the scene; and secondly, the idea that in the twentieth century, when Islam is now felt to be pulling itself out of its subsequent torpor and is once again on the move, undergoing its 'renascence,'[2] the Turks have rejected Islam.

In such a position, a narrow, inadequate concept of Islamic history is coupled with a circumscribed and rigid interpretation of Islamic faith. The richness and continuity of the former are lost, and with them the richness and variety of the latter. The attempt, in both history and faith, is to impose a small and static idea upon a large and dynamic reality. Any understanding of Islam is partial that is not comprehensive and flexible enough to embrace the Turkish instance, both past and present.

The Turks and Islamic History

Let us consider the first of these "illusions." The 'golden age'[3] interpretation of Islamic history is widespread. Indeed, it is virtually standard among non-Turks. With a narrow attention fixed on the pristine brilliance of Muslim civilization in its first centuries, it would hold that Islam, both in cultural expression and in religious interpretation, early reached its zenith; and thereafter has been either static, or decadent. In this view the earthly greatness, and almost one might say the earthly truth, of Islam lies in the remote past. Islamic history is looked upon as a grand achievement—not only for the admired attainments of its erstwhile participants, but an achievement also in the primary sense of something perfected, finished. The outworking of this thesis is that to

---

[2] On this spelling cf. ref. 11 below.

[3] The phrase is used by Muslim historians today; e.g., al-'aṣr al-dhahabī, for the early 'Abbāsī period (132-232 A.H./750-847 A.D.), Ḥasan Ibrāhīm Ḥasan, Ta'rīkh al-Islām al-siyāsī wa al-dīnī wa al-thaqāfī wa al-ijtimā'ī, 3 voll., Cairo, 1935-46 (and in subsequent edd.), introd. to the first ed. of vol. 2, p. 3.

Islamic history, in any meaningful, dynamic sense of the word, Muslims since the fall of Baghdad (1258), or the like, have been heirs rather than contributors. At some such date, it is implied, Islamic history proper comes to an end.

This interpretation, even if not so formulated into a blunt doctrine, yet underlies many a working assumption and colours many an attitude. That the Arabs are prone to it is perhaps understandable enough. Their own history can indeed be fitted into some such scheme with hardly more violence than is customary in schematizing any history. And we have already noted the situation motivating them to stress and glorify the classical period of Islamic history; and inhibiting them from giving attention to the less attractive, if no less significant, centuries that followed. The attitude is exemplified in such modern Arab works as the popular one by the recent professor of Islamic history and head of the History department at Cairo University, boldly entitled *The History of Islam*, which closes with the fall of Baghdad;[4] or the well known series of Ahmad Amin, presenting *The Dawn of Islam* ('to the end of the Umawi empire'), *The Forenoon of Islam* ('the first 'Abbasi century'), and *The High Noon of Islam* ('to the end of the fourth century *hijri*'), but stopping short of what is tacitly felt to be the darkening afternoon or evening of the community's development.[5]

It is not only the Arabs, however, who adopted this viewpoint. We stated in our outline of the history that the mediaeval efflo-

---

[4] Cf. previous ref.

[5] *Fajr al-Islām*, Cairo, 1929 (and in subsequent edd.); *Ḍuḥà al-Islām*, 3 voll., Cairo, 1933-36 (and in subsequent edd.), *Ẕuhr al-Islām*, 4 voll., Cairo, 1954-55 (and in subsequent edd.). Shortly before his death this author (1886-1954), lest he be unable to complete the series (*Yawm al-Islām*, p. 5), published *Yawm al-Islām*, Cairo, 1952. This essay might seem at first glance to contradict the point that we are here making. However, it devotes but relatively few pages to the interval between the fall of Baghdad and the rise of the modern Europe-oriented period. Its chief concerns are two: Islām's early (Arab) glory, and its modern problem *vis-à-vis* the West. It could even be said to illustrate rather than to undermine our 'renascence' hypothesis for the Arabs, developed below. On Ahmad Amin, cf. above, chap. 2, ref. 47.

For a similar point, cf. the most widely read of Arab historians in the West: "This general decline of Islamic [*sic*] culture (by the beginning of the thirteenth century) marks the end of the Middle Ages"—Philip K. Hitti, *History of the Arabs*, London, 1946 ed., p. 683n. It is interesting to note also that the first four edd. of this work (note the title) carried the story of the Arabs until 1517 only. The most recent edd. (1951ff.) append a very brief section dealing with the Ottoman and modern periods.

rescence was felt by most Muslims as less 'Islamic' than the earlier classical.[6] This can be illustrated, for instance, also from India, even though it participated in the mediaeval rather than the classical. One example is Hali's great poem *The Flow and Ebb of Islam*[7] to which we have already referred, and which is by any standard one of the most characteristic and influential literary products of nineteenth-century Muslim India. In brilliantly evoking the Muslims' triumphant past, the poet recites their glories with illustrative names drawn almost exclusively from the Arabic period.[8] The "ebb" of Islam, of which his eloquence is the lament, is that subsequent decline that set in with the fall of Baghdad, and in which he felt his people still caught. To this Indian, in considering his Islamic heritage, the accomplishments of the Mughul civilization in India, or of the post-Mongol Persians in Iran, do not come to mind; let alone those of the Ottoman Turks.[9]

Examples of this sort, and instances of similar import from the work of Western orientalists, could be multiplied, further to document our contention that for many Islamic history is in principle the story of something that happened in the past, an early period of creativity that came to an end long since.

In contrast, for the Turks Islamic history is neither remote nor stable. Like the Arab Muslims and unlike the Indian, the modern Turks have tended to be interested greatly in their own part in the history of Islam. That part, distinctively, has been both recent and continuing. Unlike the Arabs, who ignore or in principle almost deny the history of Islam in the period after the initiative

[6] Above, chap. 1, pp. 35-38.

[7] *Madd-o Jazr-i Islām*, popularly known as *Musaddas-i Ḥālī*; cf. above, chap. 2, ref. 20.

[8] Of the various persons paraded in the poem, Nāṣir al-Dīn Ṭūsī is the most recent: born 1201 A.D., he sided with Hūlāgū in the overthrow of the 'Abbāsī empire, and leaving works both in Arabic and Persian, died 1274— the only one of the great men recalled by Ḥālī who lived even part of his life this side of the fall of Baghdad. So far, indeed, does Ḥālī go in tacitly equating Islamic with Arabic culture that he is willing to include two Christian Arab intellectuals of Baghdad, Ḥunayn ibn Isḥāq and 'Alī ibn 'Īsà (ninth and early tenth centuries) among his representatives of the 'flow' of Islām indicating erstwhile Muslim greatness.

[9] Further on this point, cf. the present writer's "Development of the Historical Consciousness among the Muslims of India in the Modern Period," a paper read at the Conference on Indian Historiography, School of Oriental and African Studies, University of London, 1956; the conference papers are to be published presently in a volume by that School.

in it had been lost by themselves, Turkish Muslims can hardly ignore and certainly cannot deny Islamic history before its destiny was committed to Turkish hands. True, the nationalist, even chauvinist, climate of the first post-Revolution age tended to concentrate their attention on the history of the Turks as Turks. For some, this may have taken the marginal form of regarding the Turko-Islamic period as a chapter in Turkish history rather than in Islamic. Even so, it is the most brilliant and important chapter. The Turks became great as Muslims. Others, more Islamic-minded, might devote attention to the formative Arabic era of the religion's development, or be culturally concerned with the Persian contributions. Still, they could hardly fail to be interested also, or even primarily, in the Turks' activities in this field. The Turks have been concerned with the Turkish share in the evolution of Islam.

However one may approach it, that part is impressive. The impartial observer finds it considerable enough. Turkish thinkers themselves have been pushed by patriotic enthusiasm into finding it massive. The Turks became great as Muslims. And their greatness was dedicated to the cause of Islam, which they adopted with fervour and served with piety and skill.

They see Turks as reviving, in the Selcuk empire, the then crumbling Muslim world on which they advened; reintegrating that world at home, and presently, by brilliant conquests under various dynasties, taking Islam into wide expansion. As they view it, it was Turks (Ghaznavi) who carried Islam to India; as it was again a Turk (Babur) who five centuries later revitalized Islamic rule there by founding the radiant "Mughul" dynasty. For some, it was Turks who essentially threw back the Crusades; and again Turks who finally, on the other hand, stemmed the sweep of Mongol devastation. Certainly it was they who pushed back and then overthrew the mighty Byzantine empire, Islam's longest-standing foe; and took Islamic dominion into southeastern Europe. They see themselves as having supplied Egypt with ruling houses (from the Mamluks to the latest dynasty), as well as having for long directly ruled it and other major sections of the Muslim world.

Not only have they contributed this political might and social vitality to Islam, and built for Islam and of it great civilizations, like the Ottoman with its sixteenth-century splendour. In the development of Islam's cultural and religious activities also they have played their part. Not only have they provided Sufism with orderfuls of devout members; they have also adorned and advanced it with great creative poets. They have produced not only generations of zealous Sunnis, but also many a significant doctor of the Law. They have worshiped in the mosques, but also have raised magnificent mosques in which to worship.

It would be easy, and even imperative, to dispute details of this historical interpretation. Non-Turkish Muslims would be quick, for instance, to protest the wide casting of the 'Turkish' net. Al-Farabi, for example, is a Turk only in a sense in which Muhammad 'Ali is not: the one Arab by culture, the other Albanian by birth, the claim to both is confused. However, the details are not, for the moment, at issue. More important, it might be alleged that this reading of the past may be dismissed as simply one more instance of a characteristically nationalist-romantic glorification of one's own background, no more responsible or significant than comparable efforts on the part of numerous peoples, Arab and many others, propagandizing for their past achievements.

Against this, some discrimination is in order. Whatever the romanticism, nonetheless Turks have since the Revolution actually been engaged in what seems a greater production of serious, critical historiography than any other Muslim people.[10] And their reading of Islamic history, whatever its validity, is not fundamentally apologetics. They genuinely feel the determinative role of Turks in Muslim development; and are not merely trying, like many modern Arabs, to persuade themselves and others that they have been significant. In fact, under the first impact of revolutionary iconoclasm they were not particularly proud of this role; and many even deprecated the energy that Turks had "wasted" on being leaders of Islam.

They have not only glorified: their self-criticism has been striking, and probably unique in contemporary Islam. Their Islamic past has been continuous, but not uniformly great. While Europe, once far below them in attainment, plunged lustily forward with creative energy, Turkey was losing its vitality, and Turks cor-

[10] Cf. Halil Inalcik, "Some Remarks on the Study of History in Islamic Countries," *The Middle East Journal*, Washington, 7:451-55 (1953); and Bernard Lewis, "History-writing and National Revival in Turkey," *Middle Eastern Affairs*, New York, 4:218-27 (1953).

rupted what they had previously accomplished. Turkish Islam on earth became harsh and awry. If Turks have been proud of the height of their culture in the sixteenth century, they have recognized that they allowed it to degenerate and encrust in the eighteenth and nineteenth.

The fundamental point here is this: that the modern Turkish sense of Islamic history is of an unterminated process, with themselves as active participants. They see it as a long-range development, with much of which they have latterly been intimate, and for much of which they have latterly been responsible.

All this has religious corollaries. A larger, fuller, truer understanding of Islamic history means, whether tacitly or obviously, another interpretation of the faith. To see Islamic history not decapitated but continuing, and to feel it not exteriorized but existentially, is perhaps to face its modern period with more personal integration and effectiveness?

However that may be, certainly with divergent attitudes to history go differing understandings of what Islam is. And any answer, conscious or implicit, seriously given in the modern world to the question as to what Islam really is, is important. The Turks' particular understanding is, therefore, worth considerable effort to discern.

Concomitant with the distant-golden-age feeling about Islamic history has usually been the conviction or assumption that Islam as a religion was fully worked out in its early centuries. For such a position, Islam is what the Arabs long ago made it.

In the more dynamic view, human understanding of Islam is a long-range evolution, still in process.

The distinction cannot be pressed too rigidly. There are many exceptions, and many shades of variation. Yet the question of the general direction of loyalties is, we believe, significant. The Arabs glorify classical Arabism, which produced, or even is summated in, classical—that is orthodox—Islam. Persian sophisticates glorify the Achaemenians, who were not Muslim at all. The Pakistanis and Indonesians have not yet defined their past, yet think of erstwhile Islamic greatness as something, if not remote from themselves as a people, at least transcending them greatly. Against this the Turks, if they would glorify—in addition to whatever fantasies of Turkish or pseudo-Turkish pre-Muslim history they may allow themselves—so far as Islam is concerned glorify a period whose evolution produced no fixed form, and that can be looked upon as still incomplete.

It is perhaps not misleading to epitomize the divergence in a discrimination between the concepts 'renascence' and 'reformation.' Taking these terms as signifying respectively the reviving of an ancient reality that has lapsed, and the modifying of an existing one that has gone wrong, then the former idea applies more aptly to the modern mood of other Muslims, particularly Arabs and Indo-Pakistanis, the latter to the Turks. The others, in their attitude to Islamic society on earth, are thinking of an ancient glory that they wish to recapture; the Turks of a recent misdevelopment that they wish to rectify.

It is standard in modern Arabic to use the same term (*nahdah*) for the European Renascence[11] and for the age of modern revitalization through which the Arabs are now conscious of living. Similarly in Indo-Pakistan, Iqbal is typical when he writes: "If the renaissance of Islam is a fact, and I believe it is a fact. . . ."[12]

Nonetheless, there is an important difficulty here. Analogies are seldom close, and it is hazardous to correlate too firmly. Indeed, the very differences can be illuminating. For the Renascence in Europe, the re-birth of classicism, was a revival of ideas and attitudes, particularly humanist. The Greek achievement was primarily intellectualist. These ideas and attitudes proved immensely creative, in their second birth as in their first. But what they created in the second instance, the social institutions, laws, etc., were new; relevant to the new age of the Modern West. The renascence of Islam, on the other hand, has to a significant degree meant to many Arabs and Pakistanis a revival of the *institutions*

[11] The French spelling *Renaissance* was adopted also in both German and English when this concept of the French romantics was introduced into European thought in the nineteenth century and popularized greatly by Burckhardt and Symonds—even though these concentrated on Italy as its source (Jules Michelet, *Histoire de France*, vol. 8, *Renaissance*, Paris, 1855; Jacob Burckhardt, *Die Cultur der Renaissance in Italien*, Basel, 1860; J. A. Symonds, *The Renaissance in Italy*, London, 1875-86). Matthew Arnold pled for the form "Renascence" (*Culture and Anarchy*, London, 1869, § 4). There has been some hesitation in accepting the anglicized form of the metaphor to designate the European instance. Yet it seems clear that the neutral term is more reasonable for other 're-births' in human history; and we prefer it in all cases.

[12] Muhammad Iqbal, *The Reconstruction of Religious Thought in Islam*, 1944 ed., Lahore, p. 153.

of their classical age. We have stressed throughout that Islam is less an intellectualist religion than a sociological. Its tangible manifestation is laws and social structure. Perplexity ensues because the very problem of modernity lies in the fact that the institutions of the seventh to tenth centuries do not seem effective or relevant in the twentieth. Some would perhaps argue that the notion of renascence is more valid for philosophies; that of reformation for religions.[13]

The latter concept also cannot, of course, be correlated too closely with the European instance. The 'Reformation' in Christian history used the notion of a chronologically pristine purity in the church as a criterion for judging and reforming, re-fashioning, what had grown old and inadequate. The Protestant reformers were in fact innovating when they thought that they were resuscitating. In contrast, part of our point here has precisely been that whereas the Arab dream is of restoration, the modern Turks consciously talk of novelty (*teceddüt*, later *yenilik*).

The content of this novelty, and the talk about it, we shall later explore. For the moment, we simply call attention to the Turkish disposition to revise.

When European armies began to defeat theirs on the battlefield, and European diplomatic, economic, and much other pressure began to crush and threatened to overwhelm them, the Turks did a quite remarkable thing. They started to ask themselves what was wrong with their own way of life, what were the weaknesses that allowed this to happen. They set about—in the end successfully—to remedy those weaknesses, to transform their society into one that would be viable in the modern world as it is. They are not unaware that this stern realism (as well as its success) stands in contrast to the moralizing response which certain other Muslim peoples and other orientals made to a similar situation: the offended cry—quite valid, of course, but not necessarily effective—that this Western encroachment ought not to happen, and the appeal, to God, to the world at large, or to the conscience of the conquerors, to reverse it because it was wrong. The Turks' deter-

---

[13] However, it would also be possible to argue that a true renascence for Islām would consist in a renewal not of the particular judgements and institutions of early Muslims, but of their sense of moral imperative, of their overwhelming reverence before the 'oughtness' of things. Yet without the supplement of a discerning intelligence and rational restraint in the implementation of this sense of duty, the dynamist movements show, this too fails.

mination was to reverse it themselves, because their self-preservation was at stake.

For self-preservation they were determined—and, surprisingly, also willing—to go to any lengths requisite in re-fashioning themselves and their community. While other Muslims, suffering from the domineering of Europe, insisted that something was wrong with Europeans, the Turks devoted their attention to finding out what was wrong with themselves.

One of their judgements was that a major obstacle not only to progress but to the very continuance of their life as a nation was the form into which they had been building Islam. That form, then, must be undone.

Few deny that the Turks have been dramatically successful in re-making themselves into a dynamic nation able to stand on its own feet in the modern world. The indictment, however, voiced both by orthodox Muslims in the East and by observers such as Toynbee[14] in the West, is that in the process they are losing their own soul.

This brings us to our second "illusion": the belief that the Republican Turks of our day have renounced Islam.

Islam in Turkish Secularism

Not only are the Turks thought by some to have entered the course of Islamic history in the past after that history was, significantly, over. In the present they are supposed to have withdrawn from it just as it is significantly recommencing. Far from being credited, then, with playing a significant and determinative role in Islamic development, they are quietly disqualified from any role at all.

That the modern Turks, in choosing secularism, have thereby rejected Islam, has not had much support from serious students of the subject, either in the East or in the West. It is, however, a general impression of wide prevalence, amongst both Europeans and Muslims of other lands.

The reference is not to the Turkish masses, particularly the peasants of Anatolia. These may be presumed to be conservative, even tautly so; and may be but slightly or hardly affected by the

[14] Cf. the essay "Islam, the West, and the Future," in his *Civilization on Trial*, London, 1948, pp. 184-212.

new un-Islamic outlook that the lay government has, in this view, been thought to be seeking to impose. It is a question rather of the ruling class, Atatürk ("Mustafa Kamal," as he is still mostly known to the rest of the Muslim world) and his modernizing entourage—men who in the Revolution threw over the old Turkey and all its ways and are seen as deliberately and powerfully setting out to build a new, Western, secular (or irreligious, or anti-religious) state and society in place of the old Islamic ones. It is with this group, the intelligentsia, the bourgeois élite, the men who made the Revolution and have been carrying through its ideals and practical implications, and have enjoyed its fruits—it is with this group that our own study is concerned. This is the class of persons who in the rest of the Muslim world are earnestly facing the quandary of what to do, as Muslims, with life in this inordinate world of ours today; or what to do, as moderns, with Islam—how to revitalize the traditions and values of their religious heritage so that these may be not only meaningful but creative in the new environment. In Turkey, it is widely thought, they evaded the dilemma by stoutly opting for modernity *in toto*. In this, as in much else, they would have mimicked the West, or at least that large group there who, rather than solve the problem posed by the tensions of religion in the modern world, have cut the Gordian knot and rejected religion.

This judgement, we believe, is false. But it is not weak. To refute it, arguing that the modern "emancipated" Turks have freed themselves of much but not fundamentally of Islam, is not superficially easy. The facts that have lent colour in the popular mind to the accusation are well enough known: the abolition of the *khilafah*, 1924; the forcible dissolution of the Muslim religious orders and closure of the *tekkes*, 1925; the substitution of Western-based legal codes for the *shari'ah*, 1926; the emendation of the constitution, 1928, deleting the clause that read: "the religion of the Turkish state is Islam,"[15] and establishing instead "laicism" as one of the six cardinal principles of that state; the substitution of the Latin for the Arabic alphabet, 1928, and of the Turkish for the Arabic call to prayer, 1933; and altogether the general and

[15] Constitution of the Republic of Turkey, April 20, 1924, Article 2: as given in Arnold J. Toynbee and Kenneth P. Kirkwood, *Turkey*, New York, 1927, p. 302.

firm circumscribing by law of the role in the country's life of Islam's traditional representatives and symbols.[16]

These and related actions by the new Turkish Republic make an imposing list. Patently, they are of a critical significance. So, too, is the general attitude to religious matters of the dominant group of Turks, which such actions expressed. Whether they must together be interpreted as a rejection of Islam is, however, a question to which divergent answers have been given.

The significant fact is that to this question the answer of the Turks themselves is a hearty negative.

Our observation, in conversations with many representative of the group, has been[17] that with few exceptions they denied, and even ridiculed[18] the notion that, singly ·or nationally, they had renounced Islam.[19] Even those individuals who, personally free-thinking, sceptic, or wistful, would except themselves, yet have considered the Turkish educated group as a whole to be Muslim. For the rest, their claim to be Muslims has been emphatic; its sincerity persuasive.

Manifestly, these Turks have taken great liberties with their religion. Yet they have not, one may believe, abandoned it. And, in this view, it is precisely because they have been willing and able to take liberties with it, but have not abandoned it, that one may insist that they are a significant group for the modern inter-

[16] A full and careful account of this will be found in Gotthard Jäschke, "Der Islam in der neuen Türkei," *Die Welt des Islams*, Leiden, 1:1-174 (1951); cf. also the supplementary material, *ibid.*, 1:195-228; 2:25-61, 126-35, 143-214, 278-87.

[17] The material that here follows is based in part on the present writer's conversations with a number of Turks of the educated classes during a visit to Turkey in the autumn of 1948. A preliminary draft of the analysis was multilithed and circulated to these and other Turks, and this draft discussed with them further in a subsequent visit in 1951. Since these conversations were personal and frank, not intended for individual publication, quotations from them are given in the remainder of this chapter without the mention of any names, and indeed without further reference. The writer feels particularly indebted for the openness with which these Turks were willing to talk with him of fundamental things. Readers who question the scientific validity of undocumented evidence are face to face with one aspect of the general problem of the scientific study of religion, on which we touched above, chap. 1, reff. 4 and 5.

[18] As often as a denial, any suggestion that the Turks had rejected Islām or become irreligious provoked genuine laughter.

[19] "No, there are no atheists amongst us. Certainly no one is preaching atheism; or anti-religious ethics. We are *laik*, not pagan."

pretation of Islam. The reformulation of religious truth so as to be meaningful and persuasive in the modern world is a serious business. It might well seem, in any faith, impossible without substantial liberties. Believers among the other Muslims may feel that the Turks have gone too far. There are signs that many Turks have begun to feel so. But that is a different matter. For the moment, our contention is only that Turkish vitality is evident also in the religious field.

The question turns, basically, on whether their vigorous handling of religious developments since the Revolution has been effected against Islam, or within Islam. This, in turn, is a question of whether that revolutionary class, the men and women who have brought about "the Turkish transformation"[20] and those who now participate in it and approve it, are, or are not, Muslims. Individuals, of course, may vary either way. But our submission is that, by and large, as a group they *are* Muslims; that what they have done in the last twenty-five years to the status and form of religion in Turkey is one more development within Islam, a new emergence within its historical, Turkish evolution.

It would then follow, that what they may yet do—and they have by no means finished with their treatment of it—may well prove worthy of attention.

To hold it to be a development within Islam (within historical Islam) is not to rule out the possibility that it is a deplorable development. Muslims in other lands, and perhaps other classes of Muslims within Turkey, may view it so. Modernist Turks may be thought heretics. But the discrimination between an heretical Muslim and a non-Muslim is vital. The difference is that of whether the Turks have perverted Islam or abandoned it. On careful reflection, the latter alternative can hardly be seriously maintained.

From the point of view of other Muslims who are content that they have an adequate and final criterion for discerning 'true' Islam, not only in the past but for all time, it is the former alternative that may be chosen. Also for those (Muslims or outside observers) who are in quest of such a criterion, who are uncertain as to the best or truest form for Islam or for religion in general

[20] The phrase is a reference to Henry Elisha Allen, *The Turkish Transformation; a study in social and religious development*, Chicago, 1935. This is the chief earlier study of the issues here under consideration.

in the contemporary flux, the discussion becomes one as to whether the new interpretation of Islam that Turkish society is in process of creating will be in fact a perversion or, perhaps, an advance.

Amongst those Turks who firmly believe themselves to be Muslim, the view of several is, at heart, simply this (and it is held with a remarkable unpretentiousness): that they are Muslims—in the modern, enlightened manner. What they have got rid of, they unaffectedly feel, is not Islam, but on the contrary the distortions of Islam under which their country was, for a time, sorely labouring, and that still weigh on most of the other Islamic lands; and the outgrown formal expressions of the religion's true spirit. Chiefly, they feel, they have rid themselves and their religion of that tie between church and state which, they believe, gave pernicious power to religious authorities ("sunk in vice"), to interfere in political developments and to obstruct the nation's progress; and which, they also believe, corrupted those authorities and indirectly perverted the religion. Islam, essentially a religion with no priesthood, had, they feel, produced in its historical evolution a crust of bigoted, reactionary clergy who exploited the people, debauched the government, and misinterpreted the faith. Islam, essentially a progressive religion, had, they feel, evolved institutions and vested interests whose rigidity had for long and with great effect obstructed Turkey's progress; and, when at last a dynamic government came to power intent on activating the country into a forward movement of new life and expanding horizons, these had led a bristling opposition to all change and striven to sabotage progress. If, then, even though it were for political reasons, for the sake of the country and of the new ideals, Turkey had crushed those clerical authorities, abrogated those institutions and interests, it had at the same time liberated and rediscovered true Islam.

"Certainly the Turks have not renounced Islam. That is an Arab idea. But it is the Arabs who do not know what Islam is."

"There are three Islams: the religion of the Qur'an, the religion of the *ulema*, and the religion of the masses. This last is superstition, obscurantism, fetishism. The second is bogged down with the whole weight of out-of-date legalism—impossible stuff making it necessary to get a *fetva* before one can have one's teeth filled by a dentist. Turkey has got rid of the second. It was time to abolish it; we have thus led the way for the Muslim world. Islam needs a reformation. To this extent Turkey is still in the forefront of the Islamic world. The Arabs and others—silly people, still tied down with their outworn narrowness—thought that Turkey was repudiating Islam. Not at all. Turkey simply took the today necessary, salutary, reforming step of making religion what it should be, an individual, personal matter, a thing of the conscience, a matter of private faith. The religious feeling is much too strongly imbedded in the human soul for religion to be abolished. We have simply freed it."

"Certainly we have not renounced Islam. On the contrary, we have in Turkey what we believe to be the true Islam—that taught by Muhammad (a man, the greatest of men). We have got rid of the intermediacy of priests; their contemplation, mediation, is not true Islam at all. We really want to understand the religion. With the Qur'an in Turkish, we are able to understand better."

There is little new in the claim to be purging a religion of accretions, to be rediscovering its pristine or essential spirit. Such is standard with reformers. More modern, more profound, more sensitive, are doubtless those Turkish Muslims who concede the original legitimacy of the old religious forms and expressions for their own time, but see the new Islam of Turkey as in quest of new forms and expressions relevant to the novel modern world. For such, it is not a question of calling the old forms formalities, distortions, non-essentials; but simply old. They expressed for previous generations, perhaps most felicitously and adequately, the truth of Islam; but modern man has evolved into a situation where these are no longer either felicitous or adequate, where they no longer express that truth. They are therefore discarded even by those who, warmly, are convinced that that truth is there, and is important. But in this case the task of the reformer is very much more delicate and responsible; for it is creative. It is not simply a matter of going back to an erstwhile purity in religious history; but rather of going on, to discover, or to hammer out, new forms and new expressions that may embody for our generation the truths and values that the heritage has enshrined.

Some Turkish thinkers feel, as many sensitive thinkers in Christendom are feeling, that the religious problem of today is how to reinterpret and restate the religious traditions, how to reclothe their vitality, so that the modern world in all its poignancy may participate in and prolong that living experience of which the community's history, theology, and art are the expression; and have been, in the past, also the ground.

In these terms, then, the reformer today is engaged not only in rediscovering the original meaning of old symbols but also in finding new symbolizations to convey that meaning anew. At its simplest, this is exemplified in translating the call to prayer, and even the Qur'an itself, into Turkish. This is obviously a new development. Yet it is one that, they claim, expresses for them what the old—perfectly valid, of course, for its own situation—expressed for others. "Take a scripture passage such as this: 'A book whose verses have been made clear as a Qur'an in Arabic . . .'—that is: in the vernacular, in the language of the people concerned."[21]

More controversially, this spirit can be detected in suggestions or assumptions that the institutions of Islam can and should be replaced with new ones more in tune with contemporary conditions. Already during the 1920's radical changes in the rites and observances of Islam, including its prayer ritual and mosque services, were being officially discussed.[22] Turks are prepared to consider such proposals seriously. "Islam was progressive for its time; but times and conditions meanwhile have changed." On the theological level, thinkers are to be found who recognize that the logic, basically Aristotelian, through which orthodoxy was earlier expressed has ceased to be an accepted mode of thought, and ceased to be an effective instrument of communication. Therefore, they feel, if Islam or any any other religion is to make itself understood, let alone acceptable, to educated men, its propositions will have to be formulated in a quite new way.

As one university official put it: "The classical scholarship of traditional Islam, for all its learning, is finished. With it, one can today get nowhere; it has been tried and it has failed. It is necessary to begin all over again with entirely new methods: scientific, liberal." He added: "But I believe that one should base it on feeling, not on reason." Another educationalist of weight said: "The Muslim world is waiting for a purified, true Islam. We in Turkey are ripe for it. . . . We need a new interpretation; and it must be

[21] The tendency has been to go back to the use of Arabic for the call to prayer, since this was made legally permissible again from 1950. The use of Turkish had been compulsory since 1933.

[22] Cf. Allen, *op. cit.*, pp. 179-80.

based on values. A religion that does not base itself on love and goodness is nothing. Cleanliness, love amongst men, human honesty, and the like. No, the new interpretation cannot be built on Aristotelian logic. But then, neither can it be built on scientific logic. Science has shown itself incapable of dealing with values. The more it advances, the more stark is the realization that it is helpless before that side of life. We need a new logic for religion. And such a logic will be found—eventually; certainly not swiftly. It will be found once we have the men, sensitive and competent, really looking for it. It is the men who are lacking."

It is only among a few intellectuals that this creative quest is self-conscious, this search for new expression of the ancient truth. Still rarer is the explicit recognition that, in some senses, the religious task today is creative not only of form but of essence. The truth of religion is itself developing. This is implied, whether recognized or not, in the attitude of those many Turks to whom the Islamic tradition is valuable—perhaps in the extreme—without being finally authoritative. For them, to be Muslim in the modern world means not only to recover the essential or original elements of the Islamic tradition; not only to give those elements a new form; but to carry forward the development. The tradition is capable of expansion; it may be enriched by the discovery of new truth.

It was partly in order to make intelligible this seemingly so daring premiss to belief, this almost unconsciously accepted vitalism, that we insisted above on the continuity of Islamic history in the Turkish case. Here is illustrated the fact there brought forward: that unlike other modern Muslims, Turks have not been accustomed to think of Islam as something that in the past was completed before their own participation in it. Here we begin to see the potential consequences of the fact that to many of them Islamic history, even Islam itself, is an active process, a process in which their forefathers have for long played a creative and leading part, and for which they themselves in the new circumstances of the twentieth century may, or even must, choose or carve for themselves a new and appropriate role.

Such an attitude is immensely reinforced by the success of their contemporary revolution. These are men who have made the revolution; who, labouring with devotion to actualize a vast and radical ideal, have seen a new Turkey arise before their eyes.

Their sense of accomplishment is major. And it is real. No in-sincere romanticism, it is rather a self-critical attitude emerging from the facts, and integrated with them. They set out to effect the reformation of their country and they are in process of achiev-ing it. They have made mistakes, for which they make no move to skirt responsibility; they have made triumphs, which they see as their own. They do not talk, perhaps do not clearly think, of this sense of accomplishment. More convincing, it unwittingly under-lies their conversation; and informs their thought. In nothing has the leadership of Turkey differed more profoundly from that of other Muslim countries in the last twenty-five years than in this: that they speak, with an unassuming naturalness, as a group ac-customed to seeing their will effective.[23]

Modern Turks have been accused of aping Europe, imitating the outward ways and appropriating the thoughts of an essentially disparate culture. Yet on this point there is no mere imitation, no superficial copying of results. These Turks have actually shared in what is perhaps the fundamental experience of modern West-ern civilization: the experience of remaking one's environment. Man's heritage is found to be in flux, and man is found able to influence or control that flux. Within limits, no doubt. Yet the development of society is in the hands of society. Modern Turks, like modern occidentals, have through brilliant hard work and well-applied intelligence come to feel themselves directors of destiny.

"This is arrogance; this is man's final sin," certain religious voices arraign. The protest is made both in the name of Chris-tianity in the West, where the new attitude has wider prevalence and longer standing; and by certain Muslim observers in the Orient. An intelligent Cairene Muslim commented to us: "The Turks, whatever they themselves may feel about it, have rejected Islam with a vengeance. For the essence of religion is to submit to God's will, and to accept His revelation—to humble oneself be-fore His glory. The Turks, like you Europeans, have defied Him, have claimed to order their own lives according to their own wishes, as well as to pronounce, themselves, on what is right and wrong. Now, in final blasphemy, they would lay hands on religion

[23] For example: several, when asked if the *tekke*s might be reopened, or again if the *sharī'ah* might be reintroduced, said quite simply, "We will not allow it."

itself: they attempt to fashion Islam into what *they* would like to see it be, and to bend even religion to serve human purposes." Western liberals, too, are familiar with such criticism; and, chastened by man's vast failure to build on earth a Kingdom of Heaven, pause before it. The disillusionment of liberalism's splendid hopes, the culmination of "progress" in two world wars and the near devastation of Europe, have sobered dreams, and induced attention to those preaching that man's nature is inherently sinful, and that all his proudest works must, being human, go awry. The greater man's ambition, we are told, the greater the scope of his sin. The attempt to transform the world, to direct history, to determine destiny, is the greatest of all man's conceits—and its end, the greatest corruption.

Turkish society, still on its upgrade, has not yet advanced beyond goodness and promise into horror; has not yet reached the dénouement where ex-Christendom's unbridled passions led: the standardless achievements of the Nazis, the immense human degradation of the monolithic state, the despair of the faithless libertine. Should Turkey, then, here as in so many other fields, profit from the West's example? Should it, before it is too late, learn that, to avoid destruction, men must avoid *hubris* and grandiose ambition, and must submit in humble piety to jurisdiction of a divinely, not humanly, given order?

We raise the question at this point only to clarify a matter for our present purpose, which is that of describing, analysing, and attempting to understand what actually is happening in the Muslim countries—whether it should be or not. In this connection, we may say that man's new freedom to create, his power to control, may involve a sin; they are nonetheless a fact. And that freedom and power, however sinful, cannot be exorcised by denunciation. An operative religion today must be one that has learned to assimilate rather than to decry them. People in Western Christendom and in Turkey, and incipiently now throughout the world, *are* determining their own and their nations' future; for good or ill. They may be bungling; that is, creating badness. But that is vitally different from not being creative at all. While one may wish to distinguish between men who exercise such creativity and those who do not, who do not know it or do not accept it, it would seem inept to call religious (or Muslim) only the uncreative. One must distinguish further, amongst those engaged in directing the course of history, even religious history, between men who do so religiously and those who do not.

When we agree with the Turkish modernists that, however radical, they are indeed Muslims; when we insist that most of those whom we have met and with whom we have discussed these things are, however undogmatic, religious persons; part of what we mean is this. They seem to us to be adopting the new interpretations of Islam—and even to be creating or seeking to create or hoping that there may be created still newer interpretations—not arrogantly but devoutly. Their sense of freedom, acquired through the events of their recent history, is fused with a sense of responsibility, acquired through Islam.

They are creating something new in the development of Turkey, are moulding themselves and their nation into new patterns not derived but invented. Yet they are doing so not simply according to their own desires,[24] but according to what, they feel, is *good*—good, that is, we would argue, in an objective, transcendent sense; good in the theological sense, as in accord with the will of God. They are creating something new in Islam, evolving out of their religious and social heritage new concepts not deduced but induced. Yet they are doing so not simply according to their own fancies, but according to what, they feel, is true—divinely true. They themselves would hardly use this terminology, and the whole process is not nearly so self-conscious as this analysis might suggest. But the fundamental submission to an absolute criterion is there; and is, we feel, of crucial import.

One of the most creative, and at the same time disastrous, movements in modern human history is the Communist; which has been used, it would seem, in Russia, and potentially throughout the world, to build up the gigantic and ruthless power of a nihilist

---

[24] There is involved here quite a major theological problem, eventually a major political and social problem; in the interpretation of human choice. This problem impinges throughout the Muslim world, not always consciously. The classical Islamic view has been that man chooses (or judges: *ḥakama*) either according to revelation or else according to his own desires, passions (*ahwā'*). The third alternative, that he choose or judge according to reason, is not fully understood by the representatives of the classical Muslim tradition. (An illustration of their consequent refusal to accept it: cf. above, chap. 3, ref. 194.) This is the Greek element, rejected by Islamic orthodoxy. In theological terms, we should say that reason is neither subjective nor objective, but is the transcendent immanent in man.

minority in the Kremlin. It has succeeded (politically) because it is creative, calling on man in his poverty and oppression to use the new powers that history has acquired, to transform the world and to build a new society in accord with his noblest dreams. It has failed (morally) because it has been, not in a formal sense but basically and really, irreligious. It has rejected not only the forms of the world's religion and their theologies—many need rejection, and modern man responds—and not merely the name of God; but His reality. For it has recognized no criterion by which it may itself be judged.

In the rank-and-file Party members, there has been often but a shallow atheism, a disallegiance to the overt ideas and institutions of the historical religions, but with it a fervent piety, pursuing justice and beauty without knowing them to be divine. But the power in the massive movement has rested with men at the top who, apparently, have been not superficially but profoundly atheist, have actually repudiated truth and repudiated goodness. Except as instruments of power, these have to them been bourgeois delusions. These men, standing then at the top of a hierarchy rigidly controlling a party that is the vanguard of the class that is the highest product so far of the universe's dialectical process— these men are supreme. They bow down to no higher authority.

To use the Arabic term, *la yuslimuna.*

In this sense, then, the leadership of Turkey is not, we submit, irreligious. And in this sense, it would seem of fundamental significance that it is not irreligious. It would seem to be of significance, for instance, even for an orthodox Muslim who may deplore the modernist Turks' not submitting to God in the way that he believes God has revealed, but could yet welcome the fact that they have not, like the true atheist, rejected submission in principle.

The Content and Problems of Modernism

Let us not, however, push the argument too far. Turkish non-irreligiousness is, we feel, important. Nonetheless, it is, as such, negative; and what it represents is at best tenuous and vague. This is somewhat true of the whole modernist movement in Turkish Islam. Our endeavor to call attention to that movement, and our belief that its implications are important, must not mislead us into overestimating its substance. Implications are no final substitute for content.

Indeed, it might be objected that to use the term "movement" here is overgenerous. There is in Turkey among the élite a felt need for modernism, a growing sense that something is to be searched for. But there is remarkably little positive endeavour to meet that need, remarkably little serious searching.

With an historical approach, it might be contended that the present generation of Turkish leaders, though they have jettisoned the paraphernalia of Islam, are themselves operating on the momentum of its inner spirit, imbibed through the forms and symbols in their childhood training; whereas the next generation, deprived of the institutions, will prove itself devoid of the spirit as well. In this view, the freedom of a quintessential religion evinced by today's dynamic Turks would be not the beginning of a new Islamic *élan* but an ethereal end of its long and now disembodied tradition. Certainly however much one may think one has outgrown, or however much one may deplore, the almost standard confusion between religious symbols and their meaning, still it is not easy to transmit a faith apart from the symbols in which it has traditionally been enshrined.

It is not easy; and, apart from some accepted symbols, perhaps it is impossible.

Anyway, if religion is going to be not only compatible with but a guide to creative living, it must not merely rid itself of "impediments to progress" but must develop new forms of self-expression.

Something of this sort has, perhaps, been agitating Turkish minds of late. The interpretation that sees the events bearing on religion after the Revolution as constituting a Turkish rejection of Islam, is currently supplemented by a reading of recent moves as indicating a Turkish 'return to religion.' In our interpretation, these new moves[25] are rather the second and constructive stage in

[25] For accounts of recent developments by outside observers, the first mentioned being a Muslim Arab, see the following: A. L. Tibawi, "Islam and Secularism in Turkey Today," *Quarterly Review*, London, 609: 325-37 (1956); Howard A. Reed, "Turkey's New Imam-Hatip Schools," *Die Welt des Islams*, Leiden, 4:150-163 (1955) and "Revival of Islam in Secular Turkey," *The Middle East Journal*, Washington, 8:267-82 (1954); Lewis V. Thomas, "Turkish Islam," *The Muslim World*, Hartford, 44: 181-85 (1954) and "Recent Developments in Turkish Islam," *The Middle East Journal*, Washington, 6:22-40 (1952); Bernard Lewis, "Islamic Revival in Turkey," *International Affairs*, London, 28:38-48 (1952). (Since this was compiled there has appeared the symposium Richard N. Frye, ed., *Islam and the West*, 's-Gravenhage, 1957,

the continued process of renewal. The first, over some twenty years, signalized the Muslim's repudiation of whatever in the Islamic concretion was, for him now, not vital, was not *his* true religion.[26] With this repudiation effected, to say that there was nothing left is, we have contended, to ignore what is, after all, of any religion the chief element: what was in his heart. The religion that lives in men's hearts is of eternal reference. Nonetheless a religion that is only in men's hearts will, in the temporal world, presently run dry.

However interpreted, the recent facts are these. At the end of 1946 the Republican Government, which for many years had prohibited serious public discussion of Islamic matters, allowed the question of religious education to be publicly raised; and considered it favourably. It decided to reintroduce Islamic instruction in the public schools. In 1948 schools to train religious functionaries (*imam*s and *khatib*s) were opened, under state auspices. The following year a Faculty of Theology was instituted in the University of Ankara.

Meanwhile, a number of periodicals, chiefly weeklies, of a religious sort began to appear and were allowed. In 1947, for the first time in years, Turks—to whom getting an exit visa and foreign exchange is always a considerable formality—were given permission and funds and facilities to go on the pilgrimage to Makkah. Religious programmes on the state radio were instituted. The visitation of mausolea (*turbe*) of sultans and saints was permitted again in 1950. And so on.

On the unofficial side, some of the sophisticated began to find themselves invited to weddings that included a religious ceremony as well as the civil. It was reported that a certain increase in mosque-attendance, prayer-ritual observance, and fasting, was evident; for instance, among college students—though such reports were difficult to check, and many Turks claimed that they noted no change, were aware of no religious 'revival.' As several put it,

---

with a section TURKEY, pp. 41-148, with very important articles and bibliography.)

[26] Not that the process was so deliberate as this might suggest. The revolutionizing Turks were aiming not at preserving Islām, or some vital core of Islām, but at preserving themselves. They were ruthless in rejecting from their society whatever seemed to stand in the way of that society's survival. In the face of this repudiation, only the vital part of their religion persisted; and only because it was vital.

"There has never been any lapse in religion; hence there cannot now be a revival." Others, however, explained, "The revolutionaries were in a hurry, and shattered much. We are now repairing and rebuilding."

This much, clearly, has been happening. The public expression of religion (as distinct from its inward hold on men), for long carefully circumscribed by law though never suppressed, has been allowed greater scope. The historical transmission of religion from one generation to another, through the instruction in forms and the training and setting aside of experts, a transmission interrupted at the revolution (and, with the gradual dying out of the old generation, in danger of being altogether broken) is being reinstituted. Finally, means have been being provided for working out an expression of the new faith that amorphously or potentially the liberals are harbouring. This last provision is found in the general freedom for publication and discussion and the new public atmosphere, but chiefly and most significantly in the new university Faculty of Theology.

Reasons for these developments are various. Our observation would suggest at least four. First, there is the wide philosophic trend away from secular positivism, a trend evident throughout Western culture since the First and more strikingly since the Second World War; the Turkish development is one instance of this.[27] Secondly, there has been the Turkish governments' conviction that the new régime introduced by the revolution, and established since by a quarter-century of active reconstruction, is now so firmly entrenched that the danger of effective reaction, previously led by the traditional religious authorities and fed by the traditional religious ideology, is over. Thirdly, the increase in political democracy has given a much greater voice in the control of policy to the peasants, who had throughout been much more traditionally Islamic than the previously dictatorial ruling class.[28]

[27] To the present writer, it is interesting to compare the opening in 1949 of a Faculty of Theology in the University of Ankara (over the relentlessly modern main portal of this university strikingly stands the bold quotation from Atatürk, "The truest guide in life is science") with the opening in 1948 of a Faculty of Divinity in McGill University. One may note also the recent instituting of a chair of Religious Thought in Benjamin Franklin's secular University of Pennsylvania, and similar developments in a number of institutions previously insistent on their scientific and secular orientation.

[28] This popular pressure first operated by inducing the governmental

Fourthly, the dominating and vivid menace to Turkey of Soviet expansionism after the Second World War led the leaders to bethink themselves with a new seriousness of a moral and social force to strengthen the community against external attack and internal disruption—an overt and organized Islam constituting, perhaps, just such a force.

These conditioning factors are interrelated; and, together and singly, could interestingly be discussed and commented upon at length. Basically, however, they are important as developments in the history of Turkey, while our interest is rather in the recent phenomena viewed as new developments within the history of Islam. And here one must be on guard against a tendency to discount any phenomena that can apparently be 'explained away': to regard a religious development for which extrinsic causes may be found as not really a religious development. The reactionary role of the Muslim clergy in Turkish society towards the end of the Ottoman régime, the intimate tie between official religion and the then decadent state, some have dismissed as "merely" the result of the Sultan Abdul Hamid's political manoeuvring, his attempt to make use of public religion for his very worldly purposes. So to dismiss it is to overlook the fact that that attempt, though it may have been insincere, was also successful. Again, the Kemal government, on coming to power through the Revolution, when it suppressed the influence of those same religious authorities and seriously checked the overt expression of Islam that they mediated, did so largely or wholly for political reasons—they representing and leading the chief opposition to the new régime. So serious was their opposition that the government (quite apart from any religious feeling by which it might be held) had to choose either to suppress it forcibly or to jeopardize its own cause. What is more significant, every Turk who approved the revolution in principle had, if he were honest, to approve also that suppression; had to approve in his (Muslim) heart that stringent curbing of tradi-

People's Party to take "pro-Islamic" measures on its own initiative, lest the opposition gain sweeping votes by posing as champion of (traditional) religion. The Democratic Party, by platform a firmer advocate of the so-called return to religion, was successful in the 1950 elections; and since then this matter has been one of the direct issues in Turkish political life, though careful steps have been taken to control its expression within limits set by other considerations.

tional Islam. To dismiss the development as "merely" expedient, a merely political measure, is therefore superficial (as superficial, indeed, in its own way as the exactly opposite view, which we have challenged, according to which the government abolished Islam). Governments, certainly, tend to take actions for political reasons. But this is not to gainsay that those actions may well have non-political and even deeply religious results or implications; may even be symptoms or evidences of deeply religious movements.

To dismiss, therefore, the recent actions of the Turkish government again allowing greater expression to religion as "merely" a makeweight to communism or "merely" the vote-catching of demagogy, is to miss the potential significance of the move. Islam, which in the course of its historical evolution has latterly in Turkey undergone a vigorous reorientation of its external and social forms and a concomitant and in many cases profound reorientation of its inner personal being in men's lives and hearts, is now being given there the opportunity to re-express itself. In what forms it will do so, and whether with a new vitality, are matters that will, in the future, prove significant to watch.

One possibility, of course, is that it will be re-expressed once more in the old forms—something between those of the decadence of the immediate past, when Ottoman corruption was dominant, and, ideally, the classical 'pure' forms of orthodox Islam. To some extent this is actually happening, and is welcomed with legitimate applause by the orthodox elsewhere. The call to prayer has again been made legal in Arabic. And so on. The trend, however, is evident chiefly in renewed religious activity of the masses: men whose participation in the Revolution and all its works was at best limited, so that all their life, and not only their religion, has been of the old school. For example, the new religious weeklies have apparently been *popular* both in the sense of having a quite considerable circulation and appeal and in the sense of avoiding all deep problems and serious issues. They are not addressed to either intellectuals or modernists. More extreme: a minor but inflammatory dynamist movement calling itself Ticani broke out in violent defiance of law in support of ancient fundamentalism.

If such trends, in their widest ramifications, should become dominant, it would mean primarily that those classes within Turkey who have on the whole been passive in the social transformation, if not opposed to it, were using their democratic power and religious freedom to re-establish another point of view. At its most extreme, if carried out not only in the 'religious' sphere (which cannot finally be isolated) but also in the social, political, and what not, this could mean that the Revolution, in the end, had failed. Some, whether inside or outside Turkey, would welcome that reversion.

We will not here pause to argue with them, nor to discuss the possibility of its happening, though manifestly we neither hope nor believe that the Turkish experiment will be overwhelmed. Our concern here, however, is with the form that the religion of the ruling class, the men of the Revolution, is likely to take. If *these* men choose orthodoxy, that will indeed be significant. If, as modern persons, living intellectually and practically in an industrial civilization; aware of science as a body of knowledge, a method of inquiry, and a technique for recasting their environment; aware, too, realistically of modern war (and the threat of it from their massive Russian neighbour); conscious of their free responsibility in the present moment of human history—if such Muslims find, after two decades of wandering, that their religion can be expressed best, or expressed only, or can best or only be recovered or revitalized, through the traditional forms and institutions; that will be profoundly instructive.

It would also be of wide consequence, not only in Turkey but throughout the Muslim world. And while it would mean a repudiation of the Revolution in many of its aspects, it would be quite a different matter from the failure adumbrated above. Whereas that envisaged the overpowering of the builders of the new society by the lower classes, and the rejection of their unfamiliar handiwork by outsiders unconvinced, this possibility sees rather the revolutionaries themselves deciding from within that the new direction was wrong, and deliberately choosing to go back to earlier models.

However, as we have seen, the dominant and emphatic conviction of this class itself is that such will not be the case. For them, the old type of religion is gone, and ought to be gone; and they are consciously in search of a new. Many individuals are such that, if offered only the old, they would, whether with an insouciant disparaging or with a vast sorrowing reluctance, take none at all (like those liberals in the West whose religiousness is frustrated by a resurgence of [neo-]orthodoxy that keeps them from being Christians).

Another possibility is that, in their quest for new forms, the Turks will fail. This would be indeed serious; meaning, as it would, that Islam in its first major experience of living in the fully modern world had been unable to find any interpretation for itself compatible with that modernity. For anyone, Muslim or alien, to predict such failure ahead of time would be rash as well as presumptuous.

More optimistic is the belief that the present development will continue and the Turkish intelligentsia soon or gradually will elaborate a new diction in which to speak their faith and through which Islam, or should we say God, may speak to them. In favour of this possibility is the religious quality of the persons themselves and the tenor of their immediate society's progress, as well as, perhaps, the world-wide search for religious reinterpretation in which they might participate, both profiting and contributing.

Of any group that sets out to "reform" Islam, or indeed any religion, it may well be asked, as Professor Gibb reminds us,[29] by what authority they propose to do so. Turkish modernism differs, perhaps, on this point from the Islamic modernism of all other countries, in that it has, whether explicit or no, an answer. The modernist Turk proceeds on the authority of the Revolution. This is the great dominating event of his society and his life, which he sees as having given a new birth to his nation, transforming it from decadence and disrepute into strength, honour, and—in an ultimate, though far from static, sense—virtue. What the Revolution has done and is doing to the Turkish community is to him fundamentally and monumentally good. To say that it is, to him, religiously good is tautological yet relevant.

To the Revolution and its ideal many modern Turks give their loyalty, and even, it might seem, their supreme loyalty. The discussion amongst the intellectuals regarding the new religious freedom turned largely on the question of whether or not it endangered the Revolution. Those opposed were opposed on the grounds that it opened the door to social reaction, and might put in jeopardy the whole progress thus far achieved. Those in favour, as already indicated above, defended it on the grounds that the

[29] *Modern Trends in Islam*, Chicago, 1947, p. 104.

new régime was sufficiently established that going back was no longer thinkable. Of all this, a critical Muslim could make a serious charge. For, to judge and regulate a religion in terms of some accepted social progress (rather than vice-versa) goes, one could say, beyond secularism and impiety into sacrilege.

A related indictment could be that the Turks give their loyalty to Turkey, or Turkishness, rather than to Islam.

This is a matter of profound import. To make Islam subordinate to nationalism, religion to society, is dangerous in the extreme. Yet the matter is not simple. To give one's final loyalty to anything but God is indeed—as Islam has long well taught—sin; and devastatingly such. It is disruptive not only of the personality that succumbs to this distortion of its own true nature. It is disruptive also, within history, of any society that thus loses its vision of transcendent goals. Nonetheless there are two considerations that must be urged against too quick an interpretation of the Turkish venture as irreverent.

First, there is the somewhat subtle but utterly crucial question, already adumbrated, as to whether the nationalist's loyalty is to the Revolution, social progress, Turkishness, or what not, *under God*, or whether it is to these things absolutely. Are one's values ultimately transcendent or empirical? To put the query more pragmatically: is there meaning in the question whether the Revolution, historical progress, Turkishness, etc., could go wrong?

Men to whom the word 'wrong' in that question can convey significance, have, whether they know it or not, a transcendent reference for their loyalty—a reference with which they are, ultimately, saved; and without which they are ultimately lost. The Russian intellectual Radek, presumably, was sufficiently mistaken in supposing himself a dialectical *materialist* that actually he unwittingly believed in and worked for not, finally, the revolution itself and its empirical results but the *ideal* of the revolution. He thought that the results of the revolution in actuality had deviated from the results as they ought to be. That is, though in a small and doubtless distorted way—as is varyingly true of all human beings—yet he apprehended something of the will of God. His loyalty to transcendence, however, brought him into conflict with empirical reality; and in his ruthlessly empirical, materialist, society, he paid for it with his life.

Similarly with Turkey, one may ask whether the nationalist's allegiance to nationalism is ultimately to the new status quo, come what may, the Turkey that is, or to the Turkey that ought to be. And in the latter case, one may ask what the phrase means; what gives it meaning.

It is important to realize, however, that a similar subtlety and crux are possible with regard to religion itself. It is the aim of the religions to elicit loyalty to what is transcendent. It is sometimes their nemesis to attract it only to themselves. In the particular case of Islam, we may see this in certain developments of modernist thought in other Muslim countries. If, even unconsciously, one defines a Muslim as one whose supreme loyalty is to extant Islam, especially as an empirical community but even as an empirical set of institutions and traditions, one is in the same danger of bowing down before something other than the transcendent God, and therefore of ending up with fascism. There are many Muslims throughout the world today who believe in Islam more than they believe in God.

It is our conviction, already expressed, that the loyalty of the dominant group in Turkey, for all their nationalism, has not been so earth-bound. Nonetheless, it is important to bear in mind how easily and almost imperceptibly all our group loyalties can, and perhaps must, vacillate between divine ideals and the earthly symbols and processes that embody them. It is important also to recognize the lengths to which these men's Turkishness has gone.

This is evident also in our second consideration, according to which, we would contend, Turkish nationalism is not altogether un-Islamic—even though the religious novelty is such here that it raises perhaps as many questions as it solves. We refer to the point, touched upon already in an earlier chapter, that there has been here a substitution not of something else for a Muslim grouping but of a part for the whole. Turkish nationalism is itself to a certain degree inherently Muslim, in that it is concerned with a nation that is constituted of Muslims. It is the idealization of a Muslim (though not of *the* Muslim) group. This point is of considerable significance, including religious significance. We believe that it in fact has religious overtones even when those involved are unaware or insouciant of any Islamic implication.

However, these overtones seem to some to become shrill when certain aspects of the religious implications are made explicit. This is most manifest in the aim being openly formulated by several, and said by some to be already in existence, of a Turkish Islam. As one Turk put it: "We want to construct a Turkish Islam, which will be ours, relevant to and integrated with our (new) society, just as Anglicanism is Christianity in a thoroughly English fashion. Anglicanism is not Italian, not Russian. Yet no one accuses it of not being Christian. Why should we not have an Islam of our own?"

This is new in Islamic history, and to outside Muslims is shocking. Europeans, who know from sad experience the devastating potentialities of conflicting nationalisms, as well as Muslims who know from proud tradition the integrating potentialities of Islamic universalism, may be sorry to see the cosmopolitanism of classical Muslim civilization broken up. The Turks, however, are not sorry. Their separatism is deliberate, and its success is welcomed with enthusiasm. They view that breaking up as inevitable anyway and for themselves good.

Moreover, they view the international society in which Turkey will and should participate as something other than, or larger than, the community of Islamic nations. (To this fundamental matter, we shall return.) Whether one agrees with their evaluation or no, it is important to recognize this Turkish view. Once again, what appears to others as a Turkish repudiation of Islam, or secession from it, is in fact, for good or ill, a new development of very considerable importance within Islam.

It is an internal development, which from certain points of view orthodox or alien Muslims might reasonably regard as more dangerous to Islam than repudiation or secession. For it must be recognized that the price being paid by Turkey for elaborating an Islamic interpretation of its own, is the negating, both in form and in substance, of the human community of Islam. If the one purest essence of Islam is submission to God, who is transcendent, certainly Islam as a visible religion has had in its history until now—as we have throughout stressed—a cardinal concern about the earthly society constituted by Muslims. The Turks, in pursuit of the former in today's new world, find that it (and their Turkishness) has led them away from the latter. The feeling of other members of Muslim society that the modern Turks have renounced Islam is rooted, perhaps, most deeply in their sense of the Turks' having renounced that wider society both in fact and in principle. The two points at which Turkish liberalism has most disruptively strained modern world Islam, are the Turkish Muslim's attitude to other Muslims, and the Turkish Muslim's attitude to the *shari'ah*. The Turks are, Islamically, isolationist. What is more, in rejecting the Law, they are rejecting the very notion of Islamic social integration.

Both points demand consideration.

On few subjects are modernist Turks so emphatic as in asseverating that pan-Islam is dead. We may leave aside here the historical reasons underlying this. ("We do not want to be burdened with other people's problems. We have bitter memories of that.") We may may leave aside as well present political implications. ("To stand—*viz.*, against Russia—we need powerful friends, not weak ones.") So far as religion is concerned, on few Islamic matters are their emotions so quick as in disclaiming any religious involvement with the modern Arabs. Of Indonesians, Pakistanis, and other remoter Muslims they scarcely take time to be aware; with Iran they recognize certain ties, perhaps close but certainly not strong, cultural but not political, poetic rather than religious. To most of them, 'other Muslims' means, at once, Arabs. And to many of them Arabs are, if not repellent or contemptible, at least alien.

Again, our concern is not with the historical background, perspicuous enough ("We have had too much experience with the Arabs"), nor with contemporary political relations ("We voted for the Arabs against Zionism, certainly. But we would not dream of sending troops"). For our present purposes, what is significant is the deep gap that the modern Turks find, or dig, between themselves and the Arabs *religiously*.

It is hardly an exaggeration to say that some Turks consider Arab Muslims much as an American Protestant might look on an Ethiopian Orthodox Christian: politically irrelevant and religiously benighted. Any suggestion that the new Faculty of Theology at Ankara would be 'another Azhar' is either laughable or shocking. ("A shambles. We would certainly never allow such a thing to be repeated here"—"We intend to make it something that will compare, rather, with Union Theological Seminary.") In fact, one of the impulses behind the desire for a religious reform in Turkey is the felt need for an overt differentiation of Turkish Islam from Arab.

The depth of Turkish isolationist feeling is an important fact in the modern Islamic world.

If taxed with this introversion, Turkish defence would be spirited. For one thing, Turks are well aware that their own refusal to continue their role of active championship of the Islamic world is matched by an equal reluctance on the part of other Muslims today to acknowledge Turkish hegemony.[30] (After all, they abolished the Khilafah only after the Arab Revolt.) Secondly, with their sociological bent, they emphasize that Turkish society is radically both separate from and different from the societies of other Muslims today and a difference in religion is involved. Thirdly, their whole venture in self-renewal, embodied in the Revolution (with its renunciation of empire) and still prosecuted with high mettle, is essentially a *self*-renewal. For the Turks to reform other people's Islam would seem to them as gratuitous as it would seem to them recreant not to reform their own.[31]

On the question of the Law, there is involved not only a secession from even lip-service to the notion of pan-Muslim social solidarity. The issue raises internal questions also, of serious import.

Islamic society, community consciousness, and social conscience are not merely an historical phenomenon, which Turkey, in the process of creating new history, is choosing to alter. They are also the ideal, as they are largely the result, of the *shari'ah* Law, which too Turkey has rejected.[32] Turkish modernists seem to have given little thought to the theological and moral aspects of its rejection as an ideal. They have contented themselves with a positive judgement, both theological and moral, in favour of its rejection as a practice. This is, in part, indicative of the telling failure—by no

[30] Yet they feel themselves, quite simply, the most advanced and most powerful Muslim nation. "For many a long year we have been cogitating why the Orient is backward, Europe advanced. We observe that we are the most advanced of the Muslims. . . ."

[31] Cf. Gibb, *op. cit.*, pp. 103-04, where, questioning Iqbāl's claim for Muslim liberals to reinterpret Islām, he asks, with the religious leaders, on what authority a small, self-constituted minority proposes to "remodel the social institutions of one-seventh of the human race." The Turks are remodelling those institutions, they would point out, only for themselves.

[32] The discussion, primarily, is of the *shari'ah* only as a governmental code. It is sometimes said, also by the Turks themselves, that the Republic's action has affected only those aspects of the *shari'ah*, the *mu'āmalāt*, that deal with civil or social affairs, or relations between men. Those dealing with personal affairs, the relation of each man to God, *'ibādāt*, are untouched by state action; Turks are free to accept these or not, as each sees fit. The accuracy of such an analysis is only approximate.

means confined to Turkey—of its exponents to make the ideal compelling or even intelligible or even obvious in the modern Muslim world.

Striking, certainly, in Turkey is the earnest conviction, the almost grim determination, that the recent freedom for religious expression shall not and will not lead to a return to the Law. The remarkably wide agreement on this point includes the devout as well as the sophisticated. Many on being questioned seem never to have conceived the possibility; and react to an enquiry with dismay, followed by rejection. If the new Islam in Turkey, however resurgent, were to include a revived *shari'ah* officially imposed, it would mean either that an entirely different group had gained the ascendant or that those presently dominant had been metamorphosed.

Indeed, one view of the recent enlarging of scope for religious thought is this: the new "laicism"—a sort of controlled separation of church and state—having now been worked out (and imposed) satisfactorily from the standpoint of the state, it is time for it to be worked out from that of the church. Turkish society, this argument runs, has adopted, approved, and become accustomed to, the new role for religion in modern life; but Turkish religion has not yet formally done so.

The old officiating representatives of Islam administered an Islam that sought control of politics, law, and social custom. The Republican government, suppressing that group, took matters into its own hands and itself determined what religion's role should be. Now it would seek to train a new class of officiant who will administer the new Islam within the bounds set for it. The step indicates, *inter alia*, the confidence of the modernizers that Turkish Islam has in fact, among the educated classes, been so changed that, given freedom of expression, it will express itself in this sense. (The freedom is, of course, far from absolute. The state continues its control, if not its guidance.)

Yet a problem remains. The crucial matter is, perhaps, that the Turks, in rejecting the *shari'ah*, think of themselves as having discarded only the equivalent of what in Western civilization might be thought of as ecclesiastical positive law. They do not think of having abandoned the equivalent of what is embodied in Western tradition as the concept of natural law. If there is no transcendent justice in the universe to which a man's conscience can appeal, against the empirical actions and even the laws of a society, that man and that society are precarious in the extreme. Whether Turkey can generate an effective substitute, in this realm, for the divine Laws of Islam—for Turks grown, in this realm also, ineffective—is not yet clear.

The actual regulations of the *shari'ah* the Turks have replaced, in civil matters, with those of the Swiss code. They are at no loss to argue that the change has proven itself good. But with what, if anything, have they replaced the principles on which the *shari'ah* is based? This is a question to which they have given little thought, let alone much answer. We refer not to the immediate principles, of deduction, the overt sources, etc.; for these they have explicitly substituted induction, the needs of society, and the like. Our reference is to the ultimate principles, of man's rights and duties as related to the very structure of the universe.

If today the members of the Grand National Assembly have replaced the *shari'ah* with a foreign code, because it seemed to them good, what is to keep them tomorrow from replacing this by fascist laws, if it seem to them, as a ruling group, profitable? Again, if the individual is not bound, by any eternal or internal principle, to obey or honour the laws of the *shari'ah*, by what is he bound, except an efficient police, to obey or honour the laws of the state?

We have suggested that, for individual Turks, their informal religiousness and their nationalism are serving this purpose for the moment. Their own recent measures indicate their feeling that, for the long run and for new generations, something more concrete is needed, some crystallization of their numinousness. The sociological problem is whether a society, even when consisting of members individually Muslim, their religion a personal moral affection, can be held together and made good by nationalism; or whether a principle of integration more transcendent, divine, in this case Islamic, is (also?) needed.

The theological problem is twofold. One aspect is the counterpart of the above: whether man's relation to man, an integral part of any true religion, can be left religiously unformulated. The other is a question with more timeless implications, potentially emergent in all religions and in Islamic history raised particularly by *tasawwuf*, the faith of the mystics. It is that of whether man's relation to God can subsist without the mediation of a tangible sacredness. We have earlier suggested that, as the mediator between God and man has been in Christianity Christ, so in' Islam it has been the *shari'ah*. As liberal Christianity, in completely humanizing Jesus, has run, it is said, the risk at last of losing touch with God, so it may be asked whether Muslim liberals, by enacting an avowedly man-made code of laws, may be courting a similar estrangement.

To press this point, however, is valueless for those for whom the erstwhile embodiment of the divine has, for good or ill, already ceased to mediate eternity. The Law has served as a carefully constructed and beautifully structured bridge between this world and the next; many generations of Muslims have with sureness found their way across it. But today, when the stream of life is ever quickening its tempo, that bridge, in the eyes of many Turks, has proven to be a pontoon, and under the impact of the new torrential swiftness is seen to be breaking from its moorings—*on both sides*. The bridge is receding from them; not only has it been wrenched loose from the solid ground of everyday things that make up mundane life on this shore, but also it no longer seems in contact with the divine on the other side.

On *tasawwuf*—which, one might say, has through the Islamic centuries for the individual Muslim paralleled or dispensed with the community's legal bridge—Turkish opinion is unclarified. An occasional intellectual dismisses it as "contemplation, quietism, withdrawal from life—it has nothing to do with us, with the modern world. Sufism was imported from India, anyway; and is ridiculous. It is dead in Turkey. And it ought to be dead." This type seems, however, rare, remarkably so in contrast with the Arab world. The Sufi tradition has been strong and conspicuous in Turkish history; today in an inconspicuous way it seems still religiously strong or at least active. The Turks have vigorously shattered the social institutions that it developed. The historians recognize the major role played in the past by the orders in Turkey's culture; the alert modernists recognize the similarity of aim between the true Sufi and themselves; the most sophisticated respond to a recitation of the *mawlud*.[33] Almost all, however,

[33] Süleyman Chelebi, *The Mevlidi Sherif*, translated by F. Lyman Mac-Callum, London, Wisdom of the East Series, 1943. The translation's introduction is of interest; it was written well before the present "revival," as well as before the present writer came into touch with Turkish sophisticated society to observe for himself something of the place of this poem in its

agree in denouncing the *tekke*'s (mystic orders) roundly; as at the least degenerate, as well as politically reactionary.[34] The question of reopening them has not been raised. Certainly many are, almost grimly, against it.

Yet the modernists argue, cogently, that *tasawwuf*, surely, is in principle religion without organization, without forms: in this case, if anywhere, surely in sloughing off the formalism nothing essential is lost, and very much gained. And it is precisely a rationale of inner, personal religion that the Turkish intelligentsia is seeking. They have already had, in Ziya Gökalp and in the government actions, an emphasis on religion as a social phenomenon; this emphasis has been influential in their thinking, and to some extent is supported by the general *sunni* tendency to stress the group. For all the resurgence of activity in modern Turkish Islam, there would perhaps be little prospect of a truly religious vitality were this emphasis not supplemented by the significant degree to which the orientation of individual Turks is Sufi. Moreover, the Sufi concern for human brotherhood beyond the bounds of the closed religious group is important to the Turks, who, for political, economic, ideological, and other reasons are endeavouring, while preserving their Turkish culture and their Muslim religion, to become members of Western or world civilization rather than of an Islamic bloc.

As one Turk expressed himself on this whole subject: "Certainly the *tekke*'s were finished; and should be gone for ever. But *tasavvuf* is essential, is what we need. At heart, it is imperative [this said with conviction, sadness, sincerity and an almost poetic earnestness] that we find that inner nature of religion, unencumbered by the formal accoutrements of a bygone day, and the divisive particularities of the diverse creeds. Man needs this, or all is lost. This is the moral, spiritual crisis of mankind today; and if

---

affection; one may note MacCallum's remarks on p. 15, on the continued use of the poem in Republican Turkey. The present writer was most interested to find one or two Turks surprised and even incredulous at his referring to this work as Ṣūfī, so totally has it been accepted into standard Turkish Islām.

34 The immediate occasion for dissolving the orders and closing the *tekkes* and *zaviyes* was the Kurdish Revolt of 1925, the most formidable internal threat with which the Republic was faced; it was led by the *derviş* Şeyh Said, "hereditary Abbot of the Nakhshbendi Order" (Toynbee and Kirkwood, *op. cit.*, p. 265).

we do not solve it, we are finished. And mysticism can never be a science. Science can aid it; in fact the new mysticism must use science; the new Faculty must make use of scientific methods and science's results. But the thing that we are looking for is beyond and above science. And it will bring in all mankind." The remarks were capped with an appropriate Persian couplet, traditional, vital, Sufi.

Professor Gibb has touched on the tie between Sufism and romanticism;[35] and indicated the incidence also in the modern Muslim world of that between romanticism and nationalism. It would be vain to deny a prominent strain of romanticism in the Turks' national movement—as, for instance, Cahun and the 'Sun Language Theory' illustrate.[36] It would be idle also to deny the explosive dangers of unchecked romanticism, on which he insists.

Nonetheless, the Turks are far and away the most realistic and self-critical group in present-day Islam. For one thing, despite the relation on which we have insisted between their Turkish nationalism and their Muslimness, yet there is a certain immediate conflict between the two romanticisms, so that each tends to check the other. Secondly, as Gibb himself indicates,[37] while romanticism may be checked by rationalism (which in the Islamic case has in the past been represented by the orthodox 'ulama'), it may be checked also by science and the historical method; and with these, particularly the former, the Turks have become more intimate, in their modernity, than any other Muslim people. Chiefly, however, their romanticism is disciplined by a tellingly honest viewing of their world as it is. Their imagination, though vivid, is checked by the facts of their social progress. Not only are they dreaming of an ideal Turkey; also they are busy bringing it into being. (Contrast those Arabs who are dreaming of an ideal Arab world of a thousand years and more ago.)

[35] Op. cit., pp. 110ff. Cf. that whole chapter for the discussion that here follows.

[36] See Léon Cahun, Introduction à l'histoire de l'Asie: Turcs et Mongols des origines à 1405, Paris, 1896. A Turkish translation appeared in 1899. For passing remarks regarding the significant influence of this work on historiography in Turkey for a time, and regarding the Sun Theory (Guneş-Dil Teorisi), see Bernard Lewis, op. cit. (at ref. 10 above), esp. p. 221-22; Uriel Heyd, "Language Reform in Modern Turkey," Middle Eastern Affairs, New York, 4: 402-08 (1953); and the latter's book by the same title, Jerusalem, 1954, esp. pp. 33-36.

[37] Op. cit., p. 108.

The zest with which the Turks are pursuing the national aim that they have set, and the success that they are achieving, are indications of their realism and sincerity. The whole tone of their conversations on religious subjects, quite unique in the modern Muslim world, is another. If life consists in a balance between dreams and prosaic reality, creative freedom and discipline, the modern Turks can claim a sizable measure of success.

The significance of the Turkish development can be well grasped in the terms of Professor Gibb's own analysis. For that development differs most strikingly from that of the rest of the modern Muslim world precisely in those points that he characterizes as the other Muslim modernists' chief weakness. He speaks of "the intellectual confusions and the paralyzing romanticism which cloud the minds of the modernists of today."[38] He deplores those modernists' elaboration of ideal solutions to their social problems, out of relation to the actual societies in which they live; and writes that when those societies in fact change "by the forces of internal evolution, they will find their own appropriate solutions. These solutions will not necessarily coincide with our Western solutions but will be based on the proved experience and needs of the Muslim people."[39] These observations point to the relative strength of Turkey's reinterpretation. The modernist Islam that is being gestated by the Turks has been fathered not, like the Arabs', by paralysing romanticism but by the actual social changes within their country.

As one educational official put it: "Islam among the Arabs, in India, etc., is in sharp contrast with ours in Turkey. And obviously so. For they have not had their social revolution. Amanullah did not have the social basis for his reforms; therefore he failed. Similarly in Iran: the sociological substructure had not developed far enough to accept the changes. That is why you are hearing now of the veil coming back in Tehran. Take this question of the veil. It is not possible that we shall go back to it. Everything depends on economic life; and in Turkey women are working, in banks, as teachers, professors, judges, chemists, lawyers. There are more than twenty women lawyers practising here in Ankara right now. And this applies to the provinces as well. The process has gone much too far for the old ideas to come back. Much has changed;

---

[38] *Ibid.,* p. 105, repeated p. 106 (cf. above, chap. 3, ref. 179).
[39] *Ibid.,* p. 105.

as democracy advances, there will be more change still. The religion is developing; we earnestly hope that it will continue to develop. But we have no need of a reformer: *the life of society will take care of its reformation.*"

To this question of a reformer we shall presently return. In the meantime we may note that this sociological basis for the new religion is found in the realms not only of social life but also, incipiently, of religious. There are a few signs of a new economic-social pattern emerging in explicitly Islamic life in Turkey. In the past, the religious institutions have been sustained economically chiefly by the state and by *Waqf* endowments. In Turkey at present in a few instances money is being collected for the repair or even construction of mosques by public subscription, neighbourhood or otherwise; and the office of a religious functionary is being brought potentially closer to the status of a modern profession by such practices as the paying of unprecedented sums for his services at weddings, funerals, *mawluds,* and the like, within the modernized classes. These are but precarious and minor first steps in a matter that is, in fact, of crucial importance, if a modern religion is to become not only an idea but a living force in Turkey. It is too early yet to say whether they may develop into something comparable to a 'congregation,' economically self-sustaining. If they do so develop or if otherwise a situation emerges wherein a university graduate in theology has some prospect of becoming an *imam* in a mosque with a financial and socio-cultural position comparable to that of his fellows who are doctors, lawyers, professors, and the like, the significance will clearly be great.

The state itself is moving in this direction.[40] Whether its control will offset its economic support has yet to be seen.

This, combined with the intellectual rethinking, would make not fanciful the inspiring vision of the Turkish leader who foresaw the Istanbul mosques of Süleymaniye and Sultan Ahmet—surely houses of worship magnificent and sublime—"filled with modern and educated worshipers, and with first-class preachers trained in our new Faculty and with subsequent further degrees from Oxford; honoured, modern, intelligent, serious."

Even those Turks who so dream are well aware that the task

[40] It now receives into state employment the graduates of the new religious training schools and Faculty on the same principle of salary scale (the *barem*) as those trained in other fields.

before them is far from easy and is far from completed. Most, indeed, affirm that it has not yet been begun. "There must be a reform of Islam. But at present there is no indication of such a reform: I see no one on the horizon capable of doing it, or essaying to do it. It may take years. Yes, I myself have thought much on these matters; but I have no pretensions whatever as a religious reformer. I am an ordinary simple man. All that we can do, and this we are doing, is to lay the foundations, to set up the circumstances in which a reform would be possible." So genuine is the search for a new statement of faith, and so successful the adjustment to the disestablished, unclerical, personal-moral Islam of the post-Revolution years, that the Turkish intelligentsia is less conscious of the degree of reform already accomplished than is an outside observer.

One final observation on Turkish modernism, before we move on. This concerns its relation with the West. That relation has two aspects, internal and external, each of which is of major importance. Those who had been afraid that Turkey was drifting into a spurious Westernism, away from its own authentic spirit, have doubtless been relieved to see the resurgence of an overt Islam. On the other hand, the Turks might still be accused of now aping the West even in religion, in seeking to reproduce in Islam a Reformation that Christendom effected in earlier times and different circumstances. Certainly it is startling to hear the name of Luther on many Turkish lips that could scarcely discourse on the work of al-Ash'ari or al-Ghazzali or Iqbal.

However, the answer here, we should suggest, is twofold. First, the modernizing Turks are Westernizers not in a superficial imitative sense but with deep deliberation—in contrast, for instance, to those Cairo Muslims who, while they shout down Western books, are avid of Western tinsel. Secondly, the Turks are consciously and seriously facing in religion a specific and difficult problem: which is, how to relate their inherited religion to the quite new life and society that make up the modern world. They know that they are the first Muslims to be fully confronted with this particular problem (and therefore do not expect guidance on how to solve it from a study of past Islamic history). They know also that a comparable problem has been met already in the West, and therefore bethink themselves of studying how Christians have dealt with it. They are looking to the West not for religious inspiration, which for them remains Islamic; but for, as it were, techniques in the religious field. The assumption would be that such techniques involve questions not of being Christian or Islamic, but of being modern rather than mediaeval.

The larger aspects of the Westernism of Turkey's new Islam raise issues of more than Turkish, and even more than Muslim, import. We have essayed to consider the Turkish movement as a development in the history of Islam. Another way of looking at it, both legitimate and important, is in terms of the history of civilizations. The question, essentially, is this: can a non-Christian nation be a member of Western civilization.

The question has profundities. In them the Turks find themselves involved. The question has world-wide implications, but only in Turkey is it being seriously thought out.[41] We have already remarked on the choice of the Turks not to belong to a community of Muslim nations. It is their will to participate in the Western community. As Ziya Gökalp put it, French and Germans have separate cultures, but both constitute Western civilization; so would Turks, while stressing and vitalizing their Turkish nationalism.[42] And if for a time in seeking membership they seemed to keep quiet about their religion, or even in some Western eyes to relinquish it, now they are quite explicitly Muslim though admittedly searching for what that means in the new context. If it is a question whether Islam can adjust itself to Western civilization, it is also a question whether Western civilization is able to develop so as to include Islam.

How the process will evolve we do not venture to predict. Our only insistence is, once more, that the process is significant. Coming back to our major standpoint, the development from the point of view of the Turks themselves as Muslims, we find them,

[41] Japan deliberately adopted Western methods for its own purposes; but never wished to become a member of a Western community—or, if it did, was shamefully insulted and rejected by that community, largely on the grounds of colour. The Jews, apart from being a nation only in an unusual sense, and despite their immense contribution to that civilization, have been accepted as members of Western civilization in a sense the contemplation of which gives one pause, and a Westerner shame.

[42] See the forthcoming ed. of Gökalp's writings (cf. above, chap. 2, ref. 30). Cf. also, Uriel Heyd, *The Foundations of Turkish Nationalism*, London, 1950, p. 65 and *passim*; Niyazi Berkes, "Ziya Gökalp: His Contribution to Turkish Nationalism," *The Middle East Journal*, Washington, 8:375-90 (1954), esp. pp. 387ff.

in other fields competent and effective, in this field serious and sincere.

One thing seems sure. If a Luther—to borrow their own metaphor—were to appear, he would get a ready hearing amongst the educated classes of Turkey. Emotionally and intellectually, sociologically and religiously, they seem ready to follow new ventures of Islamic development. However, whether such a reformer will indeed appear is another matter. Can one generate a Reformation by fiat?—even when providing the milieu?

The Turks seem creative enough to understand and to accept, creative enough to implement and to develop, a new religious vision. Whether they are creative enough to produce one is the crucial question.

Chapter 5

PAKISTAN: ISLAMIC STATE

INTO the business of rehabilitating Islamic history in our day, Pakistanis, of all the world's Muslim communities, have plunged most self-consciously and clamorously. This, rather than any particular success they may have yet had in executing the enterprise, gives their case significance. Here is a group that has expressly set out to live together as Muslims. They have sought, and won, political independence: they have as a nation the formal power, and therefore the responsibility, of fashioning their community life in the modern world. Here, it was said, will unfold before our eyes the earthly outworking in our day of the religious community, the twentieth-century actualization of Islam as a social ideal. Here if anywhere in the modern world, it might be argued, is a clear opportunity to see what Islam now means in operation. Here explicitly is Islamic history once again in full swing.

In less than a decade of existence Pakistan has already gone through various phases of mood and interpretation regarding the place of Islam in the life of the nation. None of the phases has been decisive, or even clear. For a time there was exuberantly an emphasis on the close tie between religion and social life. Many were enthusiastic that the purpose of Pakistan was to realize a truly Islamic community. The nation, for them, existed so that the religion could be taken seriously, and applied to modern life. This accompanied the almost standard view on which we have already touched, that Islam and its society had gone through a period of oppression and, as it were, eclipse; the attainment of Pakistan signified the emergence from that period and the embarking on a great and glorious enterprise, the society's reimplementation of Islam in our day.

More recently, a mood of disillusionment has widely supervened. To "apply Islam" to the concrete affairs of national life quickly proved vastly more difficult than many had foreseen. And some applications of it that were tried, by devotees more zealous than wise, proved ugly. The Lahore riots of 1953, in which brutality and chaos were proffered in the name of religion, gave pause.[1] Less spectacular but almost as telling, in East Pakistan

---

[1] See below, pp. 230-31.

the Muslim League, which talked of Islam, seemed to proffer nothing at all; the party was rejected at the polls.[2] All in all, many began to feel that the concept of an 'Islamic state' was none too helpful; and turned their thoughts to other things.

It is our contention, however, that the matter remains important—and indeed crucial. The happenings of recent years have made the issue more, not less, compelling. The failure of an Islamic state would be easier than its success, but no less important. A nation cannot readily escape from religion; and it cannot escape at all from history, from mundane development. Once a people is free, it is also responsible. For good or ill, it is responsible even in face of questions so formidable as that of relating its history and its faith. And on the success and manner of this Muslim people's executing the enterprise of living together as Muslims in the modern world, turns to a significant degree the future not only of their nation but also of Islam. If Islamic history is significant at all, then the history that Pakistanis are now creating is of serious moment, both temporal and religious.

Even if on second thought they may feel that the undertaking to build an Islamic society was more onerous than they once imagined, yet in a sense there is now no going back. Indeed, so far-reaching was the commitment, so overt and explicit the endeavour, that the significance and responsibility have grown inescapable. The history on which they have embarked will, deliberately or not, be Islamic. Whether they like or regret it, the engagement is large, and has been undertaken—it cannot now be discarded or shelved. For a decision to drop the 'Islamic state' idea at this stage would be no mere diversion. Rather, it would be a religious act, a deep conclusion. For it would involve the positive assertion by a great Muslim community that the Islamic ideal for society is irrelevant or unequal to the task of contemporary living; or at least that they as a people are unable so to interpret or implement it. Even without a forthright decision, merely a drift away from this ideal or from concern about it would in fact

[2] The provincial assembly elections, March, 1954. Cf. Stanley Maron, "The Problem of East Pakistan," *Pacific Affairs*, 28:132-44 (1955); Richard L. Park, "East Bengal: Pakistan's Troubled Province," *Far Eastern Survey*, 23: 70-74 (1954). Cf. also, for the ensuing period, Richard L. Park and Richard S. Wheeler, "East Bengal under Governor's Rule," *ibid.*, 23:129-34 (1954).

involve a reassessment of, and challenge to, and comment on, their faith.

To abandon all pretence to an Islamic social ideal would be of mundane as well as religious consequence. Not only would it demand, on pain of hypocrisy, a reinterpretation of religion. It would demand also some new interpretation of mundane affairs. For no society can survive that does not have some ideal, some faith, some motivation. If the Islamic were spurned, or even allowed to slide, one might reasonably expect either that this would be accompanied by the far-reaching adoption of some other conviction, or else that it would lead to disillusionment and cynicism, and these to disintegration and chaos.

Whether Pakistan could indeed effect any practical constructive programme on the basis of Islam was a serious and exacting question—more penetrating than most of the religionists recognized. Whether it can hold together and effect any practical constructive programme at all without Islam as a basis is an equally serious and exacting question—more penetrating than most of the secularists have recognized. Liberal secularism is itself a faith, a positive conviction. It has its own foundations, moral and intellectual; its own martyrs and heroes and ideals; its own history; and its own institutions. Some expect it to appear of itself so soon as religious faith is circumscribed or dropped. This is glib. The history of Pakistan to date, as we shall presently consider, all too starkly illustrates the falsity of so facile an assumption. Pakistan may choose a liberal secular future for itself; but if it does it will be taking on, as it did with its Islamic aspiration, a mighty endeavour. This too will require a high level of devoted creativity.

In sum, we are persuaded that one must in the Pakistan case take very seriously the 'Islamic state' idea—whether in order to comprehend what has been and may yet be involved if the nation aims at 'being Islamic'; or to appreciate the religious implications if it rejects the ideal in favour of some other; or to understand what the failure to be Islamic may signify in practice.

Pakistan may succeed in becoming an Islamic state. Or it may transfer its loyalty from an Islamic to some new ideal. Or it may fail. Each of the alternatives is momentous; and the choice between them is searching and inexorable.

The Establishment of an Islamic State

The conception of an 'Islamic state' ideal, a conceptual model to serve as a possible objective for the nation's striving, will receive our attention later on. We first wish to stress that there is a sense in which Pakistan is an Islamic state already; in addition to another sense in which it is not yet an Islamic state but may, and should, become one. Apart from any question of its form, and however un-ideal its actuality, it has in a certain sense been Islamic from its inception. Its being so is one of the monumental developments of contemporary Islamic history. For Indic Islam the fundamental religious fact is the sheer existence of Pakistan.

This religious significance will be readily understood if there is general validity in the argument put forward in our opening chapter above. We suggested there that Islam is a religion whose major this-worldly expression is its self-implementation in a social order. An independent political community as the arena of religious activity is part of the very genius of Islam. The existence of such a community is not something peripheral; it lies close to the heart of the faith.

For some centuries this aspect of the religion's message has had, we may remember, no effective outward expression for most Muslims. Not finding its reality in history, it had not lapsed but been driven inward to live as part of the Muslim's dream.

It lay ready to burst forth whenever an appropriate opportunity or occasion should present itself. In the Indian case we have seen that the impulses stemming from the Waliyullah movement served to rearouse it. The so-called "Wahhabi" uprisings and their affiliates in the early nineteenth century, and to a certain extent the Mutiny (1857), were in part overt expressions of this dynamic. So in its own fashion was the Khilafat movement of the early twentieth.[3]

Similarly the response was exuberant when, in 1940, partly for their own purposes, a political party of middle-class Indo-Muslims proposed the Pakistan idea. For some decades leadership in the society had lain with those whose orientation was largely not traditionally Islamic but Westernizing and novel. It was the lower classes and other non-Westernizers who most vividly preserved and warmly cherished the inherited ideals. The modernizing bour-

[3] See above, chap. 2, ref. 18.

geoisie had to some extent lost touch with the tradition; or they harboured its dreams only vaguely, feeling somewhat their impetus but unable to formulate it. Their own dreams were largely of their immediate interests and ambitions. At the very least, they had added to their inherited ideals much new-fashioned baggage recently acquired. They were hardly in a position to give precise leadership to the popular religious urge. Yet the enthusiasm elicited was widespread and powerful, almost frenzied, when the leadership that they did proffer aimed at something[4] that the rest of the community generally could and did interpret as a programme to realize the splendid, long-standing vision of Islam.

The overwhelming, almost unanimous support eagerly offered to the Pakistan conception, the swiftness with which the idea succeeded in becoming actualized, the intensity of the emotions involved, apparently surprised even the political leaders themselves. They seemingly hardly realized on how profound an Islamic urge they were almost unwittingly touching. The longing for an Islamic state on earth blazed into rapid flame.

We do not mean to suggest that nothing else was involved in the partitioning of India. Islam's inherent drive towards a religio-political community was not the only factor at work in the hectic, complex days of the 1940's. The coming into existence of the new dominion was conditioned by the multitude of mundane matters, concrete and human, obtaining at this particular juncture of time and place. Political, economic, sociological, psychological and other factors in the separatist movement and its environment were operative and important.[5] Such matters obviously affect, and in

---

[4] On March 23, 1940, the Muslim League political party adopted the Lahore Resolution, which gave political form to the idea of a separate state for the Indian Muslims; but abstrusely. The resolution did not mention Islām, or the term Pakistan. It was the following, more than the leadership, that emphasized the Islamic aspects of the programme.

[5] These factors were studied by the present writer: up to 1942, in *Modern Islām in India: a social analysis*, Lahore, 1943; the following three years in a pamphlet, *The Muslim League 1942-45*, Lahore, 1945; these two were more or less amalgamated in a revised edition of the earlier book, London, "1946" (sc. 1947). This youthful work has many defects; among them, those of which the writer is most conscious—chiefly the inadequate understanding of Islām and also of the crucial role played in history by ideological and moral factors —are corrected so far as possible in the present study. The account of the sociological factors at work in the development, though one-sided, is perhaps not invalid so far as it went, and may still be significant. But those factors, although valid, did not of themselves add up to explain adequately what

some senses of the word determine, the course of human history; including Islamic history. The impetus from the past, the on-going striving towards a dream, is influenced, moulded, by them. Yet it is not obliterated.[6]

Without the dynamic context of specific circumstance of later British rule, the move towards Pakistan would not have developed

---

happened subsequently: neither the full cataclysm of 1947, nor the mood of vibrant stamina and creativity of Pakistan in the initial years of its existence, nor the subsequent disillusionment. The writer, it is now clear, had failed adequately to comprehend the integration of these mundane factors into significantly Islamic history. One of the advantages of studying contemporary rather than ancient history is that one may fairly quickly learn where one is wrong.

It is perhaps legitimate to point out that the work entitled *Modern Islam in India* (title-page; on the jacket, *Modern Islam in India and Pakistan*), Ripon Press, Lahore [1954], bearing the present writer's name as author, is a pirated edition made without his knowledge or consent, and includes a chapter "Towards Pakistan" that is by another hand and is entirely spurious. There are a few other interpolations also.

For other studies of the historical background of Pakistan, see the master's thesis of Mu'īnu-d-Dīn Aḥmad Khān, cited above, chap. 2, ref. 3; and A. R. Ghani, *Pakistan: a Select Bibliography*, Lahore, 1951 (this last does not include Urdū material). For literature on Pakistan since its inception, see the forthcoming revised ed. of this last; and note especially the forthcoming monograph, Keith A. Callard, *Pakistan: a Political Study*, London and New York, 1957.

[6] Indeed, certain of the external factors in the situation served to stimulate the latent religious factors in Islām at this particular point.

In Christendom, a religious emphasis on organized community life is also to be found. Yet there it has been perhaps less strong, and in any case has found its chief expression in the Church, an institution unknown in Islām. In the Western tradition, accordingly, the striving towards autonomy for the religious group has led to a struggle between church and state; in the Islamic, to a struggle for a state. Further, that same striving has in the former case led to the concept of a secular state, that recognizes a community's inherent right to religious independence, with which the state must not interfere; in the latter, to the concept of an Islamic state.

Under the British *Rāj*, the Muslim community in India was restless enough. Like other groups, it aspired to eject foreign control, and as we have noted, formulated its aspiration at times in its own religious terms. Yet that *Rāj* was secular in the sense indicated: it was willing to go quite far in defining the limits of the religious sphere within which it would not meddle. Muslims apprehended that in a united independent India they would find themselves under a considerably less "secular" régime. The religious impulse towards Islamic community autarchy, therefore, already simmering under British secularism, became ebullient at the threat of Hindu "domination." ("No, it was not Iqbal who produced Pakistan; it was the Hindus.") [Note: in this chapter unidentified quotations reproduce remarks made to us in personal conversation by Muslims in Pakistan.]

as it did. We shall see later that that particular form of the development has affected also the subsequent history of even the Islamic aspects of the venture. Yet it is also true that this emergence of Pakistan would never have happened had it not been for the Muslims' still dynamic religious orientation to this world.

The objective conditions of the moment meant that Pakistan assumed this or that specific shape, became a particular form of state. The special quality of the Muslims' inherited faith, on the other hand, meant that whatever its objective form, Pakistan was at heart an Islamic state.

It is this Islamic nature of the state (quite independent of its form) that explains the joyous and devoted loyalty that it initially aroused. The establishment of Pakistan in 1947 was greeted by its Muslim citizenry with a resonant enthusiasm, despite the catastrophic terror and chaos of its early months. Indeed, without the stamina and morale generated by religious fervour the new dominion would hardly have survived the devastations of its first disorders. Pakistan by virtue of being Islamic (in an as yet undefined sense) could call on a morale and integration that proved of prime significance not only in creating the nation but in sustaining it in hardship and in impelling it forward to energetic construction.

This enthusiasm later seemed to peter out or was frustrated, as we shall presently consider. For the moment, however, we must remember that for the early years it was exuberant.

The ardent emphasis on this new 'Islamic' state attracted the attention of outsiders. These, however, were in danger of not seeing the wood for the trees. They were puzzled by the fervour for an Islamic state seemingly accompanied by a vast obscurity as to its nature, or at least an inability on the part of those involved to declare what they had in mind. They failed to realize that fundamentally it was the fact that Pakistan existed, and not its form, that had such stirring religious significance.

To Pakistanis zealous about their Islamic state, the question was repeatedly put: What kind of state is that? In many cases, no answer could be given. In others, replies ranged widely, from historical examples taken from earlier Islam, more or less idealized, to descriptions seemingly more or less indistinguishable from patterns known or idealized in the modern West. The questioner was searching for characteristics that would distinguish an Islamic from other kinds of state: to find wherein it differed from a democratic or a secular or a liberal or, for that matter, a Christian state. Indeed, there was a temptation to conclude that the concept was meaningless except in so far as this difference could be isolated and defined. Some would even suppose that the enthusiasm was for that margin of difference. Yet in fact the enthusiasm was often for precisely those aspects of the Islamic state that seemed common to it and to the normal Western concepts: democracy, brotherhood, justice, and the like. Moreover, the supposition of course left unexplained the enthusiasm of those many who could give no answer at all.

The question is significant, and we shall have to return to it. Yet it clearly misses something fundamental in the mind and heart of the Muslim. For in the first instance, an Islamic state is not a form of state so much as a form of Islam.

It is to be distinguished not so much from other kinds of state— liberal, democratic, fascist, or whatever—as from other expressions of Islam as a religion. As there is Islamic art, Islamic theology, Islamic mysticism, so there is or may be an Islamic state. Before August 14, 1947, the Muslims of India had their art, their theology, their mysticism; but they had no state. When Jinnah proposed to them that they should work to get themselves one, they responded with a surging enthusiasm. Their attainment, on that date, of a state of their own was greeted with an elation that was religious as well as personal. It was considered a triumph not only for Muslims but for Islam.

Islam, as a living force in world history, is carried by the Muslims: their art is its art, their theology is its theology. And to some degree, their misfortunes, their suffering, their weaknesses, are its woe. Art, theology, and other such creative expressions of religion are to some extent imperishable. Mosques, miniatures, and manuals may be preserved long after the ages in which they are produced. States, however, rise and fall; and vanish, leaving only memories behind. As we have throughout stressed, Islam in its recent history, especially the eighteenth and nineteenth centuries, had after eras of brilliance and might gone through a low period in which it had lost many things, preserved many things, but in most of the world had lost its political power. In most parts, it had no state. The Muslims of India, by their struggle through the Muslim League, in 1947 gave it one.

Ideologically it was not a territorial or an economic or a linguistic or even, strictly, a national[7] community that was seeking a state, but a religious community. The drive for an Islamic state in India was in origin not a process by which a state sought Islamicness but one by which Islam sought a state.

There is a rough parallel (in some aspects, of course, very rough indeed) to the case of Communism. This prior to 1917 was an ideological movement driven by the nature of its own aspirations to seek political power, through which alone it could implement itself. When Lenin and his party seized office in the October Revolution, Communism passed from being a movement carried by an organized community of people without a state of their own, living in other people's states, and advocating that society ought to be organized in a certain way, to a new stage of development. From 1917 it could be said that Russia was a Communist state—not in the sense that it was any particular kind of state, organized from the beginning in the way that Communism advocated, for this it was not and did not claim to be; but simply because it was a state at all, and one that the Communists in charge could now endeavour to construct (or use) according to Communism's principles.[8]

We do not mean—and certainly the Pakistani devotees did not mean—that any independent state comprising Muslims is automatically Islamic. This is in fact not so. Egyptians, Turks, and other Muslims do not talk, do not feel, about their body politic as Pakistanis began excitedly to do about theirs. Indonesians have deliberated whether or not to call their republic "Islamic," and so far have decided against it. Certainly Pakistanis themselves

[7] Although the Muslim League claimed that it was. The traditional word *qawm* was used, and in English, "nation." Perhaps no other item in the platform gave rise to so much confusion and dismay as this term, and the "two-nation" theory. On one of the contradictions involved, and something of the consequent disruption, see on the nation/two-nation matter below, chap. 6, p. 256 at ref. 1 and pp. 271-72.

[8] This analogy is in part disrupted, as was the situation in the Soviet Union itself, by the inner contradictions inherent in the fact that Marxism is theoretically materialist. The ensuing distinction from Islām is profound and crucial, that while Communism may treat ideals as an instrument for attaining political power (cf. "Lenin defined Marxism as the revolutionary theory and tactics of the revolutionary class struggle of the proletariat"—V. Adoratsky, *Dialectical Materialism*, opening sentence; Indian ed., Calcutta, n.d., p. 5), Islām treats political power as an instrument for attaining ideals.

strongly felt their nation to be an Islamic state in a fashion unique in the modern world. Indeed, part of their enthusiasm was precisely for the point that they were doing something for Islam that other present-day Muslims were not doing: that they were offering it a political existence that otherwise it has not had for centuries. Yet once again, their claim was based not on what their nation had accomplished; rather, on the spirit that it embodied.

Their contention was that in other states today the people are individually, even socially, Muslims; but their political life is Western-nationalist, is alien, imported. In theory and in practice, both by statute and by intent, they are politically Egyptians, or Turks, or Indonesians, or whatever. The principle of many aspects of their lives is religion, even deeply so; but the principle of their state is not, and does not pretend to be. A nation is not more Islamic than its people intend it to be. In the Pakistan case, on the other hand, these exponents contended, the whole *raison d'être* of the state was Islam: it was Islam that first brought it into being, and that continued to give it meaning. The purpose of setting up the state was to enable Muslims here to take up once again the task of implementing their faith also in the political realm.

The Objectives Resolution, 1949, fired Muslim enthusiasm when it expressed such a purpose.[9] The Constitution, 1956, despite

[9] Objectives Resolution adopted by the Constituent Assembly of Pakistan, Karachi, March 12, 1949. The Resolution spoke of the state as an arena of Islamic democracy, justice, etc., and as a state "wherein the Muslims shall be enabled to order their lives in the individual and collective spheres in accord with the teachings and requirements of Islam as set out in the Holy Quran and the Sunna" (official English version). Subsequent years have dimmed the enthusiasm that greeted this Resolution; but one must remember that enthusiasm and its historical importance. The remarks of the Prime Minister while introducing the Resolution may also be recalled: *inter alia,* "The State is not to play the part of a neutral observer, wherein the Muslims may be merely free to profess and practise their religion, because such an attitude on the part of the State would be the very negation of the ideals which prompted the demand of Pakistan, and it is these ideals which should be the corner-stone of the State which we want to build. The State will create such conditions as are conducive to the building up of a truly Islamic Society, which means that the State will have to play a positive part in this effort"— Liyāqat 'Alī Khān, in the Constituent Assembly of Pakistan, speech of March 7, 1949, in moving the motion introducing the Objectives Resolution. (As given in the government pamphlet *Fundamentals of Freedom,* Karachi, n.d. [sc. 1949]; pp. 26-27.) The Prime Minister's entire speech will repay close study; also that in Urdū of Mawlānā Shabbīr Aḥmad 'Uṣmānī. As we indicate below, ref. 19, this Resolution and the Munir Report together

much intervening disillusionment, still gave explicit form to such an aspiration.[10]

It is the intention here involved that is decisive. We have argued that an Islamic state is not in the first instance one that conforms to a prescribed ideal pattern. Neither is it one merely in which Muslims live or rule. Rather it is a state through which Muslims' purpose is to live or rule (in a democracy, to live and rule) as Muslims. If there is an ideal Islamic state, an archetypal political form, then an actual Islamic state is one that tends towards it—though of course it will never arrive. *A state is Islamic in actuality if it aims at becoming Islamic ideally.*

That is, the degree to which a state is Islamic in a first sense depends not on the extent to which its citizens have succeeded in arriving at their goals, but on the vitality and sincerity and intelligence with which they are in pursuit of them. Pakistan came into being as already an Islamic state not because its form was ideal but because, or in so far as, its dynamic was idealist.

We are differentiating, then, between the actual and the ideal; between what is and what ought to be. One must discriminate between earth and heaven, between human history and faith's transcendent vision. Yet one must note as well that these are linked in the heart of man, who is a citizen of two worlds, and whose life and history consist of the ongoing struggle to relate them.

The work of an artist is religious art not by virtue of attaining a given religious goal but by virtue of aiming at it. It is the dream in the mind of the artist, his motivation and aspiration, that are given by his faith. To clothe these with actuality is a creative endeavour. Similarly with theology. Not every school of theological thought throughout Muslim history has given perfect intellectual expression to the faith. Indeed, none has. Doubtless it is impossible to attain such perfection, to put a religion adequately into words. Yet every attempt to express Islam in theoretical terms is in fact an instance of Islamic theology. That is, any sys-

---

represent in polar fashion much of the fundamentals of Pakistan's early religious development.

[10] Except for some interesting verbal changes, the Objectives Resolution is repeated, substantially intact, as the Preamble to the Constitution of the Islamic Republic of Pakistan, adopted by the Constituent Assembly, Karachi, February 29, 1956, and set in force as from March 23, 1956.

tem of ideas is Islamic theology in actuality in so far as its author is trying to make it Islamic theology ideally.

The same is true of any faith; Christian, Taoist, or whatever. It is always impossible to make the transcendent actual. Yet meaningful life consists in the creative endeavour to do so. One becomes a Buddhist not by living up to the teachings of the Buddha or the principles of Buddhism, but by undertaking to do so. One might say that that man is Buddhist who tries to be a Buddhist. Islamic history has never been Islamic in the ideal sense. Life is too complex for that. Nonetheless it is Islamic history; and is significant because the Muslims who created it have been inspired by Islam as an ideal. Islamic history, like the history of Christians and of others, has been less than ideal because of the complications of infinite factors from human greed to economic necessity, from indolence and error to environmental intractability and interference. But also like Christians' and indeed all human history, however consequential these mundane factors might be, Islamic history would not have taken place at all were it not for the transcendent ideal, a final cause.

To declare Pakistan an Islamic Republic was to proclaim an aspiration.

The Process of Becoming

To set up an Islamic state, then, was the beginning, not the end, of an adventure. The enthusiasm that greeted the triumph of Pakistan's establishment gradually gave way in the recognition that the very meaning of the achievement lay now in a new and ever evolving question: what was to become of it. It was not enough to achieve an Islamic state; there was still the ineluctable matter of its development. To deal with mundane existence is to deal with fluidity; even when one has, as do Muslims, a transcendent, timeless reference as one's norm. Even a religion can make no Standstill Agreement with history.

To achieve an Islamic state was to attain not a form but a process.

We allowed ourselves above an analogy between the establishment of the Soviet state in 1917 as a significant point in the history of Communism, and the establishment of Pakistan in 1947 as a significant point in the history of Islam. Such an analogy may remind us that revolutions may be betrayed.

For there is this further, inescapable aspect of the fact that the Islamic state then set up was, like all social institutions, a thing in flux. Being within history, it was in motion. It could get worse as well as better. The years that ensued for the new nation once it had come into being presented a period of development in which not only could the intention of its Muslim population to make their state Islamic in an ideal sense be carried out. The opportunity was afforded also for that intention to be compromised, frustrated, neglected, or abandoned.

We must turn, therefore, to seeing what the Muslims have made, in the first few years, of the state that they set up. Having attempted to elucidate the meaning of the actual Islamic state, we must now attempt to elucidate its history.

The first point is obvious: that that history has been complex. This was the first point brought home to the religionists themselves; although in some cases it became obvious rather painfully. The question facing the Pakistan Muslims as to what to make of their new state had many aspects. As we have seen, many fervently held that, so far as the religious aspect was concerned, the task was to make it ideally Islamic. It quickly became apparent, however, that the matter was far from simple. It was not merely that there was obscurity as to what this meant. It was not merely that there was no plan as to how to arrive even at such goals as were proffered. First of all, there was the overwhelming fact, relentlessly pushing forward from day to day, that the religious aspect was not the only aspect, or perhaps not even the prime aspect, of the question.

Delays in deciding issues at the Islamic level, obstacles thrust up by religious implications, claims put forward in the interests of Islam—all these could not stop the inexorable march of this massive reality. They could not even hide it; they seemed rather to render it more stark. Whether or not Pakistan, the actual Islamic state, was in process of becoming an ideal Islamic state, it was surely in conspicuous and unrestrainable process of becoming a great many other things.

Some of the other aspects seemed even prior, in logic and in fact. This came to the fore immediately, with the trauma of the country's birth. The cataclysm of partition, with its massacres and stupendous disruption, evoked a quick and unreflecting agony of activity, to salvage the tottering situation and to make *something* of Pakistan rather than letting it disintegrate or succumb in ruins to circumstance and foe. The imperious need to make Pakistan survive overshadowed at first all question of giving it this or that form, of selecting some shape for its destiny. This need of survival continued to be important, if not actually dominant. As the first wild months were mastered and the new dominion rose to its feet from the bludgeonings of its inauspicious inauguration, it began slowly to cast about for guidance and to consider where it wished to go. Yet one may imagine that it will be some while yet before our relentless modern world allows such a nation the luxury of choosing, or even of thinking to choose, its course very freely. It will never, of course, reach a freedom that is not within a context of viscous circumstance.

These two considerations, then, with varying force have pressed and will continue to press on the country's populace: what steps they must take if their country is not to collapse, as well as what kind of country they would like it to be.

The two differ; yet they are not unrelated. To make Pakistan viable, and to make it Islamic, might theoretically be envisaged as in certain conditions even contradictory; while in kinder circumstances supplementary. Yet in the process of history they are in fact intertwined. For the possibility of each in some fashion embraces the necessity of the other.

The viability of any nation depends on many things, including the morale of its people. In Pakistan's case, its initial Islamic quality called forth that active loyalty without which it would never have survived the nightmare of its first six months. Without some similar allegiance, persistent and constructive, one may guess that it will hardly survive the numerous other challenges with which for some time it will doubtless continue to be faced.

That Pakistan's being Islamic depends, in turn, on its viability is still more evident. Manifestly the most idealistic Muslim cannot bend the shape of Pakistan to any preconceived model or cherished goal, unless he ensures or is willing to let the government ensure the nation's continuing existence. This would seem platitudinous, but is in effect exceedingly significant, even religiously. For viability in the interdependent, competitive, technological world of today necessitates many modernities, from industrialization to intellectual flexibility, that are not explicit, and might appear not even implicit, in his preconceived model or cherished Islamic goal.

To responsible or imaginative Pakistanis it was quickly demonstrated that survival itself is no simple matter. In our day—as indeed in any day—survival demands unceasing vigilance, technical competence, creative intelligence, enormous hard work. In fields from chemical research to international finance, and from military power and economic entrepreneurship to administrative sagacity and political finesse, such ability and energy as the nation could muster were in importunate demand.

Matters such as these, then, served not only to modify ideology but also peremptorily to distract the effective leadership of Pakistan from expressly religious objectives. Moreover, there were other orders of consideration also that decisively impinged on the historical development of the new Islamic state. These too had practical, and for intelligent persons also theoretical, consequences. One was the universal matter of human fallibility. Another was the particular nature of the specific leadership that was in fact in power in Pakistan.

The former point, once presented, requires but little comment, though no little stress. National objectives, whether idealistic or pragmatic, Islamic or administrative-technological, are one thing. Individual motivation is another, and may range from self-interest and ambition on to greed and downright dishonesty, not always on a small scale. Not only are Pakistani Muslims, like the rest of us, human enough that some become so bogged down in day-to-day procedures as to lose sight of long-range objectives and ultimate visions. Not only are they human enough that some enter government service or the universities or other socially significant posts not primarily to serve a country or a cause, but to earn themselves a living. There are, as in other countries, more serious lapses from and even perversions of the goals. So much has this been so that within the first few years in the case of some of the provinces, entire governments were dismissed on charges of "maladministration, gross misconduct and corruption."[11] And throughout the country the population has repeatedly found itself confronted with instances of social immorality. These have in

[11] Press communiqué issued from the Sindh Governor's secretariat, April 26, 1948, announcing the dismissal of the provincial government.

many cases been striking enough to sober the exhilaration of the Islamicists.

As an observer penetratingly remarked: "These people may not take interest. But they can certainly take bribes. . . ."

This corruption has been of prime significance in the political and economic history of Pakistan. It has also had religious significance, in several ways. One is the growing awareness of the moral problem in matters of national conduct. This can affect the notion of an ideal Islamic state in two opposite ways. On the one hand, those who press for a radical reorientation may insist the more emphatically that the present social order is manifestly corrupt and decadent and must be replaced with a new, Islamic one, informed with the moral principles and discipline of the faith. On the other hand, some have found the political pretensions of Islamic society discredited, and have felt that the basic and certainly prerequisite task of Islam or any moral movement is to produce men of character and integrity, rather than to strive after a political organization that, however ideal in theory, men without character and integrity can and conspicuously do corrupt.

Their hesitation has been furthered by the prominent matter of hypocrisy. In instances where persons in public life abandon genuine goals, Islamic or national, to pursue their own devious ends, they have often found it possible and convenient to hide their immorality behind the paraphernalia of formal conformity, cloaking their nefarious procedure with religious symbols, playing upon religious emotions, and accusing those who would criticize them of being "against Islam." This is the old story of the cynical political exploitability of religion. As in other societies, it has been used in Pakistan both by those in office, in an attempt to maintain their power, and by those thirsting for it, in an attempt to manoeuvre their way in. In both cases, it is the outward, static elements of religious faith, its formalisms and tangibilities, that are in play; rather than the inner human qualities, the dynamic pursuit of transcendent values. Nonetheless, the excitement is real. It seems part of the genius of religious faith across the world to be easily aroused over false issues.

These developments have given food for thought to those Pakistanis concerned with the eventual Islamicization of the state; as well as providing important observations to those concerned with the interim mundane process of the nation. We turn to what is from both points of view probably one of the most decisive elements in Pakistan's history so far: namely, the nature and position of the nation's leadership.

When the new dominion came into existence, its leadership in the most general terms was constituted of the Muslim Westernizing bourgeoisie which for a century had been gradually building up in India its distinctive position, social, economic, and intellectual. This tiny minority was sharply marked off from the generality of the Indo-Muslim community by the intense experience, the virtual transformation, through which it had gone in its rapid 'modernization': its active relation to the new sources of wealth, power, and ideas in the intrusive twentieth-century world. From the rest of the Indian bourgeoisie it was sharply marked off in a growingly communalist situation by being Muslim, by being a minority, according to its own claim less advanced and severely disadvantaged. (Those Muslim members of the Indian middle class who did not choose or were not forced into separatism, emerged after 1947, not in Pakistan but in India.)[12]

Political leadership specifically lay with the recently expanded Muslim League political party. In other fields as well, economic, administrative, and intellectual, Pakistan began its career in the hands of this class of men.

The languages of the class were Urdu and English. It is not irrelevant to the development of the geographical two units that emerged, that this leadership was drawn from throughout what had been India, with a particular concentration from the United Provinces, and with but a handful from Bengal. The group was further marked off, therefore, from the mass of the Pakistan population that it was leading by deriving only in part directly from the peoples led.

The signal qualities of the leadership, however, with regard to the problem before us, were two. One was their unique fitness in the realm of making the new state viable. The other has been their inaptness for the task of rendering it Islamic.

The class concerned comprised those with a virtual monopoly of the qualifications needed for running a modern state. In the matter of knowing one's way around the modern world, both in

---

[12] For a history of the development of this class, until the eve of the attainment of Pakistan, see the material cited above at ref. 5.

general and in the elaborate, exacting business of often intricate detail, these men were incomparably ahead of the more traditionally Islamic sections of the community. They had the disposable capital, as well as the idea and tradition of economic organization. They had the administrative experience, as well as the understanding of legal, social, and political processes. They had some scientific competence, as well as some apprehension of what science is all about and what its actual and potential role is in modern life. They were trained; the rest of the community was not.

It is patent, therefore, that without their management Pakistan would have floundered quickly. They were administratively successful, in some ways brilliantly so, in the crucial task of organizing the nation and enabling it to take its place in contemporary world affairs. And they have continued to carry it forward into the immense constructive task awaiting it, of gradually rearing on austere and even friable foundations the vast structure of a prosperous modern state.

These are no mean achievements. We do not mean that their success has been radiant; the suggestion is absurd. We mean rather that the task was more than formidable; and it was not clear that any other group available could have done nearly as well.

Yet in this ongoing task of carrying the nation out of initial chaos towards eventual stability and prosperity, they have been increasingly hampered if not betrayed by their critical failure to hold the confidence and to inspire the cooperation of those whom they would lead. To many in the country they have seemed, in fact, to have clung to power but to have abdicated leadership.

We are speaking not merely of a political party but of a whole class, at least in its higher ranks; including administrators, business personnel, and professional men.

The failure has, of course, many aspects. Yet essentially, in our view, it has consisted in the inability of this group so far to give leadership to the Islamic state idea. In the circumstances, this has amounted to both a moral and political failure, with exceedingly discouraging results.

Ironically, it is the very qualification of this group to provide modern leadership at all that has disqualified it for leadership in this special field. The history of Muslim India during the past century has been such that those who acquired the competence to serve Pakistan's modern viability tended in the process to become cut off from the sources that would have enabled them to strive competently towards making it Islamic. There has thus come disquietingly into practical effectiveness the deepest recent problem of Indian Islam: the great bifurcation between the religious tradition and modernity.

When the community was first penetrated by the forces of the modern world, its reaction was much the same as that in the rest of the Muslim world. In addition to incomprehension, indifference, and resistance, some small segments of society began to adjust themselves, even creatively, to the new dynamics. The social, economic, and intellectual modernization through which these segments then went was not, however, matched on the religious plane. To these men, leadership shifted in all spheres of life— except the religious. Religious leadership remained substantially with the forms, the idiom, the milieu, the personnel of an earlier age. The Islamic tradition in the community in its central massiveness continued relatively unaffected by the new conditions. Those who adapted themselves to these latter, accordingly, tended to lose vital or at least creative contact with it.

This process is illustrated most clearly in the educational system. Training in matters other than religion was developed in one set of institutions, with one orientation; training in classical and mediaeval Islamics in and with quite another. The divergence was not only in subjects studied and pupils taught, but in method and flavour and valuation; a divergence that became fundamental to the whole social order. Even when there was a token attempt to bring the two teachings together in one school, it was rather in juxtaposition than in integration or synthesis or even harmony; so that perhaps the dichotomy only stood out more clearly.[13] By and large, persons growing up with a modern education, and persons growing up with a technical and critical competence to handle the Islamic tradition, were two different sets of people. The arrangement seemed calculated to send the former group forth into life at most respecting and feeling—often very deeply—the religious heritage, rather than thinking it.

One frequently meets the assertion that the basic religious

[13] As, for instance, at Aligarh. Cf. the present writer's "Ek Sawāl," 'Alīgaḍh Maygazīn, 1953-54, 1954-55, Aligarh, 1955, pp. 81-83.

problem of Muslims today stems from the impact of modernity[14] upon Islam. The judgement seems to us superficial. Throughout human history there has been an impact of modernity upon tradition, including religious tradition. It has never been so accelerated as today; but in principle the matter is not new. The dilemma of contemporary Muslims stems rather from the divergence of the two, each going its separate way. This has been of profound consequence in Pakistan; and in this Pakistan is not unique. One might almost argue that the fundamental religious problem for contemporary Muslims has to do with the fact that the impact of modernity upon the Islamic tradition has not been nearly strong enough.

At least, now that they are an independent people, called upon responsibly to relate their faith and their own[15] contemporary living, their difficulty is, to say the least, enhanced by the fact that for seventy-five years their religious tradition has been kept in an almost water-tight compartment. It has been relatively cut off and sheltered from the developments that have inundated the rest of their lives, and has been unattuned to humanity's new upsurge in which it is now their lively ambition to have their own 'Islamic' nation creatively participate.

The gulf widened. Yet we do not at all mean that the modernizers had become quite irreligious. In rare cases this happened; more generally religious enthusiasm, at least, remained strong. It was the function of apologetic, for instance, to keep it so; and in this it did not fail. Besides, the general momentum of a centuries old faith is powerful: Muslims do not so easily relinquish their piety. Islam remained important, even for those for whom its formulation was remote. Nor do we mean that no move at all was made to bridge the gap. In our second chapter above, surveying recent Muslim history, instances were given of some steps taken along the path of reinterpretation. We noted at the time, however, that on the whole these concerned the peripheral rather than central affirmations of the faith.[16]

The evolution of the modernizing bourgeoisie produced, then, a class of people who maintained a generalized and sometimes

[14] Or, the impact of the West. This is even more superficial.
[15] Their own, not Western; at least, not primarily and not much. Cf. the preceding ref.
[16] Cf. above, chap. 2, pp. 59, 65-66.

profound allegiance to a somewhat undefined Islam, and an operative and sometimes fiery sentiment of cohesion with the Muslim
community. Our position here is simply that they were but little
equipped to offer effective leadership in creative Islamics.

They could maintain their own religiousness, even perhaps in
an unfamiliar world, particularly in the realm of feeling. But they
have seemed unable to advance their faith significantly, and especially to advance significantly the faith of others who looked to
them for guidance in entering the brave new world of Pakistan's
aspiration.

There has been an apparent failure to generate an interpretation of Islam that could serve as an effective, realistic, meaningful
ideology, or framework for ideology, in the present situation. In
speaking of this failure, one must not underestimate the magnitude of the task against which these men were being measured.
Here, under highly distracting and difficult conditions, they found
what is the essential and universal problem of Islam in the modern
world, confronting them in a concrete and urgent form. Islam was
presented to them in a form inherited from an earlier and very
different day; the fluid complexities of modernity were embodied
for them in the immediate responsibilities of a particularly demanding national life. Their task was to relate the two realistically, creatively. They have not, as yet, discharged it effectively.

Further, when we speak of failure, we do not do so analytically.
It would obviously be presumptuous for us to seem to set up formal
or ideal criteria for assessment. Even more would it be indiscreet
to suggest any kind of moral indictment. Our statement aims
rather at attaining an objective description of what has historically
happened. It is an observable fact that in the first decade of
Pakistan's history the leadership failed to (that is, did not) lead
the Pakistani aspiration towards an Islamic quality for the state.

This is an observable fact that we believe would be disputed
by few, whether inside that leadership, or among potential followers, or among outside students. It has been also a momentous
fact. Pakistan's coming into being was such that an Islamic failure
has tended to become an ideological failure, a moral failure, and
a political failure.

The political failure lies in the degree to which the dominant
class has largely lost the confidence of the populace. Leadership
implies a following. However competent in detail, leadership is

not, cannot be, effective unless what it offers is such that those concerned are happy, or at least reasonably content, to follow. In Pakistan it was called upon to lead a people agog with a surging enthusiasm to build a better world. The dream was cast in an Islamic form. Clearly, then, the leadership either must persuade that people to change the form, to adopt some other goal, or else must choose between satisfying or frustrating the deep aspiration. The most conspicuous outcome has in fact been wide-spread frustration.

Disillusionment, not least a disillusionment with the governing class, has observably settled upon the national life. If no other group is available to take its place, this but makes for the more dejection.

More subtle, but probably still more serious, has been the internal demoralization. Within the leadership itself a failure of idealism has become manifest. Some of that small group of Indo-Muslims who voted against Pakistan did so on the grounds not that they were against the Islamic state idea but that these particular leaders were surely unfit, unable, to effect it. Others, in both India and Pakistan, have subsequently accused the leadership of insincerity. They would now dismiss as sheer bombast and patent affectation any talk from those in authority about Islamic or even national ideals. Part of the extensive disillusionment just mentioned finds expression in the view that the Muslim bourgeoisie in leading the Pakistan movement (or at least in leading it since Partition or since Mr. Jinnah's or anyway since Mr. Liyaqat 'Ali's death), has been devoted primarily to its own class or provincial or even individual interests, chiefly economic, and has been exploiting Pakistan and its own position within it to advance those selfish aims. People who hold this view are not unable to give illustrations of what they mean.

For the dominant group in the country has largely failed not only to inspire the rest of the population to a constructive and realistic Islamic striving in the national interest. They have largely failed also to inspire themselves. The absence of a meaningful and compelling social ideal for the persons occupying the key posts in the society was serious. It meant not only that those among them who devoted themselves creatively and sustainedly to the national interest formed but a tiny minority. Such a minority, however small, may achieve much if surrounded and buttressed by others in key positions whose dynamic is perhaps not lively enough to carry them significantly beyond the discharge of their assigned duties but whose honesty and loyalty are sufficient to make their routine performance reliable, and perhaps generous. The tragedy of Pakistan lay in the fact that the morale to maintain even this group was in danger of proving inadequate.

The course of events in Pakistan history so far has suggested that a significant number of the ruling class had so far lost touch with the vital, central matters in the Islamic tradition that they were not only unable to create an effective ideology for an Islamic state in the twentieth century, but were even unable to respond to moral values rather than to the temptations of personal ambition and greed.

The classical form of Islam had been conspicuously successful in rearing men of character, sensitively obedient to moral imperatives and far too courageous to be deflected by private gain. It continued this service to society long after it had ceased to sponsor political power. The modern form of Islam, on the other hand, seemed to many in Pakistan to be demonstrating the inability of the new Islamic state to come to fruition through a failure in active loyalty and even in elementary honesty.

We refer not merely to the peculation that in and out of government gave rise throughout the country to a sense of grievance or despair. Such matters as the handling of evacuee property, commercial licensing, contracts, and so on were symptoms of a deeper, more widespread malady. These were positive aspects of a fundamentally negative matter, outer and not necessarily the most important expressions of an inner failure. This is the failure of Pakistan to command the constructive fidelity of its dominant class.

Demoralization reached such a pitch that many of the intelligentsia gave serious thought to emigrating. This illumines not merely the discouraging condition of their environment. At the same time it betokens the alarming irresponsibility within their own spirits. Similarly, the complaints against 'the failure of leadership' were many, petulant, and bitter; and although the public welfare was, as we have seen, indeed threatened by the behaviour that widely elicited complaints, yet it was jeopardized no less by the inclination of others to complain rather than to strive.

The vast discouragement was a cause, as well as a result, of the national dislocation. A failure of leadership is a failure of potential as well as actual leaders. The absence of an effective motive for loyal service affected not only the latter. It meant that the former too were not stimulated to be realistically productive.

Finally, we may give specific consideration to the role of the intellectuals as a class. Perhaps it would be more precise to speak of the absence of their role. Pakistan, we have argued, has conspicuously suffered from a lack of effectual ideas. It is the task of the intellectuals in a society to supply the ideas with which the society may effectively and truly handle the problems with which it has to deal. The failure here, since the death of Iqbal, has been sad.

It is not merely that individual members of the intelligentsia often did not tackle their tasks in the realm of thinking with the vigour, honesty, and courage that were ruthlessly needed. In addition, the society as a whole seemed not to recognize how central and responsible a task that of the intellectuals was. In this there was perhaps some parallel to, and even encouragement by, other societies throughout the modern world. In some degree at least there has appeared in many places a tendency to lose sight of how critical a role they play—especially in times of stress. Amidst all the talk of economic advance and technical training, Pakistan has not been alone in failing adequately to recognize that economic and technical progress and even governmental operations and social stability cannot proceed if the intellectuals do not fulfil their function. Pakistan has, however, unfortunately had to pay the price of this error more quickly than most other nations.

The matter went deeper. For here even the intellectuals themselves seemed hardly to recognize their role even theoretically. The class had developed over the past century but had not yet been consciously and functionally integrated with the life of the community. Editors and writers and the universities gave but little impression that they realized that the nation's survival turned in significant measure on the ability of its thinkers to think correctly and creatively.

Especially there was little evidence of an operative conviction that the responsible intellect has a duty to solve also religious and moral problems; or that reason, like faith, is an intermediary between the divine and humanity's activity in history.[17]

[17] Cf. "The Intellectuals in the Modern Development of the Islamic

Some might be disposed to argue that this matter was ultimately related to the absence of an effective tradition from Greece; others, that it was but one more illustration of the general despondency that had settled on Pakistan. Whatever the cause, it was serious.

The Westernizing middle class of Pakistan, then, has failed to evolve a successful ideology. It has not succeeded in putting forward in this realm anything winsome and feasible, eliciting the intellectual assent, moral commitment, and constructive energy of its own members. It has not persuaded the masses of the population that the programme on which it has embarked is significantly related to their own convictions and aspirations, is calculated to fulfil their hopes.

We are suggesting that this fact has profoundly affected the early history of Pakistan. We have already touched on the waning morale in this class's own ranks. We may touch briefly on more concrete ramifications elsewhere.

The most striking perhaps were the fierce Panjab "disturbances" of 1953, in fact a vast heresy hunt. Many thousands of citizens, with extremely wide popular support throughout the province, rioted murderously, in almost pogrom-like fashion, against the dissident sect of Ahmadis and against the government for not declaring these to be religiously and politically outside the pale. The riots have been fully described and analysed, and the movement leading up to them has been studied, in an unusually revealing and at times brilliant report.[18] The movement, of course, had many aspects. Several[19] are illustrations of the general analysis that we have been putting forward; to some we shall later return.

World," in Sydney Nettleton Fisher, ed., *Social Forces in the Middle East,* Ithaca, 1955, pp. 190-204; a chapter by the present writer, which he now recognizes as a little too optimistic historically but on its analytical side still valid.

[18] *Report of the Court of Inquiry constituted under Punjab Act II of 1954 to enquire into the Punjab Disturbances of 1953,* Lahore, 1954. This is popularly known as the *Munir Report* (after the Court's president, Mr. Justice Muḥammad Munīr), and is so referred to in what follows.

[19] Such matters as some of the behaviour, or lack of behaviour, of leadership groups; the hypocritical exploitation of religious issues for political purposes (e.g., p. 259); etc., etc. Indeed, the whole report could serve as confirmatory documentation for much of the argument advanced in our present section. It and the Objectives Resolution (above, ref. 9) are the two basic documents for the history of Islām in Pakistan in its first decade. An understanding that can fully appreciate both is requisite, though it is difficult for both Muslims and outsiders.

At present we would call attention to that aspect of the movement in which it appears as a great popular protest. Its organizers, for their own purposes, had been able slowly to crystallize around a carefully chosen issue, emblematic of Islam, the growing and powerful discontent of the populace over the general deterioration of affairs in Pakistan after its early promise. The formal religious issue manifestly symbolized for the people their deep dissatisfaction. It had taken years of careful, plodding work on the part of the political party responsible, and considerable support from other circumstances and from authorities, to stir up the people around this particular symbol. The popular aspiration for a new and better social order had been cast in an Islamic form. Also cast in an Islamic form then was this expression of its disappointment. The movement gave vent to the bitter sense not merely that the aspiration was not being fulfilled, but that the leaders of the country were not even taking it seriously, were not trying to fulfil it.

In the anti-Ahmadi agitation and its brutalities this feeling was given a particular form that was religiously inept, ethically shocking, and practically disastrous. We but call attention here to the fact that the feeling existed. The Panjab disturbances demonstrated the failure, and some of the serious consequences of the failure, to fit a valid substance to the Islamic form of sociopolitical aspiration.

Another instance, at quite a different level, of the ramifications of the frailty of a national ideal, is the matter of provincial rights. This question, too, has been complex: clearly there could be no simple way to harmonize such formally disparate elements as East and West Pakistan. To hold these two in reasonably cheerful balance must be a process in which political acumen, economic prospects, and many other factors would surely play their part. One consideration, however, cannot be neglected: that the essential, and in fact only, point in the uniting of the two geographical wings of Pakistan lies in their Muslimness. Apart from the debilitating negativism of some joint antipathy to India, if a meaning for their collaboration is to be found at all it must be an Islamic meaning.

Certainly in the early years of the nation's history the failure of the middle class to be inspired by some realistic vision of an Islamic state was sadly apparent also in this realm—some vision of an Islamic state that East and West Pakistan might jointly become. It was illustrated in that class's failure in those years not only to evolve a national programme in which the two wings could gladly participate, but even to persuade the less advanced province that by and large they were genuinely in pursuit of such a programme.

There was, again, a failure to persuade themselves effectively that it was worth pursuing. Very few West Pakistanis, or Muslims from India, gave the impression of having the welfare of East Pakistanis genuinely at heart; of being motivated by an honest concern.

Once again it was not men's failure to arrive at their ideals that had political consequences, so much as the failure to form ideals that should seem to men worth striving for.

A further and almost dire repercussion of the failure to formulate a satisfactory ideal was important also chiefly in Bengal. It concerns the minorities. The Muslim leadership was instant in its protestations that an Islamic state did not mean oppression for non-Muslims, but on the contrary was an assurance of fair dealing. We shall advance arguments in our next section urging what we believe to be an essential validity and basic importance of this position. Moreover, the middle classes, with their Westernizing modernist education, to a significant extent believed, and their top leaders often believed deeply, in equality and fairness for minorities on humanist as well as, or rather than, on Islamic grounds. There was also, of course, the crucial question of expediency: both internally and in international relations with both India and the rest of the world. The absence of any convincing presentation, and even of any precise conviction, as to what Pakistan's being Islamic really signified, meant that some fanatical Muslims, and a great many Hindus, were left to presume that it signified its being a nation in which non-Muslims were sorely out of place.[21] Since there were eleven million of them,[22] the problem

[21] A Hindū, in private conversation with the present writer: "The men at the top are fair-minded. But among the subordinate officers the outlook is narrow: such men think it patriotism to harass the Hindūs." A Muslim: "An Islamic state . . .: these damned Hindūs have been put in their place." (Dacca, March 1949).

[22] Caste Hindū, 4,349,000; Scheduled Caste Hindū, 5,421,000; Christian, 541,000; Others, 366,000 (Census of Pakistan, 1951: population according to religion [Table 6], Census Bulletin No. 2, Karachi, 1951, p. 1). From these

was severe. Unless it were solved, the state could flounder on this one issue.[23]

The seeming inability of the modernizers to rise to the challenge of implementing Islam in twentieth-century history, did not mean that other sections in the community could offer a better lead. The 1953 riots, as we have seen, showed that large groups felt so strongly that they could on occasion be dexterously persuaded to follow any lead at all. At least they could be persuaded once. The lead then given proved false, which resulted in many turning more cautious, if not more disillusioned. The Munir Report[24] publicized further the fact that the *'ulama,'* the traditional leaders of traditional Islam, were not only unfitted to run a modern state but were deplorably unable under cross-questioning even to give realistic guidance on elementary matters of Islam. The court of inquiry, and subsequently the world, was presented with the sorry spectacle of Muslim divines no two of whom agreed on the definition of a Muslim, and who yet were practically unanimous that all who disagreed should be put to death.[25]

Into the breach left by the ever more conspicuous failure of both modernizers and classicists to offer significant Islamic leadership, a new movement was developed, represented most importantly by the Mawdudi group (Jama'at-i Islami).[26] This is the

---

figures, a total for non-Muslims may be computed as 10.677 million (14.1 per cent of total population), in 1951.

[23] No authoritative study has come to our attention on the position of the non-Muslims in East Pakistan in general, or on such matters as the important exodus across the border, acute at the present time (1956); nor have our own observations been systematic or close. That the question is serious, however, has been obvious to all concerned. The Indian Prime Minister, Mr. Nehru, was quoted as saying in Calcutta, January 16, 1957, that "nearly 4,000,000 people had already come over to India from East Pakistan and more were coming" (*Daily Indiagram*, Ottawa, 17.1.57, reproducing despatch from New Delhi). For an able analysis of earlier trouble, on both sides of the frontier, see Richard D. Lambert, "Religion, Economics, and Violence in Bengal," *The Middle East Journal*, Washington, 4:307-28 (1950).

[24] Cf. just above, ref. 18. See especially pp. 200-32 of the Report.

[25] *Ibid.*, esp. pp. 218-19.

[26] One still awaits a careful, unpartisan study of Mawlānā Sayyid Abū-l-A'là Mawdūdī (1903-   ) and his movement (*Jamā'at-i Islāmī*, 1941-   ). Yet they constitute one of the most significant developments in contemporary Islām and one of the most significant forces in contemporary Pakistan. The literature produced by the movement itself is voluminous. It has been chiefly in Urdū, but translations into Arabic and English are appearing increasingly. The monthly journal *Tarjumānu-l-Qur'ān* has appeared under the Mawlānā's

counterpart in India and now Pakistan of the Ikhwan group among the Arabs;[27] the two have recently come into tenuous mutual relation. There are, however, some important differences between them, both as to the environment in which they operate and as to ideas.

The dynamics of Pakistan society—on some parts of which only we have been commenting—obviously provided elements essential to understanding the movement. Further, such factors as we have noted in the Ikhwan case were also relevant here. Apart from these two matters, perhaps the most significant constituent of Mawdudi's position has been the gradual and continual elaboration of an impressive system of ideas. Mawdudi would appear to be much the most systematic thinker of modern Islam; one might even wonder whether his chief contribution, in the realm of interpretation, has not been for good and ill his transforming of Islam into a system—or, perhaps more accurately, his giving expression to a modern tendency so to transform it.

A great many Muslims in Pakistan and beyond who may differ from Mawdudi even radically as to the content of his interpretation, have come increasingly to premise that there is an Islamic system of economics, an Islamic political system, an Islamic constitution, and so on. It is true that in the second and third centuries *hijri* some of the moral imperatives of Islam were systema-

---

editorship from 1932; first in Haydarabad, Dakkan, then 1938-47 Pathankot, and since 1947, Lahore. The leader has written in addition a great number of books and pamphlets, and many of his speeches have been published. Among his books, one may perhaps mention as illustrative of his religious ideas *Tafhīmāt* (the edition available to us is the 4th, rev., Lahore, 1947); *Risālah'-i Dīnīyāt* (9th ed., Pathankot, n.d.); *Tafhīmu-l-Qur'ān*, Pathankot and Lahore, 1943-   , in process (2 voll. have appeared so far). For his views on specifically constitutional problems there is available an English translation of selected speeches and writings, under the editorship of Khurshid Ahmad: Syed Abul 'Ala Maudoodi, *Islamic Law and Constitution*, Karachi, 1955. An English translation of the *Risālah* is Abdul Ghani, trans., *Towards Understanding Islam*, Lahore, 1940. By outsiders, one may note the quite critical study, Shaykh Muhammad Iqbāl [pseudonym], *Jamā'at-i Islāmī par ek Naẓar*, Lahore, 1952; and two recent articles, Freeland Abbott, "The Jama'at-i-Islami of Pakistan," *The Middle East Journal*, Washington, 11:37-51 (1957), and Khalid B. Sayeed, "The *Jama'at-i-Islami* Movement in Pakistan," *Pacific Affairs*, New York, 30: 59-68 (1957).

[27] Cf. above, chap. 3, pp. 156-60. On the continuing Jamā'at in post-partition India, cf. below, chap. 6, p. 284.

tized by the then religious leaders into the Law. There are modern tendencies that would view even this system as dated, as inadequate in scope and too rigid in form to represent faithfully those imperatives for today; and would seek the truth of Islam also in this area more in the realm of values and dynamic, of principles and spirit. Over against these, Mawdudi for the first time would rather extend still further the drive to reduce Islam to a positive system—further both in the degree of reduction and in the areas covered. He presents Islam as a system, one that long ago provided mankind with set answers to all its problems, rather than as a faith in which God provides mankind anew each morning the riches whereby it may answer them itself.

Furthermore, to judge from his own expositions, it would appear that he aims at imposing his system on Pakistan, if he can contrive to get his group into a position of power, also in a rigorously systematic fashion. He evinces but scant concern both for the human beings and their individual welfare who would live under his rule, and with the human beings and their potential weaknesses who might help him enforce it. His ideology seems to make little allowance either for the wishes and even the integrity of the ruled, or for the propensity, which men in positions of authority have all too often demonstrated through human history, to distort even the finest of schemes by individual aberration.

The content of the particular system that he has been elaborating owes much, of course, to previous Islamic history, from whose flow he abstracts for his static pattern. It owes something, however, also to modern concepts and potentialities, so that he differs significantly from the unaccommodating traditionalists. Despite the consequent vitality, his movement is in this matter rather a compromise and adaptation than a creative vision. Its position has been neither modern enough to win many from the advanced sections of the bourgeoisie, nor familiar enough to enthuse the masses. Its following has been chiefly confined to the lower middle classes, the urban discontents, and to idealistic youth.

Nonetheless, one must not underestimate the force of what Mawdudi has to say. In a situation of extreme confusion his movement has propounded an intellectually coherent, almost massive case. In a situation of demoralization it has exhibited enthusiasm and an even sacrificial vigour in striving for such ideals as it professes.

It was no small matter on the Pakistan scene that here was one group of men able to state vociferously what they believed, and able to summon the moral energy to pursue it.

It was significant that such individuals within the top leadership of the nation as this movement was able even partially to influence were among the very few whose personal integrity and genuine patriotism were unquestioned. It was significant also that among university students and young graduates those attracted by this movement were among the few (outside the Communists) who were impelled to live out in practice the ideas to which intellectually they subscribed.

This contrasted with the liberalism ostensibly characterizing the bourgeoisie. In the general survey of our introductory second chapter above we noted that whereas the liberals are strong, liberalism has been weak. Again the 1953 Panjab riots illustrated this tellingly. The religious condition of Pakistan was intimated perhaps not chiefly in the fact that the outburst occurred. Fanaticism is deplorable, but may not in itself be finally significant. No less revealing was the absence of religious reply. For seventy-five years a trend in Islamic interpretation, drawing on material proffered by such men as Sir Sayyid Ahmad Khan, Amir 'Ali, Yusuf 'Ali, Iqbal,[28] as well as by the Sufi tradition, had been increasingly applauded by the middle classes—a trend that would emphasize not the outward formalities but 'the spirit of Islam.'[29] Yet in a crisis it appeared[30] that there was no major force in society to give

[28] It seems imperative to include Iqbāl's name on this list. Yet on the specific issue of the disturbances he himself had powerfully sided with and contributed to anti-Aḥmadī antagonism. See the section "Islam and Qadianism," in "Shamloo" [pseudonym], *Speeches and Statements of Iqbal*, Lahore, 2nd ed., 1948, pp. 91-144. This reproduces a series of press statements, correspondence, and articles originally published in 1935-36, which led to controversy at the time and attracted considerable attention. The chief article, "Islam and Ahmadism; with a reply to questions raised by Pandit Jawahar Lal Nehru," was reprinted (e.g., by the Anjumān-i Khuddāmu-d-Dīn) a number of times in Lahore from 1936 on, both before Partition and after in full or extracts.

[29] The phrase is the title (originally, the subtitle) of Amīr 'Alī's widely read and widely appreciated book, that has appeared in a series of editions from 1891 to 1922, and is still being reprinted. Cf. above, chap. 2, ref. 41.

[30] For example: "In the meeting of citizens at the Government House on the afternoon of 5th March [1953] no leader, politician or citizen was willing

outspoken leadership to the conviction that Islam teaches not "loot, arson and murder"[31] nor even narrow formalism, but "democracy, freedom, equality, tolerance and social justice."[32] The apprehension of this latter truth was not sufficiently vivid to enkindle those who professed it.

The riots were finally put down in the name not of Islam but of governmental stability, and maybe common sense. Religiously they seemed to elicit no rejoinder, beyond discouragement.

The Ideal

We argued that Pakistan was an actual Islamic state when it was established in 1947, by virtue of the intention to make it an ideal Islamic state. We have contended further that in the course of its subsequent history many important aspects of the nation's development have been seriously affected by (and have affected) the question of its moving or failing to move toward that goal. Yet we have delayed until now giving attention to the ideal itself. Our discussion in both cases has proceeded without a clarification of what, in fact, that final objective is whose pursuit, we have maintained, is of such far-ranging relevance.

In this, we have followed the Pakistanis themselves. They, too, were swept up by the elation of the initial establishment, and swept along in the turbulence of the following years, without the benefit of such clarification. The basic force of the Islamic state idea did not depend on its being defined.

However, again like the Pakistanis themselves, we must in the

---

to incur the risk of becoming unpopular or marked by signing an appeal to the good sense of the citizen."—Munir Report, p. 234. (One should note, however, the Jamā'at's rather unconvincing rejoinder; cf. next ref.)

[31] The phrase (sometimes, "loot, arson, and murders," or with other slight variation) is used repeatedly in the Munir Report (e.g., pp. 158, 234). The Court was convinced also, as readers of its Report must be, that the disorders were "certainly anticipated by all who were associated with, and responsible for, the movement" (p. 241), including the chief religious organizations of the country—the participants in the All Pakistan Muslim Parties Convention, Karachi, Jan. 16-18, 1953. (See, however, Mawdūdī's representations to the Court: Taḥqīqātī 'Adālat men . . . Bayān, Lahore, 1954; and the Jamā'at's reply to the Report, Taḥqīqātī 'Adālat kī Raport par Tabṣirah, Lahore, 1955.)

[32] The words are taken from the Preamble to the Constitution of 1956, echoing the Objectives Resolution of 1949. Both read: ". . . the principles of democracy, freedom, equality, tolerance and social justice as enunciated by Islam. . . ."

end come to terms with the conception. In concluding our study, we turn to the question of the ideal. What does the phrase 'Islamic state' in our second sense mean? What have Pakistani Muslims had in mind, or heart, when they have said, or felt, that Pakistan ought to be Islamic?

Their own answers have been several and diverse, and in many cases obscure. There must be elucidation also of this very divergence, and of the obscurity. Any understanding of Pakistan must be defective that does not do justice to the Islamic state ideal. Any insight into that ideal must be defective that cannot comprehend the significance of each specific answer and discern as well the totality of aspiration, making room for the fact that Pakistanis have still to determine their interpretation.

We are, therefore, brought back to the elementals; are brought face to face with the deepest issues here involved. As in our introductory chapter, we must remind ourselves that Islam is first and foremost a religion. Secondly, we must recall what particular kind of religion it is. Only so can we appreciate the dimensions of the matter; and particularly, the transcendence.

For the essential significance of the Islamic state ideal does not lie in the content of the concept. For various Pakistanis it has diverse content, and for some it would seem to have no specific content at all. Being religious, it transcends precise apprehension as well as transcending objective actuality. Man's duty is to discern as well as to implement. His mind, too, must aspire.

As a shrewd political leader put it: "Once in Cambay I saw a boy flying a kite on a misty day, so that the kite was invisible in the fog. I asked him what fun he was having, since he could not see his kite. He replied at once: 'I cannot see it; but something is tugging.' So it is with Pakistan and the Islamic state. They cannot see it. But very surely something is tugging; and they know it. No one has a clear conception; it will yet evolve."

Whether it will indeed evolve is perhaps still at issue; otherwise, the remarks are apposite. The Islamic state is the ideal to which Pakistan, it has been felt, should aspire. It is the aspiring that has been fundamental; not this or that pattern of the ideal. It is an ideal not in the immediate sense of a blueprint that Muslims have only to actualize, but an ideal in a much more ultimate sense. It is that to which final loyalty in this sphere should be given. Hence its relation to the divine; hence its ineffability. It is not a picture of what ought to be, but a criterion by which all pictures of what ought to be must be judged. In some cases it has been but the feeling that, however inaccessible, such a criterion exists. The meaning has been dynamic rather than static, moral rather than sociological; the mood imperative rather than indicative. For Muslims, so far as the social sphere is concerned, it is not a good but The Good.

The demand that Pakistan should be an Islamic state has been a Muslim way of saying that Pakistan should build for itself a good society. Not merely an independent or a strong or a wealthy or a modern society; all these things, perhaps, but also a good society.

Some opined that a good society is this, some that it is that. Others would hardly venture to say what it is, or would admit that they did not clearly know. Where they all agreed, perhaps with enthusiasm and even with commitment, was that it is worth pursuing; and that their country's fundamental significance rested upon the extent to which it so pursued.

We might even thus complete our formal definition. An *actual* Islamic state is a state that its Muslim people are trying to make *ideally* Islamic. *An ideal Islamic state is a state that its Muslims consider to be good.*

It is this transcendence of the concept that enables us to clarify our understanding, while leaving undetermined what in fact the Muslims, in this case in Pakistan, do consider good. To leave it so is essential. For one thing, it is a fact of observation that it is undetermined. They are still in process of resolving, through both discussion and experience, what they consider good. Secondly, it is essential to leave room for future development. Even if, *mirabile dictu*, all Pakistanis should solidly agree tomorrow, they would be free to revise their judgement the next day; as, like other religious communities, they have done in the past.

We do not mean that a Muslim may fall prey to any whim, may choose arbitrarily his goal and call it "Islamic." His conviction is that God determines what is good and what is evil;[33] and that

---

[33] This ultimately is what is meant by the much-discussed opening remark of the Objectives Resolution, 1949, retained as the opening remark of the 1956 Constitution: "Sovereignty over the entire universe belongs to God Almighty alone" (in the Constitution, "Allah Almighty"); or, more lucidly in the Urdū original, God is *al-ḥākim al-muṭlaq*. (Cf. the Prime Minister's remarks on this clause, in his speech moving the Objectives Resolution; see

man's discernment of these has been illuminated by His disclosures, in prophetic revelation and specifically in the religion of Islam; as we saw in our opening chapter. Indeed, the acceptance of this channel of knowledge concerning good and evil is what makes him a Muslim; and this, in turn, is what makes it verbally legitimate for us to call "Islamic" not this or that state in particular but in general the state that he deems good.

Yet it is essential for us thus to preserve, even in a definition, the determinative role of the individual person in any application of Islam to history. It is essential to preserve also, along with this finite and varying factor, the transcendence of the fixed factor, the illimitability of what is given.

One of the greatest, and gravest, of misapprehensions has been the belief that the religion of Islam—especially as an historical reality—somehow determines what a Muslim ought, and ought not, to do. This vitiates understanding, both for outside students and internally. It is the kind of fallacy that has at times threatened both the Islamic state idea and Pakistan itself. It is God, we repeat, who determines what is good and what is evil. For a Muslim, what the religion of Islam does is to elucidate this for him. Islam purports to have brought a revelation, not a confabrication, of truth. And of eternal truth—transcendent, never wholly within the grasp of man. A "Muslim" is one who submits not to Islam but to God.

The religion provided not merely an epistemology of goodness. It elucidated also its terrifying importance. It provided the motivation, as well as the axiology. The individual drive, the intense community cohesion, are no less significant elements for the Islamic state.

Moreover, the elucidation of right and wrong, although utterly important, is itself partial. This is both metaphysically necessary (because of the transcendence of goodness), and historically observable (for instance, in the variety of interpretation). Some Muslims have been arrogant or naive enough to believe that, sheerly by being Muslim, one has full access to a knowledge of what justice is, all tied up in a neat parcel. When challenged, however, as they were challenged by the circumstances of Paki-

above, ref. 9.) For an analysis of the English translation as a revealing instance of the divergence between Islamic and Western thought-worlds, see W. C. Smith, *Pakistan as an Islamic State*, Lahore, "1951" (*sc.* 1954), pp. 78-79.

240

stan, Muslims' disagreement among themselves and their hesitation before responsibility showed that it is given to man, whether Muslim or not, to discern moral truth, as well as to practice it, only in at best very partial measure.

The crucial question that Pakistan faces, therefore, is not simply whether or not it is to be Islamic. The fundamental question of immediate consequence is rather, within the framework of Islam, what its actual (human) judgements are to be.

The framework is given by history; it is relatively fixed by the fact that the great majority of Pakistan's people are Muslims. Within the forms, the actual content of the judgement is an actively personal matter for the individuals and especially the leaders concerned. That Pakistan is Islamic is given; its interpretation of Islam is the responsibility of persons who are free.

A believing Muslim is not free to interpret his faith any way that suits his, or his society's, convenience. Rather, he is free, and is or ought to be impelled if his faith is genuine, to interpret it according to what he honestly believes God's purpose to be in the twentieth century.

To discern that purpose in this situation is not easy.

Indeed the perplexity, the confusion, the strain and stress, even the failure, of Muslims in Pakistan Islamically are not simply a measure of their hypocrisy or of some religious absurdity. On the contrary, they are in part almost a measure of maturity; a sign that for these men the social aspects of religion are at last once again becoming real. As they have themselves stated, Islam is once again coming into history. For them, religion in its relation to social justice is no longer a dream, but is enmeshed with life. And life always, but especially today, is indeed a matter for perplexity and confusion, of strain and stress, even of failure.

The final truth for man lies not in some remote and untarnished utopia, but in the tension and struggle of applying its ideals to the recalcitrant and obstructive stuff of worldly sorrow.

With this perspective, we can see that much of the difficulty in the whole development, both in practice and in theory, has come from oversimplification, in some instances gross. A hurried and often irresponsible insistence that the ideal state could be readily equated with this or that has led to much disillusionment, and at times to near disaster.

At the level of practice, oversimplifications neglected the ponderous concrete difficulties. It is not simple to build a good society anywhere, Pakistan included, it being beset by stupendous problems in the practical realms of economics, sociology, health, and much more. The objective situation in all its immense and baffling intractability must be kept in mind by the administrators, inescapably; but also by such theorists and planners as might be valuable rather than merely sentimental. In the early years, there came into evidence many examples of a naïveté, fondly believing that Muslims by being Muslims were legatees of an inheritance that would of itself quickly transform the unhappy *status quo* into some radiant delight. It was easy to underestimate the practical enterprise that must stem from the fact that even valid ideals do not realize themselves. Even less maudlin expectations were in many instances prone to underestimate seriously the monumental practical issues of every sort with which the country was faced. Perception as to what is good could prove gratuitous, and even false, by being unrelated to the complex and restive circumstances that in fact obtained.

At the level of theory, the tendency to oversimplify was no less strong. It was, as well, no less telling. Impatient, some were quick to insist that the good society had been designated by Islam once for all. Some even believed in their hurry that it could be, and even had been, reduced to so comparatively simple a matter as a formal constitution.[34] Others would identify it as a society where Islamic laws are in force.[35] Still others would turn to the past, equating the Islamic State with the glorious period of Islam's community achievement in its earliest days, perhaps particularly the first forty years of Islamic history.[36] Some were ready to equate it emotionally, thoughtlessly, with their own particular 'good old

[34] This conviction presently petered out, because the test of implementation was so accessible; yet for a time it was forceful. As one of those responsible for producing the constitution put it (in private conversation to us, Karachi, 1949): "I was on a train and my fellow-traveller, when he discovered that I was in the Constituent Assembly, said that the country should have an Islamic constitution. I replied that I did not know what the term meant: what did he have in mind. This question surprised and stumped him." Again: "The people generally do not understand the difference between a constitution and laws." One youth spiritedly decried "this nonsense, that there is somewhere a hidden constitution that will solve all our problems and remedy our ills" (Karachi, 1949). Nonetheless there was persistent clamour for this solution, and books are still being written on the matter.

[35] Cf. below, p. 244, with ref. 38. [36] Cf. below, pp. 245-46, with ref. 40.

days': that traditional local culture to which they had been accustomed before modernity came to disturb the familiar patterns. Some were ready to feel almost that it was simply a state in which no non-Muslims held political office or had good jobs. More seriously, in individual instances various writers advocated their own speculative systems of Islamic definition. And so on: many interpretations have been proffered.

It matters radically in any society what in fact people do consider good. This, as much as the form in which their judgement was cast, was of day-to-day significance in Pakistan's case.

Yet it was in part the transcendence of the norm that kept any one of these interpretations from being widely or finally accepted. Because the ideal expressed the unformulated but deepest social aspiration of the individual Muslim, he was able and in some cases forced to reject any formulation, however cogently contrived, that failed to do justice to that inner longing. Though he could not say himself just what he had in mind, yet he could realize that the particular programmes being proposed would not satisfy his desire. Some Muslims, of course, were persuaded by this or that interpretation. Some, whose zeal outran their imagination, or religious commitment their moral perception, could be convinced that they ought to back this or that delineation, even though it was not in itself so winning as by its intrinsic allurement to attract their joyous support. In general, however, and particularly among the educated group whose social horizons were wide, the instinct that the Islamic state is a good state in the fullest, final sense of the term meant that no one of the specific and sometimes petty proposals put forward could command their allegiance, or even their assent.[37] The absence of any adequate positive ideology

[37] One of the difficulties in Pakistan arose from the fact that the Westernizing leadership was not quite sure in its own mind at all times but that the reactionary Muslims' interpretation of Islām might not be the right one after all. It did not think so, but lacked a positive conviction that would allow it to be confident. The most spectacular example was the Prime Minister Nāzimu-d-Dīn who in the crisis of the Disturbances in early 1953 was for long unable to bring himself to deny the 'ulamā'. "He must have felt a troublesome conflict between his own religious convictions and the implications resulting from the acceptance of the demands" (*Munir Report*, p. 234; on this point, cf. further *ibid.*, pp. 125-50, 233-35, 295-300). At the meeting of the Central Cabinet Feb. 26, 1953, "no decision could be taken" (p. 145); finally at about two o'clock the following morning another Cabinet meeting was called in the face of the threat of mob action; the demands of the 'ulamā'

was accompanied by an unhappy pervasive awareness that the specific interpretations being canvassed fell woefully short of an unformulated but important standard.

On careful inquiry it would even emerge that the quality of transcendence often persisted even in those interpretations that seemed to give, or were designed to give, a positive definition to the idea. For example, in the assertion that an Islamic state is a state with Islamic laws, it presently became apparent that these too were in part an undefined ideal. There was no precision as to just what those Islamic laws are, or ought to be. They do not, in an agreed form for enactment today, tangibly exist. In part they too are something to which, through the constructive diligence of its citizens, Pakistan ought to aspire. They are conceived as constituting in some degree the counterpart of the Western concept not of "law" so much as of "justice."[38]

---

were finally rejected and the leaders arrested. Only the most extreme situation could bring the Prime Minister to realize that the *'ulamā'* were wrong. He perhaps even then did not fully realize that this meant that they were morally wrong, Islamically wrong.

[38] The Greeks set forth the view that Justice is transcendent; human ideas of justice are fallible but cogent approximations. This is the conception by which the Western world operates. The Hindūs hold a similar position about God. Christians affirm that God is known, because (in Christ) He has revealed Himself. Muslims affirm that Justice is known, because (in the Qur'ān) He has revealed it. Neither Christians nor Muslims in theory deny transcendence, though clinging to revelation; yet Hindūs and Western jurists find them narrow and inflexible. However, within the Muslim view, as evinced in Pakistan, there has been considerable difference of opinion as to what the *sharī'ah* essentially is.

To some, the question seemed fairly simple. The Law, they felt, can be pointed to: it exists, in the books. The Laws of Islām, in their view, have been worked out by the jurists over the centuries and have been embodied in the legal tomes. Pakistan, they advocated, had only to enact this accumulated corpus into legislation. Of these, some were more, some less, ready to concede that an adaptation to the evolution of modern conditions would be required. It should be noted, however, that in any case many of these persons not only were unfamiliar in any disciplined way with modern conditions, but also did not in fact know what was in these law books. Indeed, this group included very few of the *'ulamā'* on the one hand, and very few of the governmental administration on the other. It seems to have been the position of not many serious and responsible thinkers.

The tangible law codes as extant have in fact ramified and developed over the ages. In view of this fact, some would close at one or other particular historical point the evolution of objective law that they would accept as authoritative. Some, rejecting all later growth, would feel that the fundamentals of the Law were worked out once and for all in the early golden

Similarly with the model from history. The period of the *Khilafat al-Rashidah*, the first decades of Islamic history, which was often put forward as an ideal age, not merely was advanced in highly idealized form, in a picture embodying the legendary embellishments of the subsequent pious tradition, and still today receiving favours from devout imagination. Apart from this it appears on analysis that in fact what was in mind was not the

---

age of Islām. They would then regard it as the task of Pakistan to apply these fundamentals to twentieth-century circumstances—admitting, in many cases, that to do so would be a task of imposing proportions, demanding men of the highest calibre of knowledge, acumen, judgement, and devotion.

Others would see the *sharī'ah* not as a static system but as a dynamic development, a process of which the historical stages in the past are available for study and guidance, but of which the proper present and future developments are matters of creative extrapolation. This interpretation would accept continuity and revision.

The classical *'ulamā'*, as we saw in the case of Egypt (above, chap. 3, pp. 124ff., esp. p. 128 at ref. 61), at their best view the *sharī'ah* as a transcendent norm, to which the extant version is a human approximation. A modernizing, more historically-minded counterpart of this position is the view that the classical law was the practical expression for its own time and place of that norm, for which in the new time and place of Pakistan a new expression is needed. Here again a creative task of considerable magnitude is involved.

The conception of *sharī'ah* held by some has severed all connection with a past working-out of the law by Muslims, cleaving only to the Qur'ān, or even to the principles of the Qur'ān. A senior member of the administration, with an Oxford degree, remarked: "Certainly the law of Pakistan must be the *sharī'ah*. Otherwise there was no point in having Pakistan." He elaborated this insistence with vigour and precision, and convincing sincerity. Yet on questioning, he stated that "the *sharī'ah* is the laws of the Qur'ān"; asked if it did not include also the *sunnah*, stumbled "Well . . . anyway . . . well, that has to do with the Prophet. . . . In any case, the Qur'ān is the important thing. . . ."

Except the first position that we have noted—which is content to take Islamic law for present application as already extant in detail—these interpretations evince the consensus that Islamic law has motility. ("Every thinking Musalmān agrees now with Iqbāl that *fiqh* is flexible. It is a process." "There is more talk of revising the law than there used to be." "*Fiqh* has changed, must change, and will change.")

Further, these interpretations recognize that a great creative effort would be needed on the part of Pakistan, or contemporary Muslims generally, in order to produce a version of the law for the modern world. One might emphasize each one of the words "great," "creative," and "effort."

See further the analysis in Smith, *op. cit.*, 1954, pp. 52-58. Note also that the 1956 Constitution (clause 198, para. 3) requires a Commission to go into the matter of saying what the *sharī'ah* (carefully phrased as "the Injunctions of Islam") is and ought to be; it allows five years for this task.

actuality of that age even as romantically conceived, but again a transcendent ideal, with that historical period as the most adequate and truest expression that that ideal has yet found for itself. It is not merely impossible, indeed meaningless, to reproduce in one age the activities or constructions[39] of another: manifestly Pakistan cannot relive a segment of the history of Arabia. Further, that period, even when transformed into the most roseate of its versions, was not ideal: it is well known, for instance, that three of its four successive heads of State (the *Khulafa' al-rashidun*) were done violently to death, and their régimes were disrupted by civil war, which brought the period to an end within thirty years of the Prophet's death.[40]

The Islamic state ideal, then, we would argue, cannot be understood except as an ultimate religious norm. Yet neither is it, as such, to be underestimated.

Pakistani Muslims are not alone in finding it difficult to say, in terms of the developing social process, just what it is to which final commitment is due. Neither are they alone, among men of sensitivity and perception, in being firmly persuaded that that social process has meaning; and that within and beyond it a final commitment is necessary and valid. Like other peoples, they may disagree amongst themselves as to the objective, and may individually in some cases falter or be confused. Yet what characterized the Islamic state idea was the degree to which those who held it were agreed, over against world-denying mystics on the one hand, and over against materialists and cynics on the other, that within historical development something is good, and must be pursued. For a Pakistani Muslim, to abandon the Islamic state idea is to abandon not merely the pursuit of justice, but the conviction that there is a justice to pursue.

The tragedy of the failure to find adequate content for the ideal has lain in part in the vast disenchantment with the whole social enterprise in the country. Many in coming gradually to the per-

[39] Even if from the early history one abstracts certain aspects, such as the institutions that it set up, yet these—even as forms disengaged from their actual embodiments—could be applied to twentieth-century conditions, it is clear, only with assiduously elaborate modification. On this matter, cf. the discussion on 'renascence' and 'reformation'; chap. 4, pp. 170-71 above.

[40] For a fuller analysis supporting the view that the concept of the *Khilāfat al-Rāshidah* has in fact been a concept of transcendence in Pakistanis' minds, cf. Smith, *op. cit.*, 1954, pp. 58-62.

suasion that Pakistan cannot after all be an Islamic state have in
fact been coming to the desperate conclusion that their new nation
is not worth while.

Some of the actual illustrations that Muslims in Pakistan have
given as to what in fact they have considered good, have turned
out discouraging to themselves or to their neighbours. There is
one positive judgement, however, that calls for careful attention.
In the Constitution of 1956, an interpretation of Islam that had
been lately put forward by some was given formal and concrete
approval: namely, that it is democratic. This became the first, and
so far the only, official decision as to the nature of the Islamic
state, adopted and implemented by the Constituent Assembly.
At least in the case of Pakistan, it was affirmed, the Islamic State
is to be an Islamic Republic.[41]

It is too early yet to say whether this will be maintained, either
in practice or in theory. To maintain it will not be easy. Yet the
question of whether it is maintained is at both levels immensely
significant. Theory and practice must to some degree go hand in
hand; a people cannot sustain a democracy unless they believe that
democracy is good. For democracy too is a dynamic concept, a
process. To say that a society is democratic at a given instant is to
say something about a form of government; but to say that it is
democratic for any period of time is to say something also about
the motivation and loyalty and ideals and quality of its citizens.

One can assert with assurance that democracy in Pakistan, like
democracy elsewhere, will be imperfect. Whether it will prove so
imperfect as to break down altogether is a question that Pakistanis
must constantly face—democracy is like that. Whether or not it
will break down is a question of very great significance. That this
is so religiously is perhaps not quite so obvious, but is profoundly
true. By enacting a republican constitution, the Pakistanis have
not only made democracy a part of their actual Islamic state,
rendering democratic their mundane history; they have also made
democracy a part of their ideal Islamic state, have formally chosen
to integrate it into their religio-social ideal.

The importance of both these facts would be difficult to
exaggerate, as developments within the history of Islam. It is

[41] Clause 1, para. (1), of the 1956 Constitution: "Pakistan shall be a Federal
Republic to be known as the Islamic Republic of Pakistan."

momentous enough that here many tens of millions of persons have come into at least formal power, to take responsibility for their own collective development on earth, however fragmentary may be the reality of this in its incipient stages. With this, and such comparable and fairly simultaneous instances as in Turkey and Indonesia, Islamic history in our day embarks on a new era. For the first time[42] it is taking on a democratic form, with all the immense potentialities inherent therein.

At the theoretical level also, new vistas are opened up for Islam as a dynamic system of ideals, a moral and religious ideology. For one thing, democracy if it survives must seriously affect the range of possibilities within which any effective interpretation of 'Islamic state' must hereafter in Pakistan be formulated. It must mean some kind of state that will appeal to Muslims as a whole,[43] peasants and Westernizers, trade unionists and scientists; and will involve them as a whole in its ongoing operation. The will that the state become Islamic, it has been affirmed, can be and must be implemented by a democratic process. Both these are very important religious affirmations. Not only has final political authority been accorded to the people. The Constitution represents a decision to transfer to them, not to the 'ulama' or other religiously privileged class, the responsibility, if not for making the authoritative interpretation of Islam, at least for choosing which interpretation shall become authoritative.

(This is what Pakistanis had in mind when they vigorously proclaimed that an Islamic state is not a theocracy.)[44]

[42] Some Muslims would say, "For the second time"—claiming that the *Khilāfat al-Rāshidah* was also democratic.

[43] And appeal even and at the same time to a substantial number of non-Muslims. In Pakistan these could be in theory out-voted (the Muslim demand for separate electorates is in part an attempt to outvote them). Yet in practice their influence in any election cannot be ignored.

[44] The irritation over any suggestion that an 'Islamic state' is a theocracy betrays a misapprehension of the latter term. It was coined by Josephus, after adumbrations by Philo, both Greek-speaking Jews of the first century A.D., when the mutual impact of the Hellenic philosophic tradition and the Semitic Near East's religious tradition was proving radiantly creative. These writers were endeavouring to express in terms meaningful within the classical framework, the Jewish concept of their own government under the divinely revealed Mosaic Law. The parallel with the Islamic *shari'ah* concept is not far-fetched. See Flavius Josephus, *Contra Apion,* II.16, and Philo Judaeus, *De Somniis,* II. 43,290. Cf. also H. A. Wolfson, *Philo,* Cambridge, Mass., 1947, vol. 2, chap. xiii, "Political Theory," esp. p. 382. The concept "rule by

Yet the matter goes deeper. The people may, it is true, be persuaded or inveigled to surrender their right: they may vote (or allow) into office an oligarchy or dictatorship. They are free to destroy their republic. They may equally—though not so easily—abandon its Islamic quality; we shall return to this. In the meantime, however, the Constitution implies the intention to maintain as well as to establish an Islamic Republic. This means that ongoing democracy becomes an aspect of the state's ultimate Islamic quality; it becomes a part of the final definition of an Islamic state.

Some Muslims would aver that there is nothing new in the inclusion of democracy as a social ideal of the Islamic religion. Others would recognize that Islam has long inculcated social and legal and other types of egalitarianism, but is now for the first time in a practical manner incorporating political democracy. The point is not consequential. Whether one believes the political-democracy ideal to have been all along inherent in Islam though only now becoming explicit and generally accepted; or whether one views it as a new application of Islam to modern and novel conditions, in any case the profound and significant fact is that here for the first time on a considerable scale in history, Muslims' actual conception of that community life to which they understand God, through Islam, to be calling them is stated to include parliamentary republicanism.

The matter works also in the reverse direction. We have said that to maintain democracy in Pakistan will not be easy. If a democracy breaks down, this indicates in part that the community does not adequately believe in democracy, does not rise to the demands that it implies. A breakdown of democracy in Pakistan would indicate *inter alia* a failure of these Muslims adequately to have faith in it, which in turn would mean in part a failure effectively to incorporate it in the Islam that is their living faith. In an Islamic Republic, Islam either does or does not provide the morale to keep that republic going.

How this will develop in Pakistan remains to be seen. For the moment, democracy is one thing that Pakistani Muslims have

---

ecclesiastics" or ". . . by priests," connoted for Pakistanis by the word *theocracy,* is correctly denoted by the little-used term *hierocracy.*

formally considered to be good; that is, Islamic. We turn briefly to the important question of non-Muslim minorities.[45]

Some of the non-Muslims have especially objected, and some have had compelling practical reasons to object, to the Islamic state concept. Formally, the 1956 Constitution lays down justiciable Fundamental Rights for all citizens, and also makes special provision lest these be abrogated by specifically 'Islamic' laws.[46] On the whole, the tenor of the constitution is definitely towards equality. One must not underestimate such legal safeguards. Informally, on the other hand, the actual day-to-day behaviour of the majority community, and particularly the actual interpretation of 'Islamic state' by many individuals, have often served to undermine minority confidence.[47] In a democracy, the requisite treatment of a minority is not merely a defined justice but what that minority will freely regard as justice. The challenge to the Muslims on this score was a real one. It has not yet become at all clear whether they can meet it.

In the final analysis, the rights and treatment accorded any minority or non-powerful group in any state depend on the ideal of those in power. In a Marxist state, such as the Soviet Union, the rulers recognize, they claim, no ideals; opposition groups accordingly have, in theory and practice, no rights. It is official Marxist doctrine that a person as such, "man in general,"[48] does

---

[45] The question of Muslim minorities is also important: of dissident groups within the Islamic community who wish to differ, or believe that they ought to, or that true Islām demands that one differ, from the majority view at a given moment. We cannot go into the religious aspects of this crucial problem. The political aspects were raised vividly enough by the Aḥmadī issue.

[46] Clause 198, esp. para. (4).

[47] Cf. above at reff. 21, 23. More formally: "The Indian High Commissioner in Pakistan, Mr. C. C. Desai, said that insecurity in villages, denial of equal opportunities of employment, discrimination in the grants of gratuitous relief and fishing licences and non-redress of grievances when aggrieved members of the minority community approached subordinate officials were among the many causes of migration [of Hindus from East Pakistan to India]. He had also heard complaints of seizure of crops and encroachment on lands by members of the majority community and of propaganda by fanatical people taking advantage of those provisions of the Constitution, which declared Pakistan an Islamic Republic."—quoted in *Notes on Islam*, Calcutta, 9:42 (1956).

[48] *Manifesto of the Communist Party*, 1848, derides the 'emasculating' concept of "human nature, . . . man in general, who belongs to no class, has no reality, who exists only in the misty realm of philosophical phantasy" (Authorized Indian Edition, People's Publishing House, Bombay, 1944, p. 52). Slowly men are beginning to discern again the importance of ideals, and

not exist; that a person exists only as a member of a social class. An individual condemned as being "an enemy of the working class" is regarded, then, in the U.S.S.R. as having literally no rights whatever, and is treated accordingly. Even in a democracy, the form takes its value from the ideal. Unless the majority are actively loyal to the transcendent principles of democracy, recognizing the ideal validity of every man's status as a man, then the arithmetic minority has, through the democratic form, no rights at all. Only in so far as the ideal, whether of Islamic state or otherwise, held by Pakistani Muslims includes or comes to include the notion of treating non-Muslims well—with justice, equality, or the like— only so far have those non-Muslims any *locus standi*. On a purely arithmetic basis, they would, as an outvoted and overpowerable minority, have no status at all.

Let us take a particular case, to illustrate. It was reported from a particular village, whose population since the Partition comprised a predominance of Muslims, that the Christians were refused use of the only village well. To introduce formal democratic procedures into that village would do nothing to improve the situation, since if the matter were put to a vote the decision would obviously confirm and give formal and even legal authority to an injustice. The hope for the weak group in this community is to appeal not to democratic forms, but to the laws, and finally the conscience, of the majority. The latter must be shown that, by their action, they are being *bad Muslims*; are running counter to the transcendent concept of an Islamic state.

We use this to illustrate in miniature the complexity of the entire Pakistan problem. Here too the issue has essentially been, what do the Muslims in fact consider good, and how effectively do they pursue it? This is the decisive question, in the village and in the country, as in all villages and in all countries.

We return, then, to our contention that this, rather than the formal matter of whether the state is to be Islamic or not, is Pakistan's central question.

---

to realize that it is better to have ideals, even when not lived up to, than to repudiate them outright. ("The rise of Hitler made us realize that even our English hypocrisy is of some value," it has been said in Britain.) It is important that practice be good. It is also important that, when practice lapses, good transcendent ideals be acknowledged, so that there is something to which one can appeal.

Somewhat similar considerations apply to the second great challenge to the Islamic state idea, secularism. When Pakistan was first established, only a very small minority of Muslims advocated that the state should be secular rather than Islamic. Over the years that minority has grown amongst the educated classes, chiefly because an increasing number have been sorely disillusioned and even repelled as they saw the lethargy, the fatuity, the hypocrisy, the disruption that widely prevailed; saw the enormous complexity and brute difficulty of the problems that remained unsolved; and saw the discouraging manifestations of what in the name of Islam the people in often dismal fact did consider good.

Until the time of writing, however, this sentiment toward secularism had remained inert. It was not a movement, for it lacked leaders, it lacked constructive convictions, it lacked ideals. It did not come to grips with the fact that the same people, presumably, would run Pakistan as a secular state who were running it now as an Islamic one. It proffered no evidence that these would respond more smartly to a secularist ideal than to an Islamic. Indeed there was no evidence of the ideal, of either an intellectual or moral programme in clear-cut terms to which to appeal. It was not merely that the leadership, if democracy were to be retained, would have to persuade the mass of the people that the new goals were good. Even if it jettisoned democracy, it would still have to persuade itself.[49] One cannot effect a revolution without an ideology.

To make headway secularism would not only need to be provided with both drive and content, with people actively believing it to be a good thing. It would still have to deal with the question of Islamic interpretation. As the Turks have seen, secularism implies a recognition by the religious institution that some spheres of life are outside organized religion's direct province. For the secularist the dilemma is not only that Pakistanis do not have a set of religious ideas by which they can run their nation. They also do not have a set of religious ideas that would approve of their running it on some other basis.

[49] Cf. ref. 37 above. The leadership of Pakistan includes many Muslims who are hypocritical, and many more who are in two minds about Islām and secularism. But it includes perhaps fairly few who are single-mindedly in favour of a secular régime. Whether an Atatürk may appear involves the further question of whether he would find also a sufficient coterie of lieutenants.

It would not be too absurd, perhaps, to phrase this point by saying that Pakistan will flourish as a secular state only if its Muslims are able to persuade themselves (to perceive?) that the truly Islamic state is a secular one.[50] At least this could be urged: that to set forth on the great enterprise of building a successful secular society, also, Pakistanis must first settle in their own minds what they believe.

For progress in this as in any direction, there is need for coordination of the good that they see with the Islam that they accept.

It would be a rather seismic development if any major group recognized something in society as good but un-Islamic, or as Islamic but not good. For most, the matter is more englobing. A Muslim's apprehension of goodness, as is true for everyman's, is coloured by his environment and his experience, the pressures and complexities and limitations of his particular time and place, and by his own capacities, his moral acumen, and the sensitivity and courage of his spirit. Yet it is coloured also by the fact that he is a Muslim. He believes that these all are to be integrated.

His interpretation of Islam then, as we have argued, is crucial for Pakistan. This has, precisely, become the crucial intellectual and spiritual question of the Muslim world. Pakistan Muslims would widely agree that the truth about goodness is to be known

---

[50] The idea is not, perhaps, as ridiculous as it sounds. In a sense this was the thesis of 'Alī 'Abd al-Rāziq, al-Islām wa Uṣūl al-Ḥukm, Cairo, 1925, which produced such a furore. (English and Urdū translations are to be brought out presently in Pakistan.) One may compare also, perhaps, the thinking of Ziya Gökalp. (On 'Abd al-Rāziq, cf. Charles C. Adams, Islam and Modernism in Egypt, London, 1933, esp. pp. v, 259-68; on Gökalp, cf. above, chap. 2, ref. 30.) There is a not too subtle sense in which the proper Christian state (or at least, Protestant Christian) is a secular state. It is not that a secular state is thought to embody, even imperfectly, what a Christian ideally approves. It is rather that the Christian, qua Christian, believes that a state ought to be secular. Important leaders and thinkers of the Christian Church (especially at the Reformation) have devoted energy and brains to working out a statement of the Christian faith in which the idea of a secular state fits, or at least with which it is compatible. They have worked out and built religious institutions (such as the Church) that can function religiously in a secular society. And Christian believers have accepted these things. Christians have the kind of religious beliefs and customs and organizations that allow them to live in a secular state without ceasing to be devout Christians, and without ceasing to be loyal and effective citizens. (Not always without conflict: the issue is still live.) Muslims in Turkey are engaged on a comparable problem (cf. above, chap. 4); Muslims in India bode fair to be (cf. below, chap. 6).

through Islam; but they may and do disagree as to how, even within the bounds of Islam, it is to be ascertained. One finds it through the Qur'an; one through the Qur'an and the *sunnah*; one in the early history of the *Khilafat al-Rashidah*; one in the whole unfinished history of the Islamic community; some in effect find their interpretation of Islam in Iqbal or Mawdudi. And so on and on. And undercutting all of these is for some the restless semi-awareness that the real truth of Islam lies not in the past but in the future.

Perhaps we should say, not on earth but in heaven.

At every turn, Pakistanis are harassed or coaxed by the interplay of a myriad of forces, hostile, fortuitous, or fortunate, from the Kashmir question to dollar holdings; from outside pressures to inner dishonesty; threatening to disrupt or interrupt or divert, to elaborate or circumscribe. In history there is no final result. The series of interim results must be a series of intertwinings of the multifarious circumstances that face them and of the human, moral, intellectual, and other resources that they are able to bring to bear.

The Pakistan of any moment is necessarily the child of that moment: it is one segment in the cross-section of world development at that point. Pakistanis must take their place in the phalanx of modern humanity. And one of their problems is to learn to communicate and to live in harmony with those of their contemporaries across the world who are not Muslims; and *vice versa*. Yet in addition to this transverse relationship there is the onward movement of their own more individual dynamic: their particular development, from out their special past and towards their own objectives. It is this latter relationship, between a past and a potential future, that constitutes them as Muslims and gives meaning to the Islamic aspect of their state. To be Islamic means, for Pakistan, to take its place within the moving stream of Islamic history, coming out of a distinctive past that is given and is accepted, and looking *sub specie aeternitatis* toward a future that has yet to be created. It is this stream of continuity that may serve, if anything will, to reintegrate the two senses of "Islamic state" that we have discriminated, the actual and the ideal: out of the past and towards a transcendent future.

Pakistan lives, of course, always in the present, and must deal with present problems. For these purposes and in these dealings it is a modern state. Yet in so far as, while doing so, it also keeps in conscious and deliberate touch with its Islamic past and develops it by consciously reaching out towards a better Islamic future, it is in addition an Islamic state.

Not that this outreach is only temporal. Pakistanis can appreciate their heritage, and can strive towards a better future, because or in so far as they are already, as religious men, in touch with and reaching out towards a good that is real now, though not mundanely. The transcendent surpasses, but does not exclude, actuality.

If they do not reach out at all, in some significant aspiration, the prospect is bleak.

Living in the mundane present is itself no mean task. As we have insisted, Pakistanis may not for a moment neglect the matter of making their nation viable. Yet for them, as for all men, living wholly within the mundane present is self-defeating. It is unworthy of human dignity, and disruptive of human history. They are faced, as are the rest of us in the parlous world of the latter twentieth century, with the massive problems of living at all. At the same time they are faced, as have been all communities since the dawn of history, with the further question of living well.

It has been a matter of anguish. Yet perhaps the greater tragedy would be to give up trying.

Chapter 6

INDIA: ISLAMIC INVOLVEMENT

The Indo-Muslim Community

The partition of India in 1947 involved the partitioning also of its Muslim community.

This fact shocked that community. The Indian Muslims had brought Pakistan into being on the grounds that their community was a unit. The Muslim League's suddenly advocated platform of a separate state was a corollary of its prior and more fundamental thesis: that the Muslims of the then India must stand united. With a burning intensity it proclaimed that they were a nation. They certainly succeeded in making themselves feel that they were a nation. Yet the very success of the League policy led to the fact that they are now two nations.[1]

The Muslims of what used to be India are today two nations not only in the sense that a political frontier now separates the groups—a bristling frontier across which traffic, whether of persons or of news, of trade or of understanding, has been at best difficult and at times blocked. They are two nations also in a more basic sense: they face radically different problems, and pursue not only distinct but even conflicting policy. The apparent interests of the one may seem or prove disastrous for the other. Their temporal interests, though ultimately doubtless compatible and even complementary, are far from identical. And even their spiritual interests and concerns differ. Their historical development may stridently clash. Their Islamic development may significantly diverge. The two groups now have distinct destinies, and each must be considered on its own merits as leading a self-motivating and self-responsible existence.

The Muslims of the sub-continent numbered in the 1941 census 94.4 million[2] and in 1951, approximately 104 million.[3] Of this

---

[1] Some Indian Muslims would even assert that they are now three nations: Indian Muslims, and within Pakistan those of each wing, each of these three being destined to play a distinct role.

[2] *Census of India: 1941*, Delhi, 1943.

[3] This figure has been arrived at as follows: for Pakistan, 64.96 million (*Census of Pakistan, 1951*: population according to religion (Table 6), *Census Bulletin No. 2*, p. 1); for India, 35.40 million (*Times of India Directory and*

total, some 3.3 per cent are Kashmiri[4] and therefore problematic. Slightly over half, to be precise 56.3 per cent,[5] were already resident in the area that became Pakistan. Another 6 per cent or so[6] migrated thither at the time of the partition cataclysm (mostly, the Muslims of the East Panjab; plus a much smaller but sizable group from West Bengal; plus also, from the rest of India, scattered individuals chiefly of the middle classes). About one-half per cent died in the violent upheaval.[7] Over one third, some 35 million or more,[8] emerged as residents of the new independent India.

Whether some or all of the Kashmiri Muslims are eventually to be included along with these, raising the percentage to nearly 40 and the numbers (1956 estimate) to well over 40 millions, remains to be seen. In either case, these Indo-Muslims are the group whom we must study in this chapter. Our first point, then, is that they constitute a new and distinct entity.

The identity of this new grouping has both negative and positive aspects. Many members of the community itself have been more conscious of what they are not than of what they are. Some would virtually define their group, certainly so far as their own attitudes and feelings are concerned, negatively: as that section of the erstwhile Indo-Muslim community that was not included in

---

Year Book, 1955-56, Bombay, etc., n.d. [sc. 1955], pp. 9-10); for Kashmir, 3.40 million (an estimate formed by calculating 77 per cent [the 1941 percentage was 77.11; W. Norman Brown, *The United States and India and Pakistan*, Cambridge, Mass., 1953, p. 159] of 4.41 million [*Times of India* estimate of total population for 1951, p. 7]).

[4] For 1941, the figure is 3.101 (Brown, *loc. cit.*) out of 94.389 millions, or 3.27 per cent. For 1951, the figure is 3.40 out of 103.8 millions, which gives the same percentage.

[5] This figure has been reached by taking 53.1 out of 94.389 millions. The figure 53.1 million for the 1941 population of the area that became Pakistan in 1947 has been derived by subtracting 2.8 million for Kashmir and 0.5 million for Gurdaspur from the 56.4 million that constituted the 76 Muslim-majority districts in 1941 (Kingsley Davis, *The Population of India and Pakistan*, Princeton, 1951, p. 196. This author gives 53.8 million, and 57 per cent as figures for Muslims in the Pakistan areas as of 1941; the slight difference would seem to concern Gurdaspur, which he does not mention).

[6] Exact figures are not known; this figure represents an estimate of about 6 million (cf. Davis, *op. cit.*, p. 197) out of about 100 million.

[7] Estimating 500,000; cf. preceding ref. They died "from starvation, exhaustion, disease, or murder" (Davis, *loc. cit.*). Davis's figure of one million includes Hindūs and Sikhs.

[8] Cf. ref. 3 above.

Pakistan. They have thought and felt about themselves as Pakistanis shut out from home. We ourselves have begun by stressing the dichotomy between what we have called "two nations," India's Muslims and Pakistan's. We have done this, however, not merely to suggest the truncation psychology of the former, which has indeed been dominant and which we shall later have to elaborate. More importantly, we would signalize the positive subsistence of these Muslims in their new separateness, and establish their title to consideration in their own right.

Indeed, our submission is that they constitute a very large and highly significant community, certainly one of the most significant and conceivably one of the most creative in the modern Muslim world. In our view, what they will do and will become is a much weightier question for contemporary Islam than either they or many outsiders have grasped. They have started to write one of the basically important chapters in current Islamic history.

The importance is not only economic, cultural, and other; it includes also the field of religion. This group, however unwittingly, has set forth on a new venture—to lead, to create, a new life. The Islam that will live in the hearts of the Muslims of India will be their own. It may, and almost must, prove a different form of the faith from that that the Muslims of Pakistan are developing. And conditions are such that it could well be more progressive and vital, more creative and humane and true.

In support of such a contention, various arguments will presently be adduced. In particular, for a thesis of the intrinsic import of this body of Muslims, three points seem to us striking and consequential: the size of the group, its past tradition, and its involvement in the transcending complex of India. Before elaborating these, however, we must note that one of these points—the last: the 'minority status'—has seemed to many, especially within the community itself, an argument against rather than for their own significance.

If the first obstacle to their own recognition of their selfhood has been their emotional enmeshment with Pakistan, and their obsession with having been cut off from it, the second has been their emotional enmeshment with the Hindus and their terror of being overwhelmed by them. Again, the question of what they themselves are has been repressed in the anxiety stirred by the question of their relation with those around them.

Allowing a conceit, one may see the pre-'47 Muslim community of the subcontinent as a romantic married couple living in the rather cumbersome medley of a large and strident joint family. The couple, becoming almost frenziedly sentimental about each other, and particularly repulsed also by the elder cousin who seems about to become the new head of the family on the approaching demise of the present patriarch, plot to break free from the joint family and to set up life on their own. But their plans are not clearly thought out, and prove only partly successful, partly shattering. The joint family splits up, but the lovers awake to find themselves divorced. And not divorced only, but each perforce remarried. The husband is now willy-nilly married to the frail, timid Hindu wife of East Bengal—frail and timid, yet able for all that to pose deeply embarrassing questions. The erstwhile wife is remarried, finding herself now the dismayed wife, or perhaps only the abject retainer, of that burly cousin from whom she had recoiled and of whom she had planned the whole scheme in order to be free.

Small wonder, then, that her relations with her former lover and her present husband paralysingly dominated for the moment her mind and heart. Under this dominance she had forgotten her true self, was precluded from sensing or pursuing her own development. She was afflicted with that potentially disastrous emotional insecurity and imbalance of one who thinks and feels of himself only in relation to others, not as a person in his own right.

Yet she is a person in her own right of more than ordinary stature and significance. She was in many ways the brains and even the driving force of her former marriage; and even, perhaps, has in the dénouement brought with her from that earlier marriage a greater share of the couple's personal possessions—which her partner, in his bolt from the ancestral home, was unable to take with him. More important, she has been entrusted with a new and crucial role to play in her new situation. It is one of heavy responsibility, first for her own welfare and that of coming generations. Secondly, she has responsibility also for the welfare of the new household of which she is now a part. She is a more significant member than she has learned yet to recognize; her in-laws are involved with her, as well as she with them. Thirdly, there is a responsible relationship with her own relatives outside her new home. She cannot return to her own family, but they are involved in her present destiny and will be affected and judged partly by her behaviour.

To return to prose. The Indo-Muslim community, battered by outward circumstance and gripped inwardly by dismay, has stood disconcerted, inhibited from effective self-recognition and from active vitality. Yet not only is the welfare of that community itself at stake, now and for future generations. Also the histories both of India and of Islam will in part turn on the success or failure of this community in solving its present problems, on its skill and wisdom in meeting the challenge of today.

In our allegory we allowed ourselves the words "she had forgotten her true self." To characterize the post-partition distraction of the community, its absence of realistic and critical self-awareness, the clause seems legitimate. Yet analogies are always in the end precarious, and in this case the word "forgot" betrays the inadequacy of our metaphor. For in reality the present Indo-Muslim group did not exist as a distinct entity before 1947. The individuals who now constitute it were then members of a considerably larger whole. Events have brought it about that this new grouping now exists and must be taken seriously. It is something new. She had not, then, forgotten, but rather had failed yet to discover her true self. The community had not yet recognized the validity of its own existence. It had not yet come to intellectual and emotional, let alone constructive, grips with the fact that in 1947 a new thing came to birth. It had, of course—in part painfully, and anyway with no escaping—seen and felt novelty without, a new environment. But it had hardly yet sensed the newness within, to recognize and to accept responsibility for the new creature, and its new life. The group had not yet grasped the fact that it is a new community.

The situation, its problems and challenges, are so new that one may say, as we shall presently examine, that nothing quite like this has ever happened before in the history of Islam. In one obvious sense, the Indo-Muslim community in its present form is exactly as new as the Pakistani. In another sense, as we shall presently argue, it is much older, or at least has more history behind it. In some respects, however, particularly those concerning religion, it is much newer, is more deeply an innovation.

All sections of the Islamic world find themselves today in situations that are radically unfamiliar. This is what it means to live in the twentieth century. Each section is in a situation that is also unique to itself; Islamic history in our day proceeds in segments, in diversity. The Indo-Muslim group is no exception on either score: its role in contemporary Islamic development is novel, certainly, and is very much its own. Without precedent in the past or parallel in the present, the challenge to the Muslims of India if at all adequately met will make their community one of the most significant and creative in modern Islam.

As already suggested, the principal argument for reckoning this group amongst the cardinal Islamic communities of today, rests on a combination of three factors: size, history, and situation. No one of these, quite possibly, would be sufficient in itself. But the juncture of the three seems to us to present the community with an inescapable responsibility, if not greatness, of destiny.

Numbers in themselves, of course, are not conclusively significant. Egypt, Turkey, and Iran, each with populations of somewhere about twenty millions, are not thereby the least important of the major nations in the Muslim world. Pakistan and Indonesia, the two largest bodies of Muslims today, each with just under seventy millions, are not automatically therefore the foremost, even though their potential development is manifestly great. Still, one need not overemphasize mere size to note that the numbers of the Indo-Muslim group are unquestionably impressive: in the neighbourhood of thirty-five to forty million.

On the score of history the Indo-Muslim case is equally convincing. Again, among the 'major' Muslim groups today, this community would stand at neither the top nor the bottom of the list. If in the past it has contributed less than some (for instance, the Arabs) to Islamic history, than others (for instance, the Indonesians) it has contributed more. The essential point, however, is of course not of more or less, but simply that it has contributed much—strikingly much.

It is not merely that here are two score million people, but that here are two score millions who stand at the head of a thousand-year tradition of imposing dimensions. That tradition in government, in the arts, in religious thought and practice (especially Sufi) is patently major. Indeed, no one would question the dignity of the tradition Islamically, the creation of a living and distinctive culture. What some might be found to question is the ability of the present community to continue it. But that remains to be seen. We have ourselves stressed the newness of the present situation. Yet, though new, it culminates a development that is long.

In a sense, the Pakistani and the Indian Muslims are equally successors to this past. Both have the same tradition behind them. Culturally, each is full heir to the same heritage that was Indian Islam: it is available to either, to make what they may of it.

This is largely true of the intangibles of the tradition. But in another sense the heritage is not quite so impartial. Not, as many have carelessly imagined, that Pakistan is essentially the continuator of the line of development, with the present Indo-Muslims as an offshoot or sideline. On the contrary, in many ways it is, clearly, Pakistan that is novel. Even for the sub-continent's Muslims, it is the new India that is a shrunken but true continuation of the old. Tradition is no *muhajir*; and history does not readily opt out. The present Indian Muslims fell heir to more than their share of the concrete assets and institutions of their forefathers: from the position of the Nizam[9] to the Taj Mahall, and from the traditional theological centre at Deoband to the University at 'Aligarh and the Jamia. Even the homeland of the Urdu language remained within India. More subtly but no less importantly, they fell heir to the *Indianness* of their predecessors' situation.

What they have done or might or could do with these is another question, which will occupy us later. For the moment we but stress the fact that this group began life in 1947 not as an aberration, and certainly not from scratch. The story of the Muslims in India has been a long one, with many vicissitudes. In it has been much of importance, much of grandeur, much of turmoil (both inflicted and suffered). The point is that that story is not yet over.

This brings us to the third and most characteristic feature of the Indian Muslims' position. If in numbers and in past tradition they are clearly to be compared with the other chief communities of Islam, politically their situation is unique. Of these major communities four (Turkey, Iran, Pakistan, Indonesia) have the form of independent nation-states in the modern-Western sense. The Indians and the Arabs are exceptions, each in a dis-

[9] An ambivalence in the Indo-Muslim attitude to the Nizām of Ḥaydarābād is illustrated in two poems of Ẓafar 'Alī Khān, both in his collection *Baháristán*, Lahore, 1936: "Shān-i Awrangzeb" (p. 112), which sees the dynasty as continuing Mughul glory, and "Saringāpaṭam" (pp. 123-24), which sees it as having played the traitor to it and to the Muslims, over against Tīpū Sulṭān.

tinctive way. The Arabs, though self-consciously bound together by language and culture, are politically disunited. The Indian Muslims, somewhat diverse in language (more than half speak Urdu, and about a third Bengali), somewhat integrated in culture, and highly self-conscious, are, of course, citizens of one state. Indeed, they are citizens of what is from almost every point of view one of the most important states in the modern world. What gives them a radically unique posture among the major sections of contemporary Islam, and is manifestly also the fundamental feature of their own current development, is the fact that they share citizenship in the new republic with an immense number of other people.

They constitute the only sizable body of Muslims in the world of whom this is, or ever has been, true. One may compare the Muslims in China, the U.S.S.R, or Negro Africa. Not only are these groups much smaller in size (roughly twenty millions each); and not only do they have vastly less history behind them. There is the further radical difference that they are not free.

This Indian situation is complex and needs to be elaborately explored. But at first blow it seemed to many Muslims simple: a sheer, overwhelming frustration of any hope of realizing their community's dreams. The quality of this new kind of history, in its radical and creative emergence, was lost in the stunning sense of the end of the old kind. An utter bleakness seemed to have descended.

We have suggested earlier that the basic dilemma of modern Muslims resides in the discrepancy between their faith and their contemporary history. This discrepancy seemed at its most vast for these Muslims of India. If for other Islamic groups the glories of the community's earthly career had waned and the onward march of its history faltered, for this group they appeared to have been shattered into nothingness. While other segments of Islamic history seemed inadequate to their divine theme, these men put forth a great effort to achieve a Pakistan where one part, at least, of that history might shine forth once again in true splendour. Yet from the débâcle their own, Indian, segment seemed to emerge more inadequate than ever, if not extinct. The earthly conditions of other major Muslim communities seemed to frustrate their Islamic aspirations; those of this community, derisively to mock them.

This interpretation omits many aspects of the historical situation, both concrete and potential. It omits, too, many basic considerations of the religious involvement. In our view it is, then, a hasty and inadequate understanding; we shall presently endeavour to amend it. However, it cannot be dismissed as a superficial misreading. It rests on manifest facts, and must be understood.

The community in its present form was born in bloodshed and hatred, weak in a world at war. In 1947 the riots and massacres of Partition, ghastly beyond all telling, ushered into existence the new states of India and Pakistan. If the vehemence and violence of those desperate days left their mark on the two nations, how much more on the minorities within them, who cowered in helpless fear. And it was not only the climactic outburst of destructive passion sweeping across Pakistan and India in those early months of the nations' freedom, but the years of mounting tension that had led up to it: the gradually intensifying and shrill animosity that had gripped the land as the two great communities suffered misunderstanding and estrangement, then fear and acrid anger. The rejecting and being rejected of strident, frenzied communalism provided the background from which this community came, through a holocaust, to be a minority in a dominion whose general populace they considered, and who considered them, alien and bitterly hostile.

When passions cooled, the terror passed but the difficulties remained. The new India fairly quickly pulled itself out of the morass of the early dislocation, and set itself with some enthusiasm and skill to overcome grave crises of food shortages and the like; settling down to the constructive, responsible, difficult, and at times exhilarating business of being and becoming a free nation in a perplexing but exciting world. Some individual Muslims, particularly those few who had throughout identified themselves with Indian nationalism and spurned the separatism of the Muslim League, joined in this great forward endeavour. They devoted themselves to it with sincerity and energy, and were accepted in it with equality and friendship.[10] The bulk of their community,

[10] Individual Muslim members of the cabinet were conspicuous: not only the famed Abū-l-Kalām Āzād of long standing, but the devoted, able, and much appreciated Rafi' Aḥmad Qidwā'ī, who executed a notable task in the organizing of the food-control situation in the country's early, critical years. Other Muslim persons of prominence have served their country with distinc-

however, neither trusting nor trusted, held aloof. It continued to cower; rejected, mistrusted, and afraid.

Its members felt that the new creative upsurge of Indian construction was not for them. Indian freedom they saw rather as the unchecked opportunity for their enemies to hold them down or indeed to crush them. They tended to feel that the professed secularism of the new state was an hypocrisy; at best constitutionalizing the lack of special consideration in protection for non-Hindus, and at worst, especially on the lower levels of administration, merely putting up a façade for international exhibition behind which to practise the discrimination of the liberated and disdainful and even vindictive Hindus. They tended similarly to feel that the democracy was at best but an arithmetic device, depriving their votes of effective consequence; and at worst again a false front of a caste-conscious and closed community in power.

We shall return to a discussion of these really deep issues. At this point we may observe that, whatever its validity, an understanding of how Muslims and others in their position could and did tend to such an interpretation is quite fundamental to an appreciation not only of their inner feelings and dismay, but also of their objective condition.

To the generalization that no religious minority anywhere in the world really feels secure and accepted, China was in pre-Communist days perhaps the one exception. In the existing circumstances it was inconceivable of India that it should be an exception—just as it was of Pakistan. Man has not yet devised a social system to accommodate satisfactorily those groups who do not participate fully. The Negroes in America, the Jews in Christendom, the Copts in Egypt, the deviationists under Communism, have had varying reason to be afraid. It is no easy or pleasant matter to be in a minority anywhere—even though tolerance can vary vastly, all the way from liberality to zero. It is mawkish and absurd to lose sight of the fact that rights and freedom, even if short of perfection, are extremely important in those cases where they exist at all, in whatever degree (there is a minority psychology

---

tion and happiness as ambassadors, civil service commissioners, and the like, and within the civil service; and a trusted institution such as the Jamia near Delhi found itself in full development. (It was remarked by some more humble Muslims, however, that this type of career was much easier for men of prominence than for the obscure, at top levels than in remote areas.)

that does lose sight of this, complaining of shortcomings without appreciation of degrees). It is also false to lose sight of the fact that no matter what rights and freedom obtain, it is in the nature of human society impossible for a member of a minority[11] to feel fully at home. His life is sentenced to infringement. It is among the bitternesses of human history that his personality is precluded from that free flowering to which man as a full member of a free group may have the good fortune to rise.

In the particular case of India and of the Muslim group within it, it is irresponsibly blind to underestimate the legal provisions of the Constitution, the liberal spirit of the government and society in so far as this prevails, and those factors in the past heritage and present development making for fraternity and human recognition. Secularism and its nondiscriminatory "democratic" justice have, surely, been an aspiration rather than an attainment. Yet one must recall the lesson of the rise of fascism: that even hypocritical pretensions of democracy and sadly fragmentary implementations of justice are of relative value, and disastrously worse can be no such pretensions at all, and the implementation of some other vision. Only in very limited numbers did Muslims evaluate with true appreciation the ideals and announced objectives of the nation to which they belonged, and such earnestness as the government and other leadership evinced in pursuit of these. Infinitely precious are the aspirations of sheerly human welfare irrespective of communal consideration, which the state has formally proclaimed; and also infinitely precious are those forces, Hindu and other, within the society that motivate some at least of its citizens to devote themselves to this aspiration with varying but not negligible sincerity. It was no small matter that the Hindu leaders of the nation, in the name of secularism and humanity, restrained the natural and potentially ferocious impetus of the Hindu majority to wreak vengeance on the Muslim group.

On the other hand, it is also blind not to recognize that the minority is a minority; with disabilities and frustrations and fears, and grounds for fear, that are real and large—linguistic, economic, political and other.

The community is in danger of being deprived of its language, than which only religious faith is a deeper possession. Nine years of gradual adjustment in other fields have brought no improve-

[11] By "minority" we mean, of course, socially significant minority; which perhaps renders the observation almost tautologous, though still important.

ment in this, and little prospect of improvement. And alongside the new constitutional Indian political system of democracy, and alongside such strands in Hindu thought and development as preach the worth of man as man, stands the old Hindu religious system of caste, the most highly organized, rigid, philosophically justified, and stubbornly persistent system of social discrimination and arrogant inequality that humanity throughout its long history of failure in fraternity has ever evolved.

In our insistence earlier in this discussion, still to be elaborated, that the Indian Muslim community is in a position of great import and potential creativity, we did not mean that it faces no problem.

Disruption by Pakistan

Next to Hindu communalism, the most conspicuous factor in the continuing insecurity and distress of the Muslims of India has been the behaviour of Pakistan. The Muslims of Pakistan have strikingly contributed to the dislocation of the Indian Muslims' life.

In some ways it is simply the existence of Pakistan that undermines the Muslims' position in India. Its establishment of course made them a much smaller minority than they would otherwise have been. In undivided India, caste Hindus constituted a majority of 53 per cent, with Muslims counting almost half that number; in the shrunken India of today the former aggregate 66 per cent, outnumbering Muslims over six to one. (If one extends 'Hindus' to include 'Scheduled Castes' and non-Christian 'Tribals,' these figures become: 71 per cent and over one third for undivided India; and after Partition 85 per cent, more than eight to one.[12])

Further, by voting for Pakistan's establishment, over against all other offers, the present Indo-Muslims as it were explicitly rejected all claim to special status in the new India, and almost could be seen as rejecting all claim to any status at all. ("These men made

[12] The figures in this paragraph have been calculated on the following data (in millions). For 1941: Caste Hindus, 206.1 (d); Scheduled Castes, 48.8 (a); Tribals, 25.4 (a); non-Christian Tribals, 24.3 (c); total non-Tribal Hindus, 254.93 (a); total "Hindus," 279.3 (d); Muslims, 94.4 (a); total population, 388.998 (a). For 1951: Caste Hindus, 233.9 (d); Scheduled Castes, 51.3 (b); Tribals, 19.1 (b); non-Christian Tribals, 18 (c); total "Hindus," 303.2 (b); Muslims, 35.4 (b); total population, 356.879 (b). Sources: (a) *Census of India 1941*; (b) *Times of India, op.cit.*, pp. 7, 10; (c) our own calculations from (a) and (b) as modified by the figures and reasoning of Kingsley Davis, *The Population of India and Pakistan*, Princeton, 1951, p. 251; (d) by addition or subtraction.

an intolerably large demand—and we conceded it. Let them now keep quiet.") And a Muslim peasant, who perhaps never had a political idea in his head, may be kicked about in his village with the contemptuous sneer, "Why don't you get out; why don't you go to your Pakistan?" And his cry does not reach very far.

Nonetheless, to the simple fact of Pakistan's establishment the Indian Muslims could more easily have adjusted themselves, had it not been for that "Islamic" nation's subsequent activities. The policies pursued, based in this sphere on a persistently communalist interpretation of Muslim interests, have tended to affect adversely the Muslim on the Indian side of the frontier.

This began immediately after partition, when the Pakistan Muslims massacred and raped and exiled Sikhs and Hindus by the millions. On the whole, India quickly recognized that this terrifying situation was equally damaging to both sides. Its public leaders and private citizens soon saw the outburst in human terms, and expressed penitence on ". . . the blackest chapter in the history of India."[13] Pakistan, on the other hand, seems not to have had the freedom from prejudice and the moral sensitivity and courage to acknowledge its roughly equal guilt.[14] The Muslims of that

[13] Sardār Paṭel, in an address to Congressmen at Bangalore, Feb. 25, 1949, criticized those who believed in Hindū Rāj and only Hindū culture: "Gandhiji was against that mad idea," he said, and went on, "We did not listen to [his appeal for unity], and when we got freedom, we know how the three communities, Hindus, Muslims and the Sikhs behaved. It is now a matter of history and it will always remain the blackest chapter in the history of India" —The Hindustan Times, New Delhi, Feb. 26, 1949. Apart from leaders' statements of this kind, the present writer has found ordinary citizens—Sikh taxi drivers in Calcutta, Hindū refugees whom one meets on the trains— spontaneously expressive of similar sentiments, and regretting communal ill will and its results as a shame to humanity.

[14] It is difficult to document, and indeed to be sure about, the relative distribution of murders, horrors, and the general infliction of suffering. However, in 1949 the present writer made as careful inquiry as he was able, for example among Christian volunteers working among refugees, abducted women, etc.; and became tentatively persuaded that there seemed relatively little to choose between the two sides. This much at least is certain, that enough was inflicted on both sides for regret. Government publications and private writings, however, in Pakistan still (1956) tend to speak of the 1947 holocaust self-righteously. There have been, apparently, some Urdū novels published in Pakistan portraying the 1947 situation in humanist rather than communal terms. Yet the general mood does not seem significantly to have altered. (A typical and innocuous enough example of the standard attitude: the government publication Pakistan, the Struggle of a Nation, Washington, 1949, p. 36, "At the Time of Partition.")

country have in general not been aware of the appalling suffering that the other side also underwent. It was left to the Muslims of India (into whose midst the surviving refugees poured in bitter terror) to recognize the fierce madness—to recognize it; and in part to pay its price.

However, the fearful days of 1947 passed; and gradually India has struggled forward towards forgetting them. The deep wounds then inflicted cannot readily heal; it will be long before no bitterness remains. Yet in less than ten years the Muslim community slowly found itself realizing that its worst fears could go. It would not be exterminated ("as we were in Spain") or utterly ground down, as many had apprehended. The majority community had only in part forgiven or forgotten; yet it was restrained from taking vengeance.

The goodwill of that majority, however, on which so much seemed to depend, was inhibited by various features, among which, as we have said, Pakistan behaviour continued to be prominent. At a level relatively close to the surface, this has operated in that what Pakistan does from day to day (especially *vis-à-vis* its internal Hindu community in East Bengal, and externally *vis-à-vis* India) influences the attitude of the majority Indian population to local Muslims. Any increase in hostility between the two nations, or any deterioration in the position of Pakistani Hindus, has been quickly reflected in the worsening of the Indian Muslims' situation. Contrariwise, the single most important step towards a betterment in this situation would be improvement in Pakistan-India relations (actually, one of the most important steps for the welfare of both countries in general, quite apart from any consideration of minorities). Each new Hindu discontent fleeing from East Pakistan, and each new border incident or exacerbation of canal-water dispute or refugee-property question, have had repercussions on Muslim life within India.

This had added a singular complication to the Kashmir tangle: since a transfer of Kashmir to Pakistan would, and even pressure for such a transfer does, militate against the interest of other Muslims in India. Nationalist leaders of the latter group have seen this point and expressed it;[15] but Pakistanis have been quite unable to comprehend this.[16]

[15] See the statement presented by Zākir Ḥusayn and others on the Kashmir

Kashmir is not, however, the most important issue. We have said that this sort of matter has been relatively close to the surface. The effects can go deep, and be serious. Yet the more fundamental point has been the philosophy that underlies the acts. Pakistan came into existence and has continued to operate on a communalist interpretation both of Muslims' interests and of Indian nationalism. Formally, its official policy was forced by realities fairly quickly to recognize that Pakistan has no extra-territorial claim on the Muslims of India.[17] Emotionally, however, and unofficially, the claim persisted. Pakistani attitudes to India still expressed a basic antagonism,[18] and a refusal to admit the latter's non-communal character. Its people remained still[19] incapable of recognizing, let alone of applauding and encouraging,

---

issue: *Text of Memorandum, dated August 14, 1951, submitted by Fourteen Muslim Leaders of India to Dr. Frank P. Graham, United Nations Representative.* This was subsequently bound as a pamphlet, with the cover-title *Indian Muslim Leaders' Memorandum on Kashmir,* and the indication, "Issued by Dr. Zakir Hussain, Vice Chancellor, Muslim University, Aligarh."

[16] The standard reaction in Pakistan to the "Statement" was to dismiss it as one more instance of how utterly dominated by the Hindū Indian government Muslims in India were; it was interpreted as illustrating the pressure on those Muslims, and their succumbing to it. This attitude, apart from being a gratuitous insult to a person of the moral and other stature of Dr. Zākir Ḥusayn, was politically unrealistic.

[17] April 8, 1950: an agreement between India and Pakistan, signed by the two prime ministers, on the treatment of minorities, known as the Delhi Pact, or the Liyāqat-Nehrū pact. The text will be found in *The Middle East Journal,* Washington, 4:344-46 (1950). Note especially the paragraph: "Both Governments wish to emphasize that the allegiance and loyalty of the minorities is to the State of which they are citizens, and that it is to the Government of their own State that they should look for the redress of their grievances."

[18] This fact is stridently obvious to any visitor to the country, especially to West Pakistan. It can be seen in published literature also; cf. almost any issue of the government's bi-monthly press excerpts, *Pakistan News Digest,* Karachi, and especially the editorials of the Karachi daily, *Dawn.*

[19] This continued the attitude of the pre-partition Muslim League *vis-à-vis* the Congress: an insistence by the League not only that it itself represented a religious community ("nation"), but also that the Congress did, and must acknowledge itself as doing so. The League was never able to acknowledge that the principle on which the Congress rested was different from its own, that the dispute between them was between a communal and a non-communal group. This was the actual issue on which agreement between the two primarily floundered. (Cf. W. C. Smith, *Modern Islām in India,* Lahore, 1943, pp. 293-94; London, "1946" [sc. 1947], pp. 253-54.) The basic difficulty has been and remains the long-standing and widespread one, of insisting on interpreting other people in terms of one's own presuppositions.

the secularism of the new state. Rather than coming firmly to terms with the realization that the position of India's Muslims depends primarily on two things, their aspiration towards Indianness and India's aspiration towards secularism, Pakistan has tended to deride that secularism[20] and to presume and encourage a disloyalty of Indian Muslims to their state.[21]

The whole matter is partly the normal outworking of disparate national interests, with each state pursuing its own policies quite regardless of their repercussions within the other. Yet there is more involved. The vitiation goes back to a fundamental self-contradiction in the basic idea on which the Pakistan programme was put forward. This was the Muslim League proposition that "the Muslims of India are a nation." To say that the Muslims of Pakistan constitute a nation, or the Muslims of the world, would have been coherent; whether true or false. But to posit the then term "India" as having nationalist meaning, in the very determination to negate it, was inevitably to become enmeshed in inconsistencies. These, when translated into practice, must and did mean disruption and clash. This idea still obtains; and in so far as it obtains, it continues to disrupt painfully and deeply.

It is of course not unusual that ideas, especially when not carefully thought out—this one was hardly thought out at all[22]—prove

[20] For instance, it is a fairly standard sarcasm to use quotation marks in referring to " 'secular' India"—a recent example, *Pakistan News Digest,* Karachi, 4:18, p. 6 (Aug. 15, 1956), quoting *Dawn,* Karachi. At a more serious level, one may note so responsible a thinker as Dr. Ishtiyāq Ḥusayn Qurayshī seriously writing, while a member of the Pakistan cabinet, of his hopelessness for the Muslim minority in India: "In a hundred years, perhaps in a shorter time, the Muslim people may cease to exist in that country"— I. H. Qureshi, "The Foundations of Pakistani Culture," a paper presented to the Colloquium on Islamic Culture, Princeton, 1953; reprinted in *The Muslim World,* Hartford, 44:3-11 (1954), p. 8.

[21] This takes the form not only of speeches and the general tone of references in Pakistan (chiefly West Pakistan) to Indian Muslims; but also of positive action, in that Indian Muslims even in responsible positions are actively enticed to abandon their country and their responsibilities and to accept offers from Pakistan, including the Pakistan government. The outstanding examples have been the poet Josh and Brigadier Anīs, discussed below; but the tendency has operated in countless smaller instances. Few Pakistanis have had the imagination to recognize that they are undermining the position of Muslims in India by giving employment to Muslim graduates of Indian universities immediately upon their graduation, etc.

[22] Mr. Jinnāh is usually regarded, by Pakistanis at least, as a brilliant leader. That he was a clever dialectician and lawyer seems clear. Yet is it

to have internal inconsistencies when implemented. The difficulties have in this case been rendered unusually serious not only by the vast and radical nature of the programme, and the profundity of the emotions involved, but also in that most of the consequent heavy cost fell on one section of those involved. It is the Indian Muslims who have chiefly paid for the ambiguities of Pakistan. It is they who have suffered most for the impracticalities and absurdities.[23]

Similarly in the case of the profound emotional ambivalencies. There was in the Pakistan proposal, in addition to a positive constructive element, a negative one of sheer hatred and fear. Along with the affirmative vision of actually building a new and creative community life, went a destructive fury of anti-Hindu, anti-outsider rejection. And along with the positive aspiration of the Muslims to be free went the negative impulse of Hindus not to accept them. Here again, such positive aspects as there were came to fruition on the Pakistan side of the frontier; and while there is also in Pakistan still immense play for the negative aspects, on the Indian side it is only these that could find expression. Indian Muslims pay for Pakistan's imperfections not only in present action but in original intention. They are involved with Pakistan, but inevitably with its contrarieties. They cannot share its triumphs but must suffer for its faults.

This kind of inverted relation is discouragingly visible also on

---

not perhaps time to bring into question his statesmanship, his political sagacity, in view of his apparent failure to foresee—apparently even to try to foresee—the concrete outworking of his proposals? One is left with the impression that he had never studied a map of the Panjab or Bengal; let alone envisaged the former's canal system. When asked about such problems as Kashmir, he irately insisted that only British India was under discussion in the constitutional proposals. When asked about the boundaries of the proposed Pakistan, he ridiculed as preposterous the suggestion that these should be roughly what they in fact turned out to be (cf. his part in the Gāndhī-Jinnāḥ talks, 1944; cited in Smith, *op. cit.*, London ed., p. 284). If he is to be credited with all Pakistan's achievements, as is customary, should he be exempted from responsibility for its problems?

[23] One must note the *Qurbān* theory: that the Indo-Muslims have gladly paid the price for Islām's flourishing in Pakistan. "It is good that we suffer," they say in effect, "in order that our brethren might be free." This is legitimate enough, if it be sincere and not rationalization. However, the disillusionment has been bitter with the discovery, gradually spreading, that Islām in Pakistan, rather than flourishing, has become in large measure the plaything of hypocritical and ineffective politicians.

the other side. Pakistani Muslims have had so heavy a psychological investment in the conviction that Indian Muslims are mistreated, that at times one cannot but detect a morbid welcoming of adverse news,[24] and a resistance to awareness of Indo-Muslim welfare. The emotional involvement between the two groups is still close, and is itself a further cause of their actual estrangement.

The Indian Muslims are, or appear to be, in the unenviable position of having their fate depend upon two outside groups. Their condition seems determined not only by the behaviour of their fellow citizens of a different faith, but also by that of their fellow Muslims of a different nation. They have been manoeuvred into a position where it is they who pay for the mistakes or excesses, and even the apparent mistakes and excesses, of another Muslim community. Killing of non-Muslims in Lahore wounds Muslims in India; any failure of justice in Dacca makes justice for them that much more difficult. The more "Islamic" Pakistan is in form (and especially in so far as there is form without substance), the less secure are the Muslims of India. In a crude and exteriorist and grossly unsubtle sense, a cynic might aver that the more Islam flourishes in Pakistan the more it will wilt in India.

The truth of this will be gainsaid only if Islam is taken, by the Muslims of both communities, in a lofty and interior and subtle dynamic sense. For those who fail to rise to such an interpretation, the distress is both inward and external.

Self-Inflicted Tragedy

We have said that Pakistan has been a conspicuous factor in the Indo-Muslim community's distress. The more serious factor, however, underlying this, has been rather the community's own attitudes and behaviour. The adverse effect of Pakistan's policies

[24] This is apparently chiefly in conversation, but is visible also in the way stories of Indian mistreatment are presented in the Pakistani press. In addition to genuine sympathy, there is a strand in Pakistani psychology not very far below the surface that does not want to hear well of Indo-Muslims. Still today (1956) the *Pakistan News Digest* takes pains to publish stories of unfair treatment of Christians in India, which can fulfil, clearly, only a psychological need (there would be no reason, for instance, for that government to publish stories of unfair treatment of Christians in Egypt or of, say, Jews in Argentina).

would have been incomparably less were it not for the community's own orientation. It is the idea of Pakistan, rather than its actuality, and the continuing participation of Indian Muslims in that idea, that has been emotionally and then socially disruptive.

So long as the Indian Muslims think of themselves, and by their behaviour and attitudes allow both Pakistani Muslims and Indian Hindus to think of them, not as *Indian Muslims* but as Pakistani Muslim expatriates, so long will their position be bleak. This stand incapacitates them, inevitably and desperately. It has produced, and cannot but produce, insecurity, both internal and overt, emotional and social; through inner confusion and outer mistrust. The rest of India cannot accept them so long as they appear to be 'fifth columnists.' And they cannot even accept themselves. In these terms they cannot accept and hardly dare to recognize the situation in which they are placed. It is not merely an historical but a theological dilemma. Their faith—Islam—is the one thing the present dénouement left to them, one reality to which in forlornness they can and must cling. Yet it is their Islam that, they feel, links them to Pakistan and segregates them from the India in which they live. In fact, of course, it is not Islam that does this, but a particular interpretation of Islam, an interpretation from which, during the crucial 1940's, the main understanding individuals in the present Indo-Muslim community kept themselves free, but to which most of the group succumbed, and of which it has since been able only very partially to rid itself. A new interpretation of Islam in terms realistic for the present situation, superseding pre-partition emotions and viewpoints with a dynamic that would inspire the community to come to creative grips with today's problems and opportunities, has yet to be attained.

The majority of the Muslims in India have felt that their group is helpless, the plaything of outside forces over which they have had no control. They suddenly awoke to find themselves in a situation that they abhorred, one from which with blind fury they had been struggling to be free, only to find it descending upon them all the more poignantly and crushingly.

The feeling, however, though deep and important, is essentially false. In fact the turn that their history has taken has not come through an inscrutable fate or an alien power. On the contrary, it was primarily the community's own doing. This is a development in Islamic history that the Muslims concerned themselves brought about. If the community did not choose the situation in which it finds itself, it chose the steps which led to it. In the 'forties, after long suppression, it moved toward freedom; and exercised that freedom by choosing to work for the creation of Pakistan—that is, toward the partition of India. It was primarily the Indian Muslims who were responsible for the emergence of the new state, and therefore also for the consequent position of their own community on the Indian side of the frontier. The Pakistanis followed and accepted, but the Indian Muslims led and created. It is true that they did not clearly foresee the shape into which they were moulding their own history. It is possible to be free without being either clear-sighted or wise. It is not possible to be free without being responsible.

The Indian Muslims are responsible for their own situation not only in the sense that they voted for Pakistan. This is, of course, the fundamental point. But there are others. One is the 'opting out' of leaders, at the time of the 1947 crisis. Within the community, the masses were left with drastically less than a normal quota of leadership of all kinds—in education, business, the professions, government service—simply because a high percentage of this group departed to cross the frontier at the time of partition. The Muslim League party used its persuasive powers to encourage this, enticing Muslims in positions of any significance to abandon the local community and to migrate to Pakistan, apparently without regard or sense of responsibility for the many Muslims who would be left behind. Nationally, the resulting burden was shouldered by the small group of outstanding personalities who throughout had been loyal to the Indian-nationalist ideal, seeing the Muslims' place as inevitably within the larger complex. In local situations, however, the loss could not but be severe, both in immediate practical consequence and in the example of apparent failure of moral responsibility or courage. It will perhaps take some time before the community can on a large and wide-ranging scale generate a new leadership from within its own depleted and discouraged ranks.

This matter too would have been less disruptive had the process not continued apace. The 1947 crisis came and went; those who chose to depart then had made a decision, which, sound or otherwise, could be respected. But those who chose to stay, and proclaimed a loyalty that they later betrayed, were another matter.

A persistent efflux of leaders long after 1947 not only increased the depletion, and the community's devastating sense of being left without guides. It also continued to falsify the position of those who remained, casting severe doubts on their reliability and status. There were men within India, both Hindus and Muslims, who championed the community's cause, or championed the cause of individual Muslims for promotion or honour or trust, and fought the communalism of those other Hindus who would write off all Indo-Muslims as inherently disloyal. Such men's case was repeatedly undermined by the series of illustrations by members of the Muslim community that in fact they were not loyal to India.

Numerous young Muslims graduating from the universities continued to seek jobs in Pakistan rather than in India. Several prominent Muslim political leaders, in many cases even after having taken their oath of allegiance to the new country and having accepted positions of trust, also later sought and found—or were offered and accepted—opportunities to cross over to Pakistan. Literary and even religious leaders, even after accepting special positions and distinctions from the government, transferred themselves and their loyalty to Pakistan when more highly-paid prospects were proffered from that side. Perhaps the most damaging incident was when a brigadier general in the Indian army, after having opted for India and been advanced to positions of responsibility and access to secret information, in 1955 voluntarily retired and at once settled down in Pakistan, accepting a Pakistan-government post.

It can be imagined how severely behaviour such as this worsens the situation of those Muslims who remain. Brigadier Anis's move has made it much more difficult for another Muslim to be appointed brigadier (and indeed, even to be appointed *chaprasi* or peon). The poet Josh's departure has meant that the prospects for Urdu in India, whatever they may have been before he made his decision, are much darker afterward. Pakistanis use this kind of material to prove how bleak is the Muslim position in India, how discontent are even its established and favoured leaders. We leave aside for later discussion such questions, and the wider ramifications and significance of this whole trend. At the moment we but make the obvious observation that in general the position of the community, whatever it be, has been made worse by its own disloyalties. We also leave unexplored the moral question, as to why these leaders, if indeed they had found conditions for Muslims in India dark, chose their own personal advancement rather than sensing any duty to remain, in their privileged positions, to serve their fellows.

The community's estrangement from India, and from the realities of its own present situation, has been evinced and fostered by its emotional entanglement not only with Pakistan but with its own past. There are, indeed, several ways in which the difficulties of the present community, if not 'self-inflicted,' are anyway to be traced to factors within its own situation, rather than or as well as to the adversity of outsiders. There is the complex economic situation, in whose evolution for seventy-five years the Muslims have as a group been as it were disfavoured, since their community has throughout produced fewer than its due share of individuals and groups adjusted to, or able to take advantage of, new opportunities and necessities. This disadvantage, this communal lag behind constantly developing circumstance, has operated not only to depress the economic level of individuals and groups, with all the consequent psychological and emotional disturbances.[25] It has also had far-reaching implications for standard cultural and religious activity.

To take one example: most of the productive centres of Islamic culture in India—from a semi-classical institution such as the Nadwah at Lucknow to a Westernizing journal such as *Islamic Culture* of Hyderabad—were chiefly financed either from landed property or from the *largesse* of princes; that is, from obsolescent remnants from an earlier age. The modernization of India has in substance been gathering momentum for long, but in form had been held back by British control; it made a forward spurt after 1947. In doing so it has left Muslim feudal institutions unprotected in an industrial-technological age. The supersession of *zamindari* and of the native princes have been two of the most striking achievements of modern India; they must be regarded as major steps of progress. That they have spelled hardship for Indian Islam reveals the backwardness of that community. What has seemed to Indian Muslims the inflicting of discrimination may from another point of view be regarded as the uncovering of weakness.

[25] Cf. Smith, *op. cit.*, esp. Part II, chapp. 1 and 5, for a fairly elaborate descriptive analysis of this process.

The most spectacular instance of this, and of Muslim blind fury in protest against it, was the 1948 Hyderabad tragedy.[26] This illustrates further one more attempt of the Indian Muslims not to accept their new position in a democratic India. The loss of self-respect over the vanished pomp of a prouder, mightier yesterday, and the frenzied but futile attempt to perpetuate erstwhile power, were terribly illustrated in that desperate fiasco. The Nizam and his régime symbolized for many Muslims throughout the country the earthly greatness of Islamic history in its earlier and happier days, and the imminent possibility of the régime's downfall brought home to them too distressingly the extent to which that earthly greatness had come to an end. The fanatical support that the symbol elicited from the community, like the Khilafat Movement thirty years before, was in part a genuine if shortsighted endeavour to keep Muslim power on earth from too utterly disintegrating. But it was in part also an endeavour to keep from recognizing how utterly it had, in this form, disintegrated already.

The whole affair is a sadly illuminating commentary not only on the political ineptitude to which their dispiritedness had led these Indo-Muslims. It illuminates also the moral and intellectual failure to recognize that for today and tomorrow both the earthly and the spiritual greatness of Islam must, as for the rest of us, take new and different forms. It has been painful for backward-looking Muslims to discover that neither God nor the United Nations is concerned to preserve the ancient forms of Islamic achievement. The future glory of Islam in India will be built not by those who battle or bemoan the passing of the antique and by now hollow dominions of feudal potentates, but by men who strive to ascertain and to bring appropriately to bear on modern conditions the timeless, transcendent truths of the faith.

The excruciating price that the Hyderabad Muslims paid for their misinterpretations, must also be remembered. In our attempt to understand the present dilemma and distress of the Indo-Muslim group, and even to understand how far this is engendered from within, we must not lose sight of how devastatingly each false move has worsened their situation.

Signs of Hope

Two contrasting trends have been evident among the Indian Muslim community, in the face of the developing situation in

[26] For references, cf. above, chap. 2, ref. 19.

which it has found itself. One is the vicious circle of maladjustment and insecurity, at which we have already glanced. The other has been the painful and slow victory of realism, of gradually coming to forced terms with actuality, and climbing towards deliberate, responsible, liberated participation in it. In the former way has lain despondency, and the search for escape. In the latter have appeared signs of the dawn of a new day for Islam and its community, that might mean a great new freedom and creative adjustment and progress—of significance far beyond India.

Once again we meet that fundamental crisis of Islam, lying in the radical and growing discrepancy between the new situation in which the Muslims find themselves, and the now outdated emotions and concepts with which they confront it. This discrepancy is nowhere more sharp than in India; this truth is at once the measure of the community's distress and the promise of its solution. The pressure of facts over against the inadequacy and distortion of emotions and ideas seems already to be eliciting not merely anguish but liberation.

The vicious circle has certainly not yet stopped spinning. Given the external situation constituted by the triangle of Hindus, Pakistan, and past history, Indian Muslims cannot but feel insecure. And their internal insecurity is precisely the chief factor in their failure to come to terms with their actual situation; their fleeing from it, emotionally and intellectually (and literally, when the occasion arises; to Pakistan).

For instance, we have seen that one of the basic weaknesses of the minority's position in India has resided in its tie with Pakistan. Yet it is that very weakness that has made the community on the whole unwilling to cut that tie. Unwilling, rather—or unable—to recognize that in fact it has already been cut. The more insecure its position, the more desperately it has felt impelled to hold tightly to its outside relationship, while it is that outside relationship that most vitiates its position in India.

Similarly, although Khaliqu-z-Zaman's or Josh's or Anis's fleeing to Pakistan bedevils the position of those who stay, this very fact can be (and has been) interpreted as an increased reason for (rather than against) the next man's fleeing. The abject devastation to which the Rizakar[26a] venture led, could—and did—mean that many of the Hyderabad Muslims, suffering for that calamity,

[26a] For the Riẓākār and their part in the 1948 troubles see the article cited above, chap. 2, ref. 19; cf. also chap. 2 at p. 90.

fell prey to still greater despair, still less willingness to strive for normality, still less ability to take responsibility for constructive cooperation. The intelligentsia there has showed little endeavour to struggle towards a revision of attitudes and concepts that would more adequately handle modern life.[27]

The logic of sanity could mean but little in such a condition. The emotions have been profound and pervasive, the concepts deeply ingrained.

Despite all this, the situation has in fact steadily improved. Of the two trends, the one towards despair dominated for only three or four years. During the 'fifties there has been a gradual liberation. And as we have suggested, this development seems to us to give promise eventually of memorable attainment. For events themselves have been severely, indeed mercilessly, pressing home their lesson. Not the illogicality of the false interpretations but their repeatedly and cumulatively disastrous consequences in practice, have been forcing a reassessment. And on the positive side, the constructive quality of concrete achievements, the welfare and progress actually emerging from new and bold hypotheses, have begun to tell.

It is our conviction that the welfare of the Muslim community in India, both mundane and spiritual, lies in its standing on its own feet, under God, recognizing and accepting its situation in India, and recognizing and accepting responsibility for its own destiny in that situation; able to trust others and itself, and freely, honestly, and creatively participating in the life of the new nation.

It is our observation that it has moved in this direction during the past five years—despite all troubles. Of the various factors contributing to this move, the chief has been the success of secularism. That success has, of course, been partial; yet basic. The Muslims have seen law and order prevail, have seen the police prevent riots against themselves, have watched the secular state restraining triumphant Hindus from reconverting a mosque to a temple.[28] In other words, they have found that they could live at peace with India, and were free to practice, and indeed to preach, their religion. Most Muslims in India seemed (1956)

[27] There are, of course, honourable exceptions. One example is Dr. Sayyid 'Abdu-l-Laṭif, organizer and president of the Academy of Islamic Studies and its bold, pragmatic projects mentioned above, chap. 1, ref. 3.

[28] Cf. the Ajodhya mosque incident, Fazyabad, U.P.

ready to admit that their condition has been better than they expected it to be.

There has been more to it than survival. Some have been content unconsciously to adjust themselves to survival, without analysis. Not much reflection has been needed, however, to realize that their survival and welfare depend squarely on the secularity of the state. The full theological implications of this are as yet far from worked out. But the sheer fact is striking that, whatever traditional theology may say, secularism works, and for Muslims is not a bugbear but a boon. Relatively few[29] seem to have clung to the Islamic state idea. Whatever may be the merits or meaning of the concept in the abstract, most Indian Muslims have finally come to recognize that for them in the present situation it is irrelevant and damaging.

The most stark realization in this matter came from the Hyderabad collapse. As one Muslim put it, "When I heard of the action in Hyderabad, I wept for the Musalmans. Yet in the end, despite all their tragic suffering, Hyderabad was a good thing for the Muslims of India. It meant that the last flicker of hope for that kind of absurd fantasy died down and convinced them that they must face realities of life as they exist."

Such recognition has been furthered by the realization, as communications between the two countries improved, that Pakistan too is no utopia. Just as it has gradually become clear that things in India are not so bad, so also it has begun to filter through that in Pakistan they are not so good. And some, at least, are honest enough to acknowledge that they as a minority in India have in both theory and practice a better status than the minority in the neighbouring Islamic republic.

On the positive side, joint electorates in practice have demonstrated to at least some members of the community the meaning of *national* politics, and the meaning of human rather than communal categories. The ability of independent Muslims to win municipal elections in the U.P. against Congress candidates in Hindu-majority constituencies[30] could hardly fail to educate. Simi-

[29] An exception is the Jamā'at-i Islāmī, related to the Pakistan organization of the same name under Mawdūdī; cf. above, chap. 5, pp. 233-36, at ref. 26. Cf. also below, p. 284.

[30] At Saharanpur, a Muslim was elected chairman of the municipal council against a Congress opponent, by an electorate more than half Hindū.

larly the participation of Muslims in the national elections of 1951, with their vote helping to rout the Hindu communalist parties, was a significant experience.

In the 1930's the nationalist Husayn Ahmad Madani, pronouncing India to be the nation of its Muslims, had provoked from the poet Iqbal a scornful retort in poetry insisting that a Muslim can have no nation but Islam.[31] The emotion and conviction that Iqbal expressed have sunk deep into the Muslim's being (and found there a response resting on traditions centuries old), yet recent events have at least started to dislodge them.

And even Muslim-League-type newspapers, it is said, condemned Anis and Josh when they fled the country.

For a good while after 1947 many Indian Muslims continued the long-standing custom of looking for salvation or at least support to an outside source. The tendency in the past to lean on the British, on pan-Islam, on the native princes, reappeared in a readiness to look to Pakistan, the United Nations, even conceivably the U.S.S.R. or some unknown *deus ex machina*, to salvage the community from its difficulties. And there was a submerged hope if not expectation that the situation might suddenly be redeemed by God, conceived in exteriorist rather than immanent terms. These tendencies too were inhibited by the course of events.

A failure of self-reliance took perhaps its most obvious form in a resigned dependence on the Hindus. The majority has been manifestly dominant, their goodwill crucial to the minority's welfare. Many Muslims accordingly, even after they might have outgrown fear and the sense of inevitable enmity, tended to be passive, simply waiting for and hoping for that goodwill. They did not move forward to the next step, of taking on themselves the responsibility of discerning, and the task of actively strengthening, such forces within the country—political, economic, ideological, institutional, and other—as would push men away from intercommunal discord and towards goodwill and harmony. However, even here the actual situation has been hardly static enough for

[31] Cf. the poem "Ḥusayn Aḥmad" in [Muḥammad] Iqbāl, *Armughān-i Ḥijāz*, Lahore, 1938; in the Lahore, 1948, ed., p. 278. There was correspondence both private and in the Lahore daily *Iḥsān*, some of which has been collected in the pamphlet *Naẓarīyah'-i Qawmīyat: Mawlānā Ḥusayn Aḥmad Ṣāḥib Madanī wa 'Allāmah Iqbāl*, Dera Ghazi Khan, n.d.

passivity; the dynamics of freedom and democratic interplay has encouraged participation.

For there is, finally, and not unimportant, the straightforward fact that the Indian Muslim is a citizen of *India*. This is no small matter in the modern world. Despite stupendous problems, India would seem to be embarked on one of the world's great ventures of our day, in economic, technical, social, and cultural progress. It is true that the Muslim community's perhaps biggest problem is to be able to take part economically in this advance. Whether through Hindu prejudice or Muslim backwardness, Muslim economic participation has been precarious. As long as there is unemployment, the Muslim's chance of being the one unemployed is discouragingly high. Insofar as this can be solved, the expansion of India will carry the Muslims with it.

All in all, then, the development of events has served to promote among Muslims in India a tendency towards coming to grips at fairly close range with the realities of modern life.

The Problems of Progress

The dénouement of affairs has worked to shatter false answers to modern challenges. The elaboration of satisfactory answers, however, must be the work of creative individuals. The ground is ready for such seed as they may sow. There has already been evidence of some serious and intelligent grappling with the intellectual and spiritual issues. It nonetheless remains the consensus that leadership is still sorely needed in hammering out, and illustrating in personal commitment, new interpretations of Islam that will be relevant and adequate to the community's present-day problems. If the abandonment of the old disruptive prejudices were not accompanied by the positive emergence of a constructive new version of Islam, the community would be left rudderless in a troubled sea.

On the political plane the chief lead has, of course, been given by the Muslim nationalists, men who before 1947 advocated participation by the Muslim community within the total complex of Indian nationalism (specifically, the Congress party). These men since partition and independence have continued that platform within the severely modified framework of the new day: for the shrunken community within a shrunken India. As an individualist solution this programme has in several cases worked well. From the point of view of the community as a whole, however, it is clear that the matter cannot be solved purely in political terms.

On the formally religious level, two principal lines have been put forward. The less important has been that of the Jama'at-i Islami, which maintains its link with the Pakistan movement of the same name (under Mawdudi). This group is still able to arouse some enthusiasm but surely little hope on the basis of giving an essentially traditional religious content to the political and social attitude of the "two-nation theory." The programme propounded is in process of being modified to take account of the new political situation. Their chief organ has been *Zindagi* (Rampur). They have the advantage of emotional continuity with the past and of courageous commitment. Yet the community, as we have argued above, seems less and less likely to be won over to an interpretation that, however plausible in itself, has proven so disruptive in practice, so out of touch with the moral as well as socio-political demands of the day. Of course, if progressive liberalism in general should seriously falter in the country, and secularism collapse, so that among the majority Hindu communalism in exclusive arrogance should triumph, then it is perhaps not impossible that this revived Islamic communalism might well be the form in which the Muslims would participate in India's disintegration.

The more constructive lead has been that of the Jam'iyatu-l-'Ulama'. This organization of the traditional clerics has been vigorously Indian-nationalist for forty years. After 1947 it plunged forward with renewed confidence and even semi-official support, to hammer home the thesis that Indo-Muslim welfare lay in nationalist policies. Though explicitly not a political body (Muslim political parties as such being disallowed), their leaders have been national political figures as members of Parliament and even holding cabinet office. Besides, as a religious body they have had an organizational network reaching into the villages and across the country. Their chief organ has been the Urdu daily *Al-Jam'iyat* (Delhi).

They have been able to give also a theological basis for their political platform, or at least to cast it in a specifically Islamic form. They use the concept of *mu'ahadah*, mutual contract, derived from the first few years of Islamic history in Madinah when the Prophet established a civic contract between his Muslim group and the Jews in that city. Their thesis[32] is that the Muslims and non-Muslims have entered upon a mutual contract in India since independence, to establish a secular state. The Constitution of India, which the Muslim community's elected representatives[33] unanimously supported and to which they swore allegiance, represents this *mu'ahadah*. The specifically Islamic duty of the community within India now, in their eyes, is to keep loyalty to the Constitution and to work out within the national life, as an acknowledged minority with the larger society, such personal and social aspects of the total Islamic pattern as can be directly implemented in this situation, and such socio-economic-administrative aspects as they can democratically persuade the whole nation to adopt.

To the significance of these concepts we shall presently return. Meanwhile it must be noted that this group suffers two disabilities. One is perhaps best described as their being somehow out of touch, or at least being felt to be out of touch, not only with the emotions and aspirations of the Muslim League movement—which of course they rejected—but also with the deep inner loyalties of the community on which those emotions and aspirations were wrongly built. Perhaps more important is the second fact: that the 'ulama' in general, though politically realistic and their leaders highly intelligent men, are not educated in modernity. They therefore cannot give a lead in the community's other great task, that of coming to terms with that modernity.

We turn then to the cultural level. So many of the intelligentsia departed to Pakistan that only a handful remained. The lead given by some of these has been concerned chiefly with the major question of a synthesis within Indian culture in which Islamic culture would function integrally, rather than either keeping aloof or being ignored or crushed. Historical perspective and intellectual substance have been given to this by such writers as Humayun Kabir and 'Abid Husayn.[34] This question is currently

---

[32] As expounded to the present writer personally by a group of party leaders, particularly Mawlānā Ḥifẓu-r-Raḥmān; Delhi, March, 1956.

[33] In the Constituent Assembly that drafted the Constitution and adopted it, the Muslim members were communally elected, from pre-partition days.

[34] Cf. Humayun Kabir, *Our Heritage*, Bombay, 1946; London edition, *India's Heritage*, 1947; 3rd Indian ed., revised and enlarged, *The Indian Heritage*, Bombay, 1955. Cf. Sayyid 'Ābid Ḥusayn, *Hindūstānī Qawmiyat awr Qawmī Tahẓīb*, Delhi, 3 voll., 1946; abridged and revised ed., in Urdū,

symbolized in the important issue of language: whether the nation will make Hindi its 'national' language in such a way as to exclude rather than to cherish but transcend Urdu; and whether Urdu-speaking and -reading Muslims will see Hindi as an alternative to their own language, something either to be resisted or before which to succumb, rather than learning it as their educated have learned English, an additional tongue for wider participation.

The language question is, however, but one element of a wider and perhaps deeper issue—as 'Abid Husain, for instance, despite his concentration on that element, recognizes and boldly treats.

We turn then to our fundamental concern, the religious question—the Indo-Muslim emergence within the ongoing history of Islam. We may repeat our suggestion of the possibility that Indian Islam may prove in the next fifty years more creative than Pakistani. If this proves so, it will not be because such creation is easy. On the contrary, it is agonizing. If it comes it will result from the stark difficulty of the community's more manifest involvement in the problems of modernity and a wider world.

For the issues go deep. Here as elsewhere the Muslims are confronted with the general task of reconciling their faith to modernity. In addition, here they have their special minority status. We have noted the Jam'iyatu-l-'Ulama' 's position on this matter. It has yet to be seen whether this will prove acceptable or fruitful. To us, the historical parallel does not seem close.

The question of political power and social organization, so central to Islam, has in the past always been considered in yes-or-no terms. Muslims have either had political power or they have not. *Never before have they shared it with others.*[35]

Nor are they willing to share it with others today in Pakistan,

---

1956 (not available to the present writer), and in English: S. Abid Husain, *The National Culture of India*, Bombay, 1956.

[35] In the case of the Madīnah Jews with whom the original *mu'āhadah* was established, power was not really shared; it was an agreement for each community to live its own life, rather than for the two to participate in constructing a life in common. In modern times there is the instance of Lebanon, an independent republic since 1946; the Christians formally constitute a majority, so that for the Muslim community there is a parallel with India, though on a minute scale. Yet the problems are serious and unsolved. There are also new countries such as Burma, where the tiny Muslim minorities are politically in quite a flourishing situation. These, however, seem too minor to damage our point seriously.

even with a small minority.[36] To the question, "Can Muslims be fully Muslims without a state of their own?," both Indian and Pakistan Muslims recently said "No!"—with resounding assurance. If our analysis of the main development of Islam over the centuries has approximated at all to validity, this negative answer has behind it a great weight of traditional faith. Close to the heart of Islam, as we have seen, has been the conviction that its purpose includes the structuring of a social community, the organization of the Muslim group into a closed body obedient to the Law. It is this conception that seems finally to be proving itself inept in India.

What has been thought part of the meaning of the eternal norm, turns out to be irrelevant if not incriminating in the actual situation. It is not merely that the imperative is impractical. That has often happened, and can more or less be taken in one's stride. That an ideal is unrealized, even for the moment unrealizable, is not in itself disruptive; as we said in the Arab case, religious people can live with their dreams unfulfilled. It is when the ideal seems to become meaningless, the dream insignificant or obstructive, that trouble descends. Religiously one can cope with historical developments that are an obstacle to the realization of one's ideal, more easily than with an ideal that is clearly an obstacle to one's historical development.

Muslim communities have been conquered in the past. But then the conqueror is there, to take, as it were, the blame. And conquest may be regarded as temporary: the Muslim under others' control may hope or strive for freedom. The Indian Muslims already have freedom—which is precisely their dilemma. And they can neither hope nor strive for a change in their situation.

A few romantics, clinging to the past, may dream of the reestablishment of Muslim rule over India. But this is unrealistic not only mundanely, as is all too obvious, but spiritually. For it would surrender justice to a comfortable pleasure. Some in desperation may accept as solution the idea of being ruled by Hindus, giving up their own freedom and choosing to regard themselves as a defeated community. This escapes responsibility, and allows self-pity; it would constitute, of course, not only mundane deteriora-

---

[36] Whether the Muslims of Pakistan will be willing to have a joint electorate with the Hindū minority, who want it, is until the time of writing undecided. Pressure against it is strong from the religious groups.

tion but self-inflicted inner spiritual disaster. The situation is challenging, and demands a transcending of the traditional categories of ruling or being ruled.

The position is different from that of the Muslim group within, say, the Soviet Union. They too are a minority within a vast non-Muslim domain. But they are not joint rulers; they do not participate in the choice and responsibility of the course of events. The Indo-Muslims' position differs also from that of the Turks, who have chosen a secular state of their own free will. The Turks have decided that the best way for a Muslim community, or anyway for *their* Muslim community, to live in the modern world is in a lay republic. This is their own decision, and their communal life is their own implementation of that decision. The group that constitutes the lay republic is Muslim.

The Muslims of India in fact face what is a radically new and profound problem; namely, how to live with others as equals. This is unprecedented; it has never arisen before in the whole history of Islam. It raises the deepest issues both of the meaning of man's being and of social morality. It raises the deepest issues of the significance of revelation, truth, and the relation to other peoples' faith. Yet it is a question on which the past expressions and doctrines of Islam offer no immediate guidance. And it is, of course, in this particular case immensely complicated by the discouraging fact that the caste Hindus, with whom they must live, have not yet learned to live with others either.

The problem is difficult—so difficult that in one sense the rise of Pakistan may be seen as an attempt to avoid having to face it. However, the present Indian-Muslim community, for whom that hope of evading it was bitterly illusory, and for whom it was made vastly more difficult by the rise of Pakistan, cannot escape it.

The relation between Islam and democracy is a question faced in our day most conspicuously by the Muslims of Pakistan, but most searchingly by the Muslims of India. That Islam implies democracy is a claim that has been put forward repeatedly by the Muslims in this century; often glibly, and with little sensitivity to the vast responsibilities that ensue. Of course, any religion implies democracy in so far as it is true, compelling the recognition of personal worth, freedom, responsibility, and involvement. But the distance between abstract eternal truth at this level and the creation on earth of an effectively operating fraternity is not negligible.

Historically, democracy is very new to Muslims; it is new also to Hindus, and indeed has yet largely to be created. In fact, democracy is new in the world. The long struggle in the West to attain such partial embodiments of it as have as yet been reached there, and the long path still to travel before fuller realizations are established, must be borne in mind with the complexities and particularities and traditions of both India and Pakistan in any consideration of present developments or future prospects. The drama of the move towards democracy in India since 1947 is certainly exciting, and the possible future role of the Muslim community in that drama is one of moment.

In Pakistan the attitude of Muslims to minorities is the test of sincerity and comprehension; in India, that to the majority and total nation. To what degree and in what forms and with what ideological bases will Indian Muslims set themselves to working for the welfare of the whole Indian community? How will they visualize the material and spiritual welfare of Indian Islam as integrated with the activity and loyalty of non-Muslim Indians?

These questions are not easy. As we said previously, Muslims in 1947 tried to flee from them. An Indian Muslim is both an Indian and a Muslim. The desperate attempt to deny or reject this duality has failed. An attempt to integrate the two has hardly yet been seriously put forward. Some individuals have of course succeeded in being both, and some have prospered. But the meaning of Islamic faith in the life of an Indian as a modern secular minority democrat has yet to be construed and expressed. Previous Muslims throughout the centuries have enunciated Islamic answers to situations quite other, not to this. The Muslim community in India stands alone, must solve its own problems—including fundamental problems of theology, law, and morals.

In this necessity of reaching out to new interpretations, apprehending the imperatives of today, the Indian Muslim has one advantage of major proportions: intellectual freedom. Probably nowhere in the Islamic world, perhaps not even in Turkey, is a Muslim so free as in India to put his mind honestly and earnestly to religious problems, to speak fearlessly, and to publish what he writes. Elsewhere, particularly in Pakistan and the Arab world, official censorship on the one hand and, doubtless more important, the unceasing pressure of fear and the (often hypocritical) forces of social conservatism and vested prejudice, preclude open discussion. In India, however, anyone who has anything to say, no matter how traditional or novel, how radical or constructive, may say it. Not only the pressure of obviously unsolved Muslim problems but the absence of national Islamic policy and of all official Muslim institutionalism encourage liberty. This is undergirded by the long tradition of cultural creativity, and buttressed by the deep tradition of tolerance in India and the penetration of liberalism during the British period.

Here as in other Muslim areas, the relation between religion and the modern world cannot be constructively worked out until the determination is firm to see the modern world with full and hard, close clarity. The willingness to face reality is, as always, requisite. The final wisdom is to know God; the beginning of wisdom is to face facts, to see them as they are.

Also needed is the willingness to admit that there are problems waiting to be solved. This awareness has been rare in recent Islam, which has tended to believe that problems have been solved already. That the answers have somehow, somewhere, been given, and do not have to be worked out fresh with creative intelligence—this idea has deeply gripped, almost imprisoned, the minds and souls of many Muslims. The Qur'an has been regarded as presenting a perfected pattern to be applied, rather than an imperative to seek perfection. Islamic law and Islamic history have been felt to be a storehouse of solutions to today's difficulties, to be ransacked for binding precedent, rather than a record of brave dealing with yesterday's difficulties, to be emulated as liberating challenge. Religion has seemed to confine behaviour, rather than to inspire it.

The fundamental fallacy of Muslims has been to interpret Islam as a closed system. And that system has been closed not only from outside truth, but also from outside people. The fundamental hopefulness about Indian Muslims, and therefore Indian Islam, is that this community may break through this. It may be forced to have the courage and humility to seek new insights. It may find the humanity to strive for brotherhood with those of other forms of faith.

This significance is surely major, not only for the community itself, and of course for India (which needs the loyalty and constructive energy of all its elements), but indeed for the whole Islamic world. For despite its apparent isolation, the Indo-Muslim group is representative of the total community, and even of all mankind, in two of its important problems. One, the need to advance, it shares with all the Muslim world. The other is more especially its own. Pakistan symbolizes and sums up one of the great demands on Islam in the modern world: the transmutation into contemporary idiom of the theme of social justice. Islam in India symbolizes and sums up the other: the need to construct relations with outsiders. We have said that the Indian group's situation is unique among Muslim communities. This is true in that it alone of those separate communities faces modern life from the particular standpoint of an outnumbered yet free group. Yet all Muslims taken together are in fact in a comparable situation within mankind. The relative independence of civilizations has in our day died. Each of man's cultures is called upon today to evolve a new ingredient: compatibility. The West has perhaps most to learn in this regard, but no civilization is exempt. In the past civilizations have lived in isolation, juxtaposition, or conflict. Today we must learn to live in collaboration. Islam like the others must prove creative at this point, and perhaps it will learn this in India.

For the Indo-Muslims are in India what the total Muslim group is in the world: an important minority. They have their own heritage, their own values, their own hopes for the future. But their problems they share with the rest of us. They have their own role to play but it is a role that must be integrated within a larger complex of diversity, constituted in part by other men, more numerous and perhaps more powerful, with other values and with other roles. The future of the Muslims in India, like the future of the Muslims and indeed of all groups in the world, depends upon their own inner resources and faith and creativity, and their outward relations with their fellow men.

Chapter 7

OTHER AREAS

ISLAM is in principle a universal religion, and its followers are to be found here and there throughout the world. For instance, a small community in Canada has a mosque in Edmonton. In the Philippines four per cent of the population are Muslims. In Yugoslavia the percentage is eleven; in Albania it is over fifty.

In a study of the present kind it is perhaps legitimate to have omitted consideration of these kinds of group, since our entire survey is synoptic, and perforce general. However, there are other sections of the Islamic world that ought definitely to be included in any survey no matter how general. These are Indonesia (along with Pakistan the largest Muslim society on earth[1]), Iran, and the three great minorities (China, the U.S.S.R., and Negro Africa). These are major elements in the total picture, and there is an inevitable distortion if due consideration is not accorded them.[2]

The present writer is not competent to discuss developments in these areas adequately. This is a compelling reason for omitting

[1] The Muslim population of Indonesia and that of Pakistan are so close in number that there has been uncertainty as to which is greater at a given time. The 1951 census of Pakistan gave 64,959,000 (Government of Pakistan, Karachi, Census Bulletin No. 2, *Census of Pakistan, 1951*; population according to religion [Table 6], Karachi, 1951, p. 1). The figure for Indonesia given in Harry W. Hazard, *Atlas of Islamic History*, Princeton, 3rd ed., rev., 1954, pp. 5 and 40, is 71,100,000 as an estimate for 1953; for that date Hazard's projection for Pakistan is 71,500,000. There has been no census in Indonesia since 1930. For a detailed world survey of Islām see the handbook Louis Massignon, ed., *Annuaire du monde musulman, statistique, historique, social et économique*, 4th ed., Paris, 1955.

[2] There is also Afghanistan. The writer is unfortunately not informed enough about it even to be able to place it, not knowing whether it is Islamically distinctive and creative enough to be included not in the first group mentioned above but as a separate unit for detailed study. The section "Religion" (G. Morgenstierne) in the recent article AFGHANISTAN in the new ed. of *The Encyclopaedia of Islam*, Leiden, 1955, comprises only two brief paragraphs. In Mohammed Akram, *Bibliographie analytique de l'Afghanistan*, Paris, 1947, there is a section "Vingtième siècle," pp. 331-51, under "Histoire"; there is a brief article of Donald N. Wilber, "Structure and Position of Islam in Afghanistan," *The Middle East Journal*, Washington, 6:41-48 (1952). The chapter "Religion," pp. 391-404 in the latter (ed.), *Afghanistan*, and the relevant sections of his *Annotated Bibliography of Afghanistan*, both New Haven, 1956, add but little to these.

them, but an unsatisfactory one. It seems therefore important to call attention to the omission and to the consequent inevitable distortion. Among the other serious inadequacies of our treatment this also must take its place.

The lacuna is the more serious in that, except for Iran, it has been characteristic also of others. There has in the past been too great a readiness to equate the Islamic world with the Near East. This equation is already several centuries out-of-date, and may perhaps become even less tenable in the future. It will certainly need radical revision if Indonesia and Pakistan evince vitality. It is even a possibility to be borne in mind that the centre of gravity of the Islamic world may in our day be shifting from the shores of the Mediterranean to those of the Indian Ocean. In any case, one must stress the bigness of the whole community, far transcending its original and classical homelands, and extending south into Africa and north-east, east, and south-east into and through Asia. It is much too early yet to say that the future of Islam, like the later history of Christianity, may not be significantly in its newer worlds.

The great minority segments are constituted by the twenty-five million Muslims in the Soviet Union,[3] a similar or perhaps slightly greater number in China,[4] a roughly comparable Muslim population in Negro Africa.[5] These groups are interesting enough in

[3] The figure is uncertain; estimates vary from 20 to 30 million. We know of no study specifically of the religious situation, though several works deal with it *inter alia*. See, for instance, a basic recent work on this group, Vincent Monteil "Essai sur l'Islam en U.R.S.S.," *Revue des études islamiques*, Paris, 20:5-145 (1952); and "Supplément à l'essai sur l'Islam en U.R.S.S.," *ibid.*, 21:5-37 (1953); also earlier articles in the same journal. Among earlier works Gerhard von Mende, *Der nationale Kampf der Russlandtürken*, Berlin, 1936, is significant. Of recent articles in English, note Richard E. Pipes, "Muslims of Soviet Central Asia: Trends and Prospects," *The Middle East Journal*, Washington, 9:147-62, 295-308 (1955); *id.*, "Russian Moslems before and after the Revolution," in Waldemar Gurian, ed., *Soviet Imperialism: its origins and tactics*, Notre Dame, 1953, pp. 75-89.

[4] See Claude L. Pickens, Jr., *Annotated Bibliography of Literature on Islam in China*, privately printed, Hankow, 1950 (a revised edition is currently in process for New York publication).

[5] Calculating from the figures given in Hazard, *op. cit.*, the Muslim population of the Sudan and non-Arab Africa is 33.6 millions. We know of no survey of Islām as a religion throughout this wide area. There is a considerable literature on Islām in the various parts piecemeal, chiefly in English and French for the British and French colonies respectively. Of more recent works, one may mention the series begun by J. Spencer Trimingham (and perhaps

themselves, and important in many connections. It is true that they have in modern times contributed less to each other and to the major communities, and thus to the total dynamic of world Islam, than have the half-dozen major communities. It seems quite probable that they will for a time continue to contribute less. Nonetheless, they are not without importance. Two of them are in Communism, and hence somewhat cut off from the rest of the Muslim world, as from the rest of the non-Communist world generally. Their present condition is intricately enmeshed in the situation of the Soviet Union and that of the new China, and their short-run future is in part a question of the highly problematic destinies of those states. In the Chinese case, the Muslims are scattered throughout the country, are nowhere in a compact majority, and have never been in political control. In the Soviet Union, on the other hand, the Turkic republics are solidly Muslim areas that were once major centres of Islamic power and culture. It is perhaps no small matter, especially from a religious point of view, that part of the Muslim world is within the Communist domain, even though much more attention is still given to the fact that part is still under Western domination.

So far as Africa is concerned, we can say little beyond calling attention to the obvious fact that much is stirring within that continent, and noting that Islam is a major and dynamic factor in the situation. It would seem clear that indigenous African evolution at the present time is vastly affected by the energetic intrusion of three civilizations or forces from the outside: the West, Communism, and Islam.

These minority areas, though intrinsically important, are for the moment playing little role in the drama that is our over-all concern. In contrast stand Iran and Indonesia. For the purposes of this present study and the issues that relate to it, these two are major. Iran has, throughout Islamic history, played a conspicuous and relatively well-studied role, even though in modern times the religious aspect of its development has received less than its share

---

still in process to give eventually a full coverage?): *Islam in the Sudan*, London and New York, 1949; *Islam in Ethiopia*, London and New York, 1952; *The Christian Church and Islam in West Africa*, London, 1955. See also J. N. D. Anderson, *Islamic Law in Africa*, London, 1954 (this last, despite the title, deals only with the British colonies); and the same writer's "Tropical Africa: Infiltration and expanding horizons" in Gustave E. von Grunebaum, ed., *Unity and Variety in Muslim Civilization*, Chicago, 1955, pp. 261-83.

of attention. Some writing, however, has been done;[6] the present writer does not feel in a position at this point to add anything of significance to it. In the case of Indonesia, on the other hand, there has been a very serious disregard, both by Western students and, even more striking, by Muslims of other areas. The role of Islam in contemporary Indonesia, and of Indonesia in contemporary Islam, has still to be not only assessed but noticed. Even an elementary acquaintance makes it clear that here is Islamically something distinctive and fascinating and potentially very rich.[7] Surely it will have to be increasingly recognized that the Indonesians constitute one of the cardinal communities of the Muslim world, ranking along with the Indo-Muslim, the Pakistani, the Persian, and Turkey and the Arab World.

These six are the principal cultures that are the protagonists of contemporary Islam. It is they to whom Muslim development in our day is decisively entrusted. Each has its particular selfhood.

[6] The most significant recent contributions in Western sources have been perhaps those of Ann K. S. Lambton and T. Cuyler Young. Of the former, see "The Spiritual Influence of Islam in Persia," in A. J. Arberry and Rom Landau, edd., *Islam To-day*, London, 1943, pp. 163-77; and "Persia," in *Journal of the Royal Central Asian Society*, London, 31.8-21 (1944). Of the latter, see "Interaction of Islamic and Western Thought in Iran," in T. Cuyler Young, ed., *Near Eastern Culture and Society*, Princeton, 1951, pp. 130-47; and "The Problem of Westernization in Modern Iran," *The Middle East Journal*, Washington, 2:47-59 (1948). See also the Ḥaydarī thesis noted above at chap. 2, ref. 32. For earlier studies, cf. above, chap. 2, ref. 16. Of recent articles, one should perhaps mention also William McElwee Miller, "The Religious Situation in Iran," *The Muslim World*, Hartford, 41:79-87 (1951); and Richard N. Frye, "Notes on Religion in Iran Today," *Die Welt des Islams*, N.S. 2:260-66 (1953), though both are brief. One must add the section on Iran in Richard N. Frye, ed., *Islam and the West*, 's-Gravenhage, 1957, pp. 179-97.

[7] For instance, it would seem that the Indonesians, especially in Java, are the only Muslim group in the world today who have a strong and ancient indigenous liberalism. The place of women in Indonesian Muslim life is also striking (this is, for example, the only Muslim area that has never known the veil?). On other matters also, such as the relation between the religion and politics, Indonesian Muslims' positions are of the greatest interest. Altogether there could be an argument, over against the widespread view that Indonesians are "poor Muslims," that on the contrary the rest of the Muslim world may well have something vital to learn from them, even religiously.

The present writer hopes that he may eventually have the opportunity to study developments in this area also. For a comprehensive, but uncritical, compilation of literature, chiefly Western sources, on Indonesian Islam, see above chap. 2, ref. 17.

Each is an integral and significant component of the total pattern of present-day Islam. Among them there is no gradation, no hierarchy, either of form or of spirit. No one of them is subordinate to another. Nor, indeed, with present independence, is any one subordinate even to the totality. They lead the whole; they are not led by it.

For the Islamic world today is not an organized unit, but rather a complex comprising these several distinct major communities, along with the various minor groups. It is constituted solely by their participation. The Islamic world *is* what they and others have made it in the past plus what they are now making it. Apart from them it has no separate existence of its own, no intrinsic reality; and since the abolition of the *khilāfah* (1924), even no symbolic existence.[8] Its own destiny is a dynamic fusion of its past, the whole Islamic tradition, with its evolving present, the multifarious developments of the several Muslim peoples today.

Even that past tradition is now carried primarily within and by these several and separate peoples. Also, their participation, lively or feeble, in the larger complex of Islam is in each instance not something super-added but an integral aspect of that community's own current development. It therefore becomes almost fully true to say that the current history of Islam is the current history of its component parts. If the Islamic world is what they make it, in another sense it is what they make themselves.

[8] On pan-Islām, cf. above, chap. 2, pp. 80-84.

Chapter 8

CONCLUSION

WE stated in our opening paragraph that it was not within our intention or our competence to predict the future development of Islam. The survey that we have conducted thus far leaves these disclaimers intact. Yet if our survey has attained any success, if our descriptions and analyses have approximated at all to validity, then perhaps it has served to confirm our other opening judgement: that Islam will indeed have such future development, that the religion is alive and dynamic. Something is being brought to birth. The contemporary chapter of Islamic history we have tried all too fumblingly to decipher and to translate. It is an important chapter, of absorbing interest. Surely the next chapter, still to be enacted, will also be interesting and important. It will certainly be new. And our study will have achieved much of its purpose if it has at all clarified how crucially significant a question it is, just what line of development the Muslims will next hew for Islam.

Will they perhaps leave it as an ambiguous tradition, its adherents torn between a loyalty within and a world without—a loyalty that they cherish but do not know quite how to apply, and a world by which they find themselves surrounded but with which they do not know quite how to cope? Or will they perhaps emotionalize it into a closed system, by which they retreat from modernity into a fanaticism of crippling isolationist violence? Or will they construe it into an open, rich, onward vision, an effective inspiration for truly modern living; bringing themselves spiritual integrity and fulfillment, and their societies progress, justice, and honour in the world?

On questions such as these will turn, we believe, not only the religious but also the worldly welfare of the Muslim people. Mundane problems cannot be solved by men whose ideological and moral outlook is seriously inappropriate to their solution. At the very least it can hardly be gainsaid that the direction in which Islam moves is highly relevant to all other developments.

Indeed, we believe that there is no more urgent or significant issue in the Muslim world today. For spiritual and moral matters this is obvious. For other matters also it is true. The economic, political, military, demographic, and other kinds of question that

297

unrelentingly press on each of the various Muslim nations cannot be underestimated by anyone familiar with the area or concerned with the welfare of its people. It would be absurd to belittle these issues. Yet, we contend, none of them is more consequential than the religious question. Indeed, all go hand in hand. The various factors intertwine not only in jointly determining the progress of the Islamic world, but in determining each other. Not only is the modern history of Muslims not understandable if any one major factor, economic, Islamic, or the like, is ignored. The nature and development of any one factor is itself not understandable if the operation of the others is not grasped.

In our consideration, therefore, of the Islamic factor, our attempted study of the modern evolution of the faith, we are perforce taking for granted as background the continuing evolution of Islam's environment. This includes not only the local forces at work in each particular area, on some of which we have touched in the course of our study, while others have had to be presumed. It includes also the total context of our whole evolving world—the continuing newness of modernity for all mankind. An insistence on this at the beginning was one of the starting points of our whole investigation. We may well remind ourselves of it again as we close, since Islam in each area is at the same time one specific instance of Islam in the increasingly integrated and perplexing modern world as a whole. While Islam in each locality moves in conjunction with the life of its community, the world around persists in marching too.

The massive certainties of the nineteenth century have given way to the bewildering complexity of the twentieth. The resurgence of Asia has included the strenuous, gradual emancipation of Asian countries from European political control, an emancipation by now almost but not quite complete. A radical modernity in living, Western in provenance, has shown a continually expansive, determined, seemingly irresistible penetration of all areas, including the Muslim. In this process it would be difficult to overestimate how fundamentally involved the Islamic societies in fact are; in the cities psychologically and culturally, in all parts economically and administratively. Concomitant with it is a global interdependence, whereby the opportunity of a Pakistan peasant to eat may depend on a decision made in Washington; or of any of us to live, on a decision in Geneva or Peking. The

West, still mighty, still haughty, has itself been recently challenged and frightened by another society, a black sheep of its own family, Communism. In the case of Turkey and incipiently one or two others, this rather expansive society has been felt as a new and even more menacing external and internal threat.

And so on and on. A great deal of recent Muslim history has been history of which the initiative lay with others, ineluctable developments to which Muslims could but react. Yet many of these originally outside forces have increasingly been interiorized in Asia, so that Muslims like others have come more and more to participate in them actively. Much of the 'Westernism' against which some Muslims used to protest is ceasing to be distinctively Western and is becoming simply a world-wide modernism in which for good or ill Muslims are involved. To reject it, to wish to be 'left alone,' becomes simply to dislike living in the twentieth century.

Nonetheless, a great deal also of Muslims' recent history has been, of course, a continuation of their previous history, in ways that are at least equally important, even if less spectacular and perhaps less clear to outside observers.

It is in the interaction of these two with their human freedom that what is new in the Islamic world is being generated.

One may also urge the enormous significance of the attainment of political freedom. With freedom, as has so often been noted, there is responsibility. We have noted a tendency to think of political emancipation negatively, in terms of getting rid of foreign control. This of course was important. Yet the obverse was the positive and much more telling matter of assuming responsibility for one's own destiny. Roughly since the Second World War, every major Muslim community in the world has been in charge of its own affairs—as effectively as is feasible in the kind of world in which we live. Muslims, like others, are not free from outside pressures, but they are as free as can be devised or even realistically imagined. What they now do and become is as close as possible to their own doing and being. The economic, political, social, cultural, and spiritual development on which they are now embarked constitutes a history that is Islamic history in a renewed, full sense.

Freedom and responsibility, therefore, are within a context of determined circumstance. Some have spoken as if an Islamic economic system were one that a Muslim community should or would adopt if it were isolated, were not enmeshed within the extant vortex of international commerce and world monetary exchange and dollar dominance and the like. Similarly for other aspects of social living. This approach is unfruitful; it is irrelevant on a large scale, as we noted on a small scale in the particular case of Islam in India. The form of internationalism may change; the fact of it is solid. To take the isolationist approach seriously would signify that Islam is irrelevant to the kind of world in which we all live. A truer recognition is surely that Muslims' "independence" will mean not isolation but renewed internal strength and a growing Islamic influence on the rest of mankind, as well as vice versa. Freedom is participation. A faith that is alive is a faith for men and societies that are involved.

In this total context, then, the evolution of Islam is to be seen. In this total context, we are contending also that that evolution is fundamentally significant. Of all the multitudinous things that Muslims are experiencing and doing, the kind of faith that they are evolving is a matter neither isolated nor minor.

Their whole contemporary enterprise is mighty: constructing a new life in mid-twentieth-century. To take on such a task is particularly formidable for those who for some centuries have been exempt from its responsibilities. The world has begun to recognize something of the fearsome magnitude of what is involved on the sheerly material side: of suddenly attempting to catch up with "lost centuries" in the matter of building dams, organizing complex industry, rearing technical institutions, and the rest. What has been less clearly recognized is the equally monumental task on the religious and ideological side. It is also no slight matter to make up in this sphere for the loss of some centuries. One has yet to work out what is the meaning of religion in a new world that comprises dams and complex industry and technical institutions, and responsibility for them. The task might seem less major for those who wish to dichotomize life, keeping their ideals and their daily living in water-tight compartments. But it is not slight for a religion whose genius it is to apply its moral imperatives to day-to-day living, to wed the ultimate meaning of life to the society in which one participates, to seek justice in the midst of machines.

We have suggested that the welfare of Islam, intellectual and spiritual, is widely and crucially important. It is important both spiritually and temporally primarily for the Muslims themselves —a thesis not so trite as might appear. For we may remind ourselves that Islamic civilization has been unitary, as we stressed in our opening chapter, rather than dual, in the secular-religious fashion of Western civilization. In this connection it is perhaps worth noting that of man's other great civilizations today, China, somewhat like the West, has been religiously and culturally plural; India, though transcendentally monistic, cherishes so far as this world is concerned a polymorphic monism. In all three, the religions concerned inherently recognize limitations; so that it is feasible in their case for the society to change without overtly involving religion. Not so for Islam.

We do not rule out the possibility that Islam too will evolve in this direction. A case can, for instance, be made that Toynbee-esque divisions between civilizations are no longer valid, and that modern civilization, though it got under way first in the West, is spreading throughout the world and is transforming or superseding older cultural patterns both West and East. Secularism, then, as indeed modernity in general, would be not a Western device but a new and universal one, which all civilizations are in process of assimilating. To illustrate this for Islam the Turkish instance could be cited—and even the instance of Pakistan, whose enthusiasm for an "Islamic" state might be seen as frothy but short-lived, soon routed under the shock of such developments as the 1953 riots. Similarly in Indonesia, secularism and Islamic-oriented policies could be seen as alternatives, with prognosis, or at least applause, in favour of the former. In this view, the mundane welfare of the Muslim peoples would seem to depend not on their interpretation of Islam but rather on social processes independent of religious consideration.

We do not rule this out, since no one knows the future. Yet we do contend that the development of Islam impinges also here. Secularism can be imposed by force of arms or by force of circumstance, and there is evidence that in one or other of these ways it is increasingly being introduced throughout the modern Muslim world. Yet it must be religiously tolerated. Otherwise there develop severe strains within both society and the individual person, strains that shatter harmony and inhibit the effective operation of that very secularism to the point even of potential disaster. Whether a Caesar-God dichotomy will work in the Muslim world is itself a question to which the answer turns in large part on the interpretation of Islam. If Muslims on the whole resist it, then either they or it are doomed.

Even if secularism flourishes, there are basic moral problems that remain. These tend to be overlooked by Western and Westernizing secularists who would like to see Muslims, if not abandon Islam, at least relegate it to an unobtrusive corner of their living, and build their societies as liberal humanists. That the Islamic world would cease to be Muslim seems unlikely in the extreme —and could well be disastrous for both itself and the world. Further, it could be thought that Muslims, except perhaps in Turkey,[1] are unlikely to become Western liberals or Western

[1] "The Ministry of Education regards the Humanities as the basis of present day civilization and has taken steps to promote these studies. Translations from Ancient Greek and Latin are being published regularly"—Hasan-Ali Yücel, Minister of Education of Turkey, in his foreword to the official publication *Education in Turkey*, Ankara, n.d. [sc. 1946], p. iv. The same publication, pp. 81ff., lists the works published and projected under the government's "Translations from World Literature" project, enumerating translations of 100 Greek, 22 Latin, 18 Persian, 12 Arabian, 12 ancient and Far Eastern classics, and 629 "classics" from modern European languages.

This is part of the Turkish resolve to be part of Europe. The leaders of the nation are deliberately introducing this literature into Turkish education, and one might say are aiming at incorporating its contribution into Turkish life. The effect on the language (and presumably, therefore, on thought) is, it would seem, already noticeable. The movement is an implementation of a definite decision in Turkey to become *Western* in civilization, and of a recognition that the roots of Western civilization and the continuing foundations of Western modernity is a humanism that is ultimately Graeco-Roman classicism. It is a recent fruition of a tendency that has been discernible since the early days of the Republic; for instance, Hüseyin Cahit Yalçın personally translated many works, carrying forward what was begun by Ziya Gökalp, who was a member in 1923 of the Talim ve Terbiye Heyeti formulating such policies. On Gökalp's ideas on these matters, one remembers his famous triad of objectives, to be Turkish, Muslim, Western. "Why then should we still hesitate? Can't we accept Western civilization definitely and still be Turks and Muslims?" And, as he concludes the article from which this quotation is taken, the "principle of our social policy will be this: to be of the Turkish nation, of the Islamic religion, and of European civilization" ("Medeniyetimiz," first published in *Yeni Mecmua*, Istanbul, no. 68 [1923], reprinted in *Türkçülüğün Esasları*, Ankara, 1923 under the new title "Garbe Doğru" ("Towards the West")—the English translation will be found in N. Berkes, ed., *Turkish Nationalism and Western Civilization: selected essays of Ziya Gökalp*, forthcoming. Again: "The second set of models for our literature [after Turkish folk literature] are world classics, extending as far back as Homer or Virgil. The best models for a newborn national literature are

humanists, or even secular liberal humanists in the specifically Western fashion. An uncharitable critic might even argue that the impatient expectation or insistence that they do so is in danger of seeming just as much an arrogance, a provincialism, and just as little likely to succeed, as the traditional Christian expectation or insistence that they become Christians.

Our own view is that liberalism and humanism in the Muslim world, if they are to flourish at all, may perhaps be Islamic liberalism and Islamic humanism; or that in any case, some basis must be found for matters of this weight.

Liberalism and humanism are profound movements in the Western world, deriving partly from Greece, partly from the Bible, and brought to fruition through the great upsurge in the eighteenth century with its willingness to suffer martyrdom, to effect revolutions, and to push strenuous creative intellect for this cause. Classical Arabic civilization adopted the rationalist tradition of Greek philosophy and science up to a limited point,[2] but refused altogether the humanist tradition of Greek art and poetry; and that tradition never penetrated Muslim society. Again, religiously Islam repeats many of the basic doctrines of Christianity but not the humanist one; it rejected and still rejects with all the

---

masterpieces of classical literature"—from his "Edebiyatımızın Tahris ve Tehzibi," *Türkçülüğün Esasları*, Ankara, 1923, translated *ibid*. Perhaps intellectually as well as geographically this development is open only to Turkey among the Muslims?

[2] But only to a point. The parallel between Muslim and Christian scholasticism has often been drawn, but there are major differences. Ibn Sīnā no doubt assimilated Aristotle, as did Aquinas. Yet Ibn Sīnā was a lonely figure; and was pronounced *Kāfir* by Ghazzāli (*al-Munqidh min al-Ḍalāl*: the 3rd Ṣalībah and 'Ayyād edition, Damascus, 1358/1939, pp. 88-89; English translation in W. Montgomery Watt, *The Faith and Practice of al-Ghazālī*, London, 1953, p. 32). Ghazzāli, the greatest religious thinker of Islām, also wrote a major refutation of Hellenic philosophy. Sociologically, also, it would seem that the *falāsifah* in Islamic society transmitted the Greek tradition in but a narrow stream. Outside a few cities, and outside a tiny minority class even there, their ideas had virtually no influence. Even the peasant in Europe, each Sunday morning, was presented with a Graecized theology, in a distorted and distant fashion, no doubt, but the influence was there. In the Islamic world, theology itself was suspect—or, in the villages, ignored; it was the *sharī'ah* that met the villager from day to day.

Indeed, it is interesting to speculate whether the whole spread of Islām in the Near East and its overthrow of Christianity may not be partially viewed as broadly a reassertion of the Semitic mind rejecting a religion that, being Hellenically interpreted, it could never quite appreciate.

force and even horror that it can muster the affirmation that God Himself can best be known in a human embodiment. A statue of Praxiteles, which seeks the perfection of beauty in the human form, and a doctrine of incarnation, which portrays God there, provide foundations on which the West could and did build a humanist movement but which are not immediately available to Islam. Humanism in the Muslim world need not have the same foundations. But if it is to have any at all it must find them, it would seem to us, either within Islam, or (if Islam is reinterpreted to make room for an alternative) from the West, or else from some source that is not immediately apparent.[3]

In stressing the importance of ideas and moral values for the development of Islamic society, we are urging nothing unique. The ideological question is fundamental for Pakistan, for instance, not because it is Muslim. Because it is Muslim, its ideals are Islamic. For other nations, ideals take other forms. But for all of us, in any nation, the question of ideals is of utterly crucial practical importance—of ideals and their relation to immediate history. It is quite possible, and to outsiders obvious, that North America, despite its technological prowess, material affluence, and tolerably adequate political structure, may lead itself and the world to inconceivable disaster because of intellectual shallowness, moral obtuseness, or an inadequate vitality of its ideals.

Indeed, the various intellectual and moral issues are today themselves internationalized. We would contend that a healthy, flourishing Islam is important not only for the Muslims but for all the world today. Some Western political and other leaders have seemed singularly blind to this. Some have apparently adopted in practice if not in theory the absurd as well as offensive doctrine that man lives by bread alone; or as the Marxists phrase it, everything depends on economic development. From their Asian policies, it would even appear that they believe also, as even the Marxists do not, that economic development can be treated in isolation. The West is slow in bringing to fruition its incipient realization that world peace and world progress depend on the progress of ideas and serious understanding—and in realizing that the Muslim segment of human society can flourish only if Islam is strong and vital, is pure and creative and sound,

[3] In Indonesia, exceptionally, it is immediately apparent: the indigenous tradition, especially Javanese. Cf. above, chap. 7, ref. 7.

and only if there is an at least moderately happy relation with mutual understanding between it and the rest of man's systems.

Further, Christians also might well recognize this. Their traditional interpretation of ideological dogmas has stood in the way of their perceiving otherwise obvious truths—that the spiritual welfare of Muslims lies in a spiritually strong and vital Islam, and that both love and duty demand a deep aspiration for this on the part of Christendom, and of all men of good will. It is a profoundly Christian fact that the significant realities in the Muslim world (as elsewhere) are ultimately God and men; and in this particular area Islam is the relation between them. The spiritual as well as the temporal future of the Muslims turns on whether Islam's contemporary renascence or reform succeeds in bringing a renewed vitality and power to Muslim society; and its creative vision of God and His justice become for modern life, as for ancient, vivid and personal and deep in the lives of its individual adherents.

These issues raise in one important and representative instance perhaps the crux of both Western civilization and Christianity: their relations with other men. The fundamental weakness of both in the modern world is their inability to recognize that they share the planet not with inferiors but with equals. Unless Western civilization intellectually and socially, politically and economically, and the Christian church theologically, can learn to treat other men with fundamental respect, these two in their turn will have failed to come to terms with the actualities of the twentieth century. The problems raised in this are, of course, as profound as anything that we have touched on for Islam. They are, also, as consequential. Manifestly, they are outside the scope of this study, except in reminding us that all men today, Muslim or Christian, Oriental or Western, face questions that, though differing in form, are essentially comparable: the deepest questions for all of us today are those that involve us with each other.

We return, then, to our contention that the present and future evolution of Islam is a matter of moment. Throughout our discussion, we have spoken on the assumption that, within the limits imposed by circumstance, Muslims in religious matters as in all their evolution are free, that their handling of their faith depends on them. Man's freedom raises deep questions, not all of which need be answered to let the argument proceed. It is a fact of observation that religious doctrines, institutions, and attitudes do have a history. There is development; there is flexibility. There is also stagnation. Muslims, like others, in the religious as in other realms, have at times broken through to great constructive innovations, bringing vitality and boldness to bear upon new challenges; at other times they have sunk back into unimaginative imitation, and at still other times into active degeneration. At the present time the flexibility, or at least uncertainty, is widespread and marked.

The question, then, is real and meaningful as to what kind of Islam Muslims will next construct. To this the answer is not already given. Even those who believe that there is a specific answer that Muslims ought to give, may concede that it is far from certain whether or not they will actually give it. There is nothing irreverent in noting that the future of the Muslim peoples' faith has still to be determined.

Whatever one may believe about Islam's transcendental essence, yet the earthly manifestation of Islam, both temporal and spiritual, is the creation of Muslims. Whether their activity in bringing the historical reality of their religion into renewed being is an activity that they perform with freedom, or act under the constraint of God's inscrutable and over-riding will, is a question that we may leave to an al-Ash'ari.[4] The tendency in recent Islam has been to stress man's freedom.[5] The present writer believes, as a

---

[4] Abū al-Ḥasan 'Alī al-Ash'arī (260-324/873-935), the first Muslim to give forceful formulation in doctrine to his overwhelming sense of utter dependence upon God's mercy—so utter that he intellectualized this in terms of a divine sovereignty uncomplicated by human initiative. Furthermore, like Calvin, he was systematic and ruthless enough in his logic to draw all rational conclusions from his formulation, however repugnant to other sensibilities they might be. We ourselves, while insisting that man is free, are persuaded of God's activity in history, it being virtually tautologous to say that He is the source of all that is good in human as in other life. Only, we see His activity in history as channeled (and therefore circumscribed and even distorted) through man.

[5] "There is . . . one moral-theological problem of classical Islam which has been, to some extent, reopened both by the modernists and the more progressive Ulema and towards which both have shown similar trends, although their arguments have differed widely. This is the problem of theistic determinism and free will of man. Here even the Ulema, while retaining the Koranic doctrine of God's omnipotence, have mostly tended to emphasize human freedom"—F. Rahman, "Internal Religious Developments in the Present Century Islam," in *Cahiers d'histoire mondiale/Journal of World History*, Paris, 2:870-71 (1955).

matter of warm personal conviction, of cool analysis, and of empirical observation, that man is free. In any case, man is responsible.

This applies to all fields, though our particular concern is specifically religious. What the Muslim peoples now do in every phase of life will constitute Islamic history. What they do in spiritual matters will constitute the next stage in the development of the religion of Islam.

We close, then, as we began: the relation between Islam and history has been close, and remains close. Islam as a developing process is that moving point within history at which the Muslim breaks through history to reach out towards what lies beyond.[6] Yet that point remains within history; history always colours it. The development of the rest of the historical process is closely intertwined with the very heart of the Muslims' faith. And the development of the faith, we believe, bears crucially and will continue to bear on the rest of the temporal scene. That the relation between faith and history is close, is confirmed both by doctrine and by observation.

The devout (echoed in part by outside sceptics) may protest that Islam is fixed. For, a certain type of piety holds, it is given by God.

Theologically, this bears consideration. It is a question of universal import whether the religions are given by God (or any one religion is); or whether rather God gives Himself, while the religions, as we know them, are man's response. Man begins to be adequately religious only when he discovers that God is greater and more important than religion. Certainly, as we have seen, one can find modern Muslims whose loyalty to Islam as a tangible phenomenon seems greater than their faith in God. Like modern men in other cultures, these evince little apprehension of the living reality and power and personal engagement of the divine. Yet one may perhaps be not overly bold in surmising that the creative development of Islam as a religion on earth lies rather in the hands of those Muslims whose concern for the forms and institutions evolved in Islamic history is subordinate to their lively sense of the living, active God who stands behind the religion, and to their passionate but rational pursuit of that social

[6] Or, phrased more theologically: the point at which God breaks through to reach out to him.

justice that was once the dominant note of the faith and the dominant goal of its forms and institutions.

If this be true today, it will repeat what has been true in Islamic history of the past.

The human part from day to day has ever been, amid the din of life, to hear God's message; to discern its meaning and to interpret it; and in a difficult and distracting and ever-changing world, to act. Whether more or less adequate, the Islam of history is the handiwork of Muslims.

The Islam that was given by God is not the elaboration of practices and doctrines and forms that outsiders call Islam, but rather the vivid and personal summons to individuals to live their lives always in His presence and to treat their fellow men always under His judgement.

INDEX

The Arabic article *al* is so transcribed from Arabic. In Persian and Urdū compound names, however, the elision of its vowel in favour of the ending added to the preceding element, which is uninflected, and the assimilation of its consonant to what follows, are here accepted. Osmanlı Turkish is romanized as in Republican Turkey. Indonesian names are rendered as in modern Indonesian; the contemporary and presumably increasing tendency to shift from Dutch to English patterns is here actively favoured. In multiple names and even compound names, the general rule is to enter under the final element if this is a name (provided it is not a name of God). A few cross-references have been added to be helpful. Diacriticals are ignored in alphabetizing.

'Abbād ibn Sulaymān, 18n
'Abbāsī, 164n, 165, 166n. *See also* Arabs, classical
Abbott, Freeland, 234n
'Abd al-Nāṣir, Jamāl al-Dīn, 76, 113n, 157n
'Abd al-Rāziq, al-Shaykh 'Alī, 253n
'Abduh, al-Shaykh Muḥammad, 56, 58, 63, 65-66, 68, 75
'Abdu-l-'Azīz, Shāh, 45
'Abdu-l-Ḥakīm, Khalīfah, 63
Abdülhamid II, Ottoman Sultan, 83, 187
'Abdu-l-Laṭīf, Sayyid, 280n
'Abdu-r-Rahmān, Mawlānā, 44n, 45n
'Ābidīn Palace, Cairo, 95
Abraham, 12
Abū-l-Su'ūd, 37n
Academy of Islamic Studies, Hyderabad, 5n, 280n
Achaemenian, 169
Acheh, 38
Acre, 100
Adam, 11, 12
Adams, C. C., 56n, 64n, 253n
Adnan-Adıvar, Abdülhak, 60n
Adoratsky, V., 214n
Afghānī, Jamālu-d-Dīn, 47-51, 53, 54, 56, 75, 82n, 83
Afghanistan, 84, 292n
Africa, 39, 82; Negro Africa, 35, 263, 292, 293, 294; North Africa, *see* Maghrib
Agra, 38
Agus Salim, Hajji, 58

Ahmad, Husayn, 282
Ahmad Khān, Mu'īnu-d-Dīn, 44n
Ahmad Khān, Sir Sayyid, 58, 65, 68, 236
Ahmadīyah movement (Qādiyānī), 135n, 230-31, 236n, 250n; for anti-Ahmadī movement, *see also* Panjab Riots
Ajodhya mosque, Fayzabad, 280n
'Akā, 100
Akbarābādī, Sa'īd Ahmad, 64n
Akram, Muḥammad, 292n
Albania, 168, 292
Alexandria, 95
'Alī, 'Abdullāh Yūsuf, 46n, 64, 236
'Alī, Amīr, 54, 58, 61-62, 63, 86, 236
'Alī, Karāmat, 46n
'Alī, Liyāqat, 215n, 227, 270n
'Alī, Muḥammad, Indian Khilāfat leader, 53n
'Alī, Muḥammad, khedive of Egypt, 95n, 168
'Alī ibn 'Īsà, 166n
'Alī Khān, Liyāqat, *see* 'Alī, Liyāqat
'Alī Khān, Zafar, 262n
Aligarh, 224n, 262; Aligarh movement, 58
Allen, H. E., 175n
Amānullāh Khān, 201
Ambedkar, B. R., 78n
America, 22, 70, 77n, 82, 95, 103, 108, 110, 111, 113n, 141n, 194, 265, 304
Amīn, Ahmad, 64, 165
Amīn, 'Uthmān, 56n
Amīr 'Alī, *see* 'Alī, Amīr
Anatolia, 172; *cf.* Asia Minor, 35
Anderson, J. N. D., 294n
Anglican, 19, 193
Anīs, Brigadier, 271n, 276, 279, 282
Anjuman-i Khuddāmu-d-Dīn, Lahore, 236n
Ankara, 185, 186n, 194, 201
Anṣārī, Shawkatullāh, 78n
apologetics, 55, 63n, 69, 73, 85-89, 107, 114, 115-56, 168, 225
'Aqqād, 'Abbās Mahmūd al-, 62
Aquinas, St. Thomas, 303n
Arab League, 77n
'Arābī Pāshā, 49, 95
Arabia, 15, 29, 41-44, 246
Arabic alphabet, 173
Arabic language, 15, 20, 26n, 28, 47n, 62n, 93, 94, 127n, 166n, 173, 178, 183, 188, 233n, 263, 302n
Arabs, 15; classical and mediaeval Arabs, Arab period, 32, 34, 57, 94, 117-21,